THE

BEDENBAUGH-BETENBAUGH FAMILY:

DESCENDANTS OF

JOHANN MICHAEL BIDENBACH

FROM GERMANY TO

SOUTH CAROLINA

1752

by

Brent H. Holcomb

HERITAGE BOOKS
2017

HERITAGE BOOKS

AN IMPRINT OF HERITAGE BOOKS, INC.

Books, CDs, and more—Worldwide

For our listing of thousands of titles see our website
at
www.HeritageBooks.com

Published 2017 by
HERITAGE BOOKS, INC.
Publishing Division
5810 Ruatan Street
Berwyn Heights, Md. 20740

International Standard Book Numbers
Paperbound: 978-0-7884-5795-1

CONTENTS

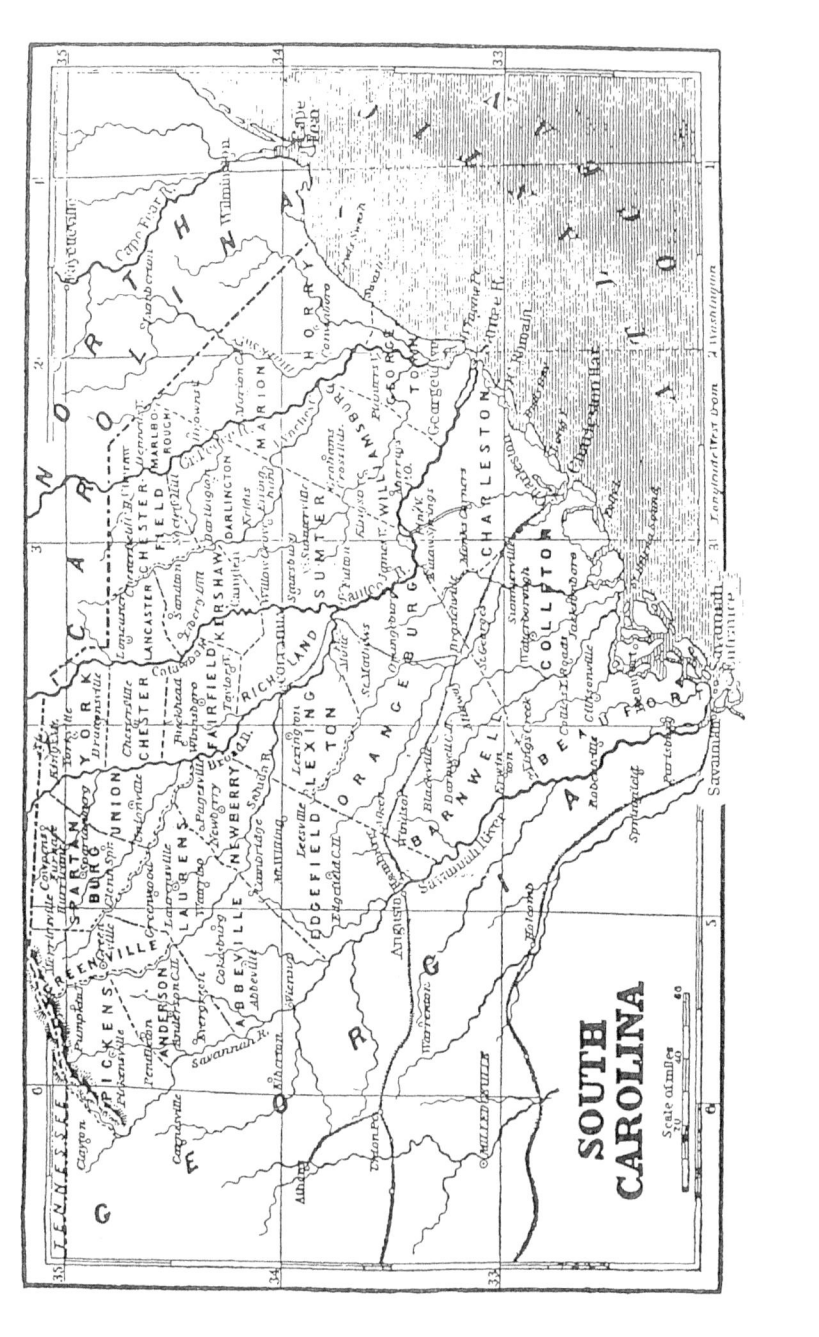

PREFACE

Ever since my first effort at publishing a genealogy of this family in 1977, I have searched for the German origins of the Bidenbach family of South Carolina. After several efforts, I was able to find a researcher in Germany who was able to solve the mystery of the origins of the Bidenbach/Bedenbaugh family of South Carolina and, at the same time, the origins of the Biddenback family of the Ebenezer settlement in Georgia, proving the two families to be related. Several descendants contributed toward the expense of the research, and all other descendants are indebted to them for their cooperation. My presentation of the results of this research comprises the first segment of this volume.

I have also been pleased to gather information and receive information on other branches of the family not included in the first publication. The information is still not complete, and I doubt that any genealogy can be complete to the last descendant. Some persons have declined to contribute information for this volume, but largely I have received excellent cooperation from descendants. My goal in the present volume was to provide information whereby any Bedenbaugh descendant could find his or her own lineage with a minimum of research of the direct lineage. With a little research into death certificates and census reports, any descendant of Adam Bedenbaugh or John Uriah Beatenbaugh should be able to trace his lineage using the information in this volume. I urge each family group to compile their own records and to publish them in some form. By doing so, families can preserve stories, traditions, and photographs, which would be too numerous to include in a volume with as wide a scope as this one. In 1990 Joyce Bedenbaugh Vorwaller published an attractive volume on the descendants of Frank Pickens Bedenbaugh, using my first volume as a starting point. I know of one other similar project in the making as of this writing (1995).

I wish to thank some persons who are not Bedenbaugh-Betenbaugh descendants but who have contributed information for this volume: Mr. Mike Becknell of Jonesville, South Carolina; Mr. Lewis A. Wood of Greenville, South Carolina; Mrs. Betty K. Johns of Union, South Carolina; Mrs. D. H. Wicker, Greenville, Mississippi; Mr. Charles W. Nicholson, Columbia, South Carolina; and Mr. J. B. Singley of Tampa, Florida.

Brent H. Holcomb

INTRODUCTION

This work is not a genealogy of a wealthy low-country plantation family, nor that of an up-country gentleman farmer, but a genealogy of the descendants of a poor German protestant who settled in the midlands of South Carolina. Many variations in the spelling and pronunciation of the name have occurred in America: Bidenbach, Peterbox, Peterbaugh, Bedenbaugh, Betenbaugh, etc. Mr. J. Moody Bedenbaugh of Prosperity, South Carolina, related to the writer that in his youth, he often heard the name pronounced as if it were spelled Peterbock. The most common pronunciations in 1995 are Betenbaw and Betenbo.

The reader should keep in mind that this family was settled on the frontier of South Carolina in 1752, where records were scant. Additionally, South Carolina kept no regular vital statistics (marriages, births, deaths) until the twentieth century. Some explanation of the political divisions of South Carolina during the time frame covered in this work is in order. In the Colonial period in South Carolina, there was no court of record outside Charleston. Counties as we know them did not exist until 1785. When Johann Michael Bidenbach arrived in South Carolina, the area in which he settled, usually called the "Dutch Fork," was usually known as the fork between the Broad and Saluda Rivers. It was sometimes considered in Craven County and sometimes in Berkley County. When the circuit court districts were established in 1769, the area was partly in Ninety Six District and partly in Orangeburgh District. The land that was granted to Johann Michael Bidenbach (as Michael Pettebay) was near the line between those two districts, which was later the line between Newberry County and Lexington County. That line was adjusted several times, because St. John's Lutheran Church (very near the land of Michael) was included in Lexington District by the *Mills' Atlas* of 1825. However, the names of his sons appear in Newberry County in 1790 and Newberry District in 1800 by the census reports. In the year 1800, the counties in South Carolina became known as districts. Lexington County had reverted to become part of Orangeburgh District in 1791 and was revitalized as Lexington District in 1804. The term *county* was resumed in South Carolina in 1868.

This volume is organized in the New England Register Method, modified to suit our needs here. The lineage in Germany to the immigrant is presented in this format, but the individuals are not numbered, except the direct lineage and that by upper case letters. The American lineage is organized by generations in each section, each person being assigned a number. (The immigrant, Johann Michael Bedenbaugh, is number 1.) Where there is information on an individual or his/her descendants further in the volume, the number is preceded by a plus sign (+). The Arabic numbers are only references points and have no significance to generations. The superscript numbers indicate the generation of the person, and the lineage of the person being discussed is given in parenthesis after his or her name. The numbers and index will aid one in following the descendants of any person or, working backwards, the lineage of any one person. The Register Method becomes tedious and repetitious, and it breaks down after a number of generations. Therefore, in the more recent generations, especially where there is little or no information other than names and dates, several generations may be listed together in outline form.

Brent Howard Holcomb
August 7, 1995

vi

THE LINEAGE IN GERMANY

The Thirty Years' War (1618-1648), a war between the Protestants and Roman Catholics, was devastating to much of Germany. The population in the war zones of Mecklenburg, Pomerania, and Wurttemberg lost over half of their inhabitants. The losses were greater in the villages than in the cities because of a lack of protection by city walls.[1] Because of the loss of population in these villages, many people moved into Germany from other areas after 1648.

We find our first probable Bidenbach ancestor in the province of Wurttemberg in the village of Bergenweiler. The church records in Bergenweiler report that the lords of Weltz in the court of the Counter Reformation left their homeland in Carynthia, the so-called "windisch Mark," which is today the region of Laibach, with their Protestant subjects and came to Bergenweiler. (Laibach is the German name for Ljubljana, capital of Slovenia, recently a part of Yugoslavia.) The church records mention Primus Bidenbach from the Wendisch Land 1659.[2] A map of Yugoslavia showing the city of Ljugljana is reproduced on page 5. The villages of Bergenweiler and Sontheim an der Brenz are near the city of Ulm, the location of which can be seen on the maps on pages 6 and 7. The map on page 7 is a detail of the map of Germany on which is indicated the approximate location of the village of Sontheim an der Brenz.

Mr. Friedrich R. Wollmershauser, a German genealogist, has done research on behalf of the writer. He provides the following information.[3]

C. Primus Bidenbach, mentioned in the Bergenweiler parish registers from 1660 onwards, married, first (before 1668), Ursula Achatz. He married, second, 20 July 1686, in Bergenweiler, Catharine Geyler, daughter of Philipp Geyler, a small farmer (Soldner) in Bergenweiler. She died, a widow, on 8 December 1732, aged 71 years and six months. He had a daughter Gertraudt, born about 1650, before the move to Bergenweiler. She died unmarried on 11 January 1716 in Bergenweiler. The children of his first marriage, born in Bergenweiler:

+ B i. Andreas, b. 18 March 1668
    ii. Christian, b. 10 Nov 1671
    iii. Regina, b. 26 Oct 1673, d. 20 March 1690
    iv. Maria, b. 25 Apr 1677
    v. Hans Michael, b. 23 Sept 1681
    vi. Anna Catharine, b. 2 Jan 1685

Children of the second marriage, all born in Bergenweiler:
    vii. Andreas, b. 13 Aug 1687, d. 9 March 1690
    viii. Catharine, b. 20 Jan 1690, d. 22 Apr 1723, unmarried
    ix. Johannes, b. 24 Nov 1697.

B. Andreas Bidenbach (Primus[C]) died 13 Jan 1731. He married, c1691, possibly in Brenz, Margaretha Crawat, who died 2 August 1731 in Bergenweiler, a widow, aged 77.

The death entry in the church register indicates that Andreas Bidenbach was aged 91 years at the time of his death. If this be correct, then he could hardly be the son of Primus Bidenbach. However, the writer suspects that this age is indeed in error, and that this Andreas Bidenbach was the son of Primus Bidenbach because no other Andreas appears in the church records (or other records searched). However, if the baptismal date of 18 March 1668 is indicative of an infant baptism, he would hardly have been old enough to have a child (Georg) born in 1679. A birth date in the 1650s seems more probable for him. Since Primus had a daughter Gertraud born about 1650, the birth of Andreas in this time frame seems logical.

Children of Andreas Bidenbach, all born in Bergenweiler:
    i. Georg, b. 17 Nov 1679, weaver, d. 25 Jan 1741 aged 62, m. 16 Sept 1701, Maria Magdalena Bidenbach, d. 26 Feb 1752. Children, born in Bergenweiler:
        a. Johanna, b. 8 May 1705
        b. Maria, b. 8 May 1705
        c. Margaretha, b. 15 Dec 1706
        d. Catharina, b. 5 March 1710,
        e. Christianus, b. 1 May 1712, and possibly others
    ii. Maria, b. 9 May 1682
    iii. Anna, b. 15 Sept 1683-- a daughter Anna Maria, d. 16 Jan 1714, aged 33.
    iv. Eva, b. 16 Jan 1685

+ A v. Andreas, b. 10 Jan 1688
    vi. Margaretha, b. 11 Nov 1690
    vii. Margaretha, b. 22 Jan 1692
    viii. Dorothea, b. 23 Apr 1694
    ix. Johannes, b. 28 Nov 1696
    x. Sebastian, b. 21 Nov 1699.

A. Andreas[A] Bidenbach (Andreas[B], Primus[C]) was born 10 January 1688 in Bergenweiler and died 9 May 1764 in Sontheim an der Brenz and was buried on 11 May. The death entry indicates that he was a citizen and farmer (on a small farm). He married, on 11 September 1714, in Bergenweiler, Waldburga Walzinger, daughter of Michael Walzinger, member of the local law-court at Sontheim an der Brenz. She died 23 December 1756 in Sontheim an der Brenz, after having been sick for six years, and she was buried on Christmas Day. (Her age is not indicated in the church register.)

There are about as many variations in the spelling of the surname in Germany as there are in America. The record of the marriage in 1714 spells the name Andreas Bittenbach. The name is also spelled Biedenbach.

There is a 1734 census of the Heidenheim area in the Hauptstaatsarchiv Stuttgart, A 213 Buschel 4782. According to Mr. Wollmershauser, it consists of a folder paper for each village. It lists the age for every male of the age of sixteen years and older. Number 22, for Sontheim, lists Andreas Bidenbach aged 47, and Christian Bidenbach (a cowherd) aged 47.

Children of Andreas[B] Bidenbach, all born in Sontheim an der Brenz:
    i. Maria, b. 14 Feb 1718
+ 1 ii. Johann Michael, b. 15 Sept 1719 (see next chapter)
    iii. Andreas, b. 30 Jan 1721
    iv. Margaret, b. 9 Oct 1722, m. 21 Oct 1755 Jacob Reinhardt

THE BEDENBAUGH-BETENBAUGH FAMILY

v. Gottfried, b. 3 Aug 1724
vi. Matthaus, b. 28 Jan 1727, m. 15 June 1751, Margaretha Hanglaiter.
vii. Christian, b. 18 July 1728.

With regard to the marriage entry for Matthaus Bidenbach, Mr. Wollmershauser states that his father is listed as Matthaus, but that it is probably an error because no record of a Matthaus, Sr., is found in that place.

Reproductions of some pertinent entries from the parish registers with the transcriptions and translations by Mr. Wollmershauser are found on pages 9 and 10.

The sponsors of Johann Michael Bidenbach at his baptism were Johannes Lindenmann and Elis. Desselbronnerin. No other information on Johann Michael Bidenbach has been located in German records. Therefore, it seems quite likely that he emigrated. The lineage continues from him in the next chapter.

Of additional interest are entries located on one Christian Bidenbach in the registers of Bergenweiler.

Christian Bidenbach married, on 1 August 1741, Sophia Elisabeth Krutschick. They had the following children born there:
i. Georg, b. 10 June 1742
ii. Catharine, b. 25 Oct 1744
iii. Johann Phillip, b. 13 Nov 1746, d. 21 Nov 1746
iv. Johann Philipp, b. 1 Dec 1747
v. Magdalena, b. 20 Sept 1749.

These names disappear from the records after the 1749 entry. This Christian Bidenbach is identical with one Christian Biddenbach, who was born c1710[4] and came to the Ebenezer settlement in Georgia about 1750 with wife Sophie. We find a baptismal entry for Christianus Bidenbach, son of George Bidenbach, dated 1 May 1712 in Bergenweiler. His daughter Catherine was married 22 February 1763 in Georgia to John Justus Grovenstein (Gravenstein, Grabenstein)[5]. Note that the daughter Catharine was baptized in German in 1744, making her about eighteen years old at the time of her marriage. The descendants of Catherine Grovenstein and Matthew Biddenbach are chronicled in *Georgia Salzburgers and Allied Families*. Matthew is indicated as a child of Christian and Sophie Biddenbach in Georgia.[6] However, it does not seem likely that Matthew or Matthaus was their son. Note that among the children listed for Andreas[B] Bidenbach is one Matthaus who married, on 15 June 1751, Margaretha Hanglaiter. We find in the Ebenezer settlement the names of Matthaeus Biddenbach and his wife Anna Margaretha associated with the Hangleiter family there.[7] The name of Andreas Biddenbach is also found in Georgia.[8] It seems more likely that this Matthaus Biddenbach was not a son of Christian Biddenbach, but a first cousin, Christian's father Georg being the eldest brother of Andreas Bidenbach, father of Matthaus and Johann Michael Bidenbach.

THE BEDENBAUGH-BETENBAUGH FAMILY

NOTES AND REFERENCES

1. Geoffrey Parker, *The Thirty Years' War*, page 211.

2. Albrecht Ritz, Nattheim und Oggenhauser im Kranz der Nachbargemeinden (Heidenheim, 1951), pages 87-88, 96. Mr. Charles W. Nicholson has kindly translated from German for the writer.

3. The information from the Bergenweiler register (1649-1832) is available on LDS microfilm, Roll 1340134, item 3. We are especially grateful to Mr. Gary T. Horlacher of Salt Lake City for additional research accomplished in this register.

4. This birth year is based on the death entry for him, which states that he died 5 May 1770 in the "60 year of his life."

5. George F. Jones and Sheryl Exley, *Ebenezer Record Book 1754-1781* (Baltimore: Genealogical Publishing Co., 1991), page 90.

6. Pearl Rahn Gnann, *Georgia Salzburgers and Allied Families*, pages 28-29, 125-138.

7. George F. Jones and Sheryl Exley, *Ebenezer Record Book 1754-1781* (Baltimore: Genealogical Publishing Co., 1991), pages 29-30, 44, 62.

8. George F. Jones, *The Germans of Colonial Georgia* (Baltimore: Genealogical Publishing Co., 1986), page 6.

Yugoslavia

International boundary
Republic boundary
Autonomous area boundary
★ National capital
◉ Republic or autonomous area capital
Railroad
Road

0 25 50 75 100 Kilometers
0 25 50 75 100 Miles

Base 504661 (545723) 1-87

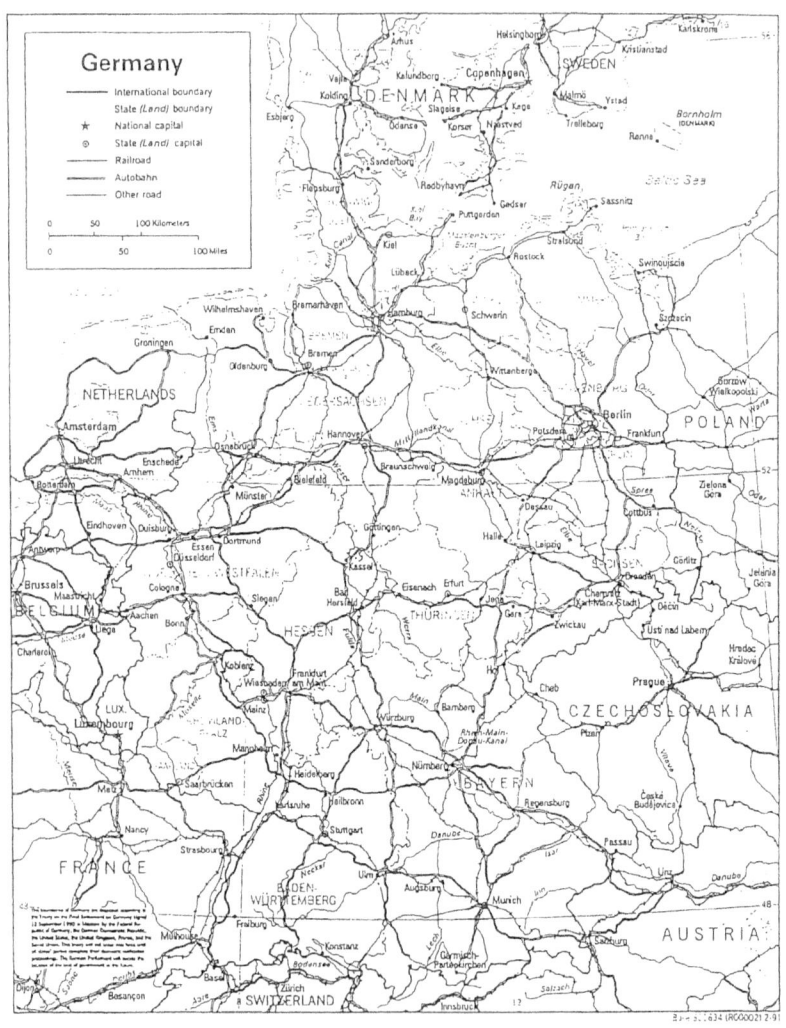

Germany

International boundary
State (Land) boundary
★ National capital
⊙ State (Land) capital
Railroad
Autobahn
Other road

0   50   100 Kilometers
0   50   100 Miles

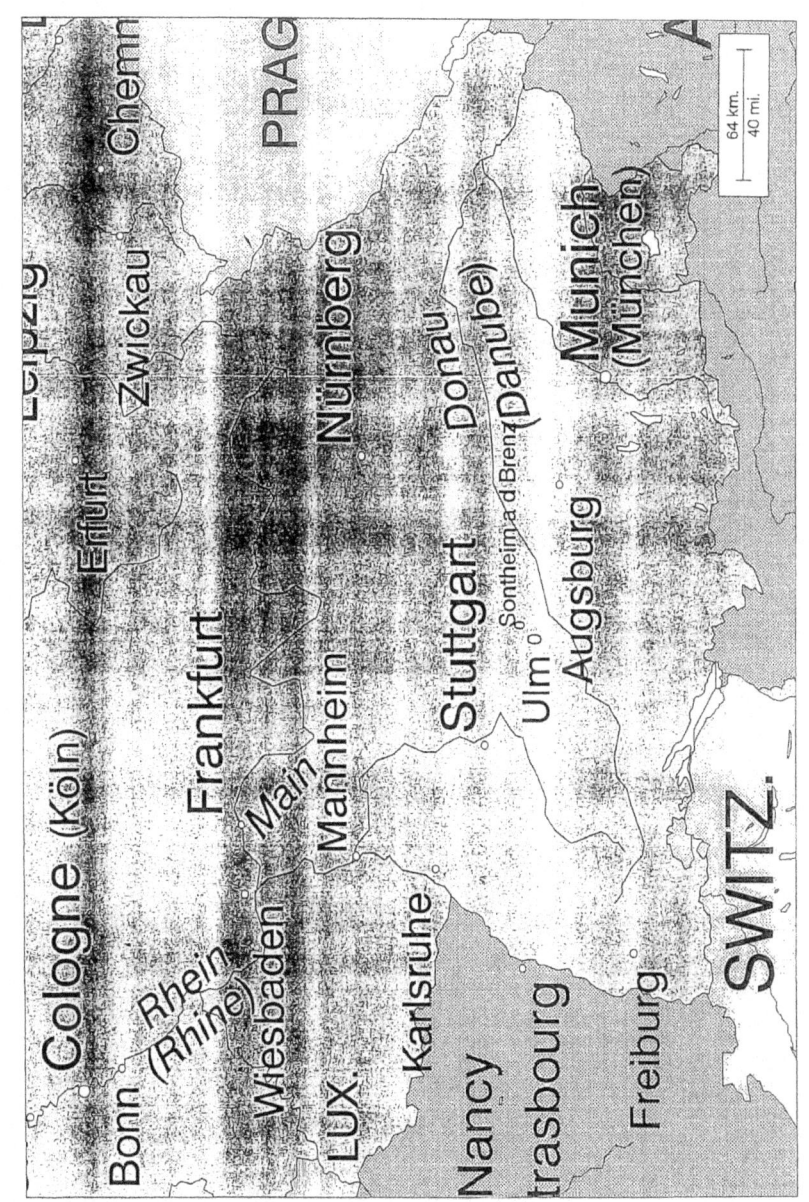

Auszug aus den Kirchenbüchern der evang. Pfarrei Bergenweiler

Eheregister 1714:

Auf hohen obrigkeitlichen Befehl sind d. 11. Sept. 1714 nach vorher gehaltener Bettstund öfentl. in der Kirchen copulirt worden: Andreas Bittenbach, ein Baurenknecht, des ehrbarn u bescheidenen Andreas Bittenbachs, Burger u. Söldners allhier, ehl. Sohn; u. Waldburga Walzingerin, des ehrsamen u. bescheidenen Michael Walzingers, Burgers u. Gerichtsmanns zu Sontheim an der Brenz ehl. Tochter.

Summary: The marriage of Andreas Bittenbach, a farmhand (son of Andreas Bittenbach, small farmer here) and Waldburga Walzinger (daughter of Michael Walzinger, member of the local law-court at Sontheim an der Brenz) has been performed on 11 Sep. 1714 in Bergenweiler upon a decree of the authorities.

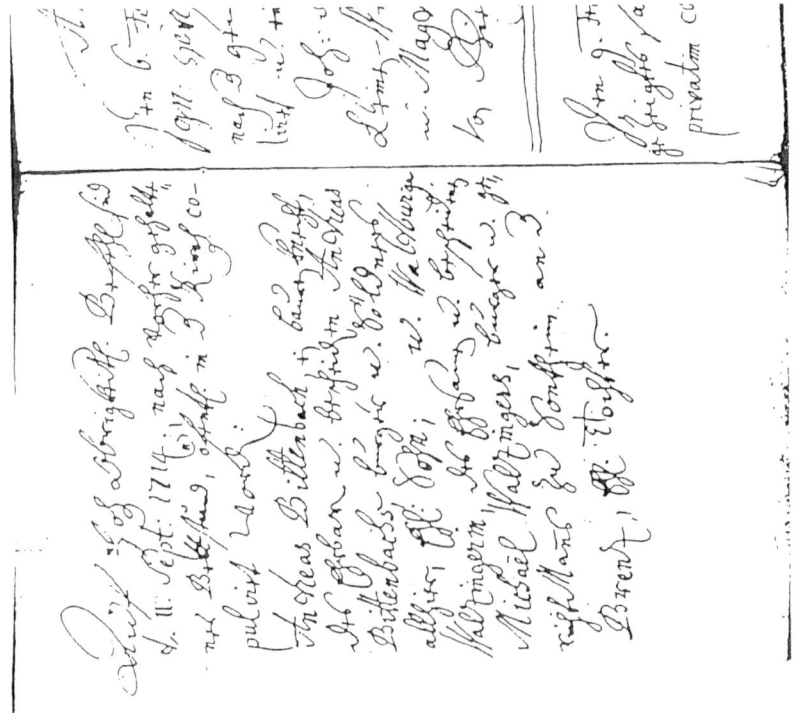

Auszug aus den Kirchenbüchern der evang. Pfarrei Sontheim/Brenz

Taufregister 1719:

Zal	Zeit	Kinder	Eltern	Gevatterleuth
27)	Sept. d. 15ten	Joh. Michael	Andreas Bidenbacb Waldburga	Johannes Lindenmann coelebs. Elis. Desselbron- nerin

Summary: Johann Michael was born (or baptized) on 15 Sept. 1719 in Sontheim an der Brenz as son of Andreas Bidenbach and Waldburga.

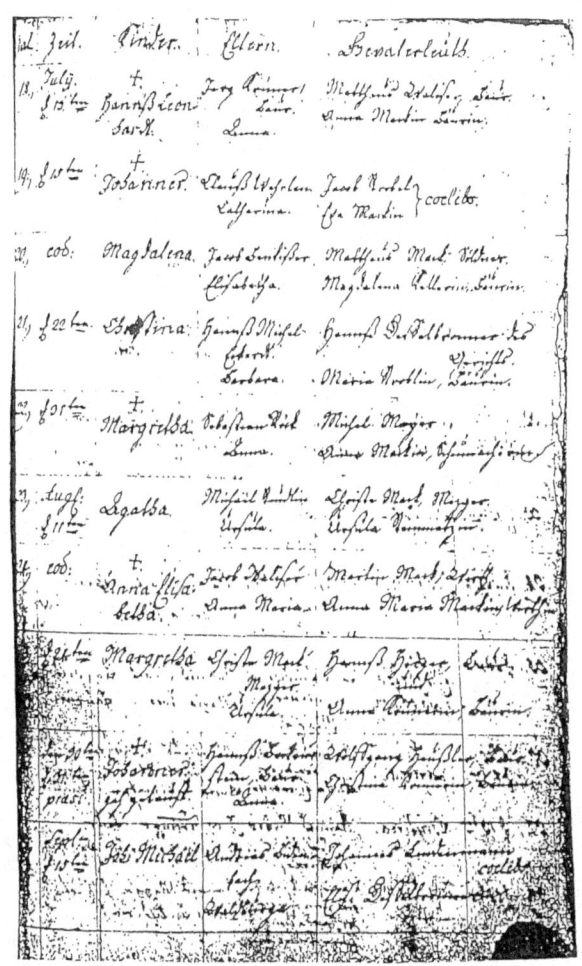

JOHANN MICHAEL BIDENBACH, THE IMMIGRANT

1. Johann Michael[1] Bidenbach (Andreas[B], Andreas[C], Primus[D]) was baptized 15 Sept 1719 in Sontheim an der Brenz, in the province of Wurttemberg, Germany. He died after 1771 in South Carolina.

There is very little record of him in America. His name is spelled Michael Pitebag in the Council Journal. It is in the Council Journal, Volume 21, pages 110-111,[1] that we find the first record of him in South Carolina:

> Read the Petition of Michael Pitebag humbly setting forth that the petitr. arrived here in the Caledonia Ship, Capt. Alexr. Harvey Commr. bound from Rotterdam to this Place and on the Encouragement given here to Forreign (sic) Protestants, and is discharged of the Freight by Messrs. Austin & Laurence and is desirous to Live in the province.
>
> That he has a wife for whom nor yet for himself has any Land been assigned him and therefore he humbly prays his Excellency and their Honors to Issue an order to the Surveyor General to Lay out or Cause to be Laid out to the petitioner 100 acres of Land free of Charges and that he may have his most Gracious Majestys provision Bounty, and the Petitioner as in Duty bound shall every pray.
>> Chas Town the 7th day of Decemr 1752. Michl Pitebag
> The said Petition being Considered and the petitioner appearing and swearing allegiance to his Majesty, and to the truth of the allegations in his said Petition the prayer thereof was granted and the Depy. Secrety. ordered to prepare a warrant and the Surveyor General to run out the 100 acres of land prayed for to the petitioner ordered also the Commissary General do pay the Charges and his Majestys Provision Bounty.

Thus Michael Bidenbach was one of approximately 1250 German immigrants to come to South Carolina and to receive Bounty Land.[2] His land was in the fork of the Broad and Saluda Rivers, which soon came to be known as the Dutch Fork. Michael's plat, dated 16 November 1753, was for 100 acres on a branch of Crim's Creek.[3] On the plat his name is spelled Petebay (a scrivenor's error in transcribing from the Council Journal, the "g" not being closed); the scrivenor added a "t" on the land grant dated 8 March 1753,[4] causing the name to appear as Michael Pettebay. With the German explosive "b" and gutteral "k" sound, Bidenbach would sound like Peatunbag or Pitebag. The next and final appearance of his name is in the Quit Rent Rolls, 1771, the only record of his ever paying them (his land was free from quit rents for ten years from 1755, as part of the "bounty"), and the name appears as Michael Pettebog.[5] His name does not appear on the 1779 Jury List, in the Minutes of the County Court of Newberry (1785-1798), or on any Federal census. The plat of Abram Chapman, dated 8 Dec 1768, shows "one Petebaugh" as an adjacent land owner,[6] and Chapman's will dated 1 June 1808 mentions this property as the Beadebaugh land[7] (see the following plat map showing the exact location of this land). Thus there can be no doubt that this Michael "Pitebag" is the original Bedenbaugh. The name of his wife is not known, but she is probably the female over 45 in the household of Uriah Pedembox in the 1800 census of Newberry District, and the female in the household of Uriah Pitinboa in 1790.[8] Only two children, being sons, can be identified for Michael. Every white person in the South (and to the best of the knowledge of the writer, anywhere) by the name of Bedenbaugh, Betenbaugh, or a variant, can be traced to one of these two sons. If there were daughters, no record has been found of them, and no record of any family in this area (even by tradition) has a female Bedenbaugh ancestor who could be a daughter of Michael. No probate record has been found for Michael under any

THE BEDENBAUGH-BETENBAUGH FAMILY

spelling. If he survived until 1781, his estate or will would have been probated in Orangeburgh District the records of which were destroyed in 1865.

Some descendants have expressed an interest in the ship *Caledonia*. Fortunately, a record is available which indicates that it departed from Charleston on December 30, 1752, and that it was a "pink" (which refers to the shape of the hull). It was a ship of two hundred tons, and the master's name was Alex. Harvey.[9]

Known children of Michael Bidenbach and his wife (name unknown):

+ 2 i. Adam[2] Bedenbaugh, b. c1760, information on his descendants begins on the following page.
+ 3 ii. John Uriah[2] Beatenbeaugh or Ulrich Bidenbach, b. c1770. His descendants are in a separate chapter in this volume, beginning on page .

NOTES AND REFERENCES

1. South Carolina copy, original at the South Carolina Archives.

2. Robert L. Meriwether, *The Expansion of South Carolina 1729-1765* (Kingsport, Tenn.: Southern Publishers, Inc., 1940), pp. 150-152.

3. South Carolina Colonial Plats, Vol. 12, p. 125, original volume at SC Archives.

4. Royal Grants, Volume 6, page 307.

5. Quit Rents, Vol. 1768-1774, p. 338.

6. Pre-Revolutionary Loose Plats, Folder 316, original at South Carolina Archives.

7. Newberry County, South Carolina, Probate Records, Box 25, Package 53, Estate #534, original in the Office of the Probate Judge, Newberry County Court House.

8. 1800 Federal Census, Newberry District, South Carolina, page 90. *Heads of Families First Census of the United States 1790 South Carolina*, page 79.

9. Colonial Office America and West Indies, Shipping Returns March 1736-January 1, 1764, page 41 (stamped number), on British Public Records Office microfilm D571 (CO 5/510), copy at South Carolina Archives.

11

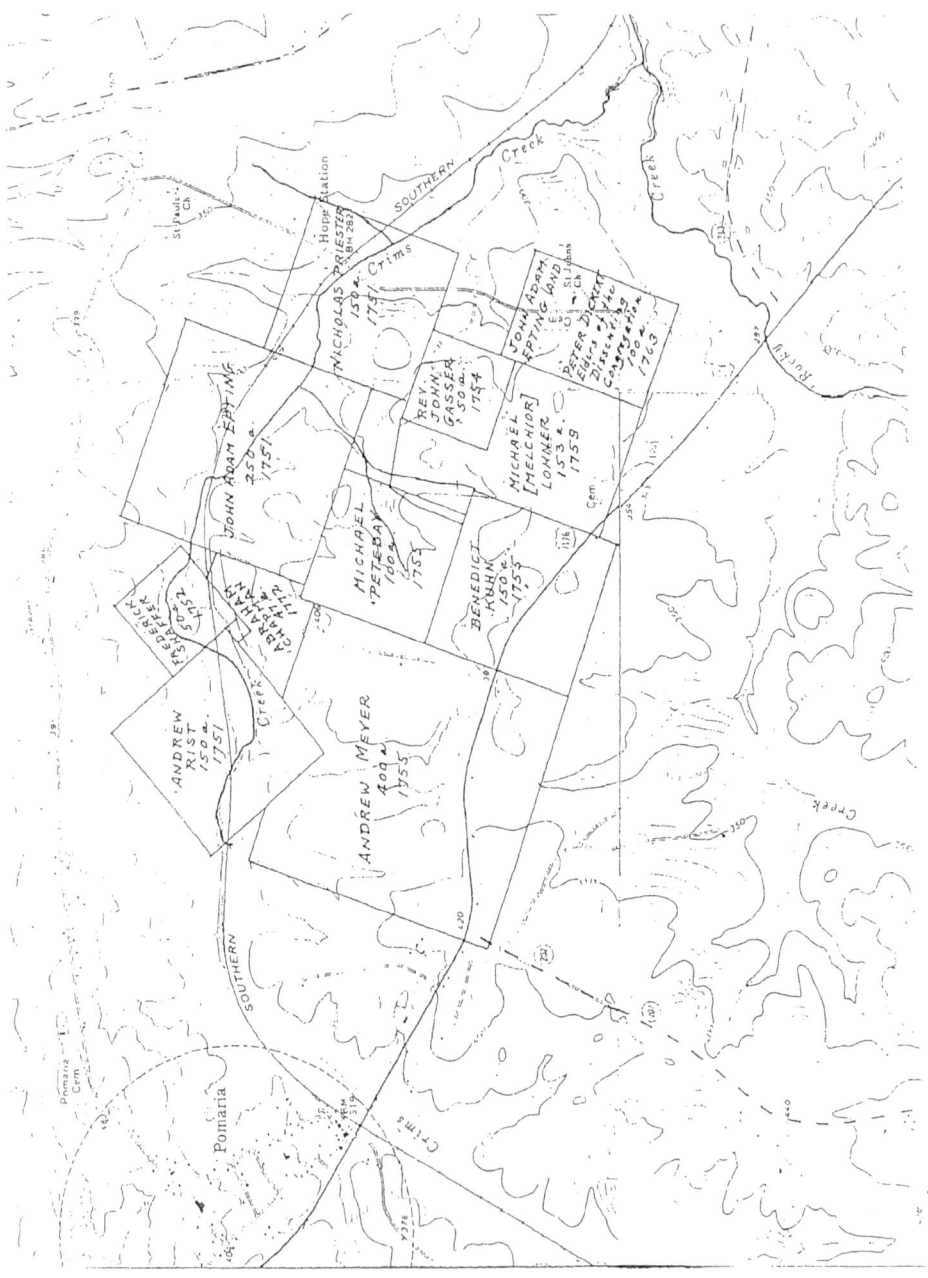

Plat map of a portion of the Crim's Creek area showing the location of the grant to Michael Pettebay and adjacent land owners.

THE BEDENBAUGH-BETENBAUGH FAMILY

SECOND GENERATION

2. Adam[2] Bedenbaugh (Michael[1]) was born c1760 and died in 1829 in Newberry District, South Carolina. He married Barbara Wertz, probably about 1781. She died in 1833.[1]

Fortunately, Adam Bedenbaugh is not the elusive person that Michael Bidenbach proved to be. His name appears on the 1790 census of Newberry County, South Carolina as Adam Pitingboa.[2] An account in the Annals of Newberry states that "Adam Bedenbaugh was born near Pomaria, S. C., of German parentage, and entered the Revolutionary war at sixteen years of age. He married a Miss Wertz and settled on Broad River. Afterwards he moved to the Stoney Hills, settling on Little Creek."[3] There are other details in the account, most of which can be documented. It was probably given to the authors by a grandson of Adam Bedenbaugh. Adam Bedenbaugh is probably buried in a cemetery on land now (1995) owned by Mr. James Earl Morris in the Stoney Hills Community, off Mother Goose Road. The only marked grave in that cemetery is that of Levi, a child of Adam (Jr.) and Mary Bedenbaugh.

Notice that the original Michael Pitebag grant was near Pomaria as indicated on the map. Adam Bedenbaugh assigned his indent for the service in the Revolution to John Adam Summer, where his name appears as Adam Bietenbach.[4] His service has been accepted by the National Society of the Daughters of the American Revolution, and National Number 686352 was assigned to his descendant Wendelyn Bedenbaugh Jamison. His name appears as John Adam Peterbaugh on a state grant dated 2 November 1789.[5] This land was eventually owned by Christena Addy, and it was conveyed to her daughters. The deed refers to land granted to Adam Beatenback.[6] However, he is most often referred to as Adam Bedenbaugh, Sr. He witnessed a deed, which he signed by mark A, from Peter Stockman to George Koone 23 December 1789, on which the name is spelled Adam Bietenbach, and the proof of which was signed in German (in Lexington County, 21 July 1792) as Adam Bidenbach.[7] He purchased land in the Stoney Battery section of Newberry County, as is evidenced by an original deed which the writer found in Newberry County Court House, Office of the Clerk of Court, in the basement of that office. (This deed is now in the South Carolina Archives).[8] The will of Adam Bedenbaugh Senr was written 5 November 1829 and proved 16 November 1829. The original is extant and is in the office of the Probate Judge of Newberry County.[9] In this will he named his wife Barbary, his sons and daughter: Henry, Adam, Michael, Jacob, Abraham, John, William, and Elizabeth Conwill. Also named is a grandson George Washington Bedenbaugh. A search of Werts and Wertz estates has not revealed a daughter Barbara or Barbary who could have been the wife of Adam Bedenbaugh, Sr.

The children of Adam[2] Bedenbaugh, Sr., and his wife Barbara Wertz:

+ 4   i. Henry[3] Bedenbaugh, b. 1 Oct 1782
+ 5   ii. Adam[3] Bedenbaugh, Jr., b. 10 Feb 1785
+ 6   iii. Michael[3] Bedenbaugh, b. c1787
+ 7   iv. Elizabeth[3] Bedenbaugh, b. 1 Dec 1790
+ 8   v. Jacob[3] Bedenbaugh, b. c1792
+ 9   vi. Abraham[3] Bedenbaugh, b. 15 July 1793
+ 10 vii. John[3] Bedenbaugh, b. c1803

THE BEDENBAUGH-BETENBAUGH FAMILY

+ 11   viii. Christian[3] Bedenbaugh, b. ___, d. 1826
+ 12   ix. William[3] Bedenbaugh, b. c1807.

THIRD GENERATION

4. Henry[3] Bedenbaugh (Adam[2], Michael[1]) was born 1 October 1782 and died 11 February 1858. He married Elizabeth Bright, who was born 21 August 1786 and died 25 May 1867. Both are buried at St. Luke's Lutheran Church, near Prosperity, Newberry County, South Carolina. *The Annals of Newberry* (pages 636-7) gives the wife's name as Elizabeth Bright.[10] A rather confusing document[11] makes it appear that one John Kinard fathered an illegitimate child, Mary M. (Polly) Bright, by this Elizabeth. The names of both Henry and Elizabeth Bedenbaugh appear as witnesses to bonds in this guardianship.

The children of Henry[3] Bedenbaugh, and wife Elizabeth Bright:[12]

   13   i. Elizabeth[4] Bedenbaugh, b. 22 Nov 1811, d. 1 April 1852, unm., bur. St. Luke's Lutheran Church.
+ 14   ii. Eve[4] Bedenbaugh, b. 11 Sept 1813
+ 15   iii. Daniel[4] Bedenbaugh, b. 7 Oct 1814
+ 16   iv. John Adam[4] Bedenbaugh, b. 11 July 1816
+ 17   v. Simeon[4] Bedenbaugh, b. 8 March 1819
   18   vi. William Pinckney[4] Bedenbaugh, b. 17 Nov 1820, d. 9 March 1880 in Newberry Co., SC,[13] m. Matilda Chapman, b. 12 Dec 1850, d. 11 Aug 1905. After the death of William P. Bedenbaugh, Matilda m. a Beachem. W. Pinckney Bedenbaugh served as a private in Co. F., 20 SC Infantry. William P. Bedenbaugh and Matilda are buried at St. Luke's Lutheran Church.
+ 19   vii. Malinda[4] Bedenbaugh, b. 6 Jan 1823
+ 20   viii. Rachel[4] Bedenbaugh, b. 12 Sept 1825
+ 21   ix. Rosanna Caroline[4] Bedenbaugh, b. 2 May 1829.

5. Adam[3] Bedenbaugh Jr. (Adam[2], Michael[1]) was born 10 February 1785, and died 25 Aug 1856. He married Mary (Polly) Kibler, who was born 25 October 1795 and died 26 August 1856 (only one day after her husband). Both are buried in the family cemetery, just off Highway 773, near Prosperity, South Carolina. Mary was the daughter of John and Nancy Kibler, buried in the Kibler cemetery, not too distant from the graves of Adam and Polly Bedenbaugh. The property including the Kibler Cemetery and Bedenbaugh Cemetery is (1995) in possession of Miss Eleanor Bedenbaugh, a descendant of Adam Bedenbaugh, Jr.. The estates papers of John Kibler[14] and that of Nancy Kibler[15] both name Adam and Polly Bedenbaugh as legatees.

The children of Adam[3] Bedenbaugh Jr., and wife Mary (Polly) Kibler, were as follows:[16]

   22   i. Levi[4] Bedenbaugh, gravemarker gives no dates, only his age as 4 years, 6 days[17].
   23   ii. Epsie[4] Bedenbaugh, b. 1821, m. Josiah Stewart; two children:
         24   a. Josiah P.[5] Stewart, b. 1 Dec 1846, d. 25 May 1869
         25   b. William Anderson[5] Stewart, b. 1 Sept 1847, d. 25 Nov 1850

+ 26 iii. John Adam[4] Bedenbaugh b. 15 April 1823
+ 27 iv. Nancy C.[4] Bedenbaugh, b. 7 June 1825
+ 28 v. Andrew Jackson[4] Bedenbaugh b. 15 Sept 1827
  29 vi. Lavina[4] Bedenbaugh died in childhood, gravemarker in family
      cemetery gives no dates, only her age as 6 years, 4 days.
  30 vii. Jacob Belton[4] Bedenbaugh b. 10 Sep 1833, d. 17 April 1915,
      unm., bur. in family cemetery with his parents
  31 viii. William C.[4] Bedenbaugh, b. 5 Nov 1836, d. 22 Apr 1860, unm.,
      bur. in family cemetery with his parents.

6. Michael[3] Bedenbaugh (Adam[2], Michael[1]) was born c1787 and died 19 April 1849. He married Magdalene (Polly) Hallman, daughter of Andrew Hallman (Holman), Jr.[18] The estate of Michael Bedenbaugh is filed in Newberry County[19] and that of his widow Polly as well.[20] His death date is stated in the estates papers, as well as the names of their children. At the request of Susannah Nichols on 16 November 1825, Michael Bedenbaugh was appointed guardian for her son James Hutchison. Michael Bedenbaugh's brothers Christian and John Bedenbaugh were his securities on the guardianship bond.[21]

+ 32 i. Katherin[4] Bedenbaugh
+ 33 ii. Laodicea[4] Bedenbaugh, b. c1820
  34 iii. William C.[4] Bedenbaugh, b. c1821, d. 1860-66, did not marry.
+ 35 iv. Elizabeth[4] Bedenbaugh, b. c1825.

7. Elizabeth[3] Bedenbaugh (Adam[2], Michael[1]) was born 1 December 1790 and died 19 March 1852 in Monroe County, Mississippi. She married Daniel G. Conwill, who was born c1790 and died 1863 in Monroe County, Mississippi. They are buried in the "Old Mound" Cemetery near Amory, Monroe County, Mississippi. They were married apparently in Newberry District, South Carolina, and had four children born in South Carolina. By 1830 we find Daniel G. Conwill with family in Monroe County, Alabama. By 1860, they were living in Mississippi. The will of Daniel G. Conwill is found in Monroe County, Mississippi.[22] The estate of his widow Elizabeth is also found in that county.[23] The original records remain at that court house in Aberdeen, Mississippi.[24]

The children of Elizabeth[3] Bedenbaugh and her husband Daniel G. Conwill:[25]
+ 36 i. John A.[4] Conwill, b. 2 May 1821, Newberry District, SC
+ 37 ii. Yates Jury[4] Conwill, b. 16 Dec 1824, Newberry District, SC
  38 iii. Anna[4] Conwill, b. c1827 SC, m. Edward Hawkins
  39 iv. Elizabeth[4] Conwill, b. June 1829 AL, d. c1900, m. 1849 John Sheley Tart
  40 v. Mary[4] Conwill, b. 1830 AL, m. James Farr
  41 vi. Sophia C.[4] Conwill, b. 1831 AL, m. John C. Rawlins
  42 vii. Adaline F.[4] Conwill, b. 1837 AL, m. John Cummings
  43 viii. William J.[4] Conwill, b. 1839 AL
  44 ix. Frances E.[4] Conwill, b. 7 Feb 1840 AL, m. W. Irving Schumpert.

8. Jacob[3] Bedenbaugh (Adam[2], Michael[1]) was born c1792 and died 28 January 1865. He married Rebecca Hair, a daughter of Mathias and Fanny Hair, who was born c1799 and died 14 October 1870.[26] The will of Jacob Bedenbaugh,[27] dated 8 Dec 1864 and proved 5 Feb 1866, names his children, including three (Levi, Mathias H., and Simeon W.) who had already received their legacies.

THE BEDENBAUGH-BETENBAUGH FAMILY

The children of Jacob[3] and Rebecca (Hair) Bedenbaugh:
+ 45   i. Levi[4] Bedenbaugh, b. 11 Dec 1812
+ 46   ii. Mathias Hare[4] Bedenbaugh, b. c 1817
+ 47   iii. Simeon Wilson[4] Bedenbaugh, b. 12 Aug 1818
   48   iv. Janie or Frances[4] Bedenbaugh, b. 1821, d. unm.
+ 49   v. Eliza[4] Bedenbaugh
+ 50   vi. Drury David[4] Bedenbaugh, b. 17 Apr 1824
+ 51   vii. Jacob Asbury[4] Bedenbaugh, b. 16 Nov 1826
+ 52   viii. Rachel[4] Bedenbaugh, b. 2 Apr 1829
   53   ix. Annie E.[4] Bedenbaugh, b. 1834, d. 1906, m. ___ Cruber.

9. Abraham[3] Bedenbaugh (Adam[2], Michael[1]) was born 15 July 1793, died 11 February 1882. He married Beersheba Nelson, who was born 25 January 1817 and died 24 June 1892. Both are buried at St. Luke's Lutheran Church. The will of Abraham Bedenbaugh, dated 15 August 1874, names his wife Bershaby and divides his estate between her and Lidy Bedenbaugh, Delphy Bedenbaugh, and John Q. A. Bedenbaugh "persons of color." The will was proved 18 Feb 1882.[28]

10. John[3] Bedenbaugh (Adam[2], Michael[1]) was born ca. 1803 and died after 1860. He married Rhoda King, who was born c1814 and died after 1860. *The Annals of Newberry* (page 637) gives his wife's name as Rhoda King.[29] A search of King estates and deeds has not revealed any Rhoda or Rhoda Bedenbaugh, but from the use of the surname King in names of her children and later generations, it would seem likely that she was a King before marriage. The children of John[3] Bedenbaugh, and wife Rhoda:[30]

+ 54   i. William J.[4] Bedenbaugh, b. 7 May 1832
+ 55   ii. James Lyttleton[4] Bedenbaugh, b. 12 June 1834
+ 56   iii. George Anderson[4] Bedenbaugh, b. 1836
+ 57   iv. Elizabeth[4] Bedenbaugh, b. 1839
   58   v. Lucinda[4] Bedenbaugh, b. 1841
+ 59   vi. Louisa Manerva[4] Bedenbaugh, b. 16 Apr 1842
+ 60   vii. Franklin S.[4] Bedenbaugh, b. c1845
+ 61   viii. Elijah King[4] Bedenbaugh, b. 1847
+ 62   ix. Rosanna[4] Bedenbaugh, b. 1850
+ 63   x. Laura Frances[4] Bedenbaugh, b. 1857.

11. Christian[3] Bedenbaugh (Adam[2], Michael[1]), birthdate unknown, died 1826, pre-deceasing his father. He married Rosemond Lester. His estate was administered by his father Adam Bedenbaugh Sr. and his widow Rosemond.[31] The estate papers state that he left only one child, George Washington Bedenbaugh, who was two years of age, 1 Jan 1832. A deed of gift of one negro slave from W. D. Lester to Rosemond Bedenbaugh, dated October 1827, is found in Newberry Deed Book U-2, page 95. The child of Christian[3] Bedenbaugh, and wife Rosemond Lester:

   64   George Washington[4] Bedenbaugh, b. 1829/30, removed to Indiana.

12. William[3] Bedenbaugh (Adam[2], Michael[1]) was born c1807 and was living in Georgia in 1888, according to the Annals of Newberry. He married, first, Hester, a daughter of John Stephens, Sr., who died prior to 1838 when a settlement of his estate indicates the amount due to the children of William Bedenbaugh by his wife Hester deceased.[32] The names of those children are not stated, nor do we know

exactly when Hester died. It seems likely, from the years of birth of the children, that Elizabeth and George Anderson Bedenbaugh were children of Hester. The name of William Bedenbaugh's second wife was Rosanna. He was still living in Newberry District, South Carolina, at the time of the taking of the 1850 and the 1860 census.[33] The children of William[3] Bedenbaugh:

+ 65 i. Elizabeth[4] Bedenbaugh, b. c1832
  66 ii. George Anderson[4] Bedenbaugh, b. c1835, killed in Confederate service, 8 July 1863. He is probably the G. A. Bedenbaugh listed as serving as a private in Co. H, Infantry, Holcombe Legion.
  67 iii. Permelia[4] Bedenbaugh, b. c1843
  68 iv. Cornelius[4] Bedenbaugh, b. c1846
+ 69 v. Benjamin F.[4] Bedenbaugh, b. 31 Dec 1849
  70 vi. Amanda[4] Bedenbaugh, b. c1851 m. 23 Dec 1869, to Arthur J. Lott.[34]
  71 vii. Simpson E.[4] Bedenbaugh, b. c1856.

FOURTH GENERATION

14. Eve[4] Bedenbaugh (Henry[3] Adam[2], Michael[1]) was born 11 September 1813 and died 8 December 1879. She married Frederick W. Boozer, Jr., who was born 10 October 1804 and died 5 February 1860. Both are buried in a Boozer family cemetery in Newberry County, South Carolina. Frederick W. Boozer had married, first, Mary (Polly) Sheppard. Two children:[35]
+ 72   i. Lemuel Lee[5] Boozer, b. 4 Oct 1832
   73   ii. Harriet H.[5] Boozer, b. 24 Mar 1836 d. 12 Aug 1868 married John Mark Wilson, b. 6 Aug 1838 d. 28 Oct 1865, buried at St. Luke's Lutheran Church.

15. Daniel[4] Bedenbaugh (Henry[3], Adam[2], Michael[1]) was born 7 October 1814 and died 18 August 1845, buried at St. Luke's Lutheran Church. He married Anna (Annie) Caroline Kinard, who was born 10 June 1822 and died 31 Jan 1889. She is buried in Fulmer Cemetery, Lafayette County, Miss. The estate papers of Daniel Bedenbaugh indicate that he left two children Simpson Kleckly Bedenbaugh and Daniel Vianna Bedenbaugh, and that the widow Anna had married John Fulmer by 3 Sept 1849.[36] The family moved to Millport, Alabama, and then to Lafayette County, Mississippi, in 1866. John Fulmer died in Confederate service. Two children:
+ 74   i. Simpson Kleckley[5] Bedenbaugh, b. 26 June 1844
   75   ii. Daniel Vianna[5] Bedenbaugh, m. John Smith.

16. John Adam[4] Bedenbaugh (Henry[3], Adam[2], Michael[1]) was born 11 July 1816 and died 5 January 1899 in Newberry County, South Carolina. He married, on 25 June 1845, Lucy Caroline Wright, who was born 21 February 1817 and died 2 September 1909. Both are both buried at St. Luke's Lutheran Church. This family were devout members of St. Luke's. The Rev. Thaddeus S. Boinest often visited in their home as is evidenced by his diary.[37] In the account of the Bedenbaugh Family in the *Annals of Newberry*,[38] the two eldest children are mentioned and the statement that two daughters died in 1865 is included. According to the St. Luke's Lutheran Church records, the two daughters died of meningitis.

Children of John Adam[4] and Lucy Caroline (Wright) Bedenbaugh:
+ 76   i. Zacheus Wright[5] Bedenbaugh, b. 15 Oct 1846
+ 77   ii. Mary Ella[5] Bedenbaugh, b. 28 Sept 1849
   78 iii. Emma Elizabeth[5] Bedenbaugh, b. 28 Sept 1849, d. 26 Feb 1865, bur. St. Luke's Lutheran Church.
   79 iv. Cleova Ursula[5] Bedenbaugh, b. 18 Mar 1853, bapt. 18 June 1853[39], d. 22 Feb 1865.

17. Simeon[4] Bedenbaugh (Henry[3], Adam[2], Michael[1]) was born 8 March 1819 and died 7 April 1893. He married, first, Rebecca Kinard, who was born 28 January 1828 and died 15 July 1854. He married, second, Catherine (Caty) Dewalt or Rikard, who was born 25 April 1823 and died 13 January 1905.[40] All three are buried at St. Luke's Lutheran Church.

Simeon Bedenbaugh served in the Confederate Army in Company A, 4th Battalion, South Carolina Reserves, enlisting on 30 December 1864.

Children by Rebecca Kinard:

80 i. Amelia[5] Bedenbaugh, b. 24 Nov 1848, d. 27 June 1933, m. 1st, 26 Dec 1893 (his 3rd wife), Archibald Basil Mills, Jr.,[41] b. 10 Feb 1825, d. 21 June 1905; m. 2nd Jacob C. Counts, b. 21 Aug 1847, d. 5 Aug 1926. No issue. Jacob C. and Amelia Counts are bur. in Prosperity Cem. Amelia was known as "Aunt Sis" to relatives.
+ 81 ii. Warren P.[5] Bedenbaugh, b. 23 April 1850
+ 82 iii. Jacob Kibler[5] Bedenbaugh, b. 21 Feb 1852

Children by Catherine Rikard:

+ 83 iv. Hawkins Kinard[5] Bedenbaugh, b. 28 July 1855
+ 84 v. John Simpson[5] Bedenbaugh, b. 4 Jan 1857
+ 85 vi. George Pettus[5] Bedenbaugh, b. 11 Apr 1860
+ 86 vii. Nancy[5] Bedenbaugh, b. 10 Aug 1862
  87 viii. Ella Caroline[5] Bedenbaugh, b. 1867, d. 4 Jan 1944, m. 18 March 1888 (Z. W. Bedenbaugh officiating),[42] Thompson Luther Morris, b. 16 June 1866, d. 16 March 1920, the son of Thomas and Rosanna (Hair) Morris.[43] Both are buried at St. Luke's Lutheran Church.

19. Malinda[4] Bedenbaugh (Henry[3], Adam[2], Michael[1]) was born 6 January 1823 and died 19 November 1899. She married Jacob Hawkins, who was born 26 July 1822 and died 9 January 1892. Both are buried at St. Luke's Lutheran Church near Prosperity, South Carolina. Children:
  88 i. Sampson Elijah[5] Hawkins, b. 11 Aug 1844, d. 19 Nov 1899, bur. St. Luke's; m. Mary Hendrix, b. 19 Apr 1834, d. 1 Dec 1912.
  89 ii. Simon Peter[5] Hawkins, b. c1846
  90 iii. Mary J.[5] Hawkins, b. c1849
  91 iv. Sarah Amelia[5] Hawkins, b. c1851 m. William Sheppard
  92 v. Pinckney[5] Hawkins, b. c1853
  93 vi. Thomas Burley[5] Hawkins, b. 13 Aug 1856, d. 25 March 1930, bur. St. Luke's Lutheran Church.
  94 vii. Jacob[5] Hawkins
  95 viii. Tilda[5] Hawkins
  96 ix. Nannie[5] Hawkins.

20. Rachel[4] Bedenbaugh (Henry[3], Adam[2], Michael[1]) was born 12 September 1825 and died 31 May 1892. She married Mathias Wicker, who was born 16 February 1816 and died 3 April 1884, natural son of Mathias Wicker. Both are buried at Colony Lutheran Church. The will of Mathias Wicker, dated 21 April 1881 and proved 6 May 1884, names his wife Rachel and their children Thomas Jefferson, Henry Pinkney and James Monroe.[44] Children[45]:
  97 i. James Monroe[5] Wicker, b. 25 Feb 1852, d. 8 Nov 1908, married Sallie L. Cook, b. 19 Oct 1853, d. 16 Feb 1930. Both bur. in Prosperity Cem; no children survived.
  98 ii. Thomas Jefferson[5] Wicker, b. 12 Sept 1860, d. 21 Dec 1937; m. Nancy L. (Nannie) Cook, b. 16 Feb 1861, d. 5 Oct 1945. Both bur. Colony Lutheran Church; no children survived.
  99 iii. Henry Pinckney[5] Wicker, b. 26 Jan 1869, d. 4 May 1951; m. 22 Nov 1900 Ella (Black) Willis, b. 21/5 May 1871, d. 3 May 1959. Both bur. Prosperity Cem. There were no surviving Wicker children.

THE BEDENBAUGH-BETENBAUGH FAMILY

21. Rosanna Caroline[4] Bedenbaugh (Henry[3], Adam[2], Michael[1]) was born 2 May 1829 and died 5 July 1897. She married, on 25 November 1846, Allen Marlow Nichols, who was born 10 April 1821 and died 29 January 1899. Both are buried at St. Luke's Lutheran Church, near Prosperity, South Carolina. Children:

100   i. Benjamin Franklin[5] Nichols, b. 7 Sept 1847, d. 2 Nov 1895
101   ii. Harriet Rebecca[5] Nichols, b. 27 Oct 1849, d. 11 Aug 1933
102   iii. James Sampson[5] Nichols, b. 2 March 1852, d. 24 June 1918
103   iv. Allen Hamilton[5] Nichols, b. 16 Nov 1854, d. 3 March 1942
104   v. Henry Luke[5] Nichols, b. 15 Oct 1857 d. 1 June 1892
105   vi. Susan Elizabeth[5] Nichols, b. 16 Feb 1860, d. 2 Aug 1943
106   vii. Emily Caroline[5] Nichols, b. 15 Oct 1864, d. 3 Nov 1951
107   viii. Joseph Mark[5] Nichols, b. 6 Sept 1867, d. 29 February 1948
108   ix. Ellen Rosannah[5] Nichols, b. 26 Jan 1870, d. 21 February 1936.

26. John Adam[4] Bedenbaugh, Sr. (Adam Jr.[3], Adam[2], Michael[1]) was born 15 April 1823 and died 20 February 1905.[46] He married Sarah D. (Sallie) Cook who was born 28 April 1825 and died 1 September 1893, the daughter of Jacob and Margaret (Aull) Cook. Both are buried at St Mark's Lutheran Church, Saluda County, South Carolina.

In 1900, John Adam Bedenbaugh, Sr., was living in the household of his son, John Adam Bedenbaugh, Jr. His photograph is reproduced on page 21.
Children:

+ 109   i. Mary Jane[5] Bedenbaugh, b. 18 Aug 1847
    110 ii. William A.[5] Bedenbaugh, 1 Sept 1849, d. 28 Sept 1888, m. Fannie E. Dominick, b. 13 Nov 1850, d. 25 Feb 1924, both bur. Union Luth. Ch.
    111 iii. Andrew[5] Bedenbaugh, b. ca. 1851
+ 112 iv. Jacob Calvin[5] Bedenbaugh, b. 10 Nov 1852
+ 113   v. Ellen R.[5] Bedenbaugh, b. 10 Jan 1854
+ 114 vi. Sarah Cornelia[5] Bedenbaugh, b. 10 Feb 1855
+ 115 vii. John Adam[5] Bedenbaugh, Jr., b. 15 Oct 1859.

27. Nancy C.[4] Bedenbaugh (Adam Jr.[3], Adam[2], Michael[1]) was born 7 June 1825 and died 7 March 1905. She married, first, John Simon Buzzard, who was born 16 July 1819 and died 14 June 1855. She married, second, Jacob Singley, who was born 21 April 1805 and died 29 November 1881. John Simon Buzzard is buried in the Buzhardt Family Cemetery.[47] Jacob Singley is buried beside his first wife (Sarah Wise) in the Singley Family Cemetery near Prosperity. Nancy Bedenbaugh Singley is buried at St. Paul's Lutheran Church, Pomaria, South Carolina. Children of Nancy (Bedenbaugh) (Buzzard) Singley:

116   i. Harriet Olivia[5] Buzzard, b. 11 Oct 1848, d. 20 Apr 1855, bur. Buzhardt Cem.
117   ii. Josephine[5] Buzzard, b. 1 Feb 1850, d. 7 Sept 1935, m. Wm. Henry Kibler, b. 20 Nov 1849, d. 15 Sept 1932, bur. St. Paul's Lutheran Church
118   iii. Mary[5] Buzzard, b. 3 Nov 1851, d. 18 Jan 1929, married Jacob L. Fellers, b. 5 June 1840, d. 27 Feb 1914, bur. St. Paul's Lutheran Church
119   iv. Jacob Calhoun[5] Singley, b. 9 Nov 1858, d. 14 Aug 1931,[48] m. 12 Sept 1884 Anna Martha Counts, b. 11 July 1861. d. 15 March 1939, both bur. St. Paul's Lutheran Church; children:
        120 a. Jacob Omerle[6] Singley, b. 18 Feb 1888, d. 21 Aug 1918 in WWI

THE BEDENBAUGH-BETENBAUGH FAMILY

John Adam Bedenbaugh, Sr.

THE BEDENBAUGH-BETENBAUGH FAMILY

Andrew Jackson Bedenbaugh

121 b. Annie Calhoun[6] Singley, b. 11 Sept 1890, d. 26 Nov 1973. m. 6 Jan 1921, James David Luther, b. 22 July 1877, d. 29 Jan 1970, bur. Prosperity Cem.

122 c. Leta Rosine[6] Singley, b. Feb 1893, d. 15 Nov 1955, m. Robert E. Carnes

123 d. Leslie Keely[6] Singley, b. 16 Dec 1895, d. 7 July 1967, m. Mildred Powell

124 e. Celeste Mower[6] Singley, b .29 July 1899, m. Lucius Herbert Harvey

125 f. George Heyward Schumpert[6] Singley, b. 5 Sept 1903, d. 7 Aug 1959, m. 23 Dec 1933 Carolyn Denby Price, b. 11 June 1904

126 v. Lillus R. Alice[5] Singley, b. 29 Oct 1860, d. 4 Jan 1947, m. David Hardin Witherspoon, b. 6 Mar 1853, d. 17 July 1921, both bur. Prosperity Cem.

127 vi. Eugenie Carrie[5] Singley, b. 27 Jan 1864, d. 17 Feb 1943, m. Jesse D. Lorick, b. 17 June 1860, d. 20 June 1940, both bur. Prosperity Cem.

128 vi. Augustus A.[5] Singley, b. 25 Apr 1866, d. 28 Jan 1934, m. Ellen M. Kibler, b. 29 Nov 1869, d. 16 Dec 1938, both bur. St. Paul's Lutheran Church

129 v. Anna F.[5] Singley, b. 7 March 1868, d. 3 March 1963, m. John Wheeler, b. Nov 1860, d. 29 May 1923, bur. St. Paul's Lutheran Church

130 vi. Pettus Claude[5] Singley, b. 22 March 1873, d. 27 March 1951, m. 5 March 1899 Phoebe Rebecca Schumpert, b. 2 Feb 1880, d. 24 Dec 1969, bur. Prosperity Cem; children:

131 a. Claude Mower[6] Singley, b. 25 March 1900, d. 29 Apr 1982, m. 22 Aug 1928, Annie S. Powell, b. 28 Aug 1908

132 b. Phebe Schumpert[6] Singley, b. 12 May 1911, m. 25 Sept 1935 m. William Oscar Callahan, b. 29 June 1908, d. 21 Nov 1967.

28. Andrew Jackson[4] Bedenbaugh (Adam Jr.[3], Adam[2], Michael[1]) was born 15 September 1827 and died 4 June 1897. He married, on 24 November 1874,[49] to Ella Rebecca (or Eleanor Rebecca) Folk, who was born 7 December 1852 and died 27 July 1939. Andrew J. Bedenbaugh is buried at Bedenbaugh Cemetery off Highway 773, near I-26. Eleanor F. Bedenbaugh is buried at St. Paul's Lutheran Church near Pomaria, South Carolina. His photograph is reproduced on page 22. Children:

+ 133 i. John Bachman[5] Bedenbaugh, b. 18 March 1876

134 ii. Annie Viola[5] Bedenbaugh, b. 2 Oct 1877, d. 14 July 1878, bur. Beden baugh Cemetery.

+ 135 iii. Grace Edith Leone[5] Bedenbaugh, b. 11 Jan 1879

136 iv. Hattie Elizabeth[5] Bedenbaugh, b. 18 Oct 1880, bapt. 24 June 1881 (Bethlehem Lutheran Church records), d. 4 Nov 1892, bur. Bedenbaugh Cemetery.

+ 137 v. William Lamar[5] Bedenbaugh, b. 8 Sept 1882

+ 138 vi. Annie Mae[5] Bedenbaugh, b. 24 Mar 1884

+ 139 vii. Ida Beatrice[5] Bedenbaugh, b. 28 Dec 1885

140 viii. Andrew Jackson[5] Bedenbaugh, Jr. (D. D. S.), b. 31 Jan 1888, bapt. 27 May 1888 (Bethlehem Lutheran Church records), died 14 Dec 1955, Columbia, SC, unm., served in the Dental Corps of the US Army in World War I.[50]

+ 141 ix. Lorane Berley[5] Bedenbaugh, b. 6 Sept 1889

142 x. Leola[5] Bedenbaugh, b. 21 June 1893, d. 28 Aug 1956, did not marry.

32. Katherine[4] Bedenbaugh (Michael[3], Adam[2], Michael[1]) died before 1850, married Robert Cutter, who was born c1815. Two children:[51]
  143 i. Andrew[5] Cutter born c1845
  144 ii. Hayne[5] Cutter, d. Dec 1861.

33. Laodicea[4] Bedenbaugh (Michael[3], Adam[2], Michael[1]) was born c1820. She married John W. Summer, Jr., who was born c1817. Children:[52]
  145 i. Jacob J.[5] Summer, b. c1839
  146 ii. Nancy Caroline[5] Summer, b. 9 July 1845, d. 28 Apr 1911. She married Franklin S.[4] Bedenbaugh in September of 1866.[53] (see under John[3] Bedenbaugh).

35. Elizabeth A.[4] Bedenbaugh (Michael[3], Adam[2], Michael[1]) was born c1825 died after 1880. She married, first, John Adam Boozer and, second, Henry Boozer.
Children by John A. Boozer:
  147 i. Henry M.[5] Boozer, b. c1845, d. 1864, m. Mary Ann Nobles
  148 ii. Benjamin Martin[5] Boozer b. 6 May 1850 d. 19 May 1882
  149 iii. Amelia or Permelia Elizabeth[5] Boozer, b. 28 June 1856 d. 28 Aug 1928
  150 iv. Mary Jane[5] Boozer, b. 4 Sept 1859, d. 17 May 1915
  151 v. Jefferson Davis[5] Boozer, b. 13 Sept 1861, d. 26 Sept 1920

Children by Henry Boozer:
  152 vi. Carrie[5] Boozer, b. c1871
  153 vii. Bessie[5] Boozer, b. c1876.

36. John A.[4] Conwill (Elizabeth[3], Adam[2], Michael[1]) was born 2 May 1821, Newberry District, South Carolina, and died 8 September 1897, in Amory, Monroe County, Mississippi. He married Melverda Jane Wiygul, who was born 27 November 1833 in Monroe County, Mississippi, and died 18 September 1897 in Nettleton, Itawamba County, Mississippi. Both are buried in the Wiygul Cemetery in Itawamba County. Eleven children, the first born in Monroe County, Alabama, and all others in Monroe County, Mississippi:
  154 i. George A.[5] Conwill, b. 3 Oct 1852, d. inf.
+ 155 ii. John Franklin[5] Conwill, b. 13 June 1854
+ 156 iii. Jesse Daniel[5] Conwill, b. 1 March 1856
  157 iv. Nancy L.[5] Conwill, b. 8 Jan 1858, d. 27 June 1913, m. Charley E. Knight
  158 v. Mary Lee[5] Conwill, b. 1 June 1860
  159 vi. A. B. Mayfield[5] Conwill, b. 10 Sept 1862, d. 1 Sept 1915, m. 24 Nov 1886 E. J. Neal
  160 vii. James T.[5] Conwill, b. 5 Apr 1865, d. 30 Nov 1939, m. 2 Dec 1885 R. Ellen Neal
  161 viii. Amanda[5] Conwill, b. 27 May 1867, d. 1944, m. Byram Sylvester Roebuck
  162 ix. F. Lula[5] Conwill, b. 8 Oct 1869, d. 17 March 1914, m. William Gordon Schumpert
  163 x. Ruth D.[5] "Dusty" Conwill, b. 21 Nov 1872, d. IL, m. Dr. Walter Hood
  164 xi. Sally M.[5] Conwill, b. 7 May 1876, m. Judge Emerson.

37. Yates Jury[4] Conwill (Elizabeth[3], Adam[2], Michael[1]) was born 16 December 1824 in Newberry District, South Carolina, and died 18 August 1860 in Monroe County, Mississippi. He married Nancy Hunter, who was born 7 March 1826 in Alabama, and died 13 March 1916 in Monroe County, Mississippi. They are buried in the Shumpert Cemetery in Itawamba County, Mississippi. Children:

165   i. Matthew[5] Conwill, b. 12 Sept 1847, Monroe Co., AL., d. 13 Sept 1911, m.
        Martha Green
166 ii. William[5] Conwill, b. Apr 1850, prob. died in childhood
+ 167 iii. Joseph Daniel[5] Conwill, b. Feb 1852, Monroe Co., AL
+ 168 iv. Yates Jury[5] Conwill, Jr., b. 18 Sept 1857, Monroe Co., MS
169   v. Timothy L.[5] Conwill, b. 15 Aug 1860, d. 28 May 1899, unm.

45. Levi[4] Bedenbaugh (Jacob[3], Adam[2], Michael[1]) was born 11 December 1812 in
Lexington District, South Carolina, and died 7 December 1879 at Senoia, Coweta
County, Georgia.[54] He married, on 28 November 1835, Barbara Rawls, who was
born 21 January 1812 in Lexington District, South Carolina, and died 5 April 1883
in Senoia, Georgia. Both are buried at Mt. Pilgrim Lutheran Church in Coweta
County, Georgia.

Levi Bedenbaugh was one of the first students of the Lutheran Theological
Seminary at Lexington, South Carolina, and was ordained by the Synod of South
Carolina in 1835. He was a pioneer of Lutheranism in middle and upper Georgia
and was a charter member of the Georgia Synod. He served several churches in
South Carolina before moving to Georgia, where he served Mt. Pilgrim Lutheran
Church. Children:
170   i. Rebecca Elizabeth[5] Bedenbaugh, b. Lexington Dist., SC, 15 October 1836,
        m. 20 May 1862 to John C. Summer; child:
        171 a. Henry Hazelius[6] Summer born 15 Oct 1864.
172 ii. Jacob Hazelius[5] Bedenbaugh, b. 4 Jan 1840, Coweta Co., Ga., d. 29 Nov
        1863 Knoxville, TN, while in Confederate service. He was a second
        lieutenant in Co. A, 7th Georgia Infantry.[55]
173 iii. Luther Melancthon[5] Bedenbaugh, b. 15 March 1849, d. 24 March 1849,
        Coweta Co., GA.
+ 174 iv. Levi William Pickens[5] Bedenbaugh, b. 20 Aug 1851.

46. Mathias Hare[4] Bedenbaugh (Jacob[3], Adam[2], Michael[1]) was born c1817 and died
January 1850 in Edgefield District, South Carolina.[56] He married Amanda
Mitchell(?), who was born c1818. The occupation of Mathias Hare Bedenbaugh was
indicated as farmer and the cause of his death was dyspepsia.
Children:[57]
175   i. Frances[5] Bedenbaugh, b. c1838
+ 176 ii. James T.[5] Bedenbaugh, b. 20 Sept 1839
177 iii. Nancy[5] Bedenbaugh, b. c1841
178 iv. Levi[5] Bedenbaugh, b. c1843
+ 179   v. Jacob P.[5] Bedenbaugh, b. Feb 1845
180 vi. Mary[5] Bedenbaugh, b. c1846
+ 181 vii. Simon Wilson[5] Bedenbaugh, b. 15 May 1846
+ 182 viii. Mathias Hare[5] Bedenbaugh, Jr., b. 12 Oct 1849.

47. Simeon Wilson[4] Bedenbaugh (Jacob[3], Adam[2], Michael[1]) was born 17 August
1818 in Newberry District, South Carolina, and died 13 June 1879 in Columbia
County, Florida. He served several Lutheran Churches in Georgia and removed to
Florida in 1872, where he served Bethlehem Lutheran Church in Columbia County,
Florida. His photograph is reproduced in the Centennial Book of that church
(1959). He married, first, Margaret Elizabeth Kinard (1819-1862) and second,
Phoebe Ann McBride.

Children by Margaret Elizabeth Kinard:

    183   i. Jacob W.[5] Bedenbaugh, b. c1840 married Mary Jane Cloud. He served as a private in Co. A, 10th Battalion, Georgia Infantry.

    184   ii. Martha[5] Bedenbaugh, b. c1842

    185   iii. Mathias H.[5] Bedenbaugh, b. 13 May 1845, d. 21 June 1920, m. Roxie Ann L. Norris. He served as a private in Co. A, 10th Battalion, Georgia Infantry.

+ 186   iv. John L.[5] Bedenbaugh, b. c1850 Macon Co., GA

    187   v. Nancy E.[5] Bedenbaugh, b. c1853 Macon Co., GA, m. Mahlor C. Wright

    188   vi. Sarah C.[5] Bedenbaugh, b. c1855 Macon Co., GA, m. Cicero Nelson

+ 189   vii. Lemuel David[5] Bedenbaugh, b. 6 March 1857

    190 viii. Levi Harris[5] Bedenbaugh, b. 1859, m. Lovonia Witt, b. 1862

Children by Phoebe Ann McBride:

    191   ix. James Kleckly[5] (Jim) Bedenbaugh, b. c1863, married Rosa Roberts

    192   x. Margaret Irene[5] Bedenbaugh, b. 1868, d. 1954, m. Buford Carrell.

49. Eliza[4] Bedenbaugh (Jacob[3], Adam[2], Michael[1]) was born _____ and died before 1864. She married Jim Sheppard and had the following children:

    193   i. James Dominick[5] Sheppard, b. c1844

    194   ii. Samuel[5] Sheppard, b. c1846

    195   iii. Elizabeth Caroline[5] Sheppard, b. c1848.

50. Drury David[4] Bedenbaugh (Jacob[3], Adam[2], Michael[1]) was born 27 April 1824 and died 30 June 1863, while in Confederate service, in Quincy, Florida. He married, on 4 March 1851, in Lexington District, South Carolina, Rebecca Smith, who was born 16 April 1828 and died 30 June 1902. He was a private in Co. G, 64th Georgia Infantry. Children:

+ 196   i. David Bachman[5] Bedenbaugh, b. 12 Aug 1858

+ 197   ii. Sarah[5] Bedenbaugh

    198   iii. Mary[5] Bedenbaugh, m. Patrick McBride

    199   iv. Annie[5] Bedenbaugh, m. 1st, Judson Chambless; 2nd, W. R. Speer

+ 200   v. Frances Drury[5] Bedenbaugh, b. 20 Sept 1863.

51. Jacob Asbury[4] Bedenbaugh (Jacob[3], Adam[2], Michael[1]) was born 16 November 1826 and died 15 January 1873. He married Amanda Emeline Long who was born 18 March 1833 and died 18 December 1917. Both are buried Zion United Methodist Church, near Prosperity, South Carolina. An obituary notice of Jacob Asbury Bedenbaugh appeared in the *Southern Christian Advocate*, the Methodist publication.[58] He served as a corporal in Co. H., Infantry, Holcombe Legion. Children:

+ 201   i. Laura Rebecca[5] Bedenbaugh, b. 5 Oct 1853

+ 202   ii. David Murchison[5] Bedenbaugh, b. 19 Nov 1855

+ 203   iii. Mark Boyd[5] Bedenbaugh, b. July 1857

+ 204   iv. Mack Wilson[5] Bedenbaugh, b. 17 Feb 1859

+ 205   v. Thomas Boston[5] Bedenbaugh, b. 1860   1862

    206   vi. Mary A.[5] Bedenbaugh, b. 7 March 1962, d. 2 Feb 1949, unm., bur. Zion United Methodist Church.

    207 vii. Nancy[5] Bedenbaugh, b. 5 Oct 1866, d. 21 Apr 1936, m. J. Bennett Dominick (1871-1948), no children.

    208 viii. Miles B.[5] Bedenbaugh, b. 2 Apr 1868, d. 6 July 1940, Laurens Co., SC

+ 209   ix. Joseph Falls[5] Bedenbaugh, b. 20 Oct 1870.

THE BEDENBAUGH-BETENBAUGH FAMILY

52. Rachel[4] Bedenbaugh (Jacob[3], Adam[2], Michael[1]) was born 2 April 1829 and died 2 June 1881. She married, on 12 November 1846, Archibald Basil (Archie) Mills, Jr., who was born 10 February 1825 and died 21 June 1905. They are buried at Zion United Methodist Church near Prosperity, South Carolina. Archie Mills married, second, Emanda Harmon, and, third, Amelia[5] Bedenbaugh (Simeon[4], Henry[3], Adam[2], Michael[1]). Children:

+ 210   i. David Newton[5] Mills, b. 12 Oct 1847
   211   ii. Jacob W.[5] Mills (1850-1905), m. Sarah Elizabeth _____
+ 212   iii. Benjamin F.[5] Mills, b. 21 Aug 1852
   213   iv. George A.[5] Mills, b. 24 July 1854, d. 22 Aug 1929, m. Frances (Fannie) Permelia Boozer, b. Oct 1851, d. 15 Jan 1929; child:
         214 a. Boston Augustus[6] Mills b. 6 April 1880, d. 30 May 1898
   215   v. Mark[5] Mills, b. 8 July 1856, d. 11 Nov 1933, m. Sallie Long b. 25 Apr 1856, d. 4 May 1935, bur. Colony Lutheran Church.
+ 216   vi. James Burr[5] Mills, b. 21 Dec 1857
   217   vii. John P.[5] Mills, b. 5 Jan 1861, d. 6 May 1942, m. Nannie Louise Cameron, b. 8 Sept 1858, d. 30 Sept 1939; child:
         218 a. Leona Lucile[6] Mills, b. 28 June 1899, d. 7 July 1899, bur. Zion.
   219   viii. Anna Estelle[5] Mills, b. 1866 m. Jake Long
+ 220   ix. Mary Ellen[5] Mills, b. 3 Sept 1863.
+ 221   x. Thomas Marion[5] Mills, b. 1 Apr 1870.

54. William J.[4] Bedenbaugh (John[3], Adam[2], Michael[1]) was born 7 May 1832 and died 31 August 1903. He married, on 3 July 1856,[59] Martha Vaughn, who was born 23 September 1836 and died 11 September 1910. Both are buried in Rosemont Cemetery, Newberry, South Carolina. Children:

+ 222   i. Mary Jane[5] Bedenbaugh, b. 2 June 1859
+ 223   ii. Nancy[5] Bedenbaugh, b. 19 Nov 1865
+ 224   iii. James Luther[5] Bedenbaugh, b. 13 Dec 1870, m. May Dobbin
+ 225   iv. Lula[5] Bedenbaugh, b. 6 June 1874
   226   v. Sallie[5] Bedenbaugh, b. 3 Oct 1877, d. 22 June 1948, m. Charles William Douglass, b. 31 Jan 1875, d. 10 Apr 1943, both bur. Rosemont Cem, Newberry, SC (no children).

55. James Lyttleton[4] Bedenbaugh (John[3], Adam[2], Michael[1]) was born 12 June 1834 in Newberry District, South Carolina, and died 12 July 1903 in Columbia County, Florida. He married Louisa Shealy, who was born 1 June 1834 in Edgefield District, South Carolina, and died 5 November 1918 in Columbia County, Florida. Their photograph appears in *The Centennial Book of Bethlehem Lutheran Church* of Columbia County, Florida. Children:

+ 227   i. Sara Emma[5] Bedenbaugh, b. 14 Apr 1852
+ 228   ii. Francis (Frank) Pickens[5] Bedenbaugh, b. 11 Aug 1859
   229   iii. Lemuel George[5] Bedenbaugh, b. 7 Dec 1863, d. July 1883, did not marry
+ 230   iv. John Nicholas[5] Bedenbaugh, b. 29 June 1867
+ 231   v. William Pinkney[5] Bedenbaugh, b. 14 Sept 1870.

56. George Anderson[4] Bedenbaugh (John[3], Adam[2], Michael[1]) was born c1836 and died 11 July 1896.[60] He married Sarah Jane Williams, who was born 18 February 1838, and died 13 March 1917, in Columbia, South Carolina, a daughter of John and Sallie (Oats) Williams.[61] There is a gravestone for S. J. Bedenbaugh in the cemetery of St. Luke's Lutheran Church, but none has been located there for George.

This couple was one of the most difficult to identify because of varying names of the children on the census reports and the lack of a tombstone for George A. Bedenbaugh. The record that paved the way to the solution was the city directory for Columbia in 1916, wherein there is a listing "Bedenbaugh, Sarah J., wid George."[62] Per the 1910 census, the mother had had fourteen children, nine of whom were still living. We can compile at least a partial list of these children[63]:

232   i. Drayton[5] Bedenbaugh, b. c1860
233   ii. Frank[5] Bedenbaugh, b. c1864
+ 234   iii. William Pierce[5] Bedenbaugh, b. 13 May 1867
235   iv. H. E.[5] Bedenbaugh (sometimes listed as Rob), b. 19 Feb 1869, d. 13 Sept 1910 in Columbia, SC, bur. St. Luke's Lutheran Church, near Prosperity.
236   v. Sparta[5] Bedenbaugh, b. c1872
237   vi. Ella[5] Bedenbaugh, b. c1874, m. Samuel Mundy. Children:[64]
        238 a. Jesse[6] Mundy, b. c1892 m. Will Klugh
        239 b. Early[6] James Mundy, b. 20 Nov 1897, d. 25 Apr 1981, bur. Rosemont Cem., Newberry, SC
        240 c. Bessie[6] Mundy, b. c1903
+ 241   vii. John Denniston[5] Bedenbaugh, b. 18 May 1875
242 viii. Sallie[5] Bedenbaugh, b. 25 May 1877, d. 1 June 1891, bur. St. Luke's Lutheran Church.
243   ix. Simon[5] Bedenbaugh, b. Apr 1880.

57. Elizabeth[4] Bedenbaugh (John[3], Adam[2], Michael[1]) was born c1839 and married John Williams. Children:
244   i. J. Luther Williams m. Jo Coon
245   ii. Rufus Williams m. Emma Buzzard
246   iii. Willie Williams
247   iv. Erma Williams.

59. Louisa Manerva[4] Bedenbaugh (John[3], Adam[2], Michael[1]) was born 16 April 1842 and died 4 June 1910. She married Nicholas Summer Merchant, who was born 9 August 1836 and died 8 February 1891. Both are buried at St. Luke's Lutheran Church near Prosperity, South Carolina. Children:[65]
248   i. George Sampson[5] Merchant, b. 14 Sept 1859, d. 25 Apr 1920 in Sumter Co., SC,[66] m. Ella Lester (1863-1909), bur. St. Luke's Lutheran Church.
249   ii. Frank[5] Merchant, m. Beatrice Cousins
250   iii. Langdon[5] Merchant m. Emma Miller
251   iv. Henry Wingard[5] Merchant, b. 30 Apr 1881, d. 5 May 1929, m. Alberta Cook, b. 10 June 1880, d. 6 Feb 1967, bur. St. Luke's Lutheran Church.
252   v. Edward[5] Merchant, m. Mary Minnick
253   vi. Allie[5] Merchant m. James Vaughn
254   vii. Mary[5] Merchant m. 1st Jim Long; 2nd Jim Dickert
255 viii. Katie[5] Merchant m. Wiley Taylor
256   ix. Flora[5] Merchant
257   x. Rhoda Roberta[5] Merchant, b. 12 July 1885, d. 11 Mar 1931,[67] m. Willie Elisha Schumpert, b. 22 Aug 1882, d. 11 June 1960, both bur. St. Luke's Lutheran Church.

60. Franklin S.[4] Bedenbaugh (John[3], Adam[2], Michael[1]) was born c1845 and died 5 April 1916[68]. He married, in September of 1866, Nancy Caroline Summer, who was born 19 July 1845[69] and died 28 April 1921 in Olympia, Richland County, South

Carolina,[70] the daughter of John W., Jr., and Laodicea[4] (Bedenbaugh) Summer (Michael[3], Adam[2], Michael[1]). Three children:
+ 258 i. Walter Simpson[5] Bedenbaugh, b. 8 Jan 1876
   259 ii. Elizabeth[5] Bedenbaugh, b. 21 Jan 1881, d. 25 Jan 1941, m. Charles Edward King, b. 4 March 1879, d. 15 May 1925, both bur. Rosemont Cem., Newberry, SC. Children:
     260 a. Blanche[6] King
     261 b. Bonnelle[6] King
     262 c. Laura Mae[6] King
     263 d. Frank[6] King
  264 iii. Ernest C.[5] Bedenbaugh, b. 1884, d. 10 May 1932, Charleston, SC, m. Vida Mae Smith, b. 25 Apr 1893, d. 12 Feb 1938, both bur. Rosemont Cem., Newberry, SC. Three sons:
     265 a. Ralph[6] Bedenbaugh
     266 b. Everett[6] Bedenbaugh
     267 c. Harry[6] Bedenbaugh.

61. Elijah King[4] Bedenbaugh (John[3], Adam[2], Michael[1]) was born 11 July 1847 (tombstone has 1850) and died 18 July 1910. He married, on 22 December 1870, Mattie J. Rogers, who was born 8 September 1852 and died 10 June 1926. Both are buried in the Prosperity Cemetery./The date of marriage is from "Family Record 1897" written by Elijah K. Bedenbaugh,[71] as is much of the information on the descendants of John Bedenbaugh. This record indicates that Rhoda's maiden name was King, but it does not give the names of her parents. Mrs. Joyce B. Vorwaller has provided an annotated typescript of this Family Record, which was in the possession of Lola Bedenbaugh, daughter of Elijah King Bedenbaugh. The marriage date 22 December 1870 is confirmed by the Confederate Pension Application of Mattie J. Bedenbaugh, at S. C. Archives.[72] Children:
   268 i. Alonzo Adolphus[5] Bedenbaugh, b. 16 Aug 1870, died 17 Jan 1936, unm., bur. Prosperity Cem.
+ 269 ii. Allen Lester[5] Bedenbaugh, b. 9 Feb 1874
   270 iii. Dudley Rothwell[5] Bedenbaugh, b. 10 June 1878, d. 6 June 1913, bur. Prosperity Cem.
   271 iv. Lola[4] Bedenbaugh, b. 12 Sept 1883 or 1886(?), d. 27 Feb. 1964, unm.

62. Rosanna[4] Bedenbaugh (John[3], Adam[2], Michael[1]) was born 1849-50 and married John Rikard. Children:
   272 i. Bennie[5] Rikard
   273 ii. Willie[5] Rikard
   275 iii. Elbert[5] Rikard
   275 iv. Clarence[5] Rikard
   276 v. Johnnie[5] Rikard
   277 vi. Legion[5] Rikard
   278 vii. Nannie[5] Rikard.

63. Laura Frances[4] Bedenbaugh (John[3], Adam[2], Michael[1]) was born 1857 and died 14 March 1914. She married, in 1875, Lawson Jefferson Boozer, who was born 25 February 1853 and died 21 December 1884. Lawson Jefferson Boozer is buried at St. Mark's Lutheran Church in Saluda County. Laura Frances (Bedenbaugh) Boozer is buried in Rosemont Cemetery in Newberry, South Carolina. Five children:

279   i. Rebecca Elizabeth[5] Boozer, b. 27 Nov 1876, d. 8 July 1958, m. 1891 Robert Lee Lewis, b. 5 Dec 1870, d. 5 May 1945. They had only one child, b. & d. 8 Oct 1908. All bur. Rosemont Cem., Newberry.

+ 280 ii. George Virgil[5] Boozer, b. 18 Feb 1989

+ 281 iii. John Reuben[5] Boozer, b. 20 Aug 1879, d. 24 Jan 1933

282 iv. Essa Caroline[5] Boozer, b. & d. 1881

+ 283 v. Jacob Lawson[5] Boozer, b. 28 Jan 1884.

65. Elizabeth[4] Bedenbaugh (William[3], Adam[2], Michael[1]) was born 20 November 1832 and died 2 July 1912. She married, first, Chaney H. Morris, who was born c1829, and died 6 April 1865 in prison at Point Lookout, Maryland, from a wound received at Sharpsburg, serving in Company H, Holcombe's Legion.[73] She married, second, James C. Moore, who was born 16 May 1832 and died 29 August 1909. They are buried in the Prosperity Cemetery. Children:

284   i. William Jason[5] Morris, b. 4 June 1850, d. 25 Apr 1924, m. Martha Emma Stockman, b. 6 Jan 1853, d. 17 Sept 1928, both bur. Prosperity Cem.

285 ii. George Waters[5] Morris, b. 12 Oct 1852, d. 9 Oct 1926, married Sallie Cromer.

286 iii. Edward Yarborough[5] Morris, b. c1855

287 iv. Lorenzie D.[5] Morris, b. 26 Oct 1857, d. 21 Oct 1936, m. Alice Fulmer, b. 28 Jan 1860, d. 23 May 1938, both bur. Zion United Methodist Ch.

288   v. Marion C.[5] Morris, m. Nannie Clark

289 vi. Pamela Tallulah[5] Morris, b. 22 June 1865, d. 15 Oct 1873, bur. Zion United Methodist Ch., near Prosperity, SC.

69. Benjamin F.[4] Bedenbaugh (William[3], Adam[2], Michael[1]) was born 31 December 1849, and died 18 September 1928. He married, c1873, Eliza Padgett, who was born 27 December 1857 and died 20 November 1900. Both are buried at Nazareth Methodist Church, near Leesville in Saluda County, South Carolina. This family was living in Saluda County in 1900.[74]
Children:

290   i. Berley[5] Bedenbaugh, b. March 1876, m. c1899 Lula ___, removed to Snead, FL

+ 291 ii. Lula Mary[5] Bedenbaugh, b. 23 Sept 1878

292 iii. Mattie Estelle[5] Bedenbaugh, b. 9 Feb 1881, m. Martin Fletcher[6] Bedenbaugh (see under him for descendants).

293 iv. Carrie[5] Bedenbaugh, b. June 1883, m. John Massey

294   v. Elizabeth[5] Bedenbaugh, b. March 1888, m. David Hawkins

295 vi. Lochie I.[5] Bedenbaugh, b. 17 May 1892, d. 12 May 1898, bur. Nazareth Meth. Ch.

296 vii. Joseph Ballenger[5] Bedenbaugh, b. 20 Jan 1896, d. 12 Apr 1898, bur. Nazareth Meth. Ch.[75]

THE BEDENBAUGH-BETENBAUGH FAMILY

FIFTH GENERATION

72. Lemuel Lee[5] Boozer (Eve[4], Henry[3] Adam[2], Michael[1]) was born 4 October 1832 and died 29 January 1906. He married, Jane C. Wilson, who was born 1 January 1828 and died 18 June 1902. Both are buried at St. Luke's Lutheran Church near Prosperity, South Carolina. Lemuel Lee Boozer was a private in Company H., Third Regiment, South Carolina Infantry. He was wounded 6 May 1864 in the Battle of the Wilderness, and was paroled 2 May 1865 at Greensboro, North Carolina. Children:

    297   i. T. B.[6] Boozer, b. 14 Oct 1854, d. 31 Oct 1854, bur. family cem.
    298 ii. William P.[6] Boozer, b. 18 June 1856, d. 18 Aug 1857, bur. family cem.
    299 iii. Nancy E.[6] Boozer, b. 23 Aug 1859, d. 19 Nov 1862, bur. family cem.
+ 300 iv. Pierce Franklin[6] Boozer, b. 8 May 1866
+ 301 v. Joseph Elzy[6] Boozer, b. 1868.

74. Simpson Kleckley[5] (Tech) Bedenbaugh (Daniel[4], Henry[3], Adam[2], Michael[1]) was born 26 June 1844 Newberry District, South Carolina, and died 28 October 1920, Lafayette County, Mississippi. He married Grabilla Adeline Venable, who was born 16 February 1856 and died 25 October 1953 at Oxford, Mississippi. They are buried in the Fulmer Cemetery, Teckville, MS (now Route 1, Como, MS). Simpson K. Bedenbaugh served as a private in Co. E, 25th Alabama Infantry. Simpson Kleckly (sometime Keckly) Bedenbaugh was appointed Postmaster of Teckville, MS in Oct. 1894 (original charter in possession of Mrs. Adeline B. Robinson, Meridian, Miss, who supplied some of the above information).

Children of Simpson K. Bedenbaugh:

    302   i. Daniel Moses[6] Bedenbaugh, b. 3 Sept 1877 Lafayette Co., MS., d. 21 Nov 1954 in Memphis, TN, m. Lena Speigner
    303 ii. Doxie[6] Bedenbaugh, b. 15 Sept 1879 in MS, d. 19 Dec 1969 Biloxi, MS, m. Matthew S. Fite
    304 iii. Rosa[6] Bedenbaugh, b. 11 Sept 1881 in Panola Co., MS, d. 18 Apr 1957, m. Reuben E. Wilborn
    305 iv. Lula[6] Bedenbaugh, b. 21 Sept 1883, in Panola Co., MS, d. 1 Sept 1960 Lafayette Co., MS., m. John Kitchell
+ 306 v. Marion Frank[6] Bedenbaugh, b. 27 March 1886 in Lafayette Co., Miss.
    307 vi. Milson M.[6] Bedenbaugh, b. 22 Dec 1888, Lafayette Co., MS, d. 26 Aug 1973 in Meridian, MS, m. Ruth Hargis
    308 vii. Poston G.[6] Bedenbaugh, b. 1 Apr 1891 in Lafayette Co., MS, d. 26 June 1975 Starkville, MS, m. Parkie Childress.
    309 viii. Kinard G.[6] Bedenbaugh, b. 26 Feb 1894 Lafayette Co., MS., d. 8 Nov 1947, Memphis, TN (unm.)
    310 xi. Audrey[6] Bedenbaugh born 19 March 1896
    311 xii. Virgie Anna[6] Bedenbaugh, b. 31 Oct 1898, d. 4 Feb 1976, m. Monroe Sanders of Panola County, MS.

76. Zacheus Wright[5] (Rev.) Bedenbaugh (John Adam[4], Henry[3], Adam[2], Michael[1]) was born 15 Oct 1846 and died 17 January 1921. He married, on 20 April 1874, Lula Cornelia Day. who born 20 April 1874 and died 3 January 1926. He served as a private in Co. A, 19th Battalion, South Carolina Cavalry. The Rev. Z. W. Bedenbaugh attended Newberry College (Newberry, South Carolina), Roanoke College in Virginia, and the Seminary, being ordained in 1874. He served several South Carolina Churches, among which were Ebenezer Lutheran Church (Colum-

bia) and Grace Lutheran Church (Prosperity). He is buried at St. Luke's Lutheran Church. Children:

312   i. Vida Day[6] Bedenbaugh, b. 27 July 1875 d. 9 Oct 1882

313   ii. Gerhard Day[6] Bedenbaugh, b. 16 Aug 1877, d. 9 Sept 1932

314   iii. Bertha Day[6] Bedenbaugh, b. 30 Sept 1879, d. 23 Oct 1882

315   iv. Ernest Day[6] Bedenbaugh, b. 25 Sept 1881, d. 4 Oct 1950, m. 19 Oct 1905 Hepie A. Campbell

+ 316   v. Lucy Day[6] Bedenbaugh, b. 1 Aug 1884

317   vi. Carlisle Day[6] Bedenbaugh.

77. Mary Ella[5] Bedenbaugh (John Adam[4], Henry[3], Adam[2], Michael[1]) was born 28 September 1849 and died 15 December 1892. She married James Burr Dennis, who was born 13 December 1851 and died 18 March 1922, both are buried Prosperity Cemetery, Prosperity, South Carolina. Children:

318   i. Wright Zacheus[6] Dennis, m. 22 Dec 1898 Minnie Coates

+ 319   ii. John Carl[6] Dennis, b. 11 Dec 1876

320   iii. Jesse[6] Dennis, did not marry.

321   iv. Osborne Frank[6] Dennis, b. 28 July 1886, m. Mary Hallman[6] Bedenbaugh (see under her for descendants)

322   v. Dottie[6] Dennis

323   vi. Olin[6] Dennis.

81. Warren P.[5] Bedenbaugh (Simeon[4], Henry[3], Adam[2], Michael[1]) was born 23 April 1850 and died 19 September 1929. He married Sarah Jane Rikard, widow of Cyrus Hartman, who was born 10 December 1839 and died 25 June 1914. Both are buried at St. Luke's Lutheran Church. Children:

324   i. James Ira[6] Bedenbaugh, M. D., b. 20 May 1874, d. 8 June 1960, m. Frances Elizabeth (Bessie) Wheeler, b. 13 Nov 1882, d. 26 Feb 1960, daughter of Thompson L. and Ida (Rikard) Wheeler, bur. Newberry Memorial Gardens.[76] Children:

    325 a. Ruth[7] Bedenbaugh, d. inf.

    326 b. Helen[7] Bedenbaugh, m. Fred Weir

    327 c. Frances Elizabeth[7] Bedenbaugh, m. J. W. Earhardt, Jr.

    328 d. James Arthur[7] Bedenbaugh

329   ii. J. Willie[6] Bedenbaugh, b. 22 Sept 1876, d. 22 May 1932, m. 25 Sept 1913,[77] Amelia Bowers, b. 7 Feb 1887, d. 23 March 1962, bur. St. Luke's Luth. Ch.

330   iii. Warren Forest[6] Bedenbaugh, b. 11 Nov 1878, d. 17 Apr 1912, bur. Prosperity Cem., m. Massie Williams

331   iv. Mary Talula[6] Bedenbaugh, b. 22 Aug 1871, d. 23 Apr 1915, bur. St. Luke's Lutheran Church, m. 24 Jan 1889 Drayton J. Taylor.[78] Children:

    332 a. Eula[7] Taylor

    333 b. Mamie Lee[7] Taylor

334   v. Arthur Ernest Pinckney[6] Bedenbaugh

335   vi. Emma[6] Bedenbaugh.

THE BEDENBAUGH-BETENBAUGH FAMILY

The Family of Hawkins K. Bedenbaugh, c1902-1903

[back row]: Roscoe, Thompsey, Ella, and Jim Bedenbaugh
[standing left]: Jeannette Bedenbaugh
[front row]: Mary (Mills) (Kelly) Nichols, Jacob, Hawkins, Melissa, Belle and Mattie Bedenbaugh

82. Jacob Kibler[5] Bedenbaugh (Simeon[4], Henry[3], Adam[2], Michael[1]) was born 21 February 1852 (baptised 10 September 1853, Bethlehem Lutheran Church records) and died 26 February 1933. He married Ann Mayer, who was born 26 January 1854 and died 21 June 1940. Children:

   336 i. George Simeon[6] Bedenbaugh married 14 December 1904 Bessie Irene Boozer, b. 5 July 1883, d. 25 Feb 1937, married, 2nd, her half-sister Ethel Lester Bedenbaugh on 2 January 1943. Child (by first marriage):

       337 a. Irene[7] Bedenbaugh m. Pollard Warren

   338 ii. Ernest[6] Bedenbaugh

   339 iii. Rebecca[6] Bedenbaugh

   340 iv. Lillie E.[6] Bedenbaugh born 9 April 1886, died 5 March 1930, unm., bur. St. Luke's Lutheran Church.

83. Hawkins Kinard[5] Bedenbaugh (Simeon[4], Henry[3], Adam[2], Michael[1]) was born 28 July 1855 died 23 December 1926. Hawkins Bedenbaugh was confirmed at St. Luke's 30 September 1866. He married E. Melissa Kelly, who was born 13 March 1853 and died 19 March 1916. Both are buried St. Luke's Lutheran Church. A photograph of this family group is reproduced on page 33.
Children:

   341 i. Nancy Elizabeth[6] Bedenbaugh, b. 30 July 1878, d. 6 Oct 1878

+ 342 ii. John Roscoe[6] Bedenbaugh, b. 12 Nov 1879

   343 iii. Thompsie Viola[6] Bedenbaugh, b. 19 Feb 1882 (see under John Carl Dennis for descendants)

+ 344 iv. James Simeon Simpson[6] Bedenbaugh, b. 23 Jan 1887

+ 345 v. Nancy Ella[6] Bedenbaugh, b. 17 Feb 1884

+ 346 vi. Eliza Jeannette Bedenbaugh, b. 9 July 1889

+ 347 vii. Rosa Belle[6] Bedenbaugh, b. 27 Sept 1891

   348 viii. Mattie Wytche[6] Bedenbaugh, b. 9 Oct 1894, bapt. 13 Dec 1897 (St. Luke's Records), m. Benny Epting

+ 349 ix. Jacob Hawkins[6] (Bud) Bedenbaugh, b. 5 Aug 1897.

84. John Simpson[5] Bedenbaugh (Simeon[4], Henry[3], Adam[2], Michael[1]) was born 4 January 1858 and died 15 April 1907. He married, in 1887, Nancy Adella Cook, who was born 26 October 1861 and died 30 July 1931. They are buried at Colony Lutheran Church. Children:

   350 i. Kate[6] Bedenbaugh, b. 21 Oct 1888, d. 8 June 1978, m. 9 Dec 1913 Asa Franklin Taylor, b. 19 March 1893, d. 25 Feb 1966, bur. Colony Lutheran Church. (no ch.)

   351 ii. Pettus Benjamin[6] Bedenbaugh, b. 13 March 1890, d. 16 Nov 1893.

+ 352 iii. Jefferson Holland[6] Bedenbaugh, b. 27 Dec 1892

+ 353 iv. Wendell Grady[6] Bedenbaugh, b. 22 June 1901.

85. George Pettus[5] (Pet) Bedenbaugh (Simeon[4], Henry[3], Adam[2], Michael[1]) was born 11 April 1860 and died 12 December 1942. He married, on 25 December 1888, Emily Christine Susannah Nichols, who was born 11 March 1871 and died 14 February 1944. Both buried at St. Luke's Lutheran Church. Children:

+ 354 i. Mary Hallman[6] Bedenbaugh, b. 26 Sept 1889

+ 355 ii. Tranquilla Susannah[6] Bedenbaugh, b. 1 Jan 1891

   356 iii. Andrew Chelsey[6] Bedenbaugh, b. 22 Oct 1892, d. 8 March 1893, bur. St. Luke's Church.

+ 357 iv. Charlie Simeon[6] Bedenbaugh, b. 22 Oct 1892

+ 358 v. Daisy Ophelia[6] Bedenbaugh, b. 4 Oct 1894

+ 359   vi. Jennie Beardon[6] Bedenbaugh, b. 17 Oct 1896 m. James O. Miller
+ 360   vii. Pettus Birge[6] Bedenbaugh, b. 17 Dec 1898
+ 361   viii. Horace Nichols[6] Bedenbaugh, b. 24 Apr 1901
+ 362   ix. Jones Mathias[6] Bedenbaugh, b. 17 Oct 1903
+ 363   x. Koon Maybank[6] Bedenbaugh, b. 6 Nov 1905, m. Nancy Ruth Smith
   364   xi. Hettie Hodges[6] Bedenbaugh, b. 25 Oct 1907, d. 26 Aug 1909, bur. St. Luke's Lutheran Church
   365   xii. Lucy Mae[6] Bedenbaugh, b. 6 Feb 1910, m. 6 Sept 1930 Forest A. Amick, b. 28 July 1901, d. 4 Nov 1989.
+ 366   xiii. Ruby Velma[6] Bedenbaugh, b. 18 Jan 1912
+ 367   xiv. Joseph Ira Cronk[6] Bedenbaugh, b. 18 Apr 1916.[79]

86. Nancy[5] Bedenbaugh (Simeon[4], Henry[3], Adam[2], Michael[1]) was born 10 August 1862 and died 16 November 1905. She married, on 24 August 1879, Burr W. Boozer,[80] who was born 19 February 1854 and died 2 March 1935. Both are buried at St. Luke's Lutheran Church. Children:
   368   i. Dudley[6] Boozer, d. inf.
   369   ii. Lafayette[6] Boozer, d. inf.
   370   iii. Sula Victoria[6] Boozer, b. 14 March 1884, d. 20 Dec 1917, buried St. Luke's Lutheran Church
   371   iv. Minnie Day[6] Boozer, b. 11 Oct 1886 married John Wesley Boozer
   372   v. William Gary[6] Boozer, b. 1894, d. 1919.

109. Mary Jane[5] Bedenbaugh (John Adam[4] Sr., Adam Jr.[3], Adam[2], Michael[1]) was born 18 August 1847 and died 25 October 1929. She married, on 19 December 1866, Wesley Nichols, who was born 18 April 1844 and died 10 January 1931. Both are buried at Union Lutheran Church, Lexington County, South Carolina. Children:
   373   i. Carry Lucinda[6] Nichols, b. 20 Sept 1867, d. 8 Oct 1876, bur. Union Lutheran Church
+ 374   ii. Andrew David Frederick[6] Nichols, b. 26 Dec 1869
+ 375   iii. Jasper Adam[6] Nichols, b. 10 Feb 1873
+ 376   iv. Tillman Sidney[6] Nichols, b. 25 Nov 1877.

112. Jacob Calvin[5] (Jake) Bedenbaugh (John Adam[4] Sr., Adam Jr.[3], Adam[2], Michael[1]) was born 10 November 1852 and died 10 February 1936. He married, on 18 January 1877, Nancy Marsilla (Nannie) Adams, who was born 6 March 1859 and died 9 April 1932, the daughter of William and Nancy (Boyd) Adams. Both are buried at Union Lutheran Church, Lexington County, South Carolina. Children:[81]
+ 377   i. Andrew Lonnie[6] Bedenbaugh, b. 20 Sept 1878
   378   ii. Nina Ora[6] Bedenbaugh, b. 1 Dec 1880
+ 379   iii. Ernest Wyche[6] Bedenbaugh, b. 20 March 1883
   380   iv. Lester Franklin[6] Bedenbaugh, b. 30 Sept 1885, d. 18 Jan 1884
   381   v. Forrest[6] Bedenbaugh, b. & d. 18 Jan 1887
   382   vi. Pettice Adams[6] Bedenbaugh, b. 28 Aug 1889, d. 2 March 1890
   383   vii. James William[6] Bedenbaugh, b. 27 Feb 1891, d. 18 Dec 1958, m. 9 Nov 1913 Nancy Agnes Shealy, b. 25 Mar 1893, d. 4 Aug 1949, bur. Union Lutheran Church
   384   viii. Jacob Calvin[6] (Cally) Bedenbaugh, b. 25 Oct 1895, d. 10 Oct 1918, bur. at sea

385 ix. George Willis[6] Bedenbaugh, b. 29 Dec 1897, d. 8 Jan 1966, m. 30 Nov 1919 Pearl Long, b. 18 Sept 1900, d. 29 July 1982. Both bur. Union Lutheran Church

386 x. John Allen[6] Bedenbaugh, b. 15 July 1901, d. 17 Oct 1965, m. 2 July 1932 Annie Shealy, b. 1 Nov 1901, d. 22 Oct 1981, both bur. Union Lutheran Church.

113. Ellen R.[5] Bedenbaugh (John Adam[4] Sr., Adam Jr.[3], Adam[2], Michael[1]) was born 10 January 1854 and died 8 July 1933 at New Brookland (now West Columbia), South Carolina.[82] She married Robert Calvin Moore, who was born 3 April 1952 and died 15 March 1937 in West Columbia. Both are buried in the Mt. Tabor Cemetery in West Columbia. Child (may have been others):

387 i. Alice L. Moore, b. 13 Oct 1875, d. 19 Aug 1926, m. J. Cephus Mathias, b. 31 July 1874, d. 18 May 1947, both bur. Mt. Tabor Cem.

114. Sarah Cornelia[5] (Sally) Bedenbaugh (John Adam Sr.[4], Adam Jr.[3], Adam[2], Michael[1]) was born 10 February 1855 in Newberry District, South Carolina, and died 10 September 1921 in Greenwood County, South Carolina. She married, on 7 December 1879,[83] Abner Asbill Dominick, who was born July 1857, and died 2 September 1940 in Greenwood County. They lived in Greenwood County, South Carolina. Nine children:

+ 388   i. Nancy Ophelia[6] Dominick, b. 12 Sept 1880
+ 389   ii. William Kimbrough[6] Dominick, b. 8 March 1882
+ 390   iii. Sarah Hunter[6] Dominick, b. 10 Apr 1884
   391   iv. John Nathan[6] Dominick, b. 13 March 1885, d. 17 March 1985
+ 392   v. Benjamin Tillman[6] Dominick, b. 17 May 1886
+ 393   vi. Ellen Eugenia[6] Dominick, b. 9 June 1890
+ 394   vii. Elizabeth Louise[6] Dominick, b. 29 Sept 1894
+ 395   viii. Abner Allen[6] Dominick, b. 16 Nov 1896
+ 396   ix. Wesley Jones[6] Dominick, b. 16 Feb 1899.

115. John Adam[5] Bedenbaugh, Jr. (John Adam[4] Sr., Adam Jr.[3], Adam[2], Michael[1]) was born 15 October 1859 and died 22 August 1935. He married, first, Barbara Lybrand who was born 5 October 1865 and died 24 April 1893. He married, second, about 1894, Isabelle Oxner, who was born 20 May 1871 and died 10 August 1935. They are all buried at Union Lutheran Church, Lexington County.
Children by Barbara Lybrand:

397 i. Samuel Odius[6] Bedenbaugh, b. 24 Apr 1887, killed in battle in France, 8 Oct 1918.

398 ii. Sarah Elizabeth[6] (Sallie) Bedenbaugh, b. 10 May 1889

399 iii. Jesse P.[6] Bedenbaugh, b. 29 March 1891, d. 31 Jan 1957, m. Ona Calk, b. 4 Sept 1901, d. 7 May 1968. Both bur. Union Lutheran Ch.

Children by Isabelle Oxner:

400 iv. Susie Marie[6] Bedenbaugh, b. 27 Aug 1894, d. 4 July 1980, m. 20 Oct 1912 Andrew Killian Shealy, b. 22 Nov 1886, d. 30 July 1953. Children:

401 a. Curtis Moyesse[7] Shealy, b. 22 Jan 1914, d. 5 Apr 1990

402 b. Julian Lester[7] Shealy, b. 27 May 1915, m. Gladys[7] Bedenbaugh (see under her for descendants)

403 c. Luther Dearmes[7] Shealy, b. 20 Apr 1917, d. inf.

404 d. James Colie[7] Shealy, b. 22 Mar 1923

405 e. Vaughn Hunter[7] Shealy, b. 20 Aug 1927

406 v. William Lester[6] Bedenbaugh, b. 12 Jan 1896
407 vi. Virgil Holland[6] Bedenbaugh, b. 26 Dec 1897, d. 30 Oct 1981, m. 25 Feb 1919 in Saluda Co., SC, Geneva Oswald, b. 7 Aug 1898.
408 vii. Elliott Hurley[6] Bedenbaugh, b. 22 Jan 1900, m. Gladys Shealy; child:
    409 a. Donald[7] Bedenbaugh
+ 410 viii. Purvis Hobson[6] Bedenbaugh, b. 26 Dec 1901
411 ix. Fanny Alethie[6] Bedenbaugh, b. 12 Dec 1903 m. J. Presley Eargle, Jr.
412 x. Arthur Cromwell[6] Bedenbaugh, b. 24 Dec 1905, m. Myrtie Mae Cameron; children:
    413 a. Solie[7] Bedenbaugh
    414 b. Gerald[7] Bedenbaugh
    415 c. Pauline[7] Bedenbaugh
    416 d. Mattie Bell[7] Bedenbaugh
417 xi. Haskel L.[6] Bedenbaugh, b. 7 Dec 1907
418 xii. Daisey Mae[6] Bedenbaugh, m. Gordon Earle; children:
    419 a. Iris[7] Eargle
    420 b. Nell[7] Eargle
421 xiii. John Bennett[6] Bedenbaugh, b. 3 Nov 1911, d. 25 Oct 1970.

133. John Bachman[5] Bedenbaugh (Andrew[4], Adam Jr.[3], Adam[2], Michael[1]) was born 18 March 1876, baptised 17 December 1876,[84] and died 7 June 1923. He married, on 20 November 1912, Addie Werts, who was born 16 October 1884 and died 11 October 1949. Both are buried at St. Paul's Lutheran Church, Prosperity, SC. Children:
+ 422 i. Christine[6] Bedenbaugh, b. 26 Aug 1914.
423 ii. Rebecca[6] Bedenbaugh, b. 11 Sept 1917, d. 24 Sept 1992, m. Sam Pat Boland, b. 3 Jan 1917 (mayor, Pomaria, SC). One child:
    424 a. Sandra[7] Boland, b. 28 Jan 1946.

135. Grace Edith Leone[5] Bedenbaugh (Andrew J.[4], Adam Jr.[3], Adam[2], Michael[1]) was born 11 January 1879, baptised 31 August 1879 (Bethlehem Lutheran Church records) and died, 11 February 1959. She married, on 27 November 1902, Clarence Richards, who was born 12 January 1874, and died 6 December 1955. Children:
425 i. Eleanor Mercer[6] Richards, b. 27 Apr 1905, d. 9 Aug 1933
+ 426 ii. Clarence Bedenbaugh[6] Richards, b. 3 Dec 1906.

137. William Lamar[5] (Will) Bedenbaugh (Andrew J.[4], Adam Jr.[3], Adam[2], Michael[1]) was born 8 September 1882, baptised 24 March 1883 (Bethlehem Lutheran Church records), and died 15 April 1957. He married, on 7 August 1918, Josephine Lipscomb, who was born 19 December 1897 and died 24 January 1989. William Lamar Bedenbaugh was a landowner-farmer in Newberry and Greenwood Counties, South Carolina. Two children:
+ 427 i. Mary Lamar[6] Bedenbaugh, b. 25 Dec 1920
428 ii. Virginia Carol[6] Bedenbaugh, b. 25 Dec 1923, Greenwood, SC, resides Ninety Six, SC.

138. Annie Mae[5] Bedenbaugh (Andrew J.[4], Adam Jr.[3], Adam[2], Michael[1]) was born 24 March 1884, baptised 16 July 1885 (Bethlehem Lutheran Church records), and died 3 February 1954. She married, on 23 December 1921, John Anthony Williams, who was born 5 August 1880 and died 11 August 1950. Both are buried at St. Paul's Lutheran Church, Prosperity, South Carolina. One child:

429 i. John A.[6] Williams, Jr., b. 31 Aug 1923, d. 31 July 1954, bur. St. Paul's Lutheran Church.

139. Ida Beatrice[5] Bedenbaugh (Andrew J.[4], Adam Jr.[3], Adam[2], Michael[1]) was born 28 December 1885, baptised 27 May 1888 (Bethlehem Lutheran Church records), and died 31 January 1961. She married, on 28 February 1911, George Alva Hope[85]. Ida Beatrice Hope and their child (below) are buried in Elmwood Cemetery, Columbia, South Carolina. Child:

430 i. George Alva[6] Hope, b. Mar 1912, d. Feb 1928 in an airplane crash in Columbia.

141. Lorane Berley[5] Bedenbaugh, Sr. (Andrew J.[4], Adam Jr.[3], Adam[2], Michael[1]) was born 6 September 1889 and died 20 December 1980. He married, on 23 January 1918, Quinnette Dantzler, who was born 13 April 1891 and died 19 August 1963. Both are buried at St. Paul's Lutheran Church, near Pomaria, South Carolina. Berley Bedenbaugh contributed much of information on the descendants on Adam Bedenbaugh, Jr. Two children:

431 i. Eleanor Connor[6] Bedenbaugh, b. 11 Nov 1919, lives near Prosperity, SC
432 ii. Lorane Berley[6] Bedenbaugh Jr., b. 3 May 1924, d. 30 Dec 1992, bur. St. Pauls Lutheran Church.

155. John Franklin[5] Conwill (John A.[4], Elizabeth[3], Adam[2], Michael[1]) was born 13 June 1854 and died there 30 March 1934. He married Sarah C. Green, who was born 6 January 1855 in Itawamba County, Mississippi, and died 6 December 1925 in Monroe County. Both are buried in the Carolina Cemetery in Itawamba County. Children, all born in Monroe County, Mississippi:

+ 433 i. Liza Melverda[6] Conwill, b. 9 Jan 1879
434 ii. John Ellis[6] Conwill, b. 22 Aug 1881, d. 26 Nov 1971, m. Della Sumner
435 iii. William F.[6] Conwill, b. 9 Jan 1882, d. 1967, m. Ida L.[6] Conwill (1st cousin)
436 iv. Jesse Daniel[6] Conwill
437 v. David A.[6] Conwill, b. 15 Oct 1890, d. 14 Dec 1957, m. Ruby E. Sumner
+ 438 vi. Lula Estelle[6] Conwill, b. 11 Feb 1895.

156. Jesse Daniel[5] Conwill (John A.[4], Elizabeth[3], Adam[2], Michael[1]) was born 1 March 1856 in Monroe County, Mississippi, and died in June 1902 in Itawamba County. He married, on 6 February 1879, Bellzora Green, who died 1 February 1940 in Monroe County, Mississippi. Both are buried in the Wiygul Cemetery in Itawamba County. Children, all born in Itawamba County, Mississippi:

439 i. Luther Eugene[6] Conwill, b. 16 Jan 1880, d. 24 Oct 1947, m. 16 Jan 1905 Verna Elliott
440 ii. Viola[6] Conwill, b. 9 Nov 1881, d. 13 Oct 1932, m. Mark T. Pettit
+ 441 iii. William Alvie[6] Conwill, b. 20 Dec 1883
442 iv. Tenny Lee[6] Conwill, b. 8 March 1886, d. 8 Oct 1978, m. Thomas A. Goodwin
+ 443 v. Jesse Daniel[6] Conwill, Jr., b. 5 Jan 1888.

167. Joseph Daniel[5] Conwill (Yates[4], Elizabeth[3], Adam[2], Michael[1]) was born in February 1852 in Monroe County, Alabama, and died in 1935 in Guymon, Oklahoma. He married, on 10 January 1881, in Lee County, Mississippi, Sarah Jane Herndon, who was born in May 1845 in Mississippi, and died in 1944. Children, all born in Texas:

444   i. Lula[6] Conwill, b. Dec 1882, m. Joe Lovett
445   ii. Mamie[6] Conwill, b. Dec 1884, m. William Ewing
446 iii. Chester[6] Conwill, b. Dec 1886
+ 447 iv. Joseph Dillard[6] Conwill, b. Dec 1888
448   v. Oscar[6] Conwill, b. Feb 1890, m. Neely Brown
449   vi. Tully[6] Conwill, b. June 1893, d. ch.
450 vii. Harry[6] Conwill, b. Sept 1895
451 viii. Fred Aubrey[6] Conwill, b. March 1897, m. Doris Johnson.

168. Yates Jury[5] Conwill, Jr. (Yates[4], Elizabeth[3], Adam[2], Michael[1]) was born 18 September 1857 in Monroe County, Mississippi, and died there 22 August 1922. He married, on 4 December 1879, Ellis Eugene Carpenter who was born 30 March 1861 in Alabama, and died in Itawamba County, Mississippi, 6 August 1915. Both are buried in the Wiygul Cemetery in Itawamba County. Children, all born in Itawamba County, Mississippi:
452   i. Joseph Lonnie[6] Conwill, b. 23 Sept 1880, d. 27 Feb 1911, m. Eula E.
      Pennington, b. 29 Aug 1885, d. 26 Apr 1905. Child:
      453 a. Yates Banolia[7] Conwill, b. 15 Jan 1905, d. 18 July 1905
454 ii. inf., b. & d. 19 Aug 1882
+ 455 iii. Ira Eugene[6] Conwill, b. 27 Nov 1884
456 iv. Ida L.[6] Conwill, b. 20 Oct 1886, d. 4 Apr 1943, m. William Frank[6] Conwill
      (1st cousin)
+ 457 v. Metta A.[6] Conwill, b. 18 Feb 1889
458 vi. Nancy Estella[6] Conwill, b. 23 July 1895, m. Myrtel Devall; child:
      459 a. Mary A.[7] Devall, b. March 1932, m. Charles L. Hodges.

174. Levi William Pickens[5] Bedenbaugh (Levi[4], Jacob[3], Adam[2], Michael[1]) was born 20 August 1851. He married, on 6 November 1872, Martha T. Thurmond. Children:
460   i. William Herbert[6] Bedenbaugh, b. 6 Aug 1873 m. Mary Etta Swygert.
      children:
      461 a. Fred Shields[7] Bedenbaugh m. Augusta Cole Riddlespurger
      462 b. Mary Grace[7] Bedenbaugh, m. George Lee Turner
      463 c. Rachel Theora[7] Bedenbaugh, m. Robert Whittington
      464 d. Elsie Ernestine[7] Bedenbaugh, m. Bruce Morgan Fry
      465 e. Lois Beatrice[7] Bedenbaugh, m. Douglas Wilson
      466 f. Lewis Lamar[7] Bedenbaugh, m. Elizabeth Whatley
+ 467 ii. Benjamin Franklin[6] Bedenbaugh, b. 19 July 1875
468 iii. Jesse Levi[6] Bedenbaugh, b. 15 Jan 1877
469   iv. Hattie Virginia[6] Bedenbaugh, b. 11 Nov 1878 m. 21 Dec 1904 Joel David
      Thomas. Child:
      470 a. Martha Virginia[7] Thomas, b. 3 Nov 1915
471   v. Antoinette Josephine[6] Bedenbaugh, b. 14 Apr 1881, m. 20 Dec 1899 to
      James Marion Davis. Children:
      472 a. Mary Lucille[7] Davis, b. 8 Nov 1900
      473 b. Homer Eugene[7] Davis, b. 16 Dec 1901
      474 c. Leon Walter[7] Davis, b. 25 July 1903
      475 d. Alvin Gilbert[7] Davis, b. 13 Apr 1906
      476 e. Evelyn Josephine[7] Davis, b. 27 March 1908
477   vi. Martha Elizabeth[6] Bedenbaugh, b. 22 Oct 1882 m. 18 Dec 1898 Erby
      Coates; children:
      478 a. Mary Ruth[7] Coates, b. 3 Oct 1899
      479 b. Paulina[7] Coates, b. 5 Sept 1902

480 c. Martha[7] Coates, b. 28 May 1906
481 d. Lillian[7] Coates b. 30 Aug 1908
482 e. Mildred[7] Coates, b. 20 Dec 1909
483 f. Mae Inez[7] Coates, b. 29 Aug 1911
484 vii. John Gilbert[6] Bedenbaugh, b. 23 June 1885 m. 21 April 1907 Myrtis
O'Neal; children:
485 a. James Lawrence[7] Bedenbaugh
486 b. John Clinton[7] Bedenbaugh (Spartanburg, S. C.)
487 c. Harold E.[7] Bedenbaugh (Griffin, Ga.)
488 viii. Susie Tench[6] Bedenbaugh, b. 30 Sept 1887 m. 8 June 1910 Raymond
Harris Sullivan.[86] child:
489 a. Robert Clark[7] Sullivan born 8 April 1911
490 ix. Lucy May[6] Bedenbaugh, b. 21 May 1891
491 x. Effie Pearl[6] Bedenbaugh, b. 8 Oct 1893, m. 3 Nov 1920 James Frederick
Sibley; children:
492 a. Charles Frederick[7] Sibley
493 b. George[7] Sibley
494 c. Lucy Ann[7] Sibley
495 d. Martha Jane[7] Sibley.

176. James T.[5] Bedenbaugh (Mathias Hare[4], Jacob[3], Adam[2], Michael[1]) was born 20 September 1839 and died 18 November 1920. He married, in March of 1867, Margaret Angelina (Maggie) Rhinehart, who was born 9 July 1846 and died 25 December 1919.[87] Both are buried at Nazareth Methodist Church, Saluda County, South Carolina.

James T. Bedenbaugh applied for disability payments on the basis of his having been wounded at the battle of Gettysburg (2 July 1863) while in Confederate Service in Company M, 7th Regiment South Carolina Volunteers.[88] His Confederate service record is filed under the name of J. T. Bedenbough.

Children:[89]
496 i. Angela[5] Bedenbaugh, b. 17 Feb 1868, d. 15 Oct 1937.[90] She m. 7 Feb
1889, in Batesburg, SC, by Rev. S. P. H. Elwell, Pickens Rinehart.[91]
497 ii. Levi Leroy[6] Bedenbaugh, b. 1 Feb 1870, Edgefield County, SC, d. 29 Dec
1941, Florence, SC. He m. 20 Nov 1891, Regina Whittle, b. 19 Dec 1870,
d. 19 Oct 1929, Florence, SC, dau. of M. A. Whittle, first sheriff of Saluda
County, and wife Mary Duncan. The Rev. L. L. Bedenbaugh and his wife
Regina are buried at Rose Hill Cemetery. He m. 2nd, 25 Dec 1937, Betty
(Woodham) Gwinn, widow of Abel Gwinn. L. L. Bedenbaugh was a
Methodist minister in South Carolina, licensed to preach Sept. 1888 and
retired in 1940.[92] He had four daughters:
498 a. _____ m. T. H. Lever
499 b. _____ m. Henry Lowery
500 c. Nell[7] Bedenbaugh
501 d. Laura[7] Bedenbaugh
502 iii. Birdie[6] Bedenbaugh, b. 12 March 1874, d. 3 Oct 1940, Lexington Co., SC,
m. B. Frank Mills b. 12 Sept 1860, d. 26 Dec 1927, both bur. Nazareth
Methodist Church, Saluda Co., SC.
503 iv. Evelina[6] Bedenbaugh, b. c1878
504 v. Alvin A.[6] Bedenbaugh, b. July 1877
505 vi. Barnoe A.[6] Bedenbaugh, b. Sept 1883

506 vii. Carrie J.[6] Bedenbaugh, b. Feb 1888, m. ____ Matthews
507 viii. Calhoun G.[6] (Callie) Bedenbaugh, b. 14 Nov 1888/9, d. 28 May 1960, m. Martha A. (Mattie) Walling, b. 3 Apr 1884, d. 23 Apr 1959, both bur. Nazareth United Methodist Church, Saluda Co., SC.

179. Jacob P.[5] Bedenbaugh (Mathias Hare[4], Jacob[3], Adam[2], Michael[1]) was born February 1844 and died after 1900. He married, about 1866, Louiza Mitchell[93], who was born March 1845.[94] Children (several not listed probably died in infancy):
508 i. B. Levi[6] Bedenbaugh, b. Nov 1867
509 ii. Elizabeth[6] Bedenbaugh, b. c1861
510 iii. William[6] Bedenbaugh, b. c1873
511 iv. Jackson[6] Bedenbaugh, b. c1874
512 v. Pinckney Robert[6] Bedenbaugh, b. July 1877
513 vi. Hall[6] Bedenbaugh, b. c1878
514 vii. R. Turner[6] Bedenbaugh, b. Nov 1879.

181. Simon Wilson[5] Bedenbaugh (Mathias Hare[4], Jacob[3], Adam[2], Michael[1]) was born 15 May 1846 and died 9 June 1924 in Saluda County, South Carolina. He married, first, Lorena Corley, who died in a house fire. He married, second, about 1885, Nancy Goff,[95] who was born 8 September 1868 and died 18 August 1949. Nancy is buried Nazareth Methodist Church. Simon Wilson Bedenbaugh wrote his will 3 December 1919 in Saluda County.[96]

Children by Lorena Corley:
515 i. Sarah[6] Bedenbaugh, b. c1866, prob. d. in childhood
516 ii. Amanda[6] Bedenbaugh, b. c1868, prob. d. in childhood
+ 517 iii. Benjamin Washington[6] Bedenbaugh, b. 17 Mar 1869
+ 518 iv. James Wade[6] Bedenbaugh, b. 7 March 1874
+ 519 v. William Thomas[6] Bedenbaugh, b. 25 September 1876
520 vi. Frances Caroline[6] (Fannie) Bedenbaugh, b. Nov 1876, d. before 1924, m. ____ Ruff
521 vii. Matilda E.[6] Bedenbaugh (1878-1961), m. John Crawford Perry
522 viii. Nancy[6] Bedenbaugh, (1880-1963), m. Hillary Shealy

Children by Nancy Goff:
523 ix. Mary Elberta[6] Bedenbaugh, b. 6 Nov 1885/6, d. 22 Jan 1964
524 x. Mattie Bessie[6] Bedenbaugh, b. 5 April 1888, d. unm.
525 xi. John Preston[6] Bedenbaugh, b. 10 Aug 1889, d. 19 May 1963 m. 21 Jan 1912 Florence Harman, b. 2 May 1890, d. 1 Sept 1962, both bur. Hulon Baptist Church near Batesburg, Lexington Co., SC
526 xii. Lawrence K.[6] Bedenbaugh, b. May 1892, m. Lela Mae Berry (d. 14 June 1963)
+ 527 xiii. Raymond Lee[6] Bedenbaugh, b. 3 March 1896
528 xiv. Mathias[6] (Mack) Bedenbaugh, b. March 1898
529 xv. Sadie[6] Bedenbaugh, b. 1899, m. Ernest E. Guins
530 xvi. Leila[6] Bedenbaugh, b. 1901, m. 25 Dec 1920 Hubert Smith.

182. Mathias Hare[5] Bedenbaugh, Jr. (Mathias Hare[4], Jacob[3], Adam[2], Michael[1]) was born 12 October 1849 died 21 November 1924 at Batesburg, South Carolina. He married Georgiana McCollough, who was born 23 September 1850 and died 12 October 1933. Both are buried at Nazareth Methodist Church in Saluda County, South Carolina. Children:

531   i. Roston[6] (Ross) Bedenbaugh, b. 8 Apr 1868, d. 29 March 1904,
     m. Cornelia Gibson.[97]
+ 532 ii. Drayton E.[6] Bedenbaugh, b. 2 Sept 1869 or 1870
+ 533 iii. Martin Fletcher[6] Bedenbaugh, b. 22 Feb 1873
534 iv. Mellie[6] Bedenbaugh born 22 Nov 1874, married John Allen Hare.
535 v. Charles[6] Bedenbaugh, b. 16 Jan 1877, d. 3 January 1954, bur. Nazareth
     Methodist Church, m. Mencie Temple.
536 vi. Nannie[6] Bedenbaugh, b. 19 October 1878, m. Drayton Rikard
537 vii. Mark[6] Bedenbaugh, b. 6 June 1880, married Mattie Pearl Goff
538 viii. Lucy Luvenia[6] Bedenbaugh, b. 6 Sept 1882, d. 23 Apr 1936, bur. Nazareth
     Methodist Church, m. James Lee Hare
539 ix. Sallie[6] Bedenbaugh, b. 20 Sept 1884, m. J. Wyman Riser
+ 540 x. Thomas Urastus[6] Bedenbaugh, b. 25 Nov 1888
541 xi. Bizzie[6] Bedenbaugh, b. 14 March 1887, d. 14 June 1888, bur. Nazareth
     Methodist Church.
542 xii. Gula[6] Bedenbaugh, b. 21 July 1891, m. 26 December 1912 Clarence Jacob
     Aull
543 xiii. Porter M.[6] Bedenbaugh, b. 23 July 1893, d. 14 May 1929, bur. Nazareth
     Methodist Church, m. 27 Jan 1923 in Saluda Co., SC, Madge Duke.

186. John L.[5] Bedenbaugh (Simeon Wilson[4], Jacob[3], Adam[2], Michael[1]) was born
June 1850 in Macon County, Georgia. He married, on 18 November 1875, Mary
Elizabeth Thurmond, who was born 25 May 1849 and died 28 August 1917 at Ware
Shoals, South Carolina, the daughter of John D. and Ann (Allen) Thurmond.[98] In
1900, John L. Bedenbaugh, his wife Mary, and their son Hosea were living in
Fayette County, Georgia.[99] By 1910 this family was living in Greenwood County,
South Carolina.[100] Children (one other, name unknown to the compiler):
544 i. Hosea G.[6] Bedenbaugh, b. 15 Apr 1884 Coweta Co., GA, d. 14 Oct 1940,
     Greenville, SC; bur. Springwood Cem., Greenville, SC, m. Sally Lou Wrenn;
     children (may have been others):
     545 a. Edith[7] Bedenbaugh
     546 b. Sue[7] Bedenbaugh
     547 c. Alfred[7] Bedenbaugh, b. 16 Apr & d. 17 Apr 1916, Ware Shoals, SC
     548 d. James H.[7] Bedenbaugh
     549 e. Fred L.[7] Bedenbaugh
     550 f. Charles[7] Bedenbaugh
     551 g. Evelyn[7] Bedenbaugh
     552 h. Alice[7] Bedenbaugh
     553 i. Louise[7] Bedenbaugh
     554 j. dau. m. G. B. Hendrix
555 ii. C. H.[6] Bedenbaugh.

189. Lemuel David[5] Bedenbaugh (Simeon Wilson[4], Jacob[3], Adam[2], Michael[1]) was
born in 6 March 1857 at Oglethorpe, Georgia, and died 13 November 1937 in
Alachua County, Florida. He married, on 25 December 1877, in Columbia County,
Florida, Nancy Rosa Shealy, who was born c1857 and died 14 April 1929 in Alachua
County, Florida. They had two children:
+ 556 i. Bloomer Wilson[6] Bedenbaugh, b. 13 Oct 1883, Columbia Co., FL
  557 ii. Nona[6] Bedenbaugh, m. Oliver Bryant.

196. David Bachman[5] Bedenbaugh (Drury David[4], Jacob[3], Adam[2], Michael[1]) was

born 12 August 1858 and died 9 November 1916, in Macon County, Georgia. He married, on 16 May 1895, Mary Elizabeth Allen, who was born 23 September 1875 in Marion County, Georgia, and died 22 April 1964, in Albany, Georgia. Children:

558   i. Rosa Jewel[6] Bedenbaugh, b. 22 Aug 1896, m. 1 Apr 1916 Thomas Hill Paschal; children:
- 559 a. Annie Ruth[7] Paschal, b. 26 Dec 1916
- 560 b. Rose Elizabeth[7] Paschal, b. 20 Oct 1923
- 561 c. Thomas Hill[7] Paschal, Jr. b. 22 Jan 1920

562 ii. David Allen[6] Bedenbaugh, b. 3 May 1898, d. 17 Jan 1972, m. 20 Oct 1924 Mollie Pauline McDonald.

563 iii. Eva Lois[6] Bedenbaugh, b. 22 Aug 1900 (she has supplied information on descendants of Drury David), m. 1 July 1933 Irvin Barret Callaway.

564 iv. Albert Wilson[6] Bedenbaugh, b. 31 Dec 1901, d. 8 July 1948

565   v. Mary Rebecca[6] Bedenbaugh, b. 21 May 1903, d. 12 Feb 1906

566 vi. Howard Elmore[6] Bedenbaugh, b. 23 Nov 1904, d. 18 March 1970 m. 12 June 1930 Mary Virginia Watkins

567 vii. James Henry[6] Bedenbaugh, b. 13 Jan 1907, m. 15 Aug 1961 Thelma Mims

568 viii. William Oscar[6] Bedenbaugh, b. 6 Oct 1908, m. 19 Jan 1963 Othello Edwards

569 ix. Wilbur Chessley[6] Bedenbaugh, m. 15 Aug 1931 June Willimena Christian.

197. Sarah[5] Bedenbaugh (Drury David[4], Jacob[3], Adam[2], Michael[1]) married Samuel J. Norris. Children:

570   i. Greene[6] Norris m. Lizzie Green; children:
- 571 a. Emmett[7] Norris
- 572 b. Grady[7] Norris, b. 26 Aug 1907, d. 9 July 1962, m. Maxie Ruth Potter, b. 18 July 1910
- 573 c. Harvey Daniel[7] Norris, b. 29 Oct 1910, m. 18 Dec 1937 Velma L. Bray
- 574 d. James Fred[7] Norris m. Lucille Coker
- 575 e. Paul[7] Norris m. Lillian Lashley
- 576 f. Roy[7] Norris
- 577 g. Leighton Riley[7] Norris (Rev.), b. 20 Dec 1924, m. 12 Aug 1945 Doris Devona Leedom
- 578 h. Sarah Elizabeth[7] Norris, b. 21 Jan 1921, m. 3 Apr 1942 Charles Clinton Ledger, b. 8 June 1921

579 ii. Drury[6] Norris m. Lee Jordan

580 iii. Mary Bell[6] Norris, b. 20 Feb 1895 m. 1st Henry Tarver Bragg, d. 29 Nov 1925; m. 2nd William Cash Fairbanks; children:
- 581 a. Sarah Finney[7] Bragg, b. 17 Oct 1915
- 582 b. Mary Julia[7] Bragg, b. 17 Nov 1916 m. Aug 1941 Horace Lenord Gennoe
- 583 c. Henry Norris[7] Bragg, b. 7 May 1919 m. 1 June 1940 Vera Catherine Fisher
- 584 d. Erma Louise[7] Bragg, b. 19 Aug 1925.

200. Frances Drury[5] Bedenbaugh (Drury David[4], Jacob[3], Adam[2], Michael[1]) was born 20 September 1863 and died 17 March 1945. She married, on 15 May 1894, Elias G. Bryan, who was born 22 September 1860 and died 29 July 1909. Children:

585   i. Needham David[6] Bryan, b. 1894

THE BEDENBAUGH-BETENBAUGH FAMILY

586 ii. Willie Mae[6] Bryan, b. 4 Apr 1898 m. 23 July 1923 Fred Edwards b. 19 Sept 1898
587 iii. Rebecca[6] Bryan, b. 12 Jan 1901 m. Horace Walker
588 iv. John Thomas[6] Bryan, b. 6 Sept 1905.

201. Laura Rebecca[5] Bedenbaugh (Jacob Asbury[4], Jacob[3], Adam[2], Michael[1]) was born 5 October 1853 and died 31 April 1933. She married, on 19 November 1891 Jefferson Taylor,[101] who was born 1 January 1833, and died 29 September 1904. They are buried at Zion United Methodist Church near Prosperity, South Carolina. Twin children:
589 i. Love[6] Taylor, b. 21 Jan 1894, d. 12 Feb 1978, m. George Arthur Long, b. 19 Aug 1890, d. 13 Feb 1974. Children:
590 a. Rebecca Nell[7] Long
591 b. Jefferson Haskell[7] Long
592 c. Furman[7] Long
+ 593 ii. Dove[6] Taylor, b. 21 Jan 1894.

202. David Murchison[5] Bedenbaugh (Jacob Asbury[4], Jacob[3], Adam[2], Michael[1]) was born 19 November 1855 and died 1 February 1927. He married Ellen Warner, who was born 29 July 1860 and died 2 February 1928. They are buried at Zion United Methodist Church near Prosperity, South Carolina. Children:
594 i. Elmer Ernest[6] Bedenbaugh, b. 9 Nov 1878, d. 24 May 1880, bur. Zion.
+ 595 ii. Maxcy Clifton[6] Bedenbaugh, b. 16 Jan 1881
+ 596 iii. Ola Fannie[6] Bedenbaugh, b. 20 May 1883
+ 597 iv. Pearl Estelle[6] Bedenbaugh, b. 10 March 1885, m. Peter Wesley Counts
+ 598 v. Colon Boyd[6] Bedenbaugh, b. 6 June 1887
599 vi. Dudley Lee[6] Bedenbaugh, b. 30 Oct 1889, d. 8 Mar 1974, m. 23 Dec 1912 Arley Dominick, b. 15 July 1892, d. 21 March 1974
+ 600 vii. Chester Warner[6] Bedenbaugh, b. 3 Mar 1892
+ 601 viii. Eula Lillie[6] Bedenbaugh, b. 2 June 1894
+ 602 ix. Dhent Asbury[6] Bedenbaugh b. 13 March 1897
+ 603 x. Elise Amanda[6] Bedenbaugh, b. 4 May 1900.

203. Mark Boyd[5] Bedenbaugh (Jacob Asbury[4], Jacob[3], Adam[2], Michael[1]) was born July 1857 and died 7 May 1938.[102] He married Nannie Matthews, widow of Dr. John Harmon,[103] who was born 14 October 1867 and died 21 August 1936. Both are buried in the Prosperity Cemetery. One child:
604 i. A. Lewis[6] Bedenbaugh.

204. Mack Wilson[5] Bedenbaugh (Jacob Asbury[4], Jacob[3], Adam[2], Michael[1]) was born 17 February 1859, died 27 February 1933. He married, on 1 December 1881 (Bethlehem Lutheran Church Records, Pomaria, SC), Martha Emma Derrick, who was born 5 December 1862 and died 11 February 1944. Both are buried in the Prosperity Cemetery, Prosperity, S. C. Children:
605 i. Linus Wilburn[6] Bedenbaugh, b. 5 Oct 1882, d. 27 July 1941, m. Lula Mae Bishop, b. 29 Nov 1891, d. 2 May 1981, bur. Rosemont Cem., Newberry,SC.
+ 606 ii. Jacob Moody[6] Bedenbaugh, b. 9 Sept 1884
607 iii. Gussie[6] Bedenbaugh born 19 May 1886, d. 7 May 1967, m. J. Simeon Miller, b. 9 Aug 1885, d. 2 Aug 1972. Both bur. Newberry Memorial Gardens; children:
608 a. Roy[7] Miller
609 b. Martha[7] Miller m. Earle McCullough

610 c. Virginia[7] Miller m. Ollie Hawkins
611 iv. Mary Juliette[6] Bedenbaugh, b. 12 July 1888, d. 8 Feb 1983, bur. St. Luke's
Lutheran Church, m. Augustus H. Hawkins; child:
    612 a. Ruby[7] Hawkins, b. 1907 m. Rev. Edwin Zeigler (1904-1982).

205. Thomas Boston[5] Bedenbaugh (Jacob Asbury[4], Jacob[3], Adam[2], Michael[1]) (1860-1948) married Mary Dawkins (1869-1939). Both are buried at Zion United Methodist Church near Prosperity. Children:
  613 i. Barnette[6] Bedenbaugh (1894-1960) m. Frank S. Harmon; children:
    614 a. Doris[7] Harmon m. Biddle Hawkins
    615 b. Lucille[7] Harmon m. Johnie Low
    616 c. Geneva[7] Harmon m. Melton Wall
    617 d. Nell[7] Harmon m. Joel Taylor
    618 e. Tommy[7] Harmon m. Linda Stoudemire
  619 ii. Joseph Worth[6] Bedenbaugh b. 22 June 1897, d. 16 July 1959, m. Ruth Boozer, b. 10 July 1902. Children:
    620 a. Elmina Novice[7] Bedenbaugh, b. 6 Jan 1921, m. 1st Thomas C. Covington, 2nd Henry Roberts
    621 b. Jean Ruth[7] Bedenbaugh, b. 17 Jan 1927, m. Daniel Bruce Oxner
  622 iii. T. McFall[6] Bedenbaugh, b. 24 May 1903, d. 19 Sept 1968, m. Elizabeth Barnes, b. 31 May 1903, no children.

209. Joseph Falls[5] Bedenbaugh (Jacob Asbury[4], Jacob[3], Adam[3], Michael[1]) was born 20 October 1870[104] and died 9 October 1946. He married Lela Shealy, who was born 19 August 1879 and died 25 December 1953. Both are buried at Zion United Methodist Church near Prosperity, South Carolina. Child:
+ 623 i. Lorenza Dow[6] Bedenbaugh, b. 15 Aug 1898.

210. David Newton[5] Mills (Rachel[4], Jacob[3], Adam[2], Michael[1]) was born 12 October 1847 and died 27 January 1914. He married Mary Caroline Asterwest Dominick, who was born 1 July 1849 and died 5 January 1939. Children:
+ 624 i. Simon P.[6] Mills, b. 10 Sept 1869
  625 ii. George A.[6] Mills, b. 20 Jan 1873, d. 4 Feb 1955, bur. Zion United Meth. Church
  626 iii. Hattie[6] Mills, b. 4 Nov 1874, m. G. W. Clamp, d. 31 Aug 1873, d. 19 March 1931
  627 iv. Archie[6] Mills, b. 1869
  628 v. Nancy E.[6] Mills, b. 1 Apr 1871, d. 1 Nov 1875, bur. Zion United Meth. Church.

212. Benjamin F.[5] Mills (Rachel[4], Jacob[3], Adam[2], Michael[1]) was born 21 August 1852 and died 28 August 1932. He married Martha I. Warner, who was born 25 March 1857 and died August 1922. Both are buried in Rosemont Cemetery in Newberry, South Carolina. Children:
  629 i. Ariel B.[6] Mills, b. Dec 1876
  630 ii. Levi[6] Mills, b. 1879
  631 iii. Ellen[6] Mills, b. 6 Feb 1881, d. 1 May 1931, m. Gary G. Johnson, b. 21 May 1877, d. 3 Jan 1950; both bur. Baxter Cem., Newberry, SC; children:
    632 a. Lois[7] Johnson
    633 b. Mable[7] Johnson
    634 c. Bennie F.[7] Johnson

635 d. Nettie[7] Johnson
636 e. Rufus[7] Johnson
637 f. Myrtle[7] Johnson
638 g. Dawson[7] Johnson
639 iv. Arthur C.[6] Mills, b. 4 Feb 1884, d. 18 Oct 1941, m. Annie Mae ____, b. 4 Jan 1889, d. 29 June 1968, both bur. Baxter Cem., Newberry, SC.
640 v. Ralph Erskine[6] Mills, b. 1 Aug 1886, d. 8 May 1936, m. Floy Lominick, b. 3 Aug 1891, d. 28 July 1979, both bur. Rosemont Cem., Newberry, SC.
641 vi. C. B.[6] Mills
642 vii. Christine[6] Mills, b. 17 Apr 1891, d. 29 Sept 1957, m. Eddie Cleveland Dominick, b. 24 Aug 1880, d. 8 June 1939.
643 viii. Lillie[6] Mills, b. 20 July 1892, d. 14 Aug 1947, m. Patrick A. Stockman, b. 18 Sept 1887, d. 18 Sept 1966; children:
    644 a. J. Andrew[7] Stockman, b. 5 Dec 1910, d. 10 Feb 1987, m. Mary K.
    645 b. Martha[7] Stockman
    646 c. Ruby[7] Stockman
    647 d. Helen[7] Stockman
    648 e. Dorothy[7] Stockman
649 ix. Lona Mae[6] Mills, b. 23 June 1897, d. 21 May 1980, m. Jacob Caldwell Franklin, b. 13 July 1897, d. 26 Apr 1983; child:
    650 a. Sarah[7] Franklin.

216. James Burr[5] Mills (Rachel[4], Jacob[3], Adam[2], Michael[1]) was born 21 December 1857 and died 18 April 1941. He married Mary Elizabeth Taylor, who was born 26 October 1855 and died 1 April 1946. Both are buried at Zion United Methodist Church near Prosperity. Children:
    651 i. Ola[6] Mills, m. _____ Fulmer
    652 ii. Maude[6] Mills, m. _____ Stockman
    653 iii. Thompson E.[6] Mills, b. 5 Oct 1888, d. 9 Aug 1889
+ 654 iv. Willie Lee[6] Mills, b. 2 June 1890
    655 v. Bertha[6] Mills, m. _____ Caison
    656 vi. Gussie[6] Mills
    657 vii. O. B.[6] Mills
    658 viii. Norman C.[6] Mills.

220. Mary Ellen[5] Mills (Rachel[4], Jacob[3], Adam[2], Michael[1]) was born 3 September 1863. She married John A. Nichols, who was born 8 March 1865 and died 5 June 1926. Children:
    659 i. Archie B.[6] Nichols, b. 14 May 1890, d. 4 July 1890, bur. Zion United Methodist Church
+ 660 ii. Sparta[6] Nichols, b. 15 Feb 1892
    661 iii. Inf. son, b. & D. 18 May 1897, bur. Zion United Meth. Ch.
    662 iv. Carrie Reba[6] Nichols, b. 17 Aug 1899, d. 24 Oct 1899 bur. Zion United Methodist Church.

221. Thomas Marion[5] Mills (Rachel[4], Jacob[3], Adam[2], Michael[1]) was born 1 April 1870 and died 15 February 1953. He married, first, Sally Long who was born 19 June 1871 and died 11 April 1939. He married, second, Ruth Lindler Meetze. Two children:
    663 i. Carroll Sease[6] Mills, b. 5 July 1899, d. 2 Dec 1976, m. Esther Taft (1900-1971)

664 ii. Lottie Vera[6] Mills, b. 16 June 1901, d. 18 June 1923, m. Dhent Asbury[6] Bedenbaugh (David Murchison[5]) (see under him for descendants).

222. Mary Jane[5] Bedenbaugh (William J.[4], John[3], Adam[2], Michael[1]) was born 2 June 1859 and died 10 January 1941 in Newberry, South Carolina. She married, on 28 February 1882, Newton Turner Hipp, who was born 17 September 1855 in Edgefield (now Saluda) County, South Carolina, and died 24 March 1936 in Newberry County. Both are buried at St. Luke's Lutheran Church, near Prosperity, South Carolina. Children, both born in Newberry County, South Carolina:

+ 665 i. Mattie Sula[6] Hipp, b. 8 Oct 1886
666 ii. Arthur Tillman[6] Hipp, b. 26 Sept 1890, d. 10 Nov 1939, m. 26 Dec 1918, Anna Julia Harmon.

223. Nancy[5] Bedenbaugh (William J.[4], John[3], Adam[2], Michael[1]) was born 19 November 1865 and died 21 March 1940. She married Merrit Simeon Christian (Chris) Danielson, who was born 21 February 1871 and died 18 March 1947. Three children:

667 i. Birdie Orine[6] Danielson, b. 5 Nov 1892, d. 8 June 1974, m. Albert Martin
668 ii. Theodore William[6] Danielson
669 iii. Augustus Roland[6] Danielson.

224. James Luther[5] Bedenbaugh (William J.[4], John[3], Adam[2], Michael[1]) was born 13 December 1870 and died 26 October 1954 in Newberry, South Carolina. He married Jessie Mae Dobbins, who was born 10 March 1873 and died 28 December 1957 in Newberry. Both are buried at Newberry Memorial Gardens in Newberry. One child:

+ 670 i. Etta[6] Bedenbaugh, b. 30 Jan 1983.

225. Lula[5] Bedenbaugh (James Luther[5], William J.[4], John[3], Adam[2], Michael[1]) was born 6 June 1874 and died 10 March 1947 in Newberry, South Carolina. She married, on 6 August 1891, August M. Danielson, who was born 31 July 1873 in Edgefield County, South Carolina, and died 21 July 1962. Both are buried at Rosemont Cemetery in Newberry, South Carolina. Children, all born in Newberry, South Carolina:

671 i. William Francis[6] Danielson, b. 3 Nov 1895, d. 6 March 1896
+ 672 ii. James Alvin[6] Danielson, b. 27 May 1899
673 iii. Mattie Elizabeth[6] Danielson, b. 30 July 1901, d. Sept 1901
674 iv. Infant, b. & d. 10 July 1904
+ 675 v. Augusta[6] Danielsen, b. 12 Nov 1906.

227. Sara Emma[5] Bedenbaugh (James Lyttleton[4], John[3], Adam[2], Michael[1]) was born 14 April 1852 in Newberry District, South Carolina, and died 17 October 1936 at Providence, Union County, Florida. She married, on 7 December 1879, William Luke Summers, who was born 27 May 1852 and died 10 October 1926 at Providence, Florida. Children:

676 i. Emma Lee[6] Summers, b. 9 Nov 1880, Columbia Co., FL, d. 9 Nov 1863, m. 20 May 1896 Robert Lee Rogers
677 ii. Lola Viola[6] Summers, b. 6 May 1882, Columbia, Co., FL, d. 21 Oct 1957; m. 1st Michael Lucy Colson; m. 2nd William F. Smith
678 iii. Jason Perry[6] Summers, b. 8 Nov 1886, Columbia Co., FL, d. 27 Jan 1943, m. Minnie Lee Sullivan.
679 iv. Fannie[6] Summers, b. 9 Sept 1888, Union Co., FL, d. 8 Feb 1961, m. Charles M. Smith

THE BEDENBAUGH-BETENBAUGH FAMILY

680   v. Jessie Lon[6] Summers, b. 8 May 1891, Union Co., FL, d. 24 Oct 1972, m. 11 Aug 1915, Edith Agner
681 vi. Cora May[6] Summers, b. 3 May 1893, d. 14 Dec 1989, m. 20 Dec 1908 John Matthew Douglas
682 vii. Elder Drew[6] Summers, b. 28 Jan 1899, d. 20 Feb 1944, m. Flora Brooks.

228. Francis (Frank) Pickens[5] Bedenbaugh (James Lyttleton[4], John[3], Adam[2], Michael[1]) was born 11 August 1859 in Newberry District, South Carolina, and died 23 December 1933 in Lake City, Florida. He married, on 3 January 1884, Catha Lee Witt or Feagle, who was born 15 May 1865 and died 11 May 1953 in Lake City, Florida. Children:
+ 683   i. Raymond Artemas[6] Bedenbaugh, b. 24 Sept 1884
+ 684 ii. Sallie[6] Bedenbaugh, b. 20 Aug 1887
+ 685 iii. Amon Lyttleton[6] Bedenbaugh, b. 26 Sept 1890
+ 686 iv. Nathan Julian[6] Bedenbaugh, b. 31 Dec 1893
  687 v. George L.[6] Bedenbaugh, b. 6 Sept 1896, d. 15 Apr 1910
+ 688 vi. Frank Willoughby[6] Bedenbaugh, b. 12 March 1901
  689 vii. Minnie Lee[6] Bedenbaugh, b. 28 Jan 1904, d. 20 Apr 1905.

230. John Nicholas[5] Bedenbaugh (James Lyttleton[4], John[3], Adam[2], Michael[1]) was born 29 June 1867 in Newberry District, South Carolina, and died 31 March 1959, in Columbia County, Florida. He married, on 10 November 1887, Annie Emma Weeks, who was born 22 March 1868 in Union County, Florida, and died 17 December 1954 in Columbia County, Florida. Children, all born Lake City, Florida:
690   i. John Nicholas[6] Bedenbaugh, b. & d. 2 Aug 1888
691 ii. Edna Cardelia[6] Bedenbaugh, b. 24 Sept 1889, d. 3 June 1965, m. 25 Sept 1920 Percy Edward Taylor
693 iii. Emma Maybelle[6] Bedenbaugh, b. 30 Nov 1893, m. 1st 19 Dec 1910 Jacob Summit Witt, m. 2nd 24 Nov 1924 Harold Burns.
694 iv. Arthur Mead[6] Bedenbaugh, b. 29 Oct 1894, d. 24 Sept 1895
695 v. Jennings Read[6] Bedenbaugh, b. 2 Sept 1897, d. 28 Apr 1899
696 vi. Edgar Hugh[6] Bedenbaugh, b. 1 Oct 1899, d. 9 Oct 1965, m. 24 Dec 1917 Annie Lee Hunt
697 vii. Colson Clyde[6] Bedenbaugh, b. 2 Dec 1902, d. 9 Dec 1905
698 viii. Orban Ozena[6] Bedenbaugh, b. 11 Nov 1905.

231. William Pinkney[5] Bedenbaugh (James Lyttleton[4], John[3], Adam[2], Michael[1]) was born 14 September 1870 in Newberry County, South Carolina, and died 29 July 1938 in Columbia County, Florida. He married, on 13 October 1907, Lula Ophelia Thompson, who was born 16 November 1885 in Columbia County, Florida, and died there 20 July 1958. Children, all born in Lake City, Florida:
699   i. Naomi Clea[6] Bedenbaugh, b. 11 Aug 1908, d. 19 Apr 1985, m. 1st 21 Dec 1924 Mahlon Peeler, m. 2nd Sam Parker
700 ii. Mary Leta[6] Bedenbaugh, b. 26 Mar 1910, d. 25 June 1990, m. in 1932 Elery Dreffus Witt
701 iii. William Elijah[6] Bedenbaugh, b. 24 Oct 1913
702 iv. Melba Syble[6] Bedenbaugh, b. 3 Sept 1915, m. 1st 30 March 1936 A. D. Williams, m. 2nd 4 March 1939, Leon P. English
703 v. Winford Warren[6] Bedenbaugh, b. 16 Dec 1923, m. 4 March 1950 Eloise Drake.

234. William Pierce[5] Bedenbaugh (George[4], John[3], Adam[2], Michael[1]) was born 13 May 1867 and died 4 April 1913 in Newberry, South Carolina. He married Annie Lorain Lafayette (1871-1954). They are buried in Rosemont Cemetery in Newberry. William P. Bedenbaugh was a merchant in Newberry and a member of the Order of Red Men.[105] Children:[106]

    704   i. Lola Lee[6] Bedenbaugh, b. 30 June 1890, d. 28 Aug 1921, m. James H. Hendrix

+ 705 ii. Josie Henrietta[6] Bedenbaugh, b. 31 July 1893

    706 iii. William Edgar[6] Bedenbaugh, b. 20 Oct 1895, d. 24 Aug 1951, bur. Rosemont Cem.

    707 iv. Bessie[6] Bedenbaugh, b. March 1897

    708   v. Bynum[6] Bedenbaugh, b. 1901

    709 vi. Gladys[6] Bedenbaugh, b. 1904

    710 vii. Lillian[6] Bedenbaugh, (1906-1957), bur. Rosemont Cem., unm.

    711 viii. Ruby Christine[6] Bedenbaugh, b. 21 Aug 1909, d. 10 July 1978, m 5 June 1937 Perry Orlando Wicker, b. 21 Apr 1906, d. 21 May 1979, both bur. Rosemont Cem.

241. John Denniston[5] Bedenbaugh (George[4], John[3], Adam[2], Michael[1]) was born 18 May 1875 and died 28 June 1951. He married, on 25 October 1896, Daisy Lillie Christine Platt, who was born 16 March 1880 and died 19 August 1954. Both are buried in Rosemont Cemetery, Newberry, South Carolina.[107] Children:[108]

+ 712   i. Lottie May[6] Bedenbaugh, b. 22 July 1897

    713 ii. Mittie Lee[6] Bedenbaugh, b. 13 Nov 1898, d. 25 Dec 1974, m. 1 Aug 1915 William Pleasant King, b. 10 Oct 1891, d. 15 Sept 1948, bur. Rosemont Cem., Newberry, SC

    714 iii. Eva[6] Bedenbaugh, b. 17 Feb 1901, d. 15 July 1901

+ 715 iv. Denniston Johnnie[6] Bedenbaugh, b. 7 Jan 1910

    716   v. Simon A.[6] (Buddy) Bedenbaugh, b. 14 July 1911, m. 27 Apr 1929, Ruby Arnold; children:

         717 a. Raymond[7] Bedenbaugh

         718 b. Betty Jean[7] Bedenbaugh

    719 vi. Helen[6] Bedenbaugh, b. 29 Oct 1913, d. 27 Dec 1962, m. 17 Apr 1929 James R. Stribble; children:

         720 a. John[7] Stribble

         721 b. Peggy[7] Stribble

         722 c. Shirley[7] Stribble

         723 d. Toby[7] Stribble.

258. Walter Simpson[5] Bedenbaugh (Franklin S.[4], John[3], Adam[2], Michael[1]) was born 8 January 1876 and died 16 Dec 1950 in Columbia, South Carolina. He married Ella Florence Gilliam, who was born 16 October 1873 and died 14 September 1951 in High Point, North Carolina. Both are buried Zion United Methodist Church near Prosperity, South Carolina. Children:

    724   i. Claude Frank[6] Bedenbaugh, Sr., m. Katie Julia Coates. Children:

         725 a. Doris Louise[7] Bedenbaugh, m. Earle W. Wessinger

         726 b. Virginia Connie[7] Bedenbaugh, m. George Henry Simon

         727 c. Frances Christine[7] Bedenbaugh, m. William (Bill) Zimmerman

         728 d. Claudia Julia[7] Bedenbaugh, unm.

         729 e. Claude F.[7] Bedenbaugh, Jr.

    730 ii. Virgil[6] Bedenbaugh

    731 iii. Arthur[6] Bedenbaugh

732 iv. Bessie[6] Bedenbaugh, m. J. Evans Bowers; children:

    733 a. Eugene[7] Bowers

    734 b. Carroll[7] Bowers

    735 c. Curtis[7] Bowers

    736 d. David[7] Bowers

    737 e. Florence[7] Bowers

    738 f. Margaret[7] Bowers, m. Hoyt E. Morris.

269. Allen Lester[5] Bedenbaugh (Elijah King[4], John[3], Adam[2], Michael[1]) was born 9 February 1875 and died 18 February 1937. He married, on 3 August 1896, Ann Adams, who was born 18 April 1878 and died 11 February 1953. Both are buried in the Prosperity Cemetery, Newberry County, South Carolina. Children:

739 i. Fred Lester[6] Bedenbaugh, b. 7 May 1899, d. 19 Jan 1936

+ 740 ii. Aldon Eugene[6] (Buddy) Bedenbaugh, b. 6 Jan 1900, d. 5 March 1975, m. Ida Mae Hayes, b. 17 July 1901, d. 6 Apr 1978.

741 iii. Marie Belle[6] Bedenbaugh, b. 29 Mar 1902, d. 5 Nov 1955, m. Brooks Epting; children:

    742 a. Robert F.[7] Epting, m. Trudie Bedenbaugh

    743 b. Ralph Epting

    744 c. Harold[7] Epting

    745 d. Randall[7] Epting

746 iv. Herbert Hayne[6] (John) Bedenbaugh, b. 22 Feb 1904, d. 15 Oct 1982, m. Julia Clary

+ 747 v. Howard King[6] Bedenbaugh, b. 16 March 1906

748 vi. Violet[6] Bedenbaugh m. 1st Carl Aaron, b. 12 May 1912, d. 8 June 1944; 2nd William Fleming; child:

    749 a. William[7] Aaron

750 vii. James Manly[6] Bedenbaugh, b. 12 Dec 1910, d. 8 May 1968, m. Mary J. Andrews; child:

    751 a. Manly Gordon[7] Bedenbaugh

752 viii. Allen Lester[6] Bedenbaugh, Jr., m. Edith Boland

753 ix. Lee Lewis[6] Bedenbaugh, m. Margorie Odell

754 x. Susan[6] Bedenbaugh m. James Nelson; children:

    755 a. Ricky[7] Nelson

    756 b. James[7] Nelson

757 xi. Rosa[6] Bedenbaugh m. Roy Lee Harris; children:

    758 a. Philip[7] Harris

    759 b. Timothy[7] Harris

    760 c. Amanda[7] Harris.

280. George Virgil[5] Boozer (Laura[4], John[3], Adam[2], Michael[1]) was born 18 February 1878 and died 10 June 1926 in Columbia, South Carolina, and is buried in Elmwood Cemetery there. He married, on 25 December 1901, Bertha Addy, who was born 12 January 1879, and died 22 September 1952, a daughter of Henry F. and Olivia (Epting) Addy. Children:

761 i. Lossie Mae[6] Boozer, m. Julian E. Hair

762 ii. George Virgil[6] Boozer, Jr., m. Everett Valentine Elliott; children:

    763 a. Anne[7] Boozer, m. Allen S. Bashore

    764 b. Everett[7] Boozer, m. Jake D. Long

765 iii. John Hubert[6] Boozer, b. c1908, d. 5 Oct 1967, Bryan, TX, m. Violet Gibson; child:

    766 a. John Wesley[7] Boozer

767 iv. Pauline[6] Boozer, m. DeVere D. Reed
768 v. Edward Fulenwider[6] Boozer, m. Myra McKeown; children:
    769 a. Edward[7] Boozer
    770 b. William Reed[7] Boozer
    771 c. Beth[7] Boozer
    772 d. John Douglas[7] Boozer
    773 e. Robert Earle[7] Boozer
774 vi. James Marion[6] Boozer, m. Mary Blakely; children:
    775 a. James Marion[7] Boozer, Jr.
    776 b. George Franklin[7] Boozer
    777 c. Thomas Chappell[7] Boozer
    778 d. Mary[7] Boozer
779 vii. Margaret[6] Boozer, m. Robert Smith
780 viii. Charles Wilson[6] Boozer, m. Nell Cunningham; children:
    781 a. Jonell Olivia[7] Boozer
    782 b. Charles Wilson[7] Boozer, Jr.
    783 c. Kathy[7] Boozer
    784 d. Alton[7] Boozer
    785 e. Cindy[7] Boozer
    786 f. Teresa[7] Boozer
787 ix. Laura Addy[6] Boozer, m. Charles G. Munn.

281. John Reuben[5] Boozer (Laura[4], John[3], Adam[2], Michael[1]) was born 20 August 1879 and died 24 January 1933. He married Nancy Elmira Oxner, who was born 11 January 1879 and died 24 March 1967. They are buried in Rosemont Cemetery, Newberry, South Carolina. Children:
    788 i. John Reuben[6] Boozer, Jr., b. 6 Apr 1906, d. 14 June 1945, m. Elizabeth Louise Corley; child:
        789 a. John Reuben[7] Boozer, III, b. 1944
    790 ii. Nannie Laura[6] Boozer, b. 1908, m. Frank Pierce Hill
    791 iii. Mable Susanna[6] Boozer, b. 1991
    792 iv. Frances Rebecca[6] Boozer, b. 1913
    793 v. Robert Lawson[6] Boozer, b. 1917, d. 1 Jan 19790, m. Elizabeth Kate McAllister; child:
        794 a. Kathryn McAllister[7] Boozer
    795 vi. Myra Helen Boozer, b. 1920, m. Ralph Addison Creswell.

283. Jacob Lawson[5] Boozer (Laura[4], John[3], Adam[2], Michael[1]) was born 28 January 1884 and died 27 July 1950 in Newberry, South Carolina. He married Bessie Josephine Nesley, who was born 3 July 1889 and died 27 October 1974. They are buried in Rosemont Cemetery, Newberry, South Carolina. Children:
    796 i. Harry Eugene[6] Boozer, b. 18 Dec 19097, d. 26 June 1924, bur. Rosemont Cem., Newberry, SC
    797 ii. Sarah Elizabeth[6] Boozer
    798 iii. Mary Helen[6] Boozer, m. Roston Hare
    799 iv. Bessie Josephine[6] Boozer, m. Robert Sims
    800 v. Dorothy May[6] Boozer, m. Clay Ballentine.

291. Lula Mary[5] Bedenbaugh (Benjamin F.[4], William[3], Adam[2], Michael[1]) was born 23 September 1878 and died 22 September 1945. She married Carrell A. Aull, who was born 8 May 1880 and died 2 December 1929. They are buried at Nazareth United Methodist Church near Leesville in Saluda County, South Carolina. Children:

  801 i. Arverene[6] Aull, b. 24 June 1907, d. 25 Jan 1977, m. 25 June 1927 Grady McGee, b. 15 Jan 1905, d. 11 Apr 1962; bur. Nazareth Meth. Ch.; children:

      802 a. Mary[7] McGee, b. 14 Feb 1949, d. 26 Apr 1969, m. 19 July 1966 James E. Langford, b. 25 May 1945, d. 26 Apr 1969, no ch.

      803 b. Heyward[7] McGee, m. Amanda Trotter

      804 c. Bernice[7] McGee, m. Pat Kirkland

805 ii. infant.

THE BEDENBAUGH-BETENBAUGH FAMILY

SIXTH GENERATION

300. Pierce Franklin[6] Boozer (Lemuel[5], Eve[4], Henry[3], Adam[2], Michael[1]) was born 8 May 1866 and died 3 December 1945. He married Ella Permelia Nicholson, who was born 15 January 1876, in Edgefield (now Saluda) County, South Carolina, and died 11 March 1937, the daughter of U. C. and Julia (Clark) Nicholson. Both are buried at St. Luke's Lutheran Church. Children:

806   i. Mary Eva[7] Boozer, b. 5 March 1893, d. 10 March 1930, m. Samuel Wilbur Shealy, b. 1890, d. 1969. Both are buried at St. Luke's Lutheran Church. Children:
- 807 a. Annette[8] Shealy m. Roy Connelly
- 808 b. Ella Rae[8] Shealy m. Huber Graves
- 809 c. Carroll[8] Shealy
- 810 d. Durham[8] Shealy

811   ii. Frank Pierce[7] Boozer, b. 16 July 1894

812   iii. Esther Maude[7] Boozer, b. 13 Sept 1895, d. 27 March 1969, Greenville, SC.

813   iv. Julia Ann[7] Boozer, b. 9 Sept 1895, d. 30 Nov 1966, m. George W. Hughes. Child:
- 814 a. George[8] Hughes

815   v. Arthur Purcell[7] Boozer, b. 10 Aug 1900, m. Elise Amanda[6] Bedenbaugh (David Murchison[5]). See under her for descendants.

+ 816   vi. Ella Ruth[7] Boozer, b. 10 July 1902

817   vii. Byrd Elma Boozer, b. 14 Feb 1904, d. 27 Sept 1965, m. Thomas Aubrey Bryant. No ch.

818 viii. Olive Elaine[7] Boozer, b. 6 June 1908, m. 18 Apr 1930, Reuben Humphrey Grant, b. 2 Aug 1904, Saluda, SC; children:
- 819 a. Barbara Elaine[8] Grant, b. 16 Nov 1932, m. Connie Wright Keason
- 820 b. Mary Permelia[8] Grant, b. 26 Dec 1938, Greenville, SC, m. John Wilbur Harrell
- 821 c. Reuben Herbert[8] Grant, b. 78 Sept 1951, Greenville, SC, m. Ruth Elizabeth Johnson

+ 822   ix. James Edwin[7] Boozer, b. 30 Oct 1909

+ 823   x. Bernard Nicholson[7] Boozer, b. 27 Sept 1911

824   xi. Everett Wilson[7] Boozer, b. 17 June 1914, m. Frances Estelle Davis, b. 10 Oct 1918, d. 3 Jan 1961, bur. St. Luke's Lutheran Ch. No. ch.

825 xii. Carolyn Mae[7] Boozer, b. 8 May 1917, m. James Leonard Hendrix, b. 2 Nov 1914. Children:
- 826 a. Jimmy Leonard[8] Hendrix, b. 26 May 1939, m. Barbara Ann Bouknight
- 827 b. Gerald Rudy[8] Hendrix, b. 8 Dec 1947.

301. Joseph Elzy[6] Boozer (Lemuel[5], Eve[4], Henry[3], Adam[2], Michael[1]) was born in 1868 in Newberry County, and died 25 July 1932. He married Mary Elizabeth Nicholson, who was born 10 October 1870 in Edgefield (now Saluda) County, South Carolina, and died 4 August 1958, the daughter of U. C. and Julia (Clark) Nicholson. Both are buried at Salem Baptist Cemetery in Saluda County. Children:

828   i. Joseph Lee[7] Boozer, b. 1893

829   ii. Seth C.[7] Boozer, b. 29 Dec 1895, Saluda, SC

830 iii. Jane Pearle[7] Boozer, b. 17 Feb 1900, b. 17 Feb 1900, Newberry Co., SC, m. 31 Aug 1918, Jacob Nolan Ruff, b. 26 Oct 1895, d. 14 Sept 1955, bur. Newberry Mem. Gardens. Children:
- 831 a. Earl Dewey[8] Ruff, b. 16 Apr 1920, m. Sara Jean Darby

832 b. Mary Elizabeth[8] Ruff, b. 30 Dec 1921, m. Thomas Edward Sease
833 c. Dorothy Annette[8] Ruff, b. 11 Nov 1923, m. Walter Thomas Lake
834 d. Jacob Nolan[8] Ruff, Jr., b. 15 March 1926, m. Betty Jean Taylor
835 e. Murray Joseph[8] Ruff, b. 17 Apr 1928, m. Jean Earle
836 f. Etta Rae[8] Ruff, b. 21 May 1930, m. Harvey McConnell Jordan
837 g. Wallace Bernard[8] Ruff, b. 20 Dec 1934, m. Renetia Ann Rawls
838 iv. Julia Mae[7] Boozer, b. 24 Feb 1902, d. 24 Feb 1974, m. 27 July 1919 Kirksey
Raymond Koon, b. 15 Jan 1898, d. 27 July 1962, bur. Rosemont Cem;
children:
839 a. Helen Rae[8] Koon, b. 18 March 1921, m. James William Foy
840 b. Raymond Lee[8] Koon, b. 20 Feb 1925, m. Jean Elliott
841 v. Annette[7] Boozer, b. 4 Apr 1905, d. 2 Sept 1942, bur. Salem Cem, Saluda
Co., m. Eddie Waters, b. 21 Jan 1903. Children:
842 a. Doris[8] Waters, b. 19 Apr 1926, m. Joseph Kendrick
843 b. Lois[8] Waters, b. 11 Sept 1927, m. Hilton Douglas
844 c. Virginia[8] Waters, b. 5 Feb 1929, m. Milton Corley
845 d. Edwin[8] Waters, b. 6 June 1934
846 e. Willie Lee[8] Waters, b. 15 March 1936
847 vi. Evelyn Gertrude[7] Boozer, b. 22 July 1907, m. 17 Aug 1929 Berley Leland
Hiller, b. 4 Jan 1909. Children:
848 a. Leland Richard[8] Hiller, b. 24 July 1930 m. Vivian Clark
849 b. Joel Herman[8] Hiller, b. 20 Dec 1932, m. Bobbie Jean Rinken
850 c. Arnold Duane[8] Hiller, b. 23 Sept 1945, m. Linda Morris
851 vii. Thelma Pauline[7] Boozer, b. 17 Sept 1910, m. 23 Dec 1933 Earl Eugene
Bollinger, b. 25 Nov 1908. No ch.

306. Marion Frank[6] Bedenbaugh (Simpson[5], Daniel[4], Henry[3], Adam[2], Michael[1])was
born 27 March 1886 in Lafayette Co., Miss., and died 29 March 1959 in Jackson,
TN. He married Lillian Divola Arnold on 25 Nov 1906 in Panola County,
Mississippi. Children of Marion Frank Bedenbaugh:
852 i. Marion Naomi[7] Bedenbaugh, b. 16 Sept 1907 (who has supplied most of the
information on descendants of Daniel), m. Thomas Wingo Hillman, 27 June
1933
853 ii. Anna Mae[7] Bedenbaugh, b. 1 July 1909 Lafayette Co., MS, m. 24 Nov 1929
Daris Pete DeShazo; children:
854 a. Frances Lee[8] DeShazo, b. 27 Apr 1931, m. James Frederick
Holloman (live Winston-Salem, N. C.); children:
855 (1) Larry Dwayne[9] Holloman m. Cathy Martin
856 (2) Melina Denise[9] Holloman
857 b. Mary DeShazo, stillborn 1933
858 c. Edna Earle[8] DeShazo, b. 30 May 1934, m. (1) James Lineback (2)
Thomas A. Story (live Winston-Salem, N. C.); children:
859 (1) Charles Daris[9] (Chuck) Story
860 (2) Timothy Wayne[9] (Tim) Story.

316. Lucy Day[6] Bedenbaugh (Zacheus Wright[5], John Adam[4], Henry[3], Adam[2],
Michael[1]) was born 1 August 1884 and died 20 August 1965. She married, on 21 Dec
1905, James Herman Werts. Children:
861 i. Zacheus Herman[7] Werts, b. 1 Nov 1906, d. 3 July 1908
862 ii. Day Bedenbaugh[7] Werts (Rev.), b. 25 Nov 1908, d. 15 May 1983, m.
Gertrude Vogel, lived Spartanburg, SC
863 iii. James William[7] Werts, b. 22 Apr 1912

864 iv. Earnest Wright[7] Werts, b. 28 Sept 1917, m. 9 Mar 1946 Kathleen Moose; children:
    865 a. Ernest Day[8] Werts, b. 14 Feb 1949, m. 17 June 1972 Margaret Gessler; son:
        866 (1) Travis Day[9] Werts, b. 19 Aug 1976
    867 b. James Steven[8] Werts, b. 22 Sept 1950, m. Fonde Thompson 15 Dec 1974.

319. John Carl[6] Dennis (Mary Ella[5], John Adam[4], Henry[3], Adam[2], Michael[1]) was born 11 December 1876 and died 15 June 1962. He married Thompsie Viola[6] Bedenbaugh (a second cousin) on 25 December 1904, Rev. S. P. Koon officiating. Thompsie Viola Bedenbaugh was born 19 February 1882 and died 10 August 1961, a daughter of Hawkins[5] and E. Melissa (Kelly) Bedenbaugh (see page 34). Both John C. and Thompsie B. Dennis are buried at St. Luke's Church. Children, all born in Newberry County, South Carolina:
    868 i. Francis A.[7] Dennis, b. 8 Sept 1905, m. Clarice Dawkins
+ 869 ii. James H.[7] Dennis, b. 22 Nov 1906
+ 870 iii. Robert Zack[7] Dennis, b. 13 Nov 1908
+ 871 iv. Mary[7] Dennis, b. 31 Aug 1912.

342. John Roscoe[6] Bedenbaugh (Hawkins[5], Simeon[4], Henry[3], Adam[2], Michael[1]) was born 12 November 1879 and died 24 November 1939. He married, on 24 January 1907, Maude Boozer, who was born 21 August 1888 and died 21 February 1977. Both are buried at St. Luke's Lutheran Church near Prosperity, South Carolina. Children:
+ 872 i. Lottie Ruth[7] Bedenbaugh, b. 7 Dec 1907
+ 873 ii. William Woodrow[7] Bedenbaugh, b. 6 Oct 1912
+ 874 iii. James Roscoe[7] Bedenbaugh, b. 26 Dec 1914
+ 875 iv. Mae[7] Bedenbaugh
+ 876 v. Ollie Thomas[7] Bedenbaugh, b. 5 Aug 1920
+ 877 vi. Robert Hawkins[7] Bedenbaugh, b. 29 Apr 1923
+ 878 vii. Mildred[7] Bedenbaugh, b. 15 Oct 1927
+ 879 viii. John Adam[7] Bedenbaugh, b. 3 Jan 1931.

344. James Simeon Simpson[6] Bedenbaugh (Hawkins[5], Simeon[4], Henry[3], Adam[2], Michael[1]) was born 23 January 1887 and died 28 February 1947. He married Toye Epting, who was born 3 November 1901 and died 8 August 1993. Both are buried at Prosperity Cemetery, Prosperity, South Carolina. Children:
+ 880 i. Benjamin McFall[7] (Mac) Bedenbaugh, b. 25 Jan 1920
    881 ii. Hazel Inez[7] Bedenbaugh, b. 5 June 1922, d. 30 Jan 1989, m. 10 Aug 1946 Ewell Gray Cotney; child:
        882 a. Vickie[8] Cotney, m. Jimmy Powell
+ 883 iii. Eula Melissa[7] Bedenbaugh, b. 4 Oct 1924
+ 884 iv. Helen Ruth[7] Bedenbaugh, b. 10 Sept 1926
+ 885 v. Vera[7] Bedenbaugh, b. 1 Apr 1929
    886 vi. James Simeon[7] Bedenbaugh, Jr., b. 20 Dec 1927.

345. Nancy Ella[6] Bedenbaugh (Hawkins[5], Simeon[4], Henry[3], Adam[2], Michael[1]) was born 17 February 1884 and died 27 November 1947. She married, on 20 January 1904, David Malcolm Shealy, who was born 31 October 1882 and died 25 October 1954. Children:
    887 i. Infant son, b. 21 Dec 1906, d. 24 Dec 1906

+ 888　ii. Ethan Otway[7] Shealy, b. 26 Apr 1908
+ 889　iii. Otis Kelley[7] Shealy, b. 19 Jan 1910
　890　iv. Maggie Lena[7] Shealy, b. 13 June 1912, d. 3 March 1917
+ 891　v. Annie Laura[7] Shealy, b. 14 Dec 1913
+ 892　vi. Sarah Malissa[7] Shealy, b. 21 June 1917
+ 893　vii. Nancy Elizabeth[7] Shealy, b. 2 Jan 1924.

346. Eliza Jeannette[6] Bedenbaugh (Hawkins[5], Simeon[4], Henry[3], Adam[2], Michael[1]) was born 9 July 1889, baptized 4 May 1890 (St. Luke's Lutheran Church Records) and died in 1984. She married Killian N. Epting, who was born 6 August 1887 and died 19 October 1946. Both are buried in the Prosperity Cemetery. Children:
+ 894　i. Violet M.[7] Epting, b. 24 July 1908
+ 895　ii. Voight Milton[7] Epting, b. 28 June 1910
+ 896　iii. Bonnie Lou[7] Epting, b. 10 July 1912
+ 897　iv. Andrew Kenneth[7] Epting, b. 13 Feb 1928.

347. Rosa Belle[6] Bedenbaugh (Hawkins[5], Simeon[4], Henry[3], Adam[2], Michael[1]) was born 27 September 1891, baptized 13 December 1897 (St. Luke's Records), and died 2 March 1982. She married, on 8 December 1912, to Tira Tiller Connelly, who was born 16 August 1894 and died 11 December 1959. Both are buried at St. Luke's Lutheran Church. Five children:
+ 898　i. Clarence Eldred[7] Connelly, b. 27 May 1914
+ 899　ii. James Ira[7] Connelly, b. 20 Apr 1917
+ 900　iii. Eula Mae[7] Connelly, b. 23 Apr 1919
+ 901　iv. Juanita[7] Connelly, b. 24 Nov 1921
+ 902　v. Carol Bedenbaugh[7] Connelly, b. 13 Mar 1927.

349. Jacob Hawkins (Bud)[6] Bedenbaugh (Hawkins[5], Simeon[4], Henry[3], Adam[2], Michael[1]) was born 5 August 1897, baptized 13 December 1897 (St. Luke's Records), and died 17 July 1958. He married Carrie Morris, who was born 19 October 1894 and died 17 July 1964. Both are buried at St. Luke's Lutheran Church. Ten children:
　903　i. Viola Melissa[7] Bedenbaugh, m. Baitey Smith
　904　ii. Jakie Lee[7] Bedenbaugh, m. Janie Bedenbaugh
　905　iii. Gerald[7] Bedenbaugh
　906　iv. James W.[7] Bedenbaugh, m. Sarah Crumpton
　907　v. Estelle[7] Bedenbaugh, m. Marvin Bouknight
　908　vi. Varee[7] Bedenbaugh, m. Clyde Wicker
　909　vii. Mary[7] Bedenbaugh
　910　viii. Johnny Clarence[7] Bedenbaugh, b. 1937, d. 5 Sept 1984
　911　ix. Bobbie F.[7] Bedenbaugh, b. 14 Dec 1934
　912　x. Hawkins S.[7] Bedenbaugh.

352. Jefferson Holland[6] Bedenbaugh (John Simpson[5], Simeon[4], Henry[3], Adam[2], Michael[1]) was born 27 December 1892 and died 7 April 1961. He married, on 27 June 1923, Grace Beryl Holcombe, who was born 20 May 1898 and died 20 July 1981. They are buried at Colony Lutheran Church, near Newberry, South Carolina. Children:
　913　i. John Holcombe[7] (Jack) Bedenbaugh m. Angela Lee Owen
　914　ii. Louisa Adelle[7] Bedenbaugh m. Darol Albert Kirby
　915　iii. Eugene Holland[7] Bedenbaugh m. Mary Helen Jackson.

353. Wendell Grady[6] Bedenbaugh (John Simpson[5], Simeon[4], Henry[3], Adam[2], Michael[1]) was born 22 June 1901 and died 23 October 1975. He married Sara Alice Kinard, who was born 7 July 1909 and died 18 September 1969. They are buried at Colony Lutheran Church, near Newberry, South Carolina. Children:

916   i. John Benjamin[7] Bedenbaugh was born 13 September 1929 and died 15 May 1993 in Columbia, SC. He was a professor at Lutheran Southern Theological Seminary in Columbia for forty years. He is buried at Colony Lutheran Church.

917   ii. Adella[7] Bedenbaugh married George W. Summer

918 iii. David Rudolph[7] Bedenbaugh, m. Cheryl Elaine Reeves

919   iv. James Wendell[7] Bedenbaugh, m. Martha Kyzer

    920 a. Sabrina[8] Bedenbaugh, b. 25 Sept 1959 m. 1st 12 July 1975 Kenneth Bruce[9] Garner (see his lineage), m. 2nd Gary Manning, lives Prosperity, SC

    921 b. James Wendell[8] Bedenbaugh, Jr., b. 25 Sept 1960, m. 1st Tammy Kinard; m. 2nd Donna Riser

    922 c. Martha Tian[8] Bedenbaugh, b. 3 May 1966, m. 1st Michael Zuluaga, m. 2nd Ron Ware

923   v. Juanita[7] Bedenbaugh married Monroe E. Fulmer.

354. Mary Hallman[6] Bedenbaugh (Pettus[5], Simeon[4], Henry[3], Adam[2], Michael[1]) was born 26 September 1889 and died 27 June 1956 and is buried at St. Luke's Lutheran Church near Prosperity, South Carolina. She married, on 5 December 1909, Osborne Frank ("Bounce") Dennis (Mary Ella[5], John Adam[4], Henry[3], Adam[2], Michael[1]), a second cousin, who was born 28 July 1886 and died 25 February 1976. Children:

+ 924   i. Vera Thelma[7] Dennis, b. 22 May 1911
+ 925   ii. Jesse Frank[7] Dennis, b. 21 Sept 1913
+ 926 iii. Robert Bedenbaugh[7] Dennis, b. 28 June 1915
+ 927   iv. Herman Wright[7] Dennis, b. 15 July 1918
+ 928   v. Clara[7] Dennis, b. 17 Oct 1924
  929 vi. Christine[7] Dennis, b. 2 March 1929, d. 11 March 1929.

355. Tranquilla Susannah[6] Bedenbaugh (Pettus[5], Simeon[4], Henry[3], Adam[2], Michael[1]) was born 1 January 1891 and died 14 February 1963. She married Clarence Raymond Riser, who was born 3 September 1891 and died 13 October 1963. Both are buried at St. Luke's Lutheran Church near Prosperity, South Carolina. Children:

+ 930   i. George Pettus[7] Riser, b. 27 July 1912
+ 931   ii. Dora Opal[7] Riser, b. 4 Sept 1914
  932 iii. Robert Karl[7] Riser, b. 15 Jan 1917, m. Eula Mae[7] Connelly (Rosa Belle[6], Hawkins[5]) (see under her for descendants)
+ 933   iv. Annie Lila[7] Riser, b. 31 July 1919
+ 934   v. Heber Pickens[7] Riser, b. 5 March 1922.

357. Charlie Simeon[6] Bedenbaugh (Pettus[5], Simeon[4], Henry[3], Adam[2], Michael[1]) was born 22 October 1892 and died 11 November 1958. He married, on 26 December 1915, Gertrude Chapman,[109] who as born 22 August 1898 and died 15 October 1986. Both are buried at St. Luke's Lutheran Church near Prosperity, South Carolina. Children:

+ 935   i. Charlie Roy[7] Bedenbaugh, b. 14 May 1917, d. 3 July 1987
+ 936   ii. Clara Nell[7] Bedenbaugh, b. 25 Feb 1919

937 iii. Carroll[7] Bedenbaugh, b. 24 Aug 1923, killed in action on board the USS
    Columbia, 6 Jan 1945.
938 iv. Andrew Hugh[7] Bedenbaugh, b. 2 Aug 1928, d. 8 June 1987, m. Ella
    Wright; children:
    939 a. Michael Andrew[8] Bedenbaugh, d. 21 March 1993, Union, SC;
        children:
        940 (1) Kristie[9] Bedenbaugh
        941 (2) Angie[9] Bedenbaugh
    942 b. Rickey[8] Bedenbaugh, lives Carrollton, TX
943 v. Rachel Susanna[7] Bedenbaugh, b. 13 March 1932, m. 10 Dec 1949, James
    Robert Stuck, b. 30 Dec 1926; children:
    944 a. Mary Ann[8] Stuck, b. 7 March 1951
    945 b. Judy[8] Stuck, b. 27 Jan 1955.

358. Daisy Ophelia[6] Bedenbaugh (Pettus[5], Simeon[4], Henry[3], Adam[2], Michael[1]) was
born 4 October 1894 and died 5 March 1976. She married, on 21 December 1913,
Lindsey Drayton Smith, who was born 27 August 1891 and died 2 November 1982.
They are buried at Newberry Memorial Gardens, Newberry, South Carolina.
Children:
946 i. Curtis Pettus[7] Smith, b. 11 July 1915, m. 15 Apr 1939 Margaret Whitman,
    b. 14 Sept 1921; two children:
    947 a. Harold[8] Smith, m. Shelby Spires; children:
        948 (1) Debra Sue[9] Smith, m. Scott Finken; child:
            949 Courtney Marie[10] Finken
        950 (2) Paige[9] Smith
    951 b. Gerald[8] Smith (Rev.), m. Christie Pengra
952 ii. Hoyt Lindsey[7] Smith, b. 6 Sept 1919 m. 1st 1 June 1941, Doris Hipp, b. 19
    Nov 1921, d. 18 May 1960; m. 2nd Mary Kathleen Shull; m. 3rd Frederica
    Able (d. 11 July 1995); children:
    953 a. Larry Emmett[8] Smith, b. & d. 21 Nov 1946, bur. St. Luke's
        Lutheran Ch.
    954 b. Preston[8] Smith, b. 11 Feb 1955, Columbia, SC, m. Karen Sanford;
        children, b. Columbia, SC:
        955 (1) Shannon[9] Smith, b. 3 July 1974
        956 (2) Heather[9] Smith, b. 18 Sept 1975
    957 c. Kevin[8] Smith, b. 22 March 1960, Columbia, SC
958 iii. Cleo Geneva[7] Smith, m. William Shatterly; child:
    959 a. Sammy[8] Shatterly, m. Ellen ____; children:
        960 (1) Gena Kay[9] Shatterly
        961 (2) William Robert[9] (Robby) Shatterly
962 iv. John Boyd[7] Smith, m. Betty Fuller; child:
    963 a. Hugh Boyd[8] Smith, b. Donna ____; child
        964 (1) Aubrey Boyd[9] Smith
965 v. Mary Christine[7] Smith, m. Harry Senn; children:
    966 a. Stanley H.[8] Senn; children:
        967 (1) Bryan[9] Senn
        968 (2) Lindsay[9] Senn
    969 b. Kenneth B.[8] Senn; children:
        970 (1) Elizabeth[9] Senn
        971 (2) Zachary[9] Senn.

359. Jennie Beardon[6] Bedenbaugh (Pettus[5], Simeon[4], Henry[3], Adam[2], Michael[1]) was born 17 October 1896 and died 21 June 1978. She married, on 21 August 1914, James Oryan Miller, who was born 27 June 1892, and died 24 June 1967. They are buried at St. Luke's Lutheran Church near Prosperity, South Carolina. Four children:

+ 972 i. Marion Pet[7] Miller, b. 8 Sept 1916
  973 ii. Emily Elizabeth[7] Miller, b. 10 Apr 1919, d. 12 Sept 1930
  974 iii. Jennie Merle[7] Miller, b. 20 Sept 1921, b. 12 Apr 1940 Leon Woodrow Kinney, b. 24 Dec 1917, d. 4 Nov 1982; child:
  975 a. David Leon[8] Kinney, b. 20 Jan 1948, m. 14 Feb 1969, Sandra Louise Morris, b. 21 March 1949
+ 976 iv. James Lee[7] Miller, b. 20 Nov 1928.

360. Pettus Birge[6] Bedenbaugh (Pettus[5], Simeon[4], Henry[3], Adam[2], Michael[1]) was born 17 December 1898 and died 12 January 1973. He married Eunice Chapman, who was born 4 May 1898, and died 10 July 1975. Both are buried at St. Luke's Lutheran Church near Prosperity, South Carolina. Four children:

  977 i. Marvin Birge[7] Bedenbaugh, b. 23 June 1920, d. 9 Jan 1968, m. Annie Laura Morris; children:
  978 a. Edith[8] Bedenbaugh
  979 b. Judy[8] Bedenbaugh
  980 c. Keith[8] Bedenbaugh
  981 ii. Lola Elizabeth[7] Bedenbaugh, b. 24 Apr 1922, m. Silas Smith; children:
  982 a. Fred[8] Smith
  983 b. Robert[8] Smith
  984 c. Alfreida[8] Smith
  985 d. Jimmy[8] Smith
  986 e. Patsy[8] Smith
  987 f. Andy[8] Smith (triplet)
  988 g. Mandy[8] Smith (triplet)
  989 h. Sandy[8] Smith (triplet)
  990 iii. George Elton[7] Bedenbaugh, b. 14 March 1924, m. 25 Nov 1948, Lois Goff, b. 8 Nov 1928; children:
  991 a. Ricky Elton[8] Bedenbaugh, b. 2 Feb 1956, m. 25 March 1978 Angela DeCarolus Fuller; children:
  992 (1) Jeremy Elton[9] Bedenbaugh, b. 27 June 1979
  993 (2) Branton Alexander[9] Bedenbaugh, b. 27 June 1983
  994 b. Cynthia Dell[8] Bedenbaugh, b. & d 23 May 1959
  995 iv. Helen Beatrice[7] Bedenbaugh, b. 7 Sept 1927, m. 15 Dec 1945 J. D. Schumpert; child:
  996 a. Diane[8] Schumpert, b. 31 Jan 1948, m. 26 July 1969 Kenneth Michael Wilson, live Charlotte, NC; children:
  997 (1) Angela Nicole[9] Wilson, b. 8 Aug 1973
  998 (2) Kenneth Michael[9] Wilson, b. 12 Sept 1975.

361. Horace Nichols[6] Bedenbaugh (Pettus[5], Simeon[4], Henry[3], Adam[2], Michael[1]) was born 24 April 1901 and died 21 September 1958. He married, on 5 November 1921, Annie Colene Smith, who was born 12 December 1902 and died 10 May 1986. They are buried Mt. Pilgrim Lutheran Church near Prosperity, South Carolina. Five children:

+ 999 i. Mary Suzanna[7] Bedenbaugh, b. 29 July 1922
+ 1000 ii. Dorothy Mae[7] Bedenbaugh, b. 17 Nov 1926

THE BEDENBAUGH-BETENBAUGH FAMILY

+ 1001 iii. Betty Lucille[7] Bedenbaugh, b. 22 Oct 1931
+ 1002 iv. Annie Norine[7] Bedenbaugh, b. 21 May 1934
+ 1003 v. Paul Nichols[7] Bedenbaugh, b. 15 Aug 1936.

362. Jones Mathias[6] Bedenbaugh (Pettus[5], Simeon[4], Henry[3], Adam[2], Michael[1]) was born 17 October 1903 in Prosperity, South Carolina, and died there 22 November 1988. He married, on 23 December 1922, Leslie Rae Smith who was born 13 July 1905 in Saluda County, South Carolina, and died 6 January 1993 in Prosperity. They are buried at St. Luke's Lutheran Church. Five children, all born in Prosperity, Newberry County, South Carolina:

+ 1004 i. Hazel Mae[7] Bedenbaugh, b. 11 July 1923
  1005 ii. Luther Pettus Bedenbaugh, b. & d. 21 Jan 1925
  1006 iii. Jones Edward[8] Bedenbaugh, b. 16 July 1926, m. 13 Sept 1947 Sarah Griffith, b. 13 Sept 1928
+ 1007 iv. Clyde Eugene[7] Bedenbaugh, b. 25 Sept 1930
+ 1008 v. Doris Louise[7] Bedenbaugh, b. 5 Nov 1931
+ 1009 vi. Gladys[7] Bedenbaugh, b. 9 Jan 1934 m. Julian Lester Shealy
+ 1010 vii. Bobby Ray[7] Bedenbaugh, b. 18 May 1940.

363. Koon Maybank[6] Bedenbaugh (Pettus[5], Simeon[4], Henry[3], Adam[2], Michael[1]) was born 6 November 1905 and died 17 August 1985, buried at St. Luke's Lutheran Church. He married, on 24 December 1927, Nancy Ruth Smith, who was born 4 October 1909. Three children:

+ 1011 i. Virginia[7] Bedenbaugh, b. 28 Sept 1928
+ 1012 ii. Ralph Maybank[7] Bedenbaugh, b. 6 Sept 1929
+ 1013 iii. George Julian[7] Bedenbaugh, b. 15 Feb 1931.

366. Ruby Velma[6] Bedenbaugh (Pettus[5], Simeon[4], Henry[3], Adam[2], Michael[1]) was born 18 January 1912 and died 9 October 1985. She married, on 21 February 1931, Guerry Harvey Fulmer, who was born 24 November 1910 and died 25 January 1994. They are buried at Newberry Memorial Garden, Newberry, South Carolina. Two children:

+ 1014 i. Guerry Alvin[7] Fulmer, b. 12 Oct 1932
+ 1015 ii. Jerry Thomas[7] Fulmer, b. 15 Jan 1939.

367. Joseph Ira Cronk[6] Bedenbaugh (Pettus[5], Simeon[4], Henry[3], Adam[2], Michael[1]) was born 18 April 1916. He married, on 4 July 1936, Mamie Lou Farr, who was born 26 October 1919. They currently live (1995) in the Stoney Hills section, near Prosperity, South Carolina. One child:

  1016 i. June Levonne[7] Bedenbaugh, b. 22 June 1937, m. 1st, 12 Jan 1955, J. Hugh Minick; m. 2nd Tommy Stevenson; four children:
    1017 a. Tony Russel[8] Minick, b. 10 June 1957, d. 20 Dec 1970
    1018 b. Austin Scott[8] Minick, b. 17 Oct 1958, m. Charlotte Spehl
    1019 c. Preston Dean[8] Minick, b. 12 Jan 1960, m. Johnnie Shelton; child:
      1020 (1) Angel[9] Minick, b. 9 Dec 1984
    1021 d. Marla[8] Minick, b. 20 Dec 1964, m. 1st Tommy Rivers, m. 2nd Mitchell McDowel; children:
      1022 (1) Natashe[9] Rivers, b. 8 Oct 1982
      1023 (2) Kristen[9] McDowel, b. 18 Feb 1985.

374. Andrew David Frederick[6] Nichols (Mary Jane[5], John Adam[4], Adam Jr.[3], Adam[2], Michael[1]) was born 26 December 1869 and died 14 May 1914. He married Mary

THE BEDENBAUGH-BETENBAUGH FAMILY

Alice Derrick, who was born 3 October 1870 and died 10 October 1952. They are buried at St. Marks Lutheran Church in Saluda County, South Carolina. Children:

1024 i. Rufus Bachman[7] Nichols
1025 ii. William Wesley[7] Nichols
1026 iii. James Derrick[7] Nichols, b. 21 July 1904, d. 30 Nov 1980
1027 iv. Mary Ella[7] Nichols.

375. Jasper Adam[6] Nichols (Mary Jane[5], John Adam[4], Adam Jr.[3], Adam[2], Michael[1]) was born 10 February 1873 and died 29 May 1951 in a Columbia hospital, a resident of Saluda County, South Carolina. He married Mamie West and is buried in the Saluda Cemetery. Children:

1028 i. Clarence Osborn[7] Nichols
1029 ii. Essie Lucille[7] Nichols, married _____ Long
1030 iii. Virgil Luther[7] Nichols.

376. Tillman Sidney[6] Nichols (Mary Jane[5], John Adam[4], Adam Jr.[3], Adam[2], Michael[1]) was born 25 November 1877 and died 12 May 1967. He married Nettie Lee Shealy. They are buried at Union Lutheran Church, Lexington County. Children:

1031 i. Mozelle[7] Nichols
1032 ii. Heyward Emerson[7] Nichols
1033 iii. Cecil Guy[7] Nichols
1034 iv. Justus Bernard[7] Nichols
1035   v. Carl Woodrow[7] Nichols m. Josephine Raines; child:
         1036 a. Carl Woodrow[8] Nichols, Jr., M. D.
1037 vi. Miriam Esther[7] Nichols
1038 vii. Everett (Bud)[7] Nichols
1039 viii. Alba Novice[7] Nichols
1040 ix. Kathryn Colleen[7] Nichols.

377. Andrew Lonnie[6] Bedenbaugh (Jacob C.[5], John Adam[4] Sr., Adam Jr.[3], Adam[2], Michael[1]) was born 20 Sept 1878 and died 10 October 1954. He married Alice Risinger, who was born 2 March 1880 and died 2 June 1953. Both are buried at Union Lutheran Church, near Leesville, South Carolina. Children:

1041 i. Monroe Clyde[6] Bedenbaugh, b. 27 Feb 1902
1042 ii. Ethel Nannie[6] Bedenbaugh, b. 26 Oct 1906
1043 iii. Andrew Jacob[6] Bedenbaugh, b. 29 Oct 1907, m. 20 Aug 1929 Lou Annie Swygert
1044 iv. Julius Ray[6] Bedenbaugh (twin), b. 25 March 1910, d. 1978, bur. Mt. Hebron Lutheran Church, Saluda County, m. 3 July 1936, Virgie Mae Snelgrove
1045   v. Julia May[6] Bedenbaugh (twin), b. 25 March 1910, d. 18 May 1914.

379. Ernest Wyche[6] Bedenbaugh (Jacob C.[5], John Adam[4] Sr., Adam Jr.[3], Adam[2], Michael[1]) was born 20 March 1883 and died 25 July 1953. He married, first, Josephine K. Addy; second, on 21 July 1920, Maggie Corder; third, on 18 May 1940 Nannie C. Cockrell. They are buried at Union Lutheran Church, Lexington County, South Carolina. Three children were from the first marriage and two from the second:

+ 1046 i. Luther Jacob[7] Bedenbaugh, b. 18 Oct 1905
+ 1047 ii. Quincy Leon[7] Bedenbaugh, b. 19 May 1908

1048 iii. Berley[7] Bedenbaugh, b. 29 Sept 1909, d. 3 May 1987, m. 20 Apr 1935
Lizzie Hallman, b. 18 Jan 1905
1049 iv. Eddie C.[7] Bedenbaugh, m. Annie Laura Cannon
1050 v. Lewie M.[7] Bedenbaugh, m. Agnes Storey.

388. Nancy Ophelia[6] Dominick (Sarah[5], John Adam[4] Sr., Adam Jr.[3], Adam[2],
Michael[1]) was born 12 September 1880 in Newberry County, South Carolina, and
died 8 December 1971 in Greenwood County, South Carolina. She married, first,
Marvin E. Etheridge and, second, Willis D. Ross. Children:
1051 i. Alley James[7] Etheridge, m. Arna Hinton
1052 ii. Lila[7] Etheridge, m. Joseph Rayburn King
1053 iii. Frances Cornelia[7] Etheridge, m. W. B. Cathcart
1054 iv. Edgar Marvin[7] Etheridge, m. Frances Cannady
1055 v. Gaines Floyd[7] Ross, b. 15 Apr 1816, m. 1st Elizabeth Merritt, 2nd Buddra
Shelby.

389. William Kimbrough[6] Dominick (Sarah[5], John Adam[4] Sr., Adam Jr.[3], Adam[2],
Michael[1]) was born 8 March 1882 in Newberry County, South Carolina, and died 1
December 1935 in Greenwood County, South Carolina. He married Leila McCool,
who was born 24 June 1884 and died 15 February 1953. They are buried at
Rehoboth United Methodist Church in Greenwood County. One child:
1056 i. Hal[7] Dominick.

390. Sarah Hunter[6] Dominick (Sarah[5], John Adam[4] Sr., Adam Jr.[3], Adam[2], Michael[1])
was born 10 April 1884 in Newberry County, South Carolina, and died 10 June 1980
in Greenwood County, South Carolina. She married Willie C. Cromer, who was
born 15 October 1880 and died 21 December 1946. They are buried at Rehoboth
United Methodist Church in Greenwood County. Children:
1057 i. Edith[7] Cromer, died young, of scarlet fever.
1058 ii. Glenn[7] Cromer, unm.
1059 iii. Herbert James[7] Cromer
1060 iv. Evelyn[7] Cromer
1061 v. Thomas Abner[7] Cromer
1062 vi. Carl W.[7] Cromer
1063 vii. Sarah[7] Cromer.

392. Benjamin Tillman[6] Dominick (Sarah[5], John Adam[4] Sr., Adam Jr.[3], Adam[2],
Michael[1]) was born 17 May 1886 in Newberry County, South Carolina, and died 23
December 1971. He married Kate Stockman, who was born 17 February 1889 and
died 3 June 1973. They are buried at Rehoboth United Methodist Church in
Greenwood County. Children:
1064 i. James Lorenzo[7] Dominick, b. 3 Jan 1916, d. 7 Feb 1969, m. 16 Sept 1951
Martha Emma Stewart
1065 ii. Everett Elmer[7] Dominick, b. 30 May 1917, m. Harriet Vaughn
1066 iii. Clarence Benjamin[7] Dominick, m. Martha Turman.

393. Ellen Eugenia[6] Dominick (Sarah[5], John Adam[4] Sr., Adam Jr.[3], Adam[2],
Michael[1]) was born 9 June 1890 in Newberry County, South Carolina, and died 4
March 1943 in Greenwood County, South Carolina. She married, on 31 July 1907,
Jacob Pierce Stockman, who was born 29 February 1884 in Newberry County and
died 20 November 1964 in Greenwood County. They are buried at Edgewood
Cemetery in Greenwood. Children:

1067 i. Mary Marcella[7] Stockman, b. 4 Oct 1908, m. 1st George Holland Anderson, Jr., 2nd Alexander J. Jamros, Sr., 3rd, Jesse Altman
1068 ii. Abner Pierce[7] Stockman, b. 4 March 1910, d. 15 Oct 1987, m. Mary A. Hilton.

394. Elizabeth Louise[6] Dominick (Sarah[5], John Adam[4] Sr., Adam Jr.[3], Adam[2], Michael[1]) was born 29 September 1894 and died 8 May 1984. She married, on 7 March 1919, Doctor Price Coursey, Sr., who was born 15 November 1892 and died 12 May 1967. They are buried in Greenwood Memorial Gardens. Children:
1069 i. Florence Cornelia[7] Coursey, b. 6 Sept 1921, m. 26 July 1945 Robert Hayne Jones, b. 31 Aug 1921
1070 ii. Doctor Price[7] Coursey, Jr., b. 6 Sept 1923, unm.
1071 iii. William Abner[7] Coursey, b. 21 Oct 1928, unm.
1072 iv. Betty Lou[7] Coursey, b. 8 Dec 1930, m. 8 July 1953 Horace Tillman Warner, Jr., b. 21 July 1928.

395. Abner Allen[6] Dominick (Sarah[5], John Adam[4] Sr., Adam Jr.[3], Adam[2], Michael[1]) was born 16 November 1896 in Greenwood County, South Carolina, and died 9 May 1968 in Orangeburg County, South Carolina. He married Charlotte Etheredge (1895-1985). They are buried in Sunnyside Cemetery in Orangeburg. Children:
1073 i. Annie Ruth[7] Dominick, b. 23 Sept 1922, m. Mason Livingston
1074 ii. Allen Etheridge[7] Dominick, b. 7 Oct 1924, m. Estelle Pardue
1075 iii. Carl Eugene[7] Dominick, b. 9 Feb 1925, unm.

396. Wesley Jones[6] Dominick (Sarah[5], John Adam[4] Sr., Adam Jr.[3], Adam[2], Michael[1]) was born 16 February 1899 in Greenwood County, South Carolina, and died 12 May 1992 in Anderson County, South Carolina. He married Lucille Anderson Fant, who was born 19 January 1904 and died in July 1967. They are buried in New Silverbrook Cemetery in Anderson County. Children:
1076 i. Mary[7] Dominick, m. Lucius Weeks
1077 ii. Wesley Jones[7] Dominick, Jr., b. 3 Sept 1928, m. Barbara Glenn.

410. Purvis Hobson[6] Bedenbaugh (John Adam Jr.[5], John Adam Sr.[4], Adam Jr.[3], Adam[2], Michael[1]) was born 26 December 1901 in Saluda County, South Carolina. He married, on 11 December 1921, Eldora Shirey who was born 28 June 1906. Nine children:
1078 i. Hazel Ruth[7] Bedenbaugh, b. 25 July 1923, d. 3 Sept 1979, m. Frankie Campbell; children:
1079 a. Henry[8] Campbell
1080 b. Jimmy[8] Campbell
1081 ii. Purvis Hobson[7] Bedenbaugh, Jr., b. 28 May 1926, m. 31 July 1960 Mary Ann Manship; children:
1082 a. Purvis Hobson[8] Bedenbaugh, III, b. 11 July 1961
1083 b. Julia Ann[8] Bedenbaugh, b. 20 June 1963
1084 iii. Mildred Shirey[7] Bedenbaugh, b. Jan 1929, m. 1952 William R. Franks; children:
1085 a. Debra Carolyn[8] Franks
1086 b. Gary Richard[8] Franks
1087 c. Sherry Lynn[8] Franks
1088 iv. Harold Oxner[7] Bedenbaugh, b. 7 Nov 1931, m. 7 March 1954 Ernestine Livingston; children:
1089 a. Harold Timothy[8] Bedenbaugh

1090 b. William Russell[8] Bedenbaugh

1091 c. Zoe Ernestine[8] Bedenbaugh

1092   v. Robert Pascal[7] Bedenbaugh, b. 10 March 1934, m. 18 Nov 1958 Faye Annelle Shealy; children:

    1093 a. Robert Paul[8] Bedenbaugh

    1094 b. Carey Ann[8] Bedenbaugh

    1095 c. Jeffry Allen[8] Bedenbaugh

    1096 d. Roger Kervin[8] Bedenbaugh

    1097 e. Allison Noel[8] Bedenbaugh

1098   vi. George Clarence[7] Bedenbaugh, b. 4 March 1936, m. 24 June 1963 Brenda Maxine Maxie; children:

    1099 a. Bryan Maxie[8] Bedenbaugh

    1100 b. Andrea Machelle[8] Bedenbaugh

1101   vii. John Adam[7] Bedenbaugh, b. 11 Aug 1938, m. 1 May 1960 Elva Mae Skipper; children:

    1102 a. John Adam[8] Bedenbaugh, Jr.

    1103 b. Tracy Adam[8] Bedenbaugh

1104   viii. James Carey[7] Bedenbaugh, b. 7 May 1941, m. 22 Apr 1961 Phyllis Lillian Havird; children:

    1105 a. James Carey[8] Bedenbaugh, Jr.

    1106 b. Todd Allen[8] Bedenbaugh

1107   ix. Lucy Carolyn[7] Bedenbaugh, b. 12 Feb 1946, m. 24 Aug 1968 Cesar Mijares; child:

    1108 a. Christy Noelle[8] Mijares.

422. Christine[6] Bedenbaugh (John Bachman[5], Andrew J.[4], Adam Jr.[3], Adam[2], Michael[1]) was born 26 August 1914 and died 28 January 1986. She married, on 26 August 1936, James Wyman Ingram, Sr., who was born 28 January 1913. Christine B. Ingram was a well-known public school music teacher in Lexington, South Carolina. Two children:

1109   i. Margni[7] Ingram, b. 2 March 1940, m. Tyrone L. Shealy; children:

    1110 a. Tyrone M.[8] (Tee) Shealy, Jr.

    1111 b. Carl[8] Shealy

    1112 c. Lee[8] Shealy

    1113 d. Drayton[8] Shealy

    1114 e. Cantrell[8] Shealy

1115   ii. James Wyman[7] (Jim) Ingram, Jr., b. 4 Oct 1947, m. 7 March 1970 Sarah Lineburger, b. 23 July 1947; two children:

    1116 a. James Wyman[8] Ingram, III (Jay), b. 2 Apr 1974

    1117 b. Blake Allen[8] Ingram, b. 27 Jan 1978.

427. Mary Lamar[6] Bedenbaugh (Will[5], Andrew J.[4], Adam Jr.[3], Adam[2], Michael[1]) was born 25 December 1920 in Ninety Six, South Carolina. She married, on 21 December 1946 at the Lutheran Church of the Incarnation in Columbia, South Carolina, Lowell Burton Nelson, who was born 24 February 1921. Two children:

1118   i. Mary Jo[7] Nelson, M. D., b. 23 June 1951, bapt. First Presbyterian Church, Natchez, MS, m. 6 July 1990, at Fort Snelling Chapel, Minneapolis, MN, Michael Vernon Nass, b. 31 Aug 1950.

1119   ii. Christine Carol[7] Nelson, b. 15 May 1954, m. 3 Sept 1988 at Univ. of Michigan Luth. Chapel, Ann Arbor, Willis Callaway Lillard, b. 3 Sept 1949; children:

    1120 a. Elizabeth Christine[8] Lillard, b. 5 Oct 1989, Ann Arbor, MI

THE BEDENBAUGH-BETENBAUGH FAMILY

1121 b. Catherine Nelson[8] Lillard, b. 9 Apr 1993, Ann Arbor, MI.

433. Liza Melverda[6] Conwill (John[5], John A.[4], Elizabeth[3], Adam[2], Michael[1]) was born 9 January 1879, and died 25 October 1917, buried in the Carolina Cemetery in Itawamba County, Mississippi. She married Charlie Green, and had two children:
   1122 i. Ruby Mae[7] Green, m. Clif Tarver
   1123 ii. Kathleen[7] Green, m. Aubrey Cowan.

438. Lula Estelle[6] Conwill (John[5], John A.[4], Elizabeth[3], Adam[2], Michael[1]) was born 11 February 1895. She married Walter Murphy Minga, who was born 16 October 1892 and died 2 June 1964. Children:
   1124   i. Murphy Troy[7] Minga, b. 7 Dec 1915, m. Doris Lillian Fears
   1125 ii. Leron Eugene[7] Minga, b. 11 Feb 1919, m. Maxine Oclay Fears
   1126 iii. Thomas Eldridge[7] Minga, b. 18 Jan 1923, m. Mary Afton Weaver
   1127 iv. Sarah Estelle[7] Minga, b. 28 Jan 1925, m. James Marion Overton
   1128   v. Mary Jo[7] Minga, b. 9 July 1928, m. Charles Earl Stinson.

441. William Alvie[6] Conwill (Jesse[5], John A.[4], Elizabeth[3], Adam[2], Michael[1]) was born 20 December 1883 in Itawamba County, Mississippi, and died 23 July 1964 in Monroe County, Mississippi. he married, on 27 December 1903, in Itawamba County, Alley Pearl Farr, who was born 11 May 1883 in Monroe County, Mississippi, and died there 6 December 1955. Both are buried in the Wiygul Cemetery in Itawamba County. Children:
   1129   i. Irene[7] Conwill, b. 5 Feb 1905, Lee Co., MS, b. 6 Oct 1978, m. Dutch Oswalt
   1130 ii. Lottie Lee[7] Conwill, b. 4 Feb 1907, Lee Co., MS unm.
 + 1131 iii. George William[7] Conwill, b. 5 March 1909
 + 1132 iv. Elmer Clay[7] Conwill, b. 6 Nov 1912
   1133   v. Jimmie Catherine[7] Conwill, b. 18 June 1914, Itawamba Co., MS, m. 16 June 1934 Raymond Oswalt
 + 1134 vi. John Allen[7] Conwill, b. 12 Oct 1916
   1135 vii. Alvia P.[7] Conwill, b. 20 Apr 1919, Itawamba Co., MS, unm.
   1136 viii. X. L. Gray[7] Conwill, b. 19 June 1923, Itawamba Co., MS, d. 31 Jan 1976
   1137 ix. Minnie Ola[7] Conwill, b. 2 July 1925, m. Elbert Deason.

443. Jesse Daniel[6] Conwill, Jr. (Jesse[5], John A.[4], Elizabeth[3], Adam[2], Michael[1]) was born 5 January 1888 in Itawamba County, Mississippi, and died there in 1980. He married, on 22 December 1912, Johnnie Lee Farr, who was born 13 July 1889 in Monroe County, Mississippi, and died 3 October 1954 in Itawamba County, buried in the Carolina Cemetery in Itawamba County. Two children:
   1138 i. Beulah Mae[7] Conwill, b. 7 May 1914
   1139 ii. Jessie Bell[7] Conwill, b. 30 May 1921.

447. Joseph Dillard[6] Conwill (Joseph[5], Yates[4], Elizabeth[3], Adam[2], Michael[1]) was born in December 1888 and died in 1935 in Hutchinson, Kansas. He married Phyllis Ruth Fuhr. Two children:
   1140 i. Joseph Dillard[7] Conwill, Jr., b. 1915, Pratt, KS, d. 1 Apr 1944
   1141 ii. Allan Franklin[7] Conwill, b. 21 Oct 1921, Hutchinson, KS, m. Arolyn Frances Hodgkins; children:
         1142 a. Joseph Dillard[8] Conwill, III, b. 1954
         1143 b. Stephen Hodgkins[8] Conwill, b. 1956
         1144 c. Michael Francis[8] Conwill, b. 1960

THE BEDENBAUGH-BETENBAUGH FAMILY

455. Ira Eugene[6] Conwill (Yates[5], Yates[4], Elizabeth[3], Adam[2], Michael[1]) was born 27 November 1884, in Itawamba County, Mississippi, and died there 8 September 1944. He married, on 29 October 1905, Jessie Lee Black, who was born 17 April 1885 in Itawamba County and died 7 December 1967, at Gilmore Memorial Hospital in Amory, Mississippi. Children, all born in Itawamba County:
+ 1145 i. Leonard Eugene[7] Conwill, b. 8 Nov 1906
  1146 ii. Willie Marie[7] Conwill, b. 19 Oct 1908, d. 9 Sept 1909
+ 1147 iii. Ernest David[7] Conwill, b. 5 May 1910, d. 27 Dec 1967, m. 7 Sept 1938 Geneva Perrigen
  1148 iv. Mary Ellis[7] Conwill, b. 3 May 1916
  1149 v. Thelma Ozema[7] Conwill, b. 16 Apr 1920, m. 17 March 1947, Samuel F. McCullough, b. March 1910, d. July 1966. One child:
          1150 a. Andrew Eugene[8] McCullough, b & d. March 1948, Amory, MS
+ 1151 vi. Paul Rainey[7] Conwill, b. 11 Nov 1926.

457. Metta A.[6] Conwill (Yates[5], Yates[4], Elizabeth[3], Adam[2], Michael[1]) was born 18 February 1889 and died 26 March 1963. She married, on 26 December 1910, David Armstrong, who was born 15 May 1889 in Itawamba County. Children:
  1152 i. Mavis[7] Armstrong, b. 28 March 1912, m. 4 July 1964, Early Bee Ritter
  1153 ii. Atlas[7] Armstrong, b. 25 Aug 1914, m. 20 Feb 1937, Victor Lindsey
  1154 iii. Lee[7] Armstrong, b. 6 Apr 1916, m. 30 Jan 1970 Lestele Burdine
  1155 iv. Jury David[7] Armstrong, b. 22 Dec 1923.

467. Benjamin Franklin[6] Bedenbaugh (Levi William Pickens[5], Levi[4], Jacob[3], Adam[2], Michael[1]) was born 19 July 1875. He married, on 19 December 1897, Isadore Addy. Children:
  1156 i. Edward Ralph[7] Bedenbaugh, b. 14 Sept 1898 m. Gladys Berry
  1157 ii. Howard Levi[7] Bedenbaugh, b. 1 July 1900 m. Juvernia Ward
  1158 iii. Beulah Mae[7] Bedenbaugh, b. 20 Nov 1901 m. Henry Shirah
  1159 iv. Garnett Franklin[7] Bedenbaugh, b. 3 Aug 1904, d. 31 March 1955, New Orleans, LA, m. Nora Louise Gomez; children:
          1160 a. Norene Helen[8] Bedenbaugh, b. 12 Apr 1940, Chattanooga, TN
          1161 b. Garnett Franklin[8] Bedenbaugh, Jr., b. 16 Oct 1941, Nashville, TN, m. 1st 6 July 1963, Patricia Claire Doyle; m 2nd 7 June 1980 Kathryn Elizabeth (Coffin) Tovrea; children:
              1162 (1) Kenneth Michael[9] Bedenbaugh, b. 16 July 1964
              1163 (2) Steven Arthur[9] Bedenbaugh, b. 30 June 1965
              1164 (3) Jeannette Eileen[9] Bedenbaugh, b. 5 March 1969.

517. Benjamin Washington[6] Bedenbaugh (Wilson[5], Mathias Hare[4], Jacob[3], Adam[2], Michael[1]) was born 17 March 1869 and died 6 May 1939.[110] He married Cornelia Bowles, who was born 4 December 1869 and died 7 September 1966. They are buried in the Baxter Cemetery, Newberry, South Carolina. Children:
  1165 i. Lillie[7] Bedenbaugh, b. 21 Jan 1893, d. 1 Jan 1984, m. Joseph Edward Fulmer
+ 1166 ii. Edna Geneva[7] Bedenbaugh, b. 2 Dec 1894
  1167 iii. Julian[7] Bedenbaugh, b. 1 Apr 1897, d. 20 Aug 1950, m. Ellen Outzs
  1168 iv. Marie[7] Bedenbaugh, b. 1899
  1169 v. Anna May[7] Bedenbaugh, b. 1901
  1170 vi. Luther B.[7] Bedenbaugh, b. 23 Mar 1905, d. 22 June 1975, m. Bessie Lee Neal
  1171 vii. Infant dau. b. 9 Mar 1904, d. 14 Aug 1908

THE BEDENBAUGH-BETENBAUGH FAMILY

1172 viii. Azelle[7] Bedenbaugh, b. c1912, m. J. Y. Floyd.

518. James Wade[6] Bedenbaugh (Wilson[5], Mathias Hare[4], Jacob[3], Adam[2], Michael[1]) was born 7 March 1874 and died 21 September 1930 in Lexington County, South Carolina.[111] He married America (Rikard) Miller, who was born 7 March 1867 and died 7 October 1937 in Lexington County.[112] James W. Bedenbaugh's occupation per the 1910 census of Lexington County was butcher. Both are buried in the Batesburg Cemetery, Batesburg, South Carolina. Children[113]:

  1173 i. Pearl[7] Bedenbaugh, b. 17 Oct 1896, d. 2 June 1973, m. John A. Howard, b. 30 Dec 1892, d. 18 July 1959, both bur. Batesburg Cem. Children:
      1174 a. Helen Alice[8] Howard
      1175 b. James Marion[8] Howard
  1176 ii. George W.[7] Bedenbaugh, b. 17 July 1899, d. 7 Jan 1962, bur. Batesburg Cem.
  1177 iii. Alton B.[7] Bedenbaugh, b. 1901
  1178 iv. Helen[7] Bedenbaugh, b. 1907, m. Charles E. Cloaninger.

519. William Thomas[6] Bedenbaugh (Wilson[5], Mathias Hare[4], Jacob[3], Adam[2], Michael[1]) was born 25 September 1876 in Edgefield (now Saluda) County, South Carolina, and died 13 February 1947 at Hartsville, South Carolina. He married, on 25 December 1912, Annie Eliza Rowell. He was a Methodist minister in South Carolina beginning in 1905. Children:

  1179 i. William Thomas[7] Bedenbaugh, Jr., m. Albertine Hearl
  1180 ii. Roland Ervin[7] Bedenbaugh, m. Labruce Teal
  1181 iii. Kenneth Wilson[7] Bedenbaugh, b. 16 Oct 1917 (Methodist minister), m. Susie Frances Burns; children:
      1182 a. Suzanna[8] Bedenbaugh, b. 31 Aug 1954, Camden, SC, m. 1st 3 June 1962 George Edward Myers; m. 2nd William B. Arrington; children:
        1183 (1) George Edward[9] Myers, Jr., b. 21 March 1963
        1184 (2) Kenneth Earl[9] Myers, b. 7 Apr 1965
        1185 (3) Melissa Leigh[9] Myers, b. 15 May 1970
      1186 b. Sylvia Burns[8] Bedenbaugh, b. 7 Jan 1945, Lancaster, SC, m. 1st Scott Bradford Arledge, m. 2nd 28 Dec 1969 Herbert Bailey Hedley; children:
        1187 (1) Janice Elizabeth[9] Arledge
        1188 (2) Julie Ann[9] Arledge
        1189 (3) Herbert Bailey[9] Hendley, Jr.
        1190 (4) Holly[9] Hendley
      1191 c. Kenneth Wilson[8] Bedenbaugh, Jr., b. 21 June 1948, Sumter, SC, m. 25 March 1972 Sylvia Thornton Lazenby; children:
        1192 (1) Kenneth Wilson[9] Bedenbaugh, III, b. 15 Jan 1970 Milton, FL
        1193 (2) Frances Austin[9] Bedenbaugh, b. 18 Nov 1979, West Columbia, SC
      1194 d. Sandra Rowell[8] Bedenbaugh, b. 31 Dec 1949, Hartsville, SC, m. James D. Leitner, Jr.; one child:
        1195 (1) James D.[9] Leitner, III
  1196 iv. Mary[7] Bedenbaugh, b. 19 Dec 1921, m. 20 Sept 1941 Holland O'Neal
  1197 v. Esmond Denny[7] Bedenbaugh, d. 24 Aug 1994, m. Myrtle Britt
  1198 vi. Clemson Harvin[7] Bedenbaugh, b. 28 Oct 1923, m. Rosalie Singletary

1199 vii. Alice Betty[7] Bedenbaugh m. 1st Don Hall; 2nd Johnny Immerso; 3rd Woodrow Smith
1200 viii. Edward Ackerman[7] (Buck) Bedenbaugh, d. 19 Dec 1993, nm.

527. Raymond Lee[6] Bedenbaugh (Wilson[5], Mathias Hare[4], Jacob[3], Adam[2], Michael[1]) was born 3 March 1896 and died 31 August 1953. He married Sara Ethel Holley (1893-1936). They are buried at Union Lutheran Church in Lexington County, South Carolina. Children:
  1201 i. Jeffie Otto[7] Bedenbaugh, m. Susan Moore. Children:
        1202 a. Jeffie Gerald[8] Bedenbaugh
  1203 ii. Voight Sidney Lee[7] Bedenbaugh, b. 23 Aug 1916, d. 10 Nov 1977, m. Jimmie Sue (Trotter) Matthews. Children:
        1204 a. Ethel Nannie Mary[8] Bedenbaugh
        1205 b. Jimmy[8] Bedenbaugh
  1206 iii. Mary Odessa[7] Bedenbaugh, m. Charles C. Ramsey. Children:
        1207 a. Joyce Ruth[8] Ramsey
        1208 b. Bernice Elizabeth[8] Ramsey
        1209 c. Charles Ray[8] Ramsey
        1210 d. Robert O'Neal[8] Ramsey
  1211 iv. Ruth Elberta[7] Bedenbaugh, m. Rev. P. Homer Jeffcoat. Children:
        1212 a. Patrick Wayne[8] Jeffcoat
        1213 b. Kathryn Ann[8] Jefcoat
        1214 c. Ronald David[8] Jeffcoat
        1215 d. Russell Garrison[8] Jeffcoat
+ 1216 v. Clavis Lorhee[7] Bedenbaugh, b. 6 Dec 1927
  1217 vi. Sarah Mae[7] Bedenbaugh, m. Richard Lichtenwalter and Roy Billingslea; children:
        1218 a. Cheryl Ruth[8] Lichtenwalter
        1219 b. Richard Gordon[8] Lichtenwalter.

532. Drayton E.[6] Bedenbaugh (Mathias Hare Jr.[5], Mathias Hare[4], Jacob[3], Adam[2], Michael[1]) was born 2 September 1869 or 1870 and died 31 September 1926 in Lexington County, South Carolina. He married Ella Rhinehart, who was born 26 July 1860 and died 16 June 1943, in Aiken County, South Carolina[114] Both are buried at Enon Lutheran Church, near Leesville, South Carolina. Children:[115]
  1220 i. Beulah[7] Bedenbaugh b. 1891
  1221 ii. Frederick L.[7] Bedenbaugh, b. 1892
  1222 iii. Willer[7] Bedenbaugh, 1894
  1223 iv. Tranny[7] Bedenbaugh, b. 1896.

533. Martin Fletcher[6] Bedenbaugh (Mathias Hare Jr.[5], Mathias Hare[4], Jacob[3], Adam[2], Michael[1]) was born 22 February 1873 and died 14 June 1940. He married, c1898, Mattie Estelle[5] Bedenbaugh, who was born 9 February 1881 and died 15 January 1963, the daughter of Benjamin Franklin[4] and Eliza (Padgett) Bedenbaugh (see page 30). Both are buried at Nazareth Methodist Church, in Saluda County, South Carolina. Children:
+ 1224 i. Arlette[7] Bedenbaugh, b. 15 Dec 1899
+ 1225 ii. Annie Grace[7] Bedenbaugh, b. 5 Dec 1902
+ 1226 iii. Georgie[7] Bedenbaugh, b. 28 Nov 1905
+ 1227 iv. Brabham[7] Bedenbaugh, b. 18 July 1908
+ 1228 v. Joseph Guy[7] Bedenbaugh, b. 28 Aug 1913.

540. Thomas Urastus[6] Bedenbaugh (Mathias Hare Jr.[5], Mathias Hare[4], Jacob[3], Adam[2], Michael[1]) was born 25 November 1888 and died 18 December 1959 at Columbia, South Carolina. He married, in January 1915 at Saluda, South Carolina, Ethel Elizabeth Adams, who was born 22 July 1897 and died 15 April 1966 at Augusta, Georgia. Both are buried Sweetwater Baptist Church, Edgefield County, South Carolina. Children:

+ 1229   i.   Roy Leon[7] Bedenbaugh, b. 1 Jan 1916
+ 1230   ii.   Edith Mae[7] Bedenbaugh, b. 20 March 1917
+ 1231   iii.   Ralph Furman[7] Bedenbaugh, b. 3 Feb 1933.

556. Bloomer Wilson[6] Bedenbaugh (Lemuel David[5], Simeon Wilson[4], Jacob[3], Adam[2], Michael[1]) was born 13 October 1883 in Columbia County, Florida, and died 5 February 1971 at Gainesville, Florida. He married, on 21 October 1914, at Palatka, Florida, Alice Leila Vause, who was born 25 March 1887 at Johnson, Florida, and died 18 May 1853. Two children:

    1232   i.   Wendell Vause[7] Bedenbaugh, b. 13 Sept 1915, Palatka, FL, d. 26 Aug 1990, Gainesville, Fl., m. 30 Dec 1937 Mina Lee Williams, b. 16 Jan 1919, Ft. Worth, FL. One child:

       1233 a. Lila Wendelyn[8] Bedenbaugh, b. 22 Sept 1940, Palatka, FL, m. 16 May 1964, Frank Jimmie Jamison, III, b. 9 Oct 1939, Atlanta, GA; child:

          1234 (1) Tracy Lynn[9] Jamison, b. 23 Sept 1973, Orlando, FL

    1235 ii. Bloomer Winston[7] Bedenbaugh, b. 28 July 1919, Alachua, FL.

593. Dove[6] Taylor (Rebecca[5], Jacob Asbury[4], Jacob[3], Adam[2], Michael[1]) was born 21 January 1894 and died 5 Feb 1918 in Newberry County, South Carolina.[116] He is buried at Zion United Methodist Church, near Prosperity, South Carolina. He married, on 9 January 1916, Edna Minick[117] and had one child:

    1236 i. Mary Nell[7] Taylor, m. 24 Aug 1935 James William Boozer, b. 12 Feb 1912; children, all b. Newberry Co.:

       1237 a. Mary Dove[8] Boozer, b. 1 Aug 1936, m. 26 May 1957 Benjamin Bernard Nichols

       1238 b. Wilma Edna[8] Boozer, b. 7 Oct 1943, m. 29 May 1961 Thomas Matthew Nichols

       1239 c. Emily Nell[8] Boozer, b. 31 Dec 1945, m. 15 March 1964 Larry M. Lake.

595. Maxcy Clifton[6] Bedenbaugh (David Murchison[5], Jacob Asbury[4], Jacob[3], Adam[2], Michael[1]) was born 16 January 1881 and died 18 June 1958. He married, on 24 December 1905, Ethel Fellers, who was born 28 September 1886 and died 5 December 1965. Children:

    1240 i. Ray Ansel[7] Bedenbaugh m. Flora Belle Wilson; children:

       1241 a. Mary Ethel[7] Bedenbaugh, m. Romaine Slabbaert
       1242 b. Maxcy[8] Bedenbaugh

    1243 ii. Clyde Elmer[7] Bedenbaugh, b. 21 Oct 1909, m. 26 Dec 1934 Rebe Counts, b. 15 Nov 1910 (no ch.).

596. Ola Fannie[6] Bedenbaugh (David Murchison[5], Jacob Asbury[4], Jacob[3], Adam[2], Michael[1]) was born 20 May 1883 and died 8 January 1967. She married Jacob Andrew Bowers, Sr., who was born 20 January 1833, and died 24 June 1950. They are buried at Zion United Methodist Church near Prosperity, South Carolina. Children:

1244　i. David Murchison[7] Bowers, b. 10 Nov 1904, d. 31 Dec 1965, m. 11 Jan 1930 Daisie Sheely, b. 9 June 1903; children:
　　1245 a. Jacob W.[8] Bowers
　　1246 b. Bobbie M.[8] Bowers
1247　ii. Mary Ellen[7] Bowers, b. 29 July 1906, m. 24 Mar 1927, George Kinard Dominick; children:
　　1248 a. Cynthia[8] Dominick
　　1249 b. Kaye[8] Dominick
1250　iii. Julia Evelyn[7] Bowers, b. 4 March 1912, d. 5 Sept 1980, m. 1 Dec 1936, William Claude Powell, Jr.; child:
　　1251 a. C. J. Scott[8] Powell
1252　iv. Myra Rebecca[7] Bowers, b. 10 Nov 1913, m. 17 June 1936 Lyon Calhoun Fellers, b. 17 June 1912, d. 22 July 1982; children
　　1253 a. Glenn[8] Fellers, m. Joy Hunter
　　1254 b. Terry[8] Fellers, m. Susan Crim
1255　v. Jacob Andrew[7] Bowers, Jr., b. 26 Jan 1919, m. 19 Sept 1944, Marjorie Wilson, b. 20 Feb 1922; children:
　　1256 a. Jacob Andrew[8] Bowers, III
　　1257 b. Monte[8] Bowers
　　1258 c. David[8] Bowers
　　1259 d. Betsy[8] Bowers.

597. Pearl Estelle[6] Bedenbaugh (David Murchison[5], Jacob Asbury[4], Jacob[3], Adam[2], Michael[1]) was born 10 March 1885 and died 4 December 1961. She married Peter Wesley Counts, who was born 18 December 1882 and died 9 June 1947. They are buried at Zion United Methodist Church near Prosperity, South Carolina. Children:
+ 1260　i. Edward Guy[7] Counts, b. 21 Sept 1905
　1261　ii. George Curtis[7] Counts, b. 20 Nov 1907, m. Vanessa Long, no ch.
+ 1262　iii. Mildred[7] Counts, b. 8 July 1914
　1263　iv. Ruby[7] Counts, b. 20 Jan 1920, m. Herman G. Stockman; child:
　　1264　a. George Wesley[8] Stockman
　1265　v. Dorothy[7] Counts, b. 25 July 1922, d. 23 May 1929, bur. Zion United Methodist Church.

598. Colon Boyd[6] Bedenbaugh (David Murchison[5], Jacob Asbury[4], Jacob[3], Adam[2], Michael[1]) was born 6 June 1887 and died 19 July 1941. He married, on 19 January 1926, Eula Belle Joiner, who was born 29 November 1888 in Sparta, Georgia, and died 8 June 1982. They are buried at Zion United Methodist Church near Prosperity, South Carolina. Children:
+ 1266　i. David Edwin[7] Bedenbaugh, b. 28 Oct 1926
+ 1267　ii. Earle Joiner[7] Bedenbaugh, b. 7 March 1928.

600. Chester Warner[6] Bedenbaugh (David Murchison[5], Jacob Asbury[4], Jacob[3], Adam[2], Michael[1]) was born 3 March 1892 and died 17 August 1967. He married, on 30 November 1916,[118] Maude Lucinda Harmon, who was born 31 October 1897, and died 24 January 1991. They are buried at Zion United Methodist Church near Prosperity, South Carolina. Children:
　1268　i. Elsie[7] Bedenbaugh, b. 14 Dec 1917, d. 10 Dec 1968, m. Paul W. Nichols, b. 13 Sept 1916
　1269　ii. Edith Caroline[7] Bedenbaugh, b. 26 Nov 1919, m. James Chester Hipp
　1270　iii. Grace[7] Bedenbaugh, b. 3 Sept 1923, m. Hoyt M. Hendrix

1271 iv. Hubert Murchison[7] Bedenbaugh, b. 14 Nov 1927, m. 14 June 1949, Geraldine Riley, b. 25 Aug 1928.

601. Eula Lillie[6] Bedenbaugh (David Murchison[5], Jacob Asbury[4], Jacob[3], Adam[2], Michael[1]) was born 2 June 1894 and died 8 January 1984. She married, on 23 December 1913, Robert Bruce Bowers, who was born 19 August 1889 and died 12 August 1946. They are buried at Zion United Methodist Church near Prosperity, South Carolina. Child:

1272 i. Mattie Brunelle[7] Bowers, b. 7 Feb 1915, d. 14 March 1990, m. J. D. Hamm, b. 28 Dec 1914, d. 23 May 1965, Children:

1273 a. James Robert[8] Hamm m. Judy Hunter

1274 b. Jackie[8] Hamm m. Al Franklin.

602. Dhent Asbury[6] Bedenbaugh (David Murchison[5], Jacob Asbury[4], Jacob[3], Adam[2], Michael[1]) was born 13 March 1897 and died 27 March 1970. He married, first, on 29 July 1922,[119] Lottie Vera[6] Mills (Thomas Marion[5], Rachel[4], Jacob[3], Adam[2], Michael[1]), who was born 16 June 1901 and died 18 June 1923. He married, second, Annie Laurie (Dennis) Harmon (1907-1958). He married, third, Earline Meetze, and fourth, Ella Ruth Boozer, widow of Joseph Worth[6] Bedenbaugh. Children:

1275 i. Harold Thomas[7] Bedenbaugh, b. 25 May 1923, m. Eula Melissa[7] Bedenbaugh (see under her for descendants)

1276 ii. Dennis[7] Bedenbaugh, b. 7 Dec 1929, d. 15 Dec 1989, unm.

+ 1277 iii. Anne[7] Bedenbaugh, b. 5 Aug 1932

+ 1278 iv. Jimmy Byrnes[7] Bedenbaugh, b. 5 Sept 1936

+ 1279 v. Merle[7] Bedenbaugh, b. 18 Nov 1942.

603. Elise Amanda[6] Bedenbaugh (David Murchison[5], Jacob Asbury[4], Jacob[3], Adam[2], Michael[1]) was born 4 May 1900 and died 30 September 1991. She married Arthur Purcell[7] Boozer (Pierce[6], Lemuel[5], Eve[4], Henry[3] Adam[2], Michael[1]) who was born 10 August 1900 in Newberry County, South Carolina, and died 21 November 1981. They are buried at Zion United Methodist Church near Prosperity, South Carolina. Children:

1280 i. James Elmer[7] Boozer, b. 23 June 1920, m. 6 Aug 1943, Ruth Frick, b. 4 March 1927; children:

1281 a. James Brice[8] Boozer, b. 19 Jan 1946, m. 16 Apr 1965, Mary Alice Shealy; child:

1282 (1) Eric Brice[9] Boozer, b. 7 June 1967, Newberry, SC

1283 b. Linda Ruth[8] Boozer, b. 10 Jul 1947, m. George Paul Corley

1284 c. Dianne[8] Boozer, b. 18 June 1949, m. Douglas M. Goff

1285 ii. Arthur Milton[7] Boozer m. 1948 Dessie Rae Hipp. Child:

1286 a. Joey[8] Boozer

1287 iii. Robert Wayne[7] Boozer, m. 1952 Peggy Ann Hipp. Children:

1288 a. Kenneth[8] Boozer

1289 b. Leslie[8] Boozer

1290 iv. Charles Keith[7] Boozer, m. 1st 1957 Shirley Ann Stribble; m. 2nd Phyllis Gay.

606. Jacob Moody[6] Bedenbaugh (Mack Wilson[5], Jacob Asbury[4], Jacob[3], Adam[2], Michael[1]) was born 9 September 1884 and died 1 April 1984. He married, on 29 August 1909, Sparta Harmon, who was born 19 July 1890 and died 24 July 1983. Children:

THE BEDENBAUGH-BETENBAUGH FAMILY

1291   i. Bennett Cornell[7] Bedenbaugh, b. 1 Feb 1911, d. 8 Apr 1994, m. 11 Feb 1934 Dorothy Counts, b. 22 May 1912; children:

      1292 a. Rodney Lee[8] Bedenbaugh, b. 24 Aug 1938, m. 22 Feb 1964 Janice Bradley; m. 2nd 24 Aug 1974 Mary Ann Amick; child:

        1293 (1) Karen Renee[9] Bedenbaugh, b. 2 July 1965

      1294 b. Sallie[8] Bedenbaugh, b. 19 Apr 1943, m. 4 Apr 1965 David Govan Sease, Jr., b. 20 Oct 1942; children:

        1295 (1) Lee Ann[9] Sease, b. 4 May 1970

        1296 (2) Lauren Bennett[9] Sease, b. 2 Dec 1973

1297   ii. Jacob Asbury[7] Bedenbaugh, b. 9 July 1917, lives Prosperity, SC

+ 1298   iii. Joseph Moody[7] Bedenbaugh, b. 15 Sept 1923.

623. Lorenza Dow[6] Bedenbaugh (Joseph Falls[5], Jacob Asbury[4], Jacob[2], Adam[2], Michael[1]) was born 15 August 1898, and died 21 August 1970. He married, on 21 December 1919,[120] Ruby Lee Harmon. Children:

1299   i. Marise[7] Bedenbaugh m. Edward Carroll DeVore; children:

      1300 a. Donald C.[8] DeVore m. Martha Penland

      1302 b. Mary Jo[8] DeVore m. Michael A. Parducci

1303   ii. Lorenza Dow[7] Bedenbaugh Jr. m. Carolyn Hutchinson; child:

      1304 a. Lorenza Dow[8] Bedenbaugh, III, m. Debra McConnell

1305   iii. Joseph Falls[7] Bedenbaugh m. Doris Hawkins

1306   iv. Harmon M.[7] Bedenbaugh m. Anna Jones; children:

      1307 a. James G.[8] Bedenbaugh

      1308 b. Thomas H.[8] Bedenbaugh

      1309 c. Jana[8] Bedenbaugh.

624. Simon P.[6] Mills (David Newton[5], Rachel[4], Jacob[3], Adam[2], Michael[1]) was born 10 September 1869 and died 30 June 1955 in Newberry County, South Carolina. He married Minnie Lee Dominick, who was born 18 December 1872 and died 31 January 1944. Both are buried at Bethel Baptist Church, Newberry County, South Carolina. Children:

1310   i. Colie H.[7] Mills, b. 8 Jan 1892, d. 12 Nov 1965, m. Dora Bell Fulmer, b. 2 May 1894, d. 1 Aug 1941. They are buried at Bethel Bapt. Ch.

1311   ii. Berley W.[7] Mills, b. 19 July 1894, d. 31 Jan 1973, m. 31 Dec 1914 Mary Morris, b. 14 Oct 1899, d. 10 Oct 1962

1312   iii. Lonnie[7] Mills, b. 16 Nov 1896, d. 5 Oct 1918

+ 1313   iv. Mattie Mae[7] Mills, b. 17 Feb 1899

1314   v. Fannie Agnes[7] Mills, b. 30 Jan 1902, d. 26 Aug 1967, m. 1st Oscar Boozer, m. 2nd John Simpson Lake, b. 2 Nov 1886, d. 27 Aug 1952.

+ 1315   vi. Minnie Marie[7] Mills, b. 21 Oct 1904

1316   vii. Ben Tillman[7] Mills.

654. Willie Lee[6] Mills (James Burr[5], Rachel[4], Jacob[3], Adam[2], Michael[1]) was born 3 June 1890 and died 29 January 1972. He married, on 30 November 1916,[121] Nettie Julian Barnes who was born 12 November 1893 and died 12 June 1967. They are buried in Newberry Memorial Gardens, Newberry, South Carolina. Children:

+ 1317   i. Allene[7] Mills

+ 1318   ii. William Leslie[7] Mills

1319   iii. Edna Elizabeth[7] Mills, b. 12 Jan 1926, m. Joseph Moody[7] Bedenbaugh (Moody[6], Mack Wilson[5], Jacob Asbury[4], Jacob[3], Adam[2], Michael[1]), see under him for descendants.

+ 1320   iv. James Carlysle[7] Mills.

660. Sparta[6] Nichols (Mary Ellen[5], Rachel[4], Jacob[3], Adam[2], Michael[1]) was born 15 February 1892 and died 10 July 1982. She married Ernest T. Garrett. Children:

   1321 i. John[7] Garrett
   1322 ii. Vernon[7] Garrett
   1323 iii. Robert[7] Garrett
   1324 iv. George[7] Garrett
   1325 v. Zilla[7] Garrett
   1326 vi. Sara[7] Garrett
   1327 vii. Faye[7] Garrett
   1328 viii. Lois[7] Garrett
   1329 ix. Betty[7] Garrett, m. Ollie Dominick.

665. Mattie Sula[6] Hipp (Mary Jane[5], William J.[4], John[3], Adam[2], Michael[1]) was born 8 October 1886 in Newberry County, South Carolina, and died 11 January 1965 in Newberry. She married, on 5 February 1902, Ernest Gibson, who was born 12 July 1884 in Edgefield (now Saluda) County, South Carolina, and died 25 October 1964. Both are buried at St. Luke's Lutheran Church near Prosperity, South Carolina. Children:

   1330 i. Henrietta[7] Gibson, b. 28 Apr 1911, m. Nathan Warren
   1331 ii. Mary Varie[7] Gibson, b. 27 July 1915, m. John Kibler
   1332 iii. William Newton[7] Gibson, b. 27 Sept 1919
   1333 iv. Sarah Ruth[7] Gibson, b. 13 Sept 1921
   1334 v. Ernestine[7] Gibson, b. 18 March 1925, m. Robert Riddle
   1335 vi. Evelyne[7] Gibson, b. 16 Sept 1927.

670. Etta[6] Bedenbaugh (James Luther[5], William J.[4], John[3], Adam[2], Michael[1]) was born 30 January 1983 and died 8 May 1974. She married John Cheley Abrams, who was born 30 June 1892 in Newberry County, South Carolina. Two children:

   1336 i. Verna Mae[7] Abrams, b. 29 Oct 1913, d. 15 March 1958
   1337 ii. James Chesley[7] Abrams, b. 10 Feb 1916, m. Rebecca Pettit; one child:
         1338 a. Verna Ann[8] Abrams, b. 7 Oct 1943, Charleston, SC, m. James Ernest Paschal, b. 13 Sept 1941; child:
             1339 (1) James Ernest[9] Paschal, Jr., b. 7 Jan 1967, Columbia, SC.

672. James Alvin[6] Danielson (Lula[5], James Luther[5], William J.[4], John[3], Adam[2], Michael[1]) was born 27 May 1899 and married Nettie Willingham. Seven children, all born in Newberry, South Carolina:

   1340 i. Ned Thomas[7] Danielsen, b. 11 Aug 1919, m. 10 May 1940, Frances Bannister, b. 10 Feb 1923, Child:
         1341 a. Larry Thomas[8] Danielsen, b. 23 March 1941, d. 24 Dec 1993, m. 27 May 1962 Tommie Ann Werts, b. 28 June 1943; children. b. Newberry, SC:
             1342 (1) Laura Ann[9] Danielsen, b. 21 Jan 1967
             1343 (2) Kristy Lee[9] Danielsen, b. 13 May 1976
   1344 ii. Clara Elizabeth[7] Danielsen, b. 1 July 1921, m. 21 Nov 1945, Joel W. Wertz, b. 24 Aug 1900, d. 8 June 1952, no ch.
   1345 iii. Dorothy Louise[7] Danielsen, b. 7 May 1923, m. 13 June 1942 John W. Padgett, b. 15 Aug 1923; children, b. Newberry, SC:
         1346 a. Daniel Allen[8] Padgett, b. 26 Aug 1944, m. 190 Aug 1963 Beverly Joan Carroll, b. 11 Oct 1946; children:
             1347 (1) Daniel Allen[9] Padgett, Jr., b. 5 June 1964, Newberry, SC
             1348 (2) Patrick McKinley[9] Padgett, b. 4 Nov 1966, Cheraw, SC

1349 (3) Kristen Marie[9] Padgett, b. 27 Apr 1974, Marietta, GA
1350 b. Cathy[8] Danielsen, b. 25 Dec 1947, m. 29 March 1964 James
    Kenneth Hart, b. 25 Dec 1947; children:
    1351 (1) Tara Elizabeth[9] Hart, b. 4 March 1966 Starkville, MS
    1352 (2) James Kenneth[9] Hart, Jr., b. 23 May 1968, Atlanta, GA
    1353 (3) Tammie Sue[9] Hart, b. 24 Sept 1969, Atlanta, GA
1354 iv. James[7] Danielsen, b. 27 Nov 1927, m. 10 Nov 1956 Louise Wise, b. 20
    Apr 1934, Joanna, SC; children, all b. Newberry, SC:
    1355 a. James Rodney[8] Danielsen, b. 25 May 1957, m. 11 June 1977 Vicki
    Hinson
    1356 b. Wanda Louise[8] Danielsen, b. 29 Apr 1959, m. 22 Sept 1978, Tracy
    Taylor
    1357 c. Mona Marie[8] Danielsen, b. & d. 28 Oct 1962
    1358 d. Christopher August[8] Danielsen, b. 24 Oct 1963
1359 v. Guy[7] Danielsen, b. 6 Jan 1929, m. 2 May 1948, Barbara Mullinax, b. 23
    June 1930, Easley, SC; children:
    1360 a. Sheryl Zane[8] Danielsen, b. 23 Feb 1949, Newberry, SC, m. 3 July
    1975 Harold Everett Trammell, Jr., b. 15 June 1948; child:
    1361 (1) Haley Zane[9] Trammell, b. 23 Oct 1978, Easley, SC
    1362 b. Donna[8] Danielsen, b. 15 June 1950, Newberry, SC, m. 31 May
    1969 Randy L. Cartee, b. 9 Sept 1950, Liberty, SC; children:
    1363 (1) Joel Lee[9] Cartee, b. 4 Dec 1970, Easley, SC
    1364 (2) Jason Tyler[9] Cartee, b. 13 Oct 1972, Easley, SC
    1365 c. Suzanne[8] Danielsen, b. 20 June 1956, Greenville, SC
    1366 d. Lisa[8] Danielsen, b. 23 June 1961, Easley, SC
1367 vi. Sarah Frances[7] Danielsen, b. 25 Nov 1931, m. 30 Aug 1951 Casper Berry,
    b. 2 March 1930, Newberry, SC; children, all b. Newberry, SC:
    1368 a. Randy Joel[8] Berry, b. 12 Oct 1952, m. 12 May 1974 Joyce Marie
    Sharpe, b. 17 June 1951
    1369 b. Keith Audie[8] Berry, b. 2 July 1954
    1370 c. Deanna[8] Berry, b. 20 Nov 1955
    1371 d. Mark Steven[8] Berry, b. 16 Sept 1959
    1372 e. Timothy Scott[8] Berry, b. 9 Feb 1964
1373 vii. Betty Lou[7] Danielsen, b. 30 Nov 1933, m. 27 Dec 1953 Donald Layton, b.
    10 June 1932, Newberry, SC; children, all b. Newberry, SC:
    1374 a. Donald Alvin[8] Layton, b. 25 Sept 1954 m. 28 June 1975 Lisa Sligh;
    child:
    1375 (1) Charlene[9] Layton
    1376 b. Claire Beth[8] Layton, b. 29 Sept 1957
    1377 c. Rhyne Kent[8] Layton, b. 29 May 1964.

675. Augusta[6] Danielsen (Lula[5], James Luther[5], William J.[4], John[3], Adam[2], Michael[1])
was born 12 November 1906. She married, on 14 July 1928, Bowers Otto Creekmore, who was born 9 December 1906 in Athens, Georgia, and died 28 February
1985 in Durham, North Carolina. Three children, all born in Newberry, South
Carolina:
1378 i. Martha Barbara[7] Creekmore, b. 5 March 1929, m. 1952 Lamar Randolph
    Smith, b. 28 Jan 1931, Ware Shoals, SC; children:
    1379 a. Debra Luann[8] Smith, b. 15 Jan 1955, Durham, NC, m. 3 June
    1984 John Mitchell, Jr., b. 2 Apr 1951; children, b. Greenville, SC:
    1380 (1) Graham[9] Mitchell, b. 23 Dec 1987
    1381 (2) Avery[9] Mitchell, b. 10 July ---

1382 b. Lamar Randolph[8] Smith, Jr., b. 20 Aug 1957, Greenville, SC, m.
18 June 1983 Joann Nancy Riel, b. 11 Apr 1960; children, b.
Greenville, SC:
1383 (1) Caroline[9] Smith, b. 12 May 1985
1384 (2) Catherine Agnes[9] Smith
1385 (3) Mathew[9] Smith
1386 ii. Robert Roy[7] Creekmore, b. 12 Dec 1931, m. 11 Oct 1958 Jean Lovina
Allison, b. 27 Apr 1931, Old Fort, NC; children, b. Asheville, NC:
1387 a. Kimberly Ann[8] Creekmore, b. & d. 2 Apr 1963
1388 b. Robert Todd[8] Creekmore, b. 27 June 1965
1389 iii. Mary Lynn[7] Creekmore, b. 12 Nov 1945, m. 16 Aug 1969 Michael Dwayne
Watson, b. Prospect Hill, NC; children. b. Durham, NC:
1390 a. Michael Bowers[8] Watson, b. 25 March 1965
1391 b. David Allen[8] Watson, b. 5 Dec 1970.

683. Raymond Artemas[6] Bedenbaugh (Francis P.[5], James L.[4], John[3], Adam[2],
Michael[1]) was born 24 September 1884 in Columbia County, Florida, and died in
Lake City, Florida, 16 October 1975. He married, on 14 November 1907, in Lake
City, Mary Susan Hadden, who was born 23 January 1891 in Columbia County, and
died 25 July 1975 in Lake City, the daughter of Robert Hugh and Susan Jane
(Robarts) Hadden. Both are buried at Bethel Methodist Church in Columbia
County, Florida. Children, all born in Lake City, Florida:
+ 1392   i. Alma Zelma[7] Bedenbaugh, b. 8 Oct 1908
+ 1393   ii. Robert Frank[7] Bedenbaugh, b. 18 Feb 1911
+ 1394 iii. Susan Lee[7] Bedenbaugh, b. 12 Feb 1913
+ 1395   iv. Vera Etta[7] Bedenbaugh. b. 1 Dec 1914
+ 1396   v. Elizabeth Armada[7] Bedenbaugh, b. 14 May 1917
+ 1397   vi. Tolula Mary Jane[7] Bedenbaugh, b. 12 Jan 1919
+ 1398 vii. Mansfield Livingston[7] Bedenbaugh, b. 24 Oct 1920
+ 1399 viii. James Edwin[7] Bedenbaugh, b. 15 Oct 1922
+ 1400   ix. Annie Louise[7] Bedenbaugh, b. 5 Oct 1924
+ 1401   x. Lena Jeannette[7] Bedenbaugh, b. 1 Aug 1925
+ 1402   xi. Raymond Henry[7] Bedenbaugh, b. 22 Sept 1928
+ 1403 xii. Roy Bishop[7] Bedenbaugh, b. 14 Nov 1930
+ 1404 xiii. Jerry Hugh[7] Bedenbaugh, b. 12 May 1933.

684. Sallie[6] Bedenbaugh (Francis P.[5], James L.[4], John[3], Adam[2], Michael[1]) was born
20 August 1887 in Columbia County, Florida, and died 13 September 1971 in Lake
City, Florida. She married, on 7 February 1907, Governor Drew Hunter, who was
born 16 October 1876 in Columbia County and died 18 April 1967 in Lake City.
Both are buried in Bethlehem Lutheran Cemetery in Columbia County. Two
children, both born in Lake City, Florida:
1405   i. Cecil Drew[7] Hunter, b. 18 Aug 1914, m. 25 Dec 1949, Beatrice Belle
Tyre, b. 9 Oct 1916, Columbia Co., FL
+ 1406 ii. Armada[7] Hunter, b. 23 Dec 1917.

685. Amon Lyttleton[6] Bedenbaugh (Francis P.[5], James L.[4], John[3], Adam[2], Michael[1])
was born 26 September 1890 in Columbia County, Florida, and died 14 September
19018 in France. He is buried at St. Mihiel American Cemetery, Thiaucourt,
Merthue-et-Mosselle, France. He married, on 9 February 1918, in Lake City, Lilla
Belle Allen, who was born 26 October 1898 and died 4 December 1898. After his

death, she married Claude T. Tompkins and James J. Hammed. Amon L. Bedenbaugh had one child:
+ 1407 i. Amon Lyttleton[7] Bedenbaugh, Jr., b. 16 Jan 1919.

686. Nathan Julian[6] Bedenbaugh (Francis P.[5], James L.[4], John[3], Adam[2], Michael[1]) was born 31 December 1893 in Columbia County, Florida, and died 24 December 1922 in Lake City. He married, on 27 December 1914, Nettie Ludella Smith, who was born 12 September 1896 in Lake City, and died 16 September 1964. After his death, she married Roy Shannon and Lewis Wiley Rivers. Children, all born in Lake City, Florida:
+ 1408 i. Claude Julian[7] Bedenbaugh, b. 27 Nov 1915
+ 1409 ii. Minnie Lee[7] Bedenbaugh, b. 23 Apr 1917
+ 1410 iii. Earl George[7] Bedenbaugh, b. 29 Oct 1919
+ 1411 iv. Catherine Elizabeth[7] Bedenbaugh, b. 5 Mar 1922.

688. Frank Willoughby[6] Bedenbaugh (Francis P.[5], James L.[4], John[3], Adam[2], Michael[1]) was born 12 March 1901 in Columbia County, Florida, and died in Lake City, 20 March 1988. He married, on 8 May 1920, Emma Katie Bell Douberley, who was born 15 December 1905 in Columbia County, Florida. Children:
+ 1412 i. Arthur Nelson[7] Bedenbaugh, b. 3 Aug 1922, Lake City, FL
+ 1413 ii. Frank Pickens[7] Bedenbaugh, b. 11 May 1924, Lake City, FL
+ 1414 iii. Joyce[7] Bedenbaugh, b. 2 Apr 1930, Jacksonville, FL.

705. Josie Henrietta[6] Bedenbaugh (William Pierce[5], George[4], John[3], Adam[2], Michael[1]) was born 31 July 1893 and died 6 April 1984. She married, in 1910, Jesse S. Schumpert, who was born 4 October 1883 and died 24 January 1950. They are buried in the Williston, South Carolina, Cemetery. Children:
1415 i. Edward Jacob[7] Schumpert, m. Bessie Hall
1416 ii. Helen Roberta[7] Schumpert, b. 22 Jan 1913, d. 12 Jan 1972, m. 24 March 1936, m. Ira Winn Blanton, b. 22 Nov 1906, d. 24 Sept 1952, Columbia, SC; children:
    1417 a. Winn Schumpert[8] Blanton, b. 20 March 1938, m. 18 Nov 1966, Connie Arlene Spencer; children:
        1418 (1) Winn Spencer[9] Blanton, b. 23 June 1968
        1419 (2) Dana Shea[9] Blanton, b. 11 Jan 1971
        1420 (3) Brent Shane[9] Blanton, b. 31 Oct 1973
    1421 b. Helen Ross[8] Blanton, b. 19 Jan 1941, m. 25 March 1960 Robert Hugh Morgan; children:
        1422 (1) Robert Jeffrey[9] Morgan, b. 21 Oct 1970
        1423 (2) Ryan Lee[9] Morgan, b. 26 Oct 1972
1424 iii. Wilford Olly[7] (Buck) Schumpert, m. Imogene Bailey Thames; children:
    1425 a. Jay Simpson[8] Schumpert, b. 9 Dec 1946, m. Maria Vale Bolen; children:
        1426 (1) Bryane Mary[9] Schumpert, b. 28 Aug 1981
        1427 (2) Jarrett Clayton[9] Schumpert, b. 17 Aug 1987
    1428 b. Laura Loraine[8] Schumpert, b. 29 Oct 1951, m. James H. Stapleton; children:
        1429 (1) Jason Winfield[9] Stapleton, b. 7 Aug 1977
        1430 (2) Joel Thames[9] Stapleton, b. 17 Oct 1978
    1431 c. Russell Vernon[8] Schumpert, b. 20 Jan 1961
1432 iv. Jesse Darril[7] Schumpert (1916-1985), m. Verna Owens, b. 1931; she was Probate Judge of Barnwell County 1980-1988.

1433   v. Ralph Lafayette[7] Schumpert, m. Elma Hutto
1434   vi. Cyril Okletnea[7] Schumpert, m. Mary Risher
1435 vii. Louis Marion[7] Schumpert, b. 27 Aug 1923 m. 1st Vonette Boylston, m.
        2nd Patricia Thatcher; children:
          1436 a. Louis Marion[8] Schumpert, b. 19 July 1951, m. Kathryn
             Williams; children:
                1437 (1) Andrew Louis[9] Schumpert, b. 5 Apr 1980
                1438 (2) Stacy Maria[9] Schumpert, b. 22 June 1982
          1439 b. Thomas Obra[8] Schumpert, m. Elaine Womack; children:
                1440 (1) Jennifer[9] Schumpert
                1441 (2) Brett[9] Schumpert
          1442 c. Robin Vonette[8] Schumpert, b. 15 May 1956; m. Frank Everett
             Robinson Lee; children:
                1443 (1) Meghan Mimbres[9] Lee, b. 21 Sept 1985
                1444 (2) Everett Robinson[9] Lee, b. 26 Oct 1987
                1445 (3) Jesse Marshall[9] Lee, b. 10 July 1994
          1446 d. Vicki Lynn[8] Schumpert, b. 31 March 1958, m. Jeffery Norris
             Wooten; children:
                1447 (1) Cory Andre[9] Wooten, b. 18 Oct 1977
                1448 (2) Shelley Nichole[9] Wooten, b. 4 Jan 1981
                1449 (3) Brice Jeffery[9] Wooten, b. 25 June 1985
                1450 (4) Josie Lee[9] Wooten, b. 30 July 1987
          1451 e. Dorothy Miriam[8] Schumpert, b. 29 Jan 1963, m. Michael James
             Robidoux; children:
                1452 (1) Hannah Olivia[9] Robidoux, b. 22 Dec 1991
                1453 (2) Courtney Victoria[9] Robidoux, b. 20 July 1993
1454 viii. Lona Kathryn[7] Schumpert, b. 2 June 1925, m. Peter Luke Crouch; child:
          1455 a. Peter Michael[8] Crouch, b. 1 Apr 1951 m. Lucy Boney; children:
                1456 (1) Sonya Michel[9] Crouch, b. 31 May 1972
                1457 (2) Michael Cameron[9] Crouch, b. 3 Sept 1975
                1458 (3) Crystal Renee[9] Crouch, b. 9 Sept 1976
1459   ix. Frank Carlton[7] Schumpert, m. Ruth Bolen; children
          1460 a. Mark Schumpert
          1461 b. Cindy Schumpert
1462   x. George Ray[7] Schumpert, m. 1st Mary Francis Boyleston; m. 2nd Arnette
        (Grubbs) Miles
1463   xi. Betty Joan[7] Schumpert, b. 1 Oct 1932, m. Grady Pierce Burke; children:
          1464 a. Betty Joan[8] Burke, m. Larry D. Ledford; child:
                1465 (1) Laurie Diane[9] Ledford, b. 27 June 1986
          1466 b. Grady Pierce[8] Burke, II, b. 1 Sept 1957, m. Rebecca Ann
             Kohler; children:
                1467 (1) Michael Pierce[9] Burke, b. 19 Oct 1991
                1468 (2) Rebecca Ann[9] Burke, b. 7 March 1993
          1469 c. Jesse Schumpert[8] Burke, b. 15 July 1959
          1470 d. Cyril Dale[8] Burke, b. 17 Dec 1963; child:
                1471 (1) Ace Preston[9] Burke, b. 9 July 1989
1472 xii. Barbara Jean[7] Schumpert, m. Thomas Willis Smith.

712. Lottie May[6] Bedenbaugh (John[5], George[4], John[3], Adam[2], Michael[1]) was born
22 July 1897. She married, on 20 December 1914 Ambrose Virgil Sanders. Children:
1473   i. Jack[7] Sanders
1474   ii. Walter[7] Sanders

1475 iii. Elese[7] Sanders
1476 iv. Louise[7] Sanders
1477 v. Virgil[7] Sanders
1478 vi. Rosalind[7] Sanders
1479 vii. Ray Evertt[7] Sanders, b. 18 Jan 1930, m. Gertrude Manie Kibler, b. 29
       Sept 1931; children, born Columbia, SC:
       1480 a. Ray Evertt[8] Sanders, Jr., b. 28 July 1955, m. Susan Olivia
             Brockman; children:
             1481 (1) Morgan Olivia[9] Sanders, b. 9 Sept 1988
             1482 (2) Sierra Rae[9] Sanders, b. 21 May 1991
       1483 b. Anthony Dean[8] Sanders, b. 11 July 1957, d. 5 Nov 1980
       1484 c. Scott Alen[8] Sanders, b. 18 Nov 1961
       1485 d. Steven Todd[8] Sanders, b. 30 Dec 1963, m. 15 Oct 1988
             Elizabeth Owens; child:
             1486 (1) Josephine Sabrine[9] Sanders, b. 5 Oct 1984.

715. Denniston Johnnie[6] Bedenbaugh (John[5], George[4], John[3], Adam[2], Michael[1]) was
born 7 January 1910 in Newberry, South Carolina, and died 24 July 1971 at
Murphys, California. He married, on 14 August 1937, Helen Burton, who was born
1 March 1918. Children:
  1487 i. Patricia Ann[7] Bedenbaugh, b. 27 Aug 1938, Newberry, SC, m. 14 Feb
         1957, James Russell Logan, b. 10 Sept 1933, Los Angeles, CA; children:
         1488 a. Scott James[8] Logan, b. 21 March 19760, Chula Vista, CA, m. 3
               July 1980 Natalie Lorraine Carrillo (div); m. 2nd 5 July 1986
               Kimberly Perkin (div); child:
               1489 (1) Angelina Maria[9] Logan, b. 5 June 1978, Stockton, CA
         1490 b. Nancy[8] Logan, b. 23 May 1963, Chula Vista, CA, m. 13 March
               1983, Brett Henrik Stark, b. 20 March 1961; children:
               1491 (1) Anthony Brett[9] Stark, b. 31 Aug 1984, Stockton, CA
               1492 (2) Adam Robert[9] Stark, b. 21 March 1986, Stockton, CA
               1493 (3) Alice Elizabeth[9] Stark, b. 1 Jan 1988, Chico, CA
  1494 ii. Elivia Christine[7] Bedenbaugh, b. 21 Jan 1942, Newberry, SC, d. 15 Oct
         1974, Stockton, CA, m. 17 Dec 1960 Stanley Joseph Silva, b. 24 Aug 1938,
         Hanford, CA; children:
         1495 a. Stanley Joseph[8] Silva, Jr., b. 11 Nov 1961, San Diego, CA, m. 15
               June 1991, Tina J. Barclay
         1496 b. John Gregory[8] Silva, m. Virginia ____; child:
               1497 (1) Gregory Shawn Silva, b. 13 Sept 1985, Portland, OR
  1498 iii. Mary Helen[7] Bedenbaugh, b. 24 Jan 1951, m. 14 July 1974 Stanley Joseph
         Silva, b. 24 Aug 1938, Hanford, CA; children:
         1499 a. Matthew Joseph[8] Silva, b. 17 May 1992, Salt Lake City, UT
         1500 b. Zachary William Silva, b. 10 Feb 1994, Salt Lake City, UT.

740. Aldon Eugene[6] (Buddy) Bedenbaugh (Allen Lester[5], Elijah King[4], John[3],
Adam[2], Michael[1]) was born 6 January 1900 and died 5 March 1975. He married Ida
Mae Hayes, who was born 17 July 1901 and died 6 April 1978. Children:
  1501 i. Aldon Eugene[7] Bedenbaugh, Jr., m. Dorothy Wise; child:
         1502 a. Ameliann[8] Bedenbaugh, M. D.
  1503 ii. Emory Hayes[7] Bedenbaugh, m. Patricia Balcomb; children:
         1504 a. Michael L.[8] Bedenbaugh
         1505 b. Cathy[8] Bedenbaugh, m. Ron Gaskins
         1506 c. Tracy[8] Bedenbaugh

1507 d. Tony[8] Bedenbaugh
1508 e. Todd[8] Bedenbaugh
1509 iii. Lester Lee[7] Bedenbaugh, m. Mary Sue Shull; children:
    1510 a. Mary Lee[8] Bedenbaugh, m. John Stephen Hooks
    1511 b. Daniel Eugene[8] Bedenbaugh, m. Frances Moore.

747. Howard King[6] Bedenbaugh (Allen Lester[5], Elijah King[4], John[3], Adam[2], Michael[1]) was born 16 March 1906 and died 28 April 1981. He married, on 6 May 1936, Teressa Shealy, who was born 7 Sept 1915, and now (1995) lives in Columbia, South Carolina. Children:
1512   i. Reginald Allen[7] Bedenbaugh
1513 ii. Milton Howard[7] Bedenbaugh
1514 iii. Larry Wayne[7] Bedenbaugh
1515 iv. Gary King[7] Bedenbaugh, m. 1st Gail Bruce; m. 2nd Gwynne Sandel; children:
    1516 a. Candace[8] Bedenbaugh
    1517 b. Tammy[8] Bedenbaugh
1518   v. Glenn Shealy[7] Bedenbaugh.

THE BEDENBAUGH-BETENBAUGH FAMILY

SEVENTH GENERATION

816. Ella Ruth[7] Boozer (Pierce[6], Lemuel[5], Eve[4], Henry[3], Adam[2], Michael[1]) was born 10 July 1902. She married, first, Joseph Worth[6] Bedenbaugh, son of Thomas Boston[5] (Jacob Asbury[4], Jacob[3], Adam[2], Michael[1]) and Mary C. (Dawkins) Bedenbaugh. See entry of Joseph Worth Bedenbaugh for descendants. She married, second (as his fourth wife), Dhent Asbury[6] Bedenbaugh, son of David Murchison[5] (Jacob Asbury[4], Jacob[3], Adam[2], Michael[1]) and Ellen (Warner) Bedenbaugh. There were no children of this marriage.

822. James Edwin[7] Boozer (Pierce[6], Lemuel[5], Eve[4], Henry[3], Adam[2], Michael[1]) was born 30 October 1909 in Newberry County, South Carolina. He married, on 19 December 1837, Mattie Irene Shealy, who was born 26 April 1917 at Little Mountain, South Carolina, the daughter of Charles Edward and Melissa Melvina (Frick) Shealy. Children:
- 1519 i. James Anthony[8] Boozer, b. 19 Dec 1938, m. 1966 Ann Baird Hyler. Child:
  - 1520 a. Toni Melissa Boozer, b. 5 May 1969
- 1521 ii. Nancy Ellen[8] Boozer, b. 4 June 1940, m. 1964 William Middleton Johnston
- 1522 iii. Beverly Irene Boozer, b. 30 Aug 1941, m. 1966 James Leon Shealy. Child:
  - 1523 a. Amy Susan Shealy
- 1524 iv. Timothy Edwin[8] Boozer, b. 6 Nov 1943
- 1525 v. Judith Kaye[8] Boozer, b. 8 Feb 1953
- 1526 vi. Janice Faye[8] Boozer, b. 4 Feb 1956.

823. Bernard Nicholson[7] Boozer (Pierce[6], Lemuel[5], Eve[4], Henry[3], Adam[2], Michael[1]) was born 27 September 1911. He married, on 11 June 1938, Hattie Shealy. Children:
- 1527 i. Gloria Ann[8] Boozer, b. 26 March 1939, m. Kenneth W. Bowers
- 1528 ii. Patricia Gail[8] Boozer, b. 28 Nov 1940, m. Toby Romaine Shealy
- 1529 iii. Bernard Lowell[8] Boozer, b. 26 Jan 1942, m. 14 Feb 1965 Edna Stoudemire.

869. James H.[7] Dennis (John Carl[6], Mary Ella[5], John Adam[4], Henry[3], Adam[2], Michael[1]) was born 22 November 1906 and married Rosette Amick. One child:
- 1530 i. Linda[8] Dennis married Dr. Jaren Van Denheuvel; child:
  - 1531 a. Heather[9] Van Denheuvel.

870. Robert Zack[7] Dennis (John Carl[6], Mary Ella[5], John Adam[4], Henry[3], Adam[2], Michael[1]) was born 13 November 1908 in Newberry County, South Carolina, and died 25 March 1993 in West Columbia, South Carolina. He married, on 10 January 1942, in Columbia, Helen Ballentine, who was born 5 October 1915. Children:
- 1532 i. Robert Gerald[8] Dennis, b. 8 June 1943, Greenwood, SC
- 1533 ii. John Carl[8] Dennis, b. 6 Dec 1946, Greenwood, SC
- 1534 iii. Beverly Jane[8] Dennis, b. 15 Oct 1953 Columbia, SC, m. Joe Alexander (div). The Rev. Beverly Alexander was ordained by the Lutheran Synod of South Carolina and is a campus pastor in Raleigh, NC.

871. Mary[7] Dennis (John Carl[6], Mary Ella[5], John Adam[4], Henry[3], Adam[2], Michael[1]) was born 31 August 1912. She married, on 19 July 1936, Brabham Otis Boozer, who was born 12 March 1914 in Newberry County, South Carolina, and died 15 October 1989. Mary Dennis Boozer lives currently (1995) in Cayce, South Carolina. Children:

1535 i. Gloria Ann[8] Boozer, b. 8 Apr 1937, m. 19 Jan 1957 David S. Davis; children:
    1536 a. David Christopher[9] Davis, died inf., 1957
    1537 b. Gregory Phillips[9] Davis, b. 15 July 1958
    1538 c. Gordon Wayne[9] Davis, b. 20 Aug 1959
    1539 d. Douglas Patrick[9] Davis, b. 20 July 1961
1540 ii. David Younginer[8] Boozer, b. 22 Apr 1945, m. 25 Apr 1964 Frances Hammett, b. 5 Nov 1944; children:
    1541 a. John David[9] Boozer, b. 28 Nov 1966 West Columbia, SC
    1542 b. Clay[9] Boozer, b. 12 Nov 1969
    1543 c. Tami[9] Boozer, b. 10 Apr 1971.

872. Lottie Ruth[7] Bedenbaugh (Roscoe[6], Hawkins[5], Simeon[4], Henry[3], Adam[2], Michael[1]) was born 7 December 1907 and died 9 December 1992. She married, on 9 September 1936, William Edward Senn, who was born 10 April 1907 and died 25 March 1994. Both are buried at Bush River Baptist Church in Newberry County, South Carolina. One child:
1544 i. Patsy Ruth[8] Senn, b. 1 July 1946, m. 16 June 1968 Rev. Engrum Lee Johnson, b. 18 Sept 1944; child:
    1545 a. William Engrum[9] Johnson, b. 21 Jan 1971, m. 11 June 1995, Kathryn Victoria Bieksha, b. 26 May 1971.

873. William Woodrow[7] Bedenbaugh (Roscoe[6], Hawkins[5], Simeon[4], Henry[3], Adam[2], Michael[1]) was born 6 October 1912 and died 30 September 1972 and is buried at Newberry Memorial Garden. He married, on 12 November 1942, Martha Elise Hawkins, who was born 7 July 1920. She married, second, on 9 Jan 1993, Horace Clyde Martin, Jr., who was born 16 September 1918.

Children, all born in Newberry County, South Carolina:
1546 i. George Roscoe[8] Bedenbaugh, b. 17 Jan 1944, m. 17 Oct 1965, Peggy Ann Chapman, b. 8 Apr 1946; children, b. Newberry, SC:
    1547 a. Karman Jay[9] Bedenbaugh, b. 13 Aug 1968, m. 20 Oct 1990 Deborah Lynn Mackey, b. 30 Mar 1969
    1548 b. Bradley Dee[9] Bedenbaugh, b. 6 Sept 1972
    1549 c. Aaron Clark[9] Bedenbaugh, b. 5 July 1974
1550 ii. William Woodrow[8] Bedenbaugh, Jr., b. 12 Feb 1948, m. 25 June 1972 Iris Elizabeth Kibler, b. 17 Apr 1951; children, b. Newberry, SC:
    1551 a. Laura Elizabeth[9] Bedenbaugh, b. 12 July 1977
    1552 b. Hannon William[9] Bedenbaugh, b. 24 Aug 1979
1553 iii. Bunny Elise[8] Bedenbaugh, b. 19 May 1950, m. 17 Dec 1972, Dwight Cannon Wessinger, b. 17 March 1946, Columbia, SC; one child:
    1554 a. Lisa Ann[9] Wessinger, b. 24 June 1983, West Columbia, SC
1555 iv. Lewis Ray[8] Bedenbaugh, b. 20 June 1951, m. 28 May 1972, Nancy Carol Foy, b. 22 June 1949; child:
    1556 a. Tyla Nance[9] Bedenbaugh, b. 11 Jan 1978, Lexington, SC
1557 v. Steve Curtis[8] Bedenbaugh, b. 2 Dec 1958, m. 11 June 1988 Edith Boazman, b. 23 Aug 1960; child:
    1558 a. Maria Catherine[9] Bedenbaugh, b. 11 May 1994, Newberry, SC.

874. James Roscoe[7] Bedenbaugh (Roscoe[6], Hawkins[5], Simeon[4], Henry[3], Adam[2], Michael[1]) was born 26 December 1914. He married, on 11 September 1940, Alethia Werts, who was born 21 September 1927. Children:

1559 i. Alice Annette[8] Bedenbaugh, b. 18 Jan 1946, m. 29 Jan 1967 Terry
      Chinault Shaver, b. 5 Dec 1940; child:
      1560 a. Terry Lynn[9] Shaver, b. 16 June 1969
1561 ii. James Ralph[8] Bedenbaugh, b. 1 Feb 1947, d. 12 Feb 1983 (bur. Newberry
      Memorial Gardens) m. Elaine Faith Hannah; children:
      1562 a. Rochelle Elisha[9] Bedenbaugh, b. 23 March 1980
      1563 b. Nina Marie[9] Bedenbaugh, b. 7 Feb 1982.

875. Mae[7] Bedenbaugh (Roscoe[6], Hawkins[5], Simeon[4], Henry[3], Adam[2], Michael[1])
married Cecil Finley. Children:
1564 i. Jerry[8] Finley, m. Kay ____ ; children:
      1565 a. Michael[9] Finley
      1566 b. Angela[9] Finley
1567 ii. Roscoe[8] Finley, m. Dale Vasser; children:
      1568 a. James[9] Finley
      1569 b. Lynn[9] Finley
      1570 c. Debbie[9] Finley.

876. Ollie Thomas[7] Bedenbaugh (Roscoe[6], Hawkins[5], Simeon[4], Henry[3], Adam[2],
Michael[1]) was born 5 August 1920 and died 11 July 1980. He married Wilman
Warren, who was born 1 November 1925, and died 29 January 1982. They are buried
at Newberry Memorial Gardens. Children:
1571 i. Warren Thomas[8] Bedenbaugh, m. 1st Gayle ____, m. 2nd Deborah ____;
      children:
      1572 a. Christopher[9] Bedenbaugh
      1573 b. Ricky[9] Bedenbaugh
      1574 c. John Michael[9] Bedenbaugh
1575 ii. Herman Michael[8] Bedenbaugh, b. 31 Jan 1949, m. 7 Aug 1976 Sarah
      Margaret Douglas, b. 9 Aug 1954; child:
      1576 a. Lucy Brockman[9] Bedenbaugh, b. 7 Sept 1986.

877. Robert Hawkins[7] Bedenbaugh (Roscoe[6], Hawkins[5], Simeon[4], Henry[3], Adam[2],
Michael[1]) was born 29 Apr 1923 and died 28 October 1972. He married, on 12
February 1943, Ruby Boland, who was born 9 March 1923. Children:
1577 i. Kathy[8] Bedenbaugh, b. 27 Aug 1948, m. James Roy Kunkle; children:
      1578 a. James Christopher[9] Kunkle, m. Tammy Auton; child:
            1579 (1) Julia Cathryn[10] Kunkle
      1580 b. Rebecca Christine[8] Kunkle
1581 ii. Robert Boland[8] Bedenbaugh, b. 13 Dec 1952, m. 24 Dec 1971 Glenda
      Melton, b. 16 Nov 1952; children:
      1582 a. Robert Boland[9] Bedenbaugh, Jr., b. 13 June 1975, m. 16 July 1994
            Heather Bright, b. 3 March 1976
      1583 b. Laura Elizabeth[9] Bedenbaugh, b. 8 Feb 1980.

878. Mildred[7] Bedenbaugh (Roscoe[6], Hawkins[5], Simeon[4], Henry[3], Adam[2], Michael[1])
was born 15 October 1927. She married, on 15 June 1947, Marvin Ernest Wilson,
Jr., who was born 8 August 1923. Children:
1584 i. Marianne[8] Wilson, b. 11 Apr 1949 m. 11 Sept 1971 Robert Elton Wages,
      b. 3 Nov 1948; children:
      1585 a. John Wilson[9] Wages, b. 31 Aug 1975
      1586 b. Paul Hunter[9] Wages, b. 2 Aug 1978
      1587 c. Rebekah Elizabeth[9] Wages, b. 4 Sept 1985

1588 ii. Martha Elizabeth[8] Wilson, b. 30 Dec 1951, m. 1 Apr 1972 Michael Ernest
Perpall, b. 13 Dec 1946; children:
1589 a. David Michael[9] Perpall, b. 29 Oct 1975
1590 b. Mark Wilson[9] Perpall, b. 12 Feb 1978
1591 c. Lauren Elizabeth[9] Perpall, b. 22 May 1981.

879. John Adam[7] Bedenbaugh (Roscoe[6], Hawkins[5], Simeon[4], Henry[3], Adam[2],
Michael[1]) was born 3 January 1931, and married, on 17 May 1959, Carolyn Davis
("Judy") Mack, who was born 26 July 1941. Children:
1592 i. Kim[8] Bedenbaugh, b. 13 Apr 1961, m. 11 Sept 1983 James Martin
Armfield, b. 19 Oct 1955
1593 ii. Amy[8] Bedenbaugh, b. 1 July 1965, m. 27 Sept 1987 Joseph Brian Jackson,
b. 18 Dec 1961.

880. Benjamin McFall[7] (Mac) Bedenbaugh (James Simeon Simpson[6], Hawkins[5],
Simeon[4], Henry[3], Adam[2], Michael[1]) was born 25 January 1920 and married, on 24
December 1939, Eris Naomi Frye, who was born 29 April 1923. Children:
1594 i. M. Carole[8] Bedenbaugh, b. 11 Feb 1941, m. Neal Dailey; children:
1595 a. Robert Edward[9] Dailey, b. 13 Feb 1962
1596 b. Joan Ellen[9] Dailey, b. 18 Feb 1963, m. Doyle Lee Towels
1597 c. Charles Scott[9] Dailey, b. 26 Apr 1967
1598 ii. Anthony M.[8] Bedenbaugh, b. 9 Sept 1942, m. Patricia Ann Wham; child:
1599 a. Mark Anthony[9] Bedenbaugh, b. 20 Mar 1965, m. M. Lynn
.   Williams; child:
1600 (1) Blakely Noele[10] Bedenbaugh,b. 10 Dec 1993
1601 iii. Judy Lynn[8] Bedenbaugh, b. Sept 1944, m. Melvin Eugene Bailey, b. 22
June 1942; children:
1602 a. Jeff Eugene[9] Bailey, b. 20 Jan 1965
1603 b. Andrea Lynn[9] Bailey, b. 18 Sept 1970, m. David Todd Sims
1604 c. Christopher M.[9] (Kit) Bailey, b. 20 Apr 1973
1605 iv. S. Gale[8] Bedenbaugh, b. 21 July 1947, m. Richard Boling; child:
1606 a. Dawnna Maria[9] Boling, b. 16 Nov 1967, m. Jarred Glendon Price,
b. 7 July 1968.
1607 v. Timmie A.[8] Bedenbaugh, b. 17 March 1959, m. Barbara Ann Cason, b. 11
Jan 1960; children:
1608 a. Jessica[9] Bedenbaugh, b. 11 May 1986
1609 b. Garrett Alexander[9] Bedenbaugh, b. 20 Feb 1990.

883. Eula Melissa[7] Bedenbaugh (James Simeon Simpson[6], Hawkins[5], Simeon[4],
Henry[3], Adam[2], Michael[1]) was born 4 October 1924, near Prosperity, South
Carolina. She married, on 10 April 1944, Harold Thomas[7] Bedenbaugh, who was
born 25 May 1923, son of Dhent Asbury[6] and Lottie V. (Mills) Bedenbaugh. Eula
Bedenbaugh has contributed information on both her and her husband's lines for
this work. Three children:
1610 i. Harold Stanley[8] Bedenbaugh, b. 1 Apr 1945, m. 14 Apr 1973, Judy Diane
Godwin, b. 10 Sept 1948, Laurens, SC; children:
1611 a. Jeffrey Thomas[9] Bedenbaugh, b. 10 Sept 1976
1612 b. Joni Rene[9] Bedenbaugh, b. 25 Feb 1981
1613 ii. Russell Stuart[8] Bedenbaugh, b. 2 Jan 1948, m. 27 Nov 1969, Mary Jane
Minick, b. 21 Oct 1947; children:
1614 a. Russell Stuart[9] Bedenbaugh, Jr., b. 18 Jan 1974
1615 b. Jody Alan[9] Bedenbaugh, b. 30 Dec 1977

1616 iii. Sherry Lynnette[8] Bedenbaugh, b. 26 Oct 1952, m. 27 Aug 1971, Leonard
    Wayne Shealy, b. 29 March 1951; children:
    1617 a. Melissa Page[9] Shealy, b. 20 May 1974
    1618 b. Kristine Lynette[9] Shealy, b. 4 Nov 1978.

884. Helen Ruth[7] Bedenbaugh (James Simeon Simpson[6], Hawkins[5], Simeon[4], Henry[3],
Adam[2], Michael[1]) was born 10 September 1926 and died 10 September 1985. She
married, in June 1947, Robert Harry Martin, Sr., who was born November 1925.
Children:
    1619   i. Robert Harry[8] Martin, Jr., b. 23 Jan 1948, m. Sheila Ryan Dickert;
        children:
        1620 a. Robbie[9] Martin, b. 5 March 1973
        1621 b. Michael[9] Martin, b. 11 Dec 1976
    1622 ii. James Horace[8] Martin, b. 28 Oct 1952, m. 1st Rebecca Wicker, 2nd
        Beverly Sweezy; children:
        1623 a. James Horace[9] Martin, Jr., b. 29 Dec 1974
        1624 b. Heather[9] Martin, b. 20 Oct 1977
        1625 c. Helena Stewart[9] Martin, b. 12 June 1988
    1626 iii. Patti Denise[8] Martin, b. 15 Jan 1955, m. Randy Suber; children:
        1627 a. Jenifer[9] Suber, b. 24 May 1976
        1628 b. Monica[9] Suber, b. 5 Sept 1979
    1629 iv. Randy Stewart[8] Martin, b. 7 Feb 1957, m. Rachel Simmons; child:
        1630 a. Brittany[9] Martin, b. 3 Apr 1985.

885. Vera[7] Bedenbaugh (James Simeon Simpson[6], Hawkins[5], Simeon[4], Henry[3],
Adam[2], Michael[1]) was born 1 April 1929. She married, on 4 March 1947, Alvin Boyd
Cotney, who was born 15 August 1924, Prosperity, South Carolina. Children:
    1631 i. Susan Dianne[8] Cotney, b. 30 Jan 1948, m. Claude Calloway; child:
        1632 a. Michelle[9] Calloway, b. 16 Nov 1966, m. Gene Armstrong; child:
            1633 (1) Amanda Michelle[10] Armstrong
    1634 ii. Cynthia[8] Cotney, b. 27 June 1955, m. Ricky Roton; children:
        1635 a. Brandy[9] Roton, b. 12 Sept 1972, m. 12 Oct 1991 Daniel Price;
            child:
            1636 (1) John Dylan[10] Price, b. 27 March 1995
        1637 b. Jamie[9] Roton, b. 12 May 1976
    1638 iii. Alvin Dean[8] Cotney, b. 21 June 1962, m. Annette Gresham (div); m. 2nd
        Amy Bowers Lee; children:
        1639 a. Clay Dean[9] Cotney, b. 24 Mar 1986
        1640 b. Jason Dean[9] Cotney, b. 23 May 1987
    1641 iv. Donna[8] Cotney, b. 11 June 1963, m. John Summer, b. 2 Oct 1961; child:
        1642 a. Martin Cotney[9] Summer, b. 29 Oct 1989.

888. Ethan Otway[7] Shealy (Nancy[6], Hawkins[5], Simeon[4], Henry[3], Adam[2], Michael[1])
was born 26 April 1908 and died 6 September 1969. He married Ina Mae Wise, who
was born 3 July 1911. Children:
+ 1643   i. Katherine Jane[8] Shealy, b. 31 Nov 1931
+ 1644 ii. Keith Wayne[8] Shealy, b. 28 Apr 1935, m. Patsy Ruth King, b. 29 Jan 1934
+ 1645 iii. Ethan Wise[8] Shealy, b. 6 July 1938
+ 1646 iv. Ina Sandra[8] Shealy, b. 13 July 1944.

889. Otis Kelley[7] Shealy (Nancy[6], Hawkins[5], Simeon[4], Henry[3], Adam[2], Michael[1]) was born 19 January 1910 and died 27 July 1991. He married Rhoda Elizabeth Vaughn, who was born 15 July 1920 and died 8 November 1991. Children:
  1647 i. Susan Kay[8] Shealy, b. 14 Nov 1946, m. 1st David Jefferson Hentz, m. 2nd Sherman D. Hager; child:
      1649 a. Sally Yvonne[9] Hentz, b. 29 Dec 1969
  1649 ii. Mary Nancy[8] Shealy, b. 8 Feb 1951, m. Lt. Col. Walter P. Wise (USAF); children:
      1650 a. Matthew Charles[9] Wise, b. 1 Aug 1981
      1651 b. Kathryn Elizabeth[9] Wise, b. 17 Oct 1985
  1652 iii. Kelly[8] Shealy, b. 27 Oct 1957.

891. Annie Laura[7] Shealy (Nancy[6], Hawkins[5], Simeon[4], Henry[3], Adam[2], Michael[1]) was born 14 December 1913. She married Allen Furman Harmon, who was born 31 January 1909 and died 2 May 1981. Children:
  1653 i. Samuel David[8] Harmon, b. 3 Aug 1935, d. 12 Apr 1990, m. Evelyn Estelle Amick; children:
      1654 a. Timothy Darnell[9] Harmon, b. 22 Sept 1963, m. Lagino Gale Lingo, b. 28 Aug 1963; child:
          1655 (1) Samantha[10] Harmon, b. 20 Sept 1991
      1656 b. Rex Alan[9] Harmon, b. 17 May 1965, d. 20 May 1965
      1657 c. Sherrie Laine[9] Harmon, b. 9 June 1966, m. Jeffrey Alan Jones, b. 6 Aug 1963; child:
          1658 (1) Justin[10] Jones, b. 11 Dec 1991
      1659 d. Cynthia Kay[9] Harmon, b. 5 Sept 1968, m. Steven Blair Franklin, b. 28 Dec 1969
      1660 e. Samuel Dean[9] Harmon, b. 31 Aug 1970
  1661 ii. Margaret Alan[8] Harmon, b. 7 June 1937, m. Paul Duane Wicker, b. 27 Oct 1935; children:
      1662 a. Marcia Anne[9] Wicker, b. 1 Nov 1959, m. Alfred Carlisle Duffie, b. 10 Feb 1960; children:
          1663 (1) Laurén Elise[10] Duffie, b. 10 Sept 1986
          1664 (2) Adrianne Nicole[10] Duffie, b. 27 Feb 1988
      1665 b. Paula Dianne Wicker, b. 9 Sept 1971, m. Lorens Ivey.

892. Sarah Malissa[7] Shealy (Nancy[6], Hawkins[5], Simeon[4], Henry[3], Adam[2], Michael[1]) was born 21 June 1917. She married Clarence Hunter Vaughan, who was born 3 July 1912 and died 20 January 1980. Children:
  1666 i. Jerry Hunter[8] Vaughn, b. 2 March 1954, m. Lisa Force, b. 20 Aug 1952; children:
      1667 a. Jerry Hunter[9] Vaughn, Jr., b. 15 July 1976
      1668 b. Melissa June[9] Vaughn, b. 31 May 1981
  1669 ii. Malcolm Lee[8] Vaughn, m. 27 July 1961, m. Darlene Richardson White, b. 20 Dec 1964; child:
      1670 a. Amanda Nicole[9] Vaughn, b. 3 Feb 1992.

893. Nancy Elizabeth[7] Shealy (Nancy[6], Hawkins[5], Simeon[4], Henry[3], Adam[2], Michael[1]) was born 2 January 1924. She married Joseph Raymond Hunter, Jr., who was born 2 November 1922. Children:
  1671 i. Sheila[8] Hunter, b. 10 Aug 1957
  1672 ii. Karen[8] Hunter, b. 30 March 1962.

THE BEDENBAUGH-BETENBAUGH FAMILY

894. Violet M.[7] Epting (Jeannette[6], Hawkins[5], Simeon[4], Henry[3], Adam[2], Michael[1]) was born 24 July 1908. She married Gurdon Wright Counts, Sr., who was born 11 July 1906 and died 19 October 1952. He is buried in the Prosperity Cemetery. Children:

    1673   i. Gurdon Wright[8] Counts, Jr., M. D., b. 12 Nov 1933, m. Elizabeth Rickenbaker, b. 8 Aug 1936; children:

        1674 a. Gurdon Wright[9] Counts, III, b. 30 Dec 1960, m. Andrea Jane Abernathy

        1675 b. Karl Frederick[9] Counts, b. 26 Apr 1962, m. Kathy Marie Taylor

        1676 c. Walter Earnest[9] Counts, b. 17 Oct 1963, m. Brenda Ann Carder, b. 19 Aug 1961; children:

            1677 (1) Sarah Alexis[10] Counts, b. 4 June 1989

            1678 (2) Laura Michelle[10] Counts, b. 4 June 1989

    1679 ii. Richard Epting[8] Counts, b. 15 May 1935, d. 1 Feb 1989, m. Mary Sophronia Watkins, b. 30 June 1935; children:

        1680 a. Richard Epting[9] Counts, Jr., b. 14 July 1961, m. Melinda Carol Hunter; child:

            1681 (1) Kyle Hunter Counts, b. 10 July 1991

        1682 b. Katharine Rene[9] Counts, b. 22 Feb 1967

        1683 c. Robin Eric[9] Counts, b. 3 Aug 1974

    1684 iii. Philip Andrew[8] Counts, b. 22 Apr 1945, d. 6 Jan 1947.

895. Voight Milton[7] Epting (Jeannette[6], Hawkins[5], Simeon[4], Henry[3], Adam[2], Michael[1]) was born 28 June 1910 and died 1 June 1986. He married Vinnie Izora Bushardt, who was born 30 June 1910. Children:

    1685   i. Zoe Jeannine[8] Epting, b. 24 Apr 1936, m. Warren Holmes Wells; children:

        1686 a. Pamela Jeannine[9] Wells, b. 4 July 1969, m. 1st Frank Gary James; 2nd Joel Buche Williams; child:

            1687 (1) Paul Wells[10] James, b. 5 Dec 1983

        1688 b. Wanda Lynn[9] Wells, b. 2 March 1970, m. Joey Randall Richardson; children:

            1689 (1) Casey Lynn[10] Richardson, b. 1 Apr 1986

            1690 (2) Melissa Kelly[10] Richardson, b. 9 June 1987

        1691 c. Nancy Beth[9] Wells, b. 7 Jan 1968

    1692 ii. Voight Milton[8] Epting, Jr., b. 11 Apr 1938, m. Cynthia Ann Petty

        1693 a. Gregory Scott[9] Epting, b. 29 May 1964, m. Lydia Farr

        1694 b. Amy Elizabeth[9] Epting, b. 23 Jan 1976, m. Hoke Kimbrell.

896. Bonnie Lou[7] Epting (Jeannette[6], Hawkins[5], Simeon[4], Henry[3], Adam[2], Michael[1]) was born 10 July 1912. She married Robert Earl Reagin, Sr., who was born 13 October 1910 and died 16 September 1980. Child:

    1695   i. Robert Earl[8] Reagin, Jr., b. 28 Nov 1949, m. Joyce Sizemore; children:

        1696 a. Robert Grant[9] Reagin, b. 17 July 1973

        1697 b. Kenneth Britt[9] Reagin, b. 14 Dec 1975

        1698 c. Bonnie Elizabeth[9] Reagin, b. 10 Oct 1982.

897. Andrew Kenneth[7] Epting (Jeannette[6], Hawkins[5], Simeon[4], Henry[3], Adam[2], Michael[1]) was born 13 February 1928. He married Catherine Lucille Solomons, who was born 17 December 1926. Children:

    1699   i. Andrew Kenneth[8] Epting, Jr., b. 1 Nov 1950 m. Theresa Elizabeth Nagy, b. 2 July 1950; children:

        1700 a. Allison Elizabeth[9] Epting

THE BEDENBAUGH-BETENBAUGH FAMILY

1701 b. Amanda Catherine[9] Epting
1702 ii. Janet Solomons[8] Epting, b. 29 Apr 1952, m. Daniel Walter Shook; children:
    1703 a. Anna Catherine[9] Shook. b 17 July 1980
    1704 b. Andrew Daniel[9] Shook, b. 9 Sept 1986.

898. Clarence Eldred[7] Connelly (Rosa Belle[6], Hawkins[5], Simeon[4], Henry[3], Adam[2], Michael[1]) was born 27 May 1914. He married, on 11 July 1941, Bernice Louise Hawkins, who was born 20 September 1922. One child:
1705 i. Keith Eldred[8] Connelly, b. 31 Oct 1955, m. 17 July 1982, Tracy Morris, b. 1 Feb 1970. One child:
    1706 a. Rachel Nicole[9] Connelly, b. 7 July 1988.

899. James Ira[7] Connelly (Rosa Belle[6], Hawkins[5], Simeon[4], Henry[3], Adam[2], Michael[1]) was born 20 April 1917. He married, on 15 January 1938, Mertie Irene Hawkins, who was born 1 July 1921. They have seven children:
1707 i. James Roger[8] Connelly, b. 13 Aug 1938, m. 22 Nov 1962 Dolores May Campbell, b. 23 June 1942. Children:
    1708 a. Kimberly Dee[9] Connelly, b. 16 Aug 1968, m. 23 May 1992, Mark Conrad Benjamin, b. 20 Feb 1966
    1709 b. Kyle Roger[9] Connelly, b. 18 Aug 1970
1710 ii. Edith Ruth[8] Connelly, b. 25 Dec 1940,. m. 22 June 1958, Carlton Wendell Hite, b. 23 May 1935, Two children:
    1711 a. Crystal Leigh[9] Hite, b. 10 July 1959, m. 19 Apr 1980 James Randal Stockman, b. 15 Jan 1959. Children:
        1712 (1) Amber Leigh[10] Stockman, b. 21 May 1983
        1713 (2) Ashley Lane[10] Stockman, b. 21 May 1983
        1714 (3) Lauren Elizabeth Stockman, b. 21 Jan 1989
    1716 b. Travis Dion[9] Hite, b. 24 March 1964
1716 iii. Alvin David[8] Connelly, b. 27 Feb 1942, m. 30 Dec 1972, Susan Lynn Price, b. 17 Feb 1949. Child:
    1717 a. Jason Neal[9] Connelly, b. 15 Nov 1981
1718 iv. Carolyn Irene[8] Connelly, b. 13 March 1943, m. 14 Jan 19962, James William Kibler, b. 22 Dec 1940. Children:
    1718 a. James David[9] Kibler, b. 4 March 1964, m. 1st 1 March 1986, Milly Hough, b. 15 Jan 1963; m. 2nd, 18 March 1995 to Christina Courturier, b. 23 Apr 1966
    1720 b. Kevin Dean[9] Kibler, b. 7 June 1966, m. 19 Dec 1992 Mandy Gail Mullikin, b. 25 June 1971
1721 v. Mitchel Joseph[8] Connelly, b. 7 Apr 1945, m. 23 May 1965, Harriet Summer Taylor, b. 11 Apr 1946. Children:
    1722 a. Wanda Michelle[9] Connelly, b. 19 Dec 1965, m. 30 Nov 1991, Richard Mark Crotwell, b. 26 Nov 1963
    1723 b. Michael Scott[9] Connelly, b. 3 Feb 1968, m. 6 March 1993 to Anne Russell Molloy, b. 20 June 1971
1724 vi. Philip Hawkins[8] Connelly, b. 25 Apr 1951, m. 18 June 1971 to Wanda Stuck, b. 20 Apr 1954; five children:
    1725 a. Tammy Lynn[9] Connelly, b. 29 Dec 1972, m. 10 Feb 1992 to David Hendrix, b. 12 Oct 1977
    1726 b. Jessie (Jay) Stuck[9] Connelly, b. 6 Oct 1974
    1727 c. Maggie Lane[9] Connelly, b. 2 Aug 1984
    1728 d. Andrew Philip[9] Connelly, b. 24 Oct 1985
    1729 e. Mollie Irene[9] Connelly, b. 1 July 1992

THE BEDENBAUGH-BETENBAUGH FAMILY

1730 vii. Timothy Ray[8] Connelly, b. 30 Dec 1955, m. 20 June 1976 to Betty Jean Shealy, b. 2 July 1956; two children:
    1731 a. Christopher James[9] Connelly, b. 19 Sept 1983
    1732 b. Nicole Marie[9] Connelly, b. 2 June 1987.

900. Eula Mae[7] Connelly (Rosa Belle[6], Hawkins[5], Simeon[4], Henry[3], Adam[2], Michael[1]) was born 23 April 1919. She married, on 1 August 1936, Robert Karl Riser, who was born 15 January 1917, and died 15 October 1994. They have four children:
1733   i. Jimmy Robert[8] Riser, b. 24 June 1937, m. 24 March 1960 Ethel Mae Rowe, b. 11 Nov 1938; three children:
    1734 a. Hope Elizabeth[9] Riser, b. 22 March 1961, m. 24 March 1984 Richard Wayne Jones, b. 15 Jan 1957; child:
        1735 (1) Heather Elise[10] Jones, b. 30 Oct 1986
    1736 b. Faith Letitia[9] Riser, b. 18 Jan 1965, m. 18 May 1984 (div 1993) James Thomas Blasingame, b. 22 March 1961; child:
        1737 (1) Sarah Faith[10] Blasingame, b. 26 Oct 1988
    1738 c. Zachary Robert[9] Riser, b. 5 Sept 1972
1739 ii. Derrill Von[8] Riser, b. 9 Apr 1939, m. 19 June 1965, Delora Clancy, b. 28 Nov 1942. Three children:
    1740 a. Christopher Micheal[9] Riser, b. 19 March 1966
    1741 b. Sandra Lynn[9] Riser, b. 24 Apr 1968, m. 23 Feb 1990 Dean Richard Huffman; children:
        1742 (1) Katie Marie[10] Huffman, b. 15 Sept 1985
        1743 (2) Casey Dean[10] Huffman, b. 23 Dec 1991
        1744 (3) Brady Von[10] Huffman, b. 8 Feb 1995
    1745 c. Susan Elaine[9] Riser, b. 3 Apr 1970
1746 iii. Kerry Phillip[8] Riser, b. 2 Dec 1945. m. Cheryl Lancaster; two children:
    1747 a. Laura Ranaire[9] Riser, b. 20 Dec 1977
    1748 b. Matthew Connelly[9] Riser, b. 27 Jan 1982
1749 iv. Patricia Lynn[8] Riser, b. 5 Dec 1945, m. Dan Gilligan.

901. Juanita[7] Connelly (Rosa Belle[6], Hawkins[5], Simeon[4], Henry[3], Adam[2], Michael[1]) was born 24 November 1921. She married 20 July 1943, James Everett Kibler, who was born 9 August 1918. They live in Prosperity, South Carolina, and have one child.
1750 i. James Everett[8] (Jim) Kibler, Jr., b. 24 June 1944. He has Ph. D. from USC and is a professor at the University of Georgia in Athens.

902. Carol Bedenbaugh[7] Connelly (Rosa Belle[6], Hawkins[5], Simeon[4], Henry[3], Adam[2], Michael[1]) was born 13 March 1927 and died 3 January 1969. He married, on 25 August 1948, Iris O'Shields, who was born 2 September 1926. One child:
1751 i. Carol Bedenbaugh[8] Connelly, Jr., b. 14 Apr 1950, m. Bobbie Dianne Hendrix, b. 21 Dec 1951; three children:
    1752 a. John Hall[9] Connelly, b. 7 Dec 1969
    1753 b. Christopher Hank[9] Connelly, b. 10 Sept 1972
    1754 c. Robert Shawn[9] Connelly, b. 22 Jan 1980.

924. Vera Thelma[7] Dennis (Mary Hallman[6], Pettus[5], Simeon[4], Henry[3], Adam[2], Michael[1]) was born 22 May 1911 and died 20 February 1995. She married, on 25 December 1927, Roy Martin Guin, who was born 19 November 1908 and died 22 November 1977. Two children:

1755 i. Roy Osborne[8] Guin, b. 23 March 1932, m. 15 Dec 1951 Vera Mae Parrott; children:
 1756 a. Shirley Dianne[9] Guin, b. 29 Dec 1952
 1757 b. Brender Mae[9] Guin, b. 30 July 1956
 1758 c. Roy Neal[9] Guin, b. 4 Oct 1966, d. 3 July 1983
1759 ii. Pearl Floree[8] Guin, b. 4 Sept 1938, m. 14 July 1957 Eric Steve Davis, d. 2 Nov 1983; children:
 1760 a. Brent Steve[9] Davis, b. 28 June 1963, m. 9 Nov 1985 Tammy Belger; children:
  1761 (1) Eric Steve[10] Davis, II, b. 15 July 1990
  1762 (2) Chad Brenton Davis, b. 12 Apr 1995.
 1763 b. Blake Melvin[9] Davis, b. 28 Jan 1972.

925. Jesse Frank[7] Dennis (Mary Hallman[6], Pettus[5], Simeon[4], Henry[3], Adam[2], Michael[1]) was born 21 September 1913, and died 3 June 1982. He married, on 19 December 1936, Bertha Mae Dominick, who was born 16 July 1918. Child:
 1764 i. Frank Milton[8] Dennis, b. 29 July 1942, m. 23 Aug 1963 Judi Diane Morris, b. 26 July 1944; child:
  1765 a. Anthony Milton[9] Dennis, b. 8 Sept 1966, m. 16 Oct 1993 Malissa Hembree, b. 13 Apr 1970.

926. Robert Bedenbaugh[7] Dennis (Mary Hallman[6], Pettus[5], Simeon[4], Henry[3], Adam[2], Michael[1]) was born 28 June 1915 and married Sara Alice Wicker, who was born 5 May 1917. Child:
 1766 i. Robert Bedenbaugh[8] Dennis, Jr., b. 23 Apr 1944, m. Rosemary Abrams, b. 29 July 1945; children:
  1767 a. Robert Bedenbaugh[9] Dennis, III, b. 28 March 1970, m. Melissa Ann Sligh, b. 16 Aug 1969
  1768 b. Brantlee Inez[9] Dennis, b. 4 Oct 1973.

927. Herman Wright[7] Dennis (Mary Hallman[6], Pettus[5], Simeon[4], Henry[3], Adam[2], Michael[1]) was born 15 July 1918. He married, on 19 March 1938, Reba Inez Shealy, who was born 14 February 1921. Three children:
 1769 i. Reba Ann[8] Dennis, b. 14 July 1943, m. 1st 3 Aug 1963 Ronald Alvin Oswald, b. 16 May 1941; m. 2nd 26 May 1978, Richard L. Dehart, b. 11 Sept 1951; children:
  1770 a. Todd Dennis[9] Oswald, b. 8 Dec 1964
  1771 b. Elizabeth Ann[9] Oswald, stillborn 23 June 1966
  1772 c. Amy Denise[9] Oswald, b. 7 Apr 1969, m. 19 Dec 1992 William Hawkes Orne, Jr., b. 16 Jan 1969
 1773 ii. Jimmy Wright[8] Dennis, b. 9 June 1944, m. 21 March 1965, Mary Ann Johnston, b. 23 Sept 1944; children:
  1774 a. Deah Lynn[9] Dennis, b. 29 Oct 1966, m. 17 June 1983 Robert Mark Roberts, b. 26 Jan 1962; children:
   1775 (1) Shawn Landon[10] Roberts, b. 22 July 1987
   1776 (2) Mark Cade[10] Roberts, b. 18 May 1988
   1777 (3) Brendan Alan[10] Roberts, b. 16 Nov 1990
  1778 b. David Glenn[9] Dennis, b. 30 Jan 1968, m. 1 May 1988, Tammy Sorrow Senn; child:
   1779 (1) David Kemper[10] Dennis, b. 3 Apr 1990
  1780 c. Alain Clark[9] Dennis, b. 31 March 1971, m. 10 July 1993, Janice Kidd, b. 28 Dec 1973

THE BEDENBAUGH-BETENBAUGH FAMILY

1781 d. Jimmy Dale Dennis, b. 1 Aug 1979
1782 iii. Marshall Oris[8] Dennis, b. 26 Nov 1946, m. 4 June 1971, Dorothy Jean
Hutchinson, b. 16 July 1950; children:
1783 a. Angela Dawn[9] Dennis, b. 22 Nov 1975
1784 b. Allison Marie[9] Dennis, b. 17 March 1985
1785 c. Ashley Noel Dennis, b. 17 March 1985.

928. Clara[7] Dennis (Mary Hallman[6], Pettus[5], Simeon[4], Henry[3], Adam[2], Michael[1]) was
born 17 October 1924. She married, first, on 3 February 1945, Ervin Albert Stroud,
who died 3 September 1955. She married, second, on 8 April 1967, William Drayton
Godfrey. Children:
1786 i. Betti Ann[8] Stroud, b. 30 Nov 1945
1787 ii. Sue Andrea[8] (Andi) Stroud, b. 14 Dec 1946, m. 18 May 1968, George Mills
Grant, Jr., b. 14 May 1947; children:
1788 a. Andrea Mills[9] Grant, b. 15 Apr 1972
1789 b. George Mills Grant, III, b. 17 Dec 1973.

930. George Pettus[7] Riser (Tranquilla[6], Pettus[5], Simeon[4], Henry[3], Adam[2], Michael[1])
was born 27 July 1912 and died 22 July 1991. He married, first, Ruby Lewis, and,
second, Hazel Modean Flanery. Four children (by Ruby Lewis):
1790   i. George Pettus[8] Riser, Jr., b. 10 Jan 1935, m. Bonnie Garlick; children:
1791 a. Charlotte[9] Riser
1792 b. Peggy[9] Riser
1793 c. Pamela[9] Riser
1794 ii. Paul Wilson[8] Riser, b. 12 May 1936, m. Barbara ____; children:
1795 a. Paul[9] Riser, Jr.
1796 b. George[9] Riser
1797 c. Donna[9] Riser
1798 d. Kathy[9] Riser
1799 e. Patrick[9] Riser
1800 iii. Donald Lewis[8] Riser, b. 10 June 1938, m. Dianne Hall; children:
1801 a. Timmy[9] Riser
1802 b. Tommy[9] Riser
1803 c. Gidget[9] Riser
1804 d. Patrick[9] Riser
1805 iv. Judy[8] Riser, b. 14 July 1941.

931. Dora Opal[7] Riser (Tranquilla[6], Pettus[5], Simeon[4], Henry[3], Adam[2], Michael[1]) was
born 4 September 1914 and married James Ira Gibson. Two children:
1806 i. Billy Riser[8] Gibson, b. 5 June 1936, m. 2 Aug 1958 Sylvia Boozer; children:
1807 a. Debra Lynn[9] Gibson, b. 24 Jan 1961, m. 21 May 1984 Clark Ivy
Abrams; child:
1808 (1) Thomas Lee[10] Abrams, b. 7 May 1989
1809 b. Lisa Ann[9] Gibson, b. 23 Aug 1963, m. 6 May 1990 George Clyde
Kinard, Jr.; children:
1810 (1) George William[10] Kinard, b. 7 July 1992
1811 (2) Rebecca Elizabeth[10] Kinard, b. 12 Feb 1995
1812 c. Carole Elizabeth[9] Gibson, b. 16 June 1967, m. 8 June 1991 Thomas
Ingram Shealy
1813 d. William Michael[9] Gibson, b. 4 March 1972
1814 ii. James Corbett[8] Gibson, b. 12 Aug 1944, m. 26 Nov 1976 Helen Meredith
Marsh, b. 5 Feb 1952; children:

THE BEDENBAUGH-BETENBAUGH FAMILY

1815 a. Jeoffrey Corbett[9] Gibson, b. 20 Dec 1978
1816 b. Joel Marsh[9] Gibson, b. 5 March 1981.

933. Annie Lila[7] Riser (Tranquilla[6], Pettus[5], Simeon[4], Henry[3], Adam[2], Michael[1]) was born 31 July 1919, and married, on 6 November 1937, Hoover Woodrow Shealy. Two children:
    1817 i. Larry Woodrow[8] Shealy, b. 25 July 1938, m. 1st Dixie Lee Wilkes, m. 2nd Lizzie Lee Fowler, b. 4 Jan 1948; children:
        1818 a. Michael Woodrow[9] Shealy, b. 29 Sept 1963, m. 21 March 1995 Vickie Lynn Ainscouger, b. 17 Oct 1966
        1819 b. Sheila Ann[9] Shealy, b. 21 Dec 1969
        1820 c. Joseph William[9] Shealy, b. 19 Oct 1971
    1821 ii. Timothy Riser[8] Shealy, b. 25 Apr 1944, m. 25 Apr 1965, Elizabeth Iris Edwards; children:
        1822 a. Timothy Riser[9] Shealy, Jr., b. 6 Aug 1967
        1823 b. Angela Ray[9] Shealy, b. 13 Dec 1970
        1824 c. Randolph Woodrow[9] Shealy, b. 29 Jan 1972.

934. Heber Pickens[7] Riser (Tranquilla[6], Pettus[5], Simeon[4], Henry[3], Adam[2], Michael[1]) was born 5 March 1922, and married, on 2 May 1942, Ethel Ellen O'Quinn, who was born 30 April 1926. He married, second, on 17 November 19966, Muriel Colvin. Children:
    1825 i. Carol Joyce[8] Riser, b. 1 March 1943, m. 31 Aug 1968 Frank Raymond Liberstein, b. 22 Oct 1946; children:
        1826 a. David Michael[9] Liberstein, b. 6 Feb 1973
        1827 b. Frank Raymond[9] Liberstein, Jr., b. 12 Dec 1974, m. 22 Apr 1995 Holly Lehmann
    1828 ii. Linda Dale[8] Riser, b. 29 Apr 1945, m. 3 June 1967 Dwight Kischel Groggel, b. 19 Sept 1945; children:
        1829 a. Richard Scott[9] Groggel, b. 27 July 1968, m. 8 Apr 1995 Charity Pechacek
        1830 b. Emily Kishelle[9] Groggel, b. 9 Sept 1971, m. 19 June 1993, Jack P. Shepherd, III
    iii. infant son, b. & d. 17 July 1952
    1831 iv. Pamela Alayne[8] Riser, b. 3 Aug 1953, m. 5 Aug 1971, Ronald T. Jones; child:
        1832 a. Ronald T.[9] Jones, Jr., b. 14 March 1972.

935. Charlie Roy[7] Bedenbaugh (Charlie Simeon[6], Pettus[5], Simeon[4], Henry[3], Adam[2], Michael[1]) was born 14 May 1917 and died 3 July 1987. He married, on 17 December 1938, Sadie Elizabeth Shealy, who was born 26 January 1922. Children:
    1833 i. Jerry Wayne[8] Bedenbaugh, b. 19 July 1941, m. 4 Dec 1965 Stella Jean Campbell, b. 31 May 1943; children:
        1834 a. Charlotte Leigh[9] Bedenbaugh, b. 26 Feb 1968, m. 29 July 1989, Grayson Douglas Amick, b. 7 Dec 1967; child:
            1835 (1) Caroline Elizabeth[10] Amick, b. 25 Jan 1995
        1836 b. Jerry Wayne[9] Bedenbaugh, Jr., b. 7 Oct 1970
    1837 ii. George Robert[8] Bedenbaugh, b. 11 Aug 1944, m. 1 March 1964, Mary Elaine Johnson, b. 22 Sept 1945; children:
        1838 a. Mary Beth[9] Bedenbaugh, b. 9 Oct 1965, m. 8 Aug 1987, Cary Metts Bishop, b. 4 Sept 1963; child:
            1839 (1) Matthew Robert[10] Bishop, b. 26 Sept 1990

1840 b. George Robert[9] Bedenbaugh, Jr., b. 11 July 1971, m. 18 Feb 1995 Carla Paulette Willis, b. 14 March 1971.

936. Clara Nell[7] Bedenbaugh (Charlie Simeon[6], Pettus[5], Simeon[4], Henry[3], Adam[2], Michael[1]) was born 25 February 1919 and died 3 July 1994. She married, on 26 October 1935, Howard Bernard Shealy, who was born 11 March 1916. Two children:
1841 i. Charles Bernard[8] Shealy, b. 6 Sept 1936, m. 1st Carolyn Frick; m. 2nd Barbara Waters; m. 3rd Annette Ames; child:
1842 a. Charlene Marie[9] Shealy, b. 1 Nov 1970
1843 ii. Phyllis Carol[8] Shealy, b. 2 Aug 1948, m. 28 July 1967 Henry Tillman Auton; children:
1844 a. Dana Michele[9] Auton, b. 10 Jan 1969, m. 22 Feb 1992, William Paul Blancher
1845 b. Alicia Carol[9] Auton, b. 23 Apr 1972, m. 25 Feb 1995 Steven Wayne Cromer.

972. Marion Pet[7] Miller (Jennie[6], Pettus[5], Simeon[4], Henry[3], Adam[2], Michael[1]) was born 8 September 1916. He married, on 17 April 1936, Mary Smith, who was born 9 May 1918. Child:
1846 i. Barbara Jean[8] Miller, b. 15 Nov 1937, m. 3 January 1959, Ralph Cedric Gilliam, b. 5 July 1937; children:
1847 a. Mark Alan[9] Gilliam, b. 10 Aug 1960, m. 28 Aug 1982 Jacquelina Elaine Taylor, b. 5 May 1961
1848 b. Marion Todd[9] Gilliam, b. 2 July 1965.

976. James Lee[7] Miller (Jennie[6], Pettus[5], Simeon[4], Henry[3], Adam[2], Michael[1]) was born 20 November 1928. He married, on 24 December 1946, Helen Louise Schumpert, who was born 25 March 1931. Children:
1849 i. Cynthia Gayle[8] Miller, b. 15 June 1949, m. 8 June 1969, George Earl Leitzsey, b. 24 Dec 1949; child:
1850 a. Melissa Gayle[9] Leitzsey, b. 28 Dec 1985
1851 ii. Susan Faye[8] Miller, b. 15 May 1955, m. 4 May 1985, James William Burch, b. 9 Nov 1953; children:
1852 a. James Patrick[9] Burch, b. 4 Dec 1987
1853 b. William Brett[9] Burch, b. 19 May 1991
1854 iii. Sandra Kay[8] Miller, b. 5 Nov 1960, m. 13 March 1993, James Eric Standridge, b. 23 Aug 1965; child:
1855 a. Erica Leigh[9] Standridge, b. 17 Jan 1995.

999. Mary Suzanna[7] Bedenbaugh (Horace[6], Pettus[5], Simeon[4], Henry[3], Adam[2], Michael[1]) was born 29 July 1922. She married, on 23 November 1939, Thomas O'Merle Summer, who was born 11 April 1919. Children:
1856 i. Mary Linda[8] Summer, b. 28 July 1941, m. 1st, 26 Aug 1957, Jack Brice Shealy; m. 2nd 11 Apr 1978, Jack Blackburn; children:
1857 a. Sharon Lynn[9] Shealy, b. 4 May 1960, m. 5 Sept 1981 Timothy Eugene Tooley, b. 13 Oct 1955; children:
1858 (1) Jason Eugene[10] Tooley, b. 6 Jan 1982
1859 (2) Kristen Dianne[10] Tooley, b. 20 May 1983
1860 b. Linda Suzanne[9] Shealy, b. 4 Apr 1962, m. 1 June 1985 Daniel Walter Fulmer, b. 18 Nov 1957; child:
1861 (1) Lori Danielle[10] Fulmer, b. 17 Nov 1991
1862 c. Thomas Carl[9] Shealy, b. 10 July 1972

1863 d. Belinda Jean[9] Blackburn, b. 8 Aug 1971

1864 e. Natasha Lynn[9] Blackburn, b. 25 Sept 1976

1865 ii. Margaret Ann[8] Summer, b. 15 Sept 1945, m. 1st 12 June 1966, Don Steven Beard m. 2nd 17 Apr 1983 Daniel Monroe Harrison; children:

1866 a. Tana Michelle[9] Beard, b. 3 June 1967

1867 b. Margaret Denise[9] Harrison, b. 19 Jan 1968, m. Shane Lawton; child:

1868 (1) Steven Dean[10] Lawton, b. 1 Oct 1990

1869 c. Pamela Anne[9] Beard, b. 24 July 1970

1870 d. Robert Daniel[9] Harrison, b. 7 July 1972

1871 e. Misty Lynn[9] Harrison, b. 15 Dec 1978

1872 iii. Judy Maude[8] Summer, b. 11 March 1952, m. 2 Jan 1972 Hiram Wright McGee; children:

1873 a. Tabitha[9] McGee, b. 23 Sept 1973

1874 b. Hiram Wright[9] McGee, b. 23 July 1973

1875 iv. Lucia Merle[8] Summer, b. 12 Nov 1955, m. 1st 7 Sept 1974 Bobby Charles Turner, b. 17 Feb 1955; m. 2nd 29 Sept 1991 John William Bantum, Jr., b. 8 March 1945; children:

1876 a. Nikki Colene[9] Turner, b. 19 June 1979

1877 b. James Ryan[9] Turner, b. 5 Nov 1981

1878 v. Tommie Kay[8] Summer, b. 31 Dec 1959, m. 30 May 1981, Robert Dean Long, b. 24 Sept 1958; child:

1879 a. Mary Summer[9] Long, b. 12 July 1992.

1000. Dorothy Mae[7] Bedenbaugh (Horace[6], Pettus[5], Simeon[4], Henry[3], Adam[2], Michael[1]) was born 17 November 1926. She married, on 27 March 1948, Alva Setzler Harris, who was born 6 July 1924 and died 12 January 1995. Children:

1880 i. Donna Patricia[8] Harris, b. 13 July 1950, m. 8 May 1971 Phillip Clark Shealy; children:

1881 a. Julie Ann[9] Shealy, b. 5 May 1972

1882 b. Wesley Clark[9] Shealy, b. 19 Aug 1977

1883 c. Marjorie Janie[9] Shealy, b. 11 Jan 1983, d. 31 Jan 1983

1884 ii. Keith Setzler[8] Harris, b. 8 Aug 1955, m. 30 June 1979, Beverly Ann Gatens, b. 4 Feb 1959; children:

1885 a. Jeremy Setzler[9] Harris, b. 18 Nov 1980

1886 b. Matthew Bryan[9] Harris, b. 16 Apr 1983.

1001. Betty Lucille[7] Bedenbaugh (Horace[6], Pettus[5], Simeon[4], Henry[3], Adam[2], Michael[1]) was born 22 October 1931. She married, on 9 November 1950, Ubric Elton Frick, who was born 26 July 1930. Child:

1887 i. Charles Kenneth[8] Frick, b. 3 Oct 1951, m. 14 May 1976 Libby Crabtree Shell, b. 11 July 19--.

1002. Annie Norine[7] Bedenbaugh (Horace[6], Pettus[5], Simeon[4], Henry[3], Adam[2], Michael[1]) was born 21 May 1934. She married, on 2 June 1951, Lewis Harlan Frick, Sr., who was born 5 May 1932. Children:

1888 i. Kathie Cheryl[8] Frick, b. 22 Sept 1952, m. 12 Sept 1971 Guy Clayton Rister, b. 16 Dec 1952; children:

1888 a. David Guy[9] Rister, b. 17 Nov 1972

1890 b. Bryan Daniel[9] Rister, b. 29 Apr 1983

1891 ii. Lewis Harlan[8] Frick, Jr., b. 1 March 1960, m. 20 Nov 1982, Ann Lindler, b. 18 June 1964; child:

1892 a. Troy Elton[9] Frick, b. 29 June 1984
1893 iii. Marsha Ann[8] Frick, b. & d. 19 Dec 1964
1894 iv. Rodney Allen[8] Frick, b. 6 May 1970, m. 24 Oct 1992, Kristy Ackermann, b. 25 July 19--.

1003. Paul Nichols[7] Bedenbaugh (Horace[6], Pettus[5], Simeon[4], Henry[3], Adam[2], Michael[1]) was born 15 August 1936. He married, on 29 June 1957, Janis Rauch, who was born 1 July 1939. Children:
1895 i. Timothy Lee[8] Bedenbaugh, b. 30 May 1959, m. 14 Nov 1981, Teryl Ann Kornahrens, b. 17 Apr 1960; children:
1896 a. Joshua Lee[9] Bedenbaugh, b. 30 July 1983
1897 b. James Timothy[9] Bedenbaugh, b. 29 July 1984
1898 c. Elizabeth Teryl[9] Bedenbaugh, b. 3 Dec 1985
1899 d. Christine Carolina[9] Bedenbaugh, b. 31 May 1988
1900 e. Daniel Edward[9] Bedenbaugh, b. 15 Nov 1989
1901 f. David Nichols[9] Bedenbaugh, b. 17 July 1991
1902 g. Mary Margaret[9] Bedenbaugh, b. 5 Jan 1993
1903 h. Andrew William[9] Bedenbaugh, b. 27 July 1994
1904 ii. Michael Alan[8] Bedenbaugh, b. 29 Dec 1961, m. 15 June 1991 Karen Leah Birmingham, b. 12 March 1963; children:
1905 a. Karen Nikole[9] Bedenbaugh, b. 8 Dec 1992
1906 b. Benjamin Paul[9] Bedenbaugh, b. 18 Nov 1994
1907 iii. Paula Jane[8] Bedenbaugh, b. 31 Dec 1964, m. 25 May 1991, James Lee Hutchison, b. 30 July 1964.

1004. Hazel Mae[7] Bedenbaugh (Jones[6], Pettus[5], Simeon[4], Henry[3], Adam[2], Michael[1]) was born 11 July 1923 in Prosperity, South Carolina. She married, first, Paul W. Smith who died 24 March 1959. She married, second, Milton Eugene Blair. One child:
1908 i. Larry W.[8] Smith (Rev.), b. 8 Jan 1944, m. 8 June 1968 Deree Abrams. He is currently pastor of St. Paul's Lutheran Church, Gilbert, SC; two children:
1909 a. Warren[9] Smith, b. 9 Sept 1969, Columbia, SC
1910 b. Nancy D.[9] Smith, b. 11 Aug 1971, m. 23 Oct 1993 Scott A. Amerson.

1007. Clyde Eugene[7] Bedenbaugh (Jones[6], Pettus[5], Simeon[4], Henry[3], Adam[2], Michael[1]) was born 25 September 1930 in Prosperity, South Carolina. He married in Charleston, on 24 June 1956, L. Vernell Pevey, who was born 29 September 1936 in Charleston, South Carolina. The Rev. Clyde Eugene Bedenbaugh received a Master of Divinity degree from Lutheran Theological Southern Seminary in 1954. He has served Lutheran congregations in South Carolina and Florida, now residing in Hollywood, Florida. Three children:
1911 i. Edith Lynn[8] Bedenbaugh, b. 5 Feb 1958, Charleston, SC, m. in Hollywood, FL, 16 Aug 1981, Frank Woodrow Gibson, Jr., b. 25 Sept 1958, Hialeah, FL; children, b. Hollywood, FL:
1912 a. Frank Woodrow[9] Gibson, III, b. 21 Jan 1984
1913 b. Andrew Chase[9] Gibson, b. 21 June 1989, d. 14 Apr 1991
1914 ii. Nancy Kathryn[8] Bedenbaugh, b. 5 Nov 1959, Charleston, SC, m. 1st 6 Sept 1980, Bryan Chris Leth, m. 2nd 20 March 1992, David Piercey. Children:
1915 a. Jacquelyn Christine[9] Leth, b. 30 Oct 1983, Gainesville, FL
1916 b. Amanda Jennette[9] Leth, b. 25 March 1986, Hollywood, FL

1917 iii. Stephen Eugene[8] Bedenbaugh, b. 2 Feb 1963, Columbia, SC, m. 22 Aug 1987, Hollywood, Fl., Christine Katulka, b. 11 May 1965, Coaldale, PA; two children:
    1918 a. Michelle Nicole[9] Bedenbaugh, b. 26 June 1990, Carrolton, TX
    1919 b. Robert Stephen[9] Bedenbaugh, b. 6 Oct 1992, Plano, TX.

1008. Doris Louise[7] Bedenbaugh (Jones[6], Pettus[5], Simeon[4], Henry[3], Adam[2], Michael[1]) was born 5 November 1931 in Prosperity, South Carolina. She married, on 31 December 1951, Verbee Shealy, who was born 5 October 1926. Children:
    i. (infant), b & d. 2 June 1952
1920 ii. Marilyn Louise[8] Shealy, b. 17 Sept 1953, d. 19 Sept 1953
1921 iii. Wanda Kay[8] Shealy, b. 17 Apr 1955, m. 8 June 1980 Edward Donald Hall, Jr., b. 22 Apr 1956. Two children:
    1922 a. Edward Erik[9] Hall, b. 14 Apr 1982
    1923 b. Alyssa Louise[9] Hall, b. 20 July 1984
1924 iv. Janet Lynn[8] Shealy, b. 23 Dec 1972.

1009. Gladys[7] Bedenbaugh (Jones[6], Pettus[5], Simeon[4], Henry[3], Adam[2], Michael[1]) was born 9 January 1934 in Prosperity, South Carolina. She married Julian Lester[7] Shealy, who was born 27 May 1915 in Saluda County, South Carolina, and died 26 April 1992 in Newberry County, South Carolina, the son of Andrew Killian and Susie Marie[6] (Bedenbaugh) Shealy (John Adam[5] Jr., John Adam[4] Sr., Adam Jr.[3], Adam[2], Michael[1]) [see page 36]. Julian Lester and Gladys (Bedenbaugh) Shealy had two children, both born in Newberry County:
1925 i. Donna Jean[8] Shealy, b. 15 June 1951, m. 1st 12 Sept 1970, Jimmy Clayton Turner (d. 25 Jan 1976), m. 2nd 19 Aug 1977 Eugene Harrison Jacobs; one child:
    1926 a. James Andrew[9] Turner, b. 9 March 1974, Newberry, SC
1927 ii. Julian Michael[8] Shealy, b. 22 Sept 1953, m. 22 July 1973 Deborah Long; two children:
    1928 a. Brandon Michael[9] Shealy, b. 2 June 1977, Newberry Co., SC
    1929 b. Nathan Long[9] Shealy, b. 26 Oct 1981, Newberry Co., SC.

1010. Bobby Ray[7] Bedenbaugh (Jones[6], Pettus[5], Simeon[4], Henry[3], Adam[2], Michael[1]) was born 18 May 1940 in Prosperity, South Carolina. He married, on 12 November 1961, Barbara Faye Moore, who was born 13 May 1940 in Newberry County. Children:
1930 i. Russell Epting[8] Bedenbaugh, b. 20 Nov 1962, m. 20 June 1992 Tina (Koon) Hope, b. 31 Aug 1960
1931 ii. Kenneth Ray[8] Bedenbaugh, b. 22 March 1967, m. 4 Aug 1990 Michelle Clements; child:
    1932 a. Molly Raye[9] Bedenbaugh, b. 14 Feb 1994; Greenville, SC.

1011. Virginia[7] Bedenbaugh (Maybank[6], Pettus[5], Simeon[4], Henry[3], Adam[2], Michael[1]) was born 28 September 1928. She married, on 5 June 1950, James R. (J.R.) Cannon, who was born 5 June 1923. Children:
1933 i. Debra[8] Cannon, b. 17 March 1953, m. 27 Sept 1985, Darrell E. Pennington, b. 29 Sept 1947; child:
    1934 a. James Dewey[9] Pennington, b. 24 Apr 1991
1935 ii. Susan[8] Cannon, b. 30 Oct 1956, m. 26 Sept 1981 Dennis L. Suber, b. 27 Oct 1953; children:
    1936 a. Stephen Andrew[9] Suber, b. 2 Feb 1988

1937 b. Meredith Alyssa[9] Suber, b. 20 June 1994.

1012. Ralph Maybank[7] Bedenbaugh (Maybank[6], Pettus[5], Simeon[4], Henry[3], Adam[2], Michael[1]) was born 6 September 1929. He married, on 23 December 1955, Jo Rosemary Moore, who was born 7 May 1938. Children:
   1938 i. Karen[8] Bedenbaugh, b. 20 Oct 1957, m. Rodger Alan Steele, b. 18 June 1947; child:
      1939 a. Joseph Adam[9] Steele, b. 20 June 1993
   1940 ii. Ralph Kent[8] Bedenbaugh, b. 15 Sept 1958, m. 28 Aug 1982, Marilyn Wilson, b. 21 Nov 1957; children:
      1941 a. Michael Kent[9] Bedenbaugh, b. 24 May 1988
      1942 b. Kyle Wilson[9] Bedenbaugh, b. 8 May 1991.

1013. George Julian[7] Bedenbaugh (Maybank[6], Pettus[5], Simeon[4], Henry[3], Adam[2], Michael[1]) was born 15 February 1931. He married, on 17 March 1951, Julia Ann Stockman, who was born 27 May 1935. Children:
   1943 i. Sandra Diane[8] Bedenbaugh, b. 13 Aug 1952, m. 20 June 1971, Stanley Harold Lominack, b. 23 Sept 1946; children:
      1944 a. Laurie Lee[9] Lominack, b. 28 Oct 1976
      1945 b. Will Seth[9] Lominack, b. 24 Sept 1983
   1946 ii. Lisa Renee[8] Bedenbaugh, b. 31 Jan 1960, m. 24 Aug 1980 James Thomas Sligh, b. 17 July 1954; child:
      1947 a. Joshua Thomas[9] Sligh, b. 23 Sept 1989
   1948 iii. George Steve[8] Bedenbaugh, b. 3 May 1961, m. 19 Apr 1985 (div), Dawn Marie Nelson, b. 14 July 1965; children:
      1949 a. Amber Nicole[9] Bedenbaugh, b. 30 Dec 1987
      1950 b. George Stephen Julian[9] Bedenbaugh, b. 23 June 1989.

1014. Guerry Alvin[7] Fulmer (Ruby[6], Pettus[5], Simeon[4], Henry[3], Adam[2], Michael[1]) was born 12 October 1932. He married, on 26 November 1953, June Moore, who was born 9 November 1935. A Lutheran pastor, he was ordained in 1956 by the South Carolina Synod, and has served several congregations in South Carolina as well as being a National Guard Chaplain. Children:
   1951 i. Valerie[8] Fulmer, b. 1 Sept 1954, m. 5 June 1976 John Brady Waites, b. 11 Jan 1953; children:
      1952 a. Justin Brady[9] Waites, b. 19 Nov 1980
      1953 b. Jonathan Guerry[9] Waties, b. 30 March 1983
      1954 c. Rebecca Lauren[9] Waites, b. 11 May 1989
   1955 ii. Stephen Luther[8] Fulmer, b. 16 Nov 1956, m. 30 Apr 1988 Elizabeth Phelps, b. 21 May 1954.
   1956 iii. Beth[8] Fulmer, b. 11 March 1965, m. 29 Oct 1988, Ralph Benjamin Haggard, b. 1 Dec 1965; children:
      1957 a. Benjamin Tyler[9] Haggard, b. 6 July 1991
      1958 b. Caroline Olivia[9] Haggard, b. 5 May 1995.

1015. Jerry Thomas[7] Fulmer (Ruby[6], Pettus[5], Simeon[4], Henry[3], Adam[2], Michael[1]) was born 15 January 1939. He married, on 27 August 1961, Nancy Elizabeth Amick, who was born 21 October 1938. Child:
   1959 i. Pamela Gayle[8] Fulmer, b. 30 Nov 1964, m. 24 Oct 1992, Paul Franklin Berrian, b. 14 Dec 1967; child:
      1960 a. Sara Elizabeth[9] Berrian, b. 17 Dec 1993.

1046. Luther Jacob[7] (Dick) Bedenbaugh (Ernest W.[6], Jacob C.[5], John Adam[4], Adam Jr.[3], Adam[2], Michael[1]) was born 18 October 1905, in Lexington County, and died 13 February 1990. He married first, on 24 January 1925, Bertie Mae Shealy, who was born 3 November 1909 and died 12 March 1930. He married, second, on 18 October 1930 Ada Elizabeth Rawl; and, third, Ruth May (Miller) Storey. He is buried at Union Lutheran Church Cemetery, Lexington County. Children:

    1961 i. Jacob Calvin[8] Bedenbaugh, b. 25 Nov 1925, m. 15 Sept 1945 Robbie Lee Wilds; children:

        1962 a. Karen[9] Bedenbaugh, b. 21 July 1948

        1963 b. Susan[9] Bedenbaugh, b. 2 Apr 1950

    1964 ii. Myrtis Rachel[8] Bedenbaugh, b. 17 Dec 1927, m. 1st 6 Jan 1946, Robert Omar Mitchell, b. 19 Apr 1920; m. 2nd Larry Helms; children:

        1965 a. Robert Omar[9] Mitchell, Jr., b. 22 Dec 1946

        1966 b. Amy Marie[9] Mitchell, b. 20 Dec 1956

    1967 iii. Josephine Katherine[8] Bedenbaugh, b. 12 Dec 1929, m. 1st 18 Jan 1947 Milton Mitchell Frye, b. 3 July 1929; m. 2nd Clarence Barnes; children:

        1968 a. Renell Leona[9] Frye, b. 22 Dec 1947

        1969 b. Julia Anne[9] Frye, b. 20 Oct 1953

    1970 iv. Margaret[8] Bedenbaugh, m. Bruce Kepler

    1971 v. Naomi[8] Bedenbaugh, m. 1st Oneal Hallman, 2nd Kenneth Screws

    1972 vi. Bowman Asbury[8] Bedenbaugh, b. 30 Jan 1942, m. 2 Aug 1963, Ellie Anna Miller; children:

        1973 a. Bowman Joel[9] Bedenbaugh, b. 13 Jan 1970

        1974 b. Stacy Lynn[9] Bedenbaugh, b. 1 Apr 1975.

1047. Quincy Leon[7] Bedenbaugh (Ernest W.[6], Jacob C.[5], John Adam[4], Adam Jr.[3], Adam[2], Michael[1]) was born 19 May 1908 and died 2 May 1963. He married, first, on 19 November 1927, Velma Tarcy Keisler, who was born 30 April 1910 and died 8 July 1929 in Lexington County, South Carolina, the daughter of Julian and Emma (Long) Keisler. She is buried at Union Lutheran Church near Leesville, South Carolina.[122] He married, second, on 1 March 1930, Annie Margaree Koon, who was born 23 December 1907. There was one child by the first marriage.

    1975 i. Velma Emma Louise[8] Bedenbaugh, b. 28 June 1929 m. 1st 29 Nov 1946 Robert Floyd[8] Bundrick (Edna Geneva[7], Benjamin[6], Wilson[5], Mathias Hare[4], Jacob[3], Adam[2], Michael[1]), b. 8 July 1922, d. 8 Jan 1986 (see under him for descendants); m. 2nd Herbert H. Keisler

    1976 ii. George Allen[8] Bedenbaugh, b. 15 June 1932

    1977 iii. Ernest Doyle[8] Bedenbaugh, b. 28 Apr 1934

    1978 iv. Doris Lynette[8] Bedenbaugh, b. 11 Dec 1935, m. Julius Smith

    1979 v. Marvin Leon[8] Bedenbaugh, b. 22 Jan 1938

    1980 vi. David Eugene[8] Bedenbaugh, b. 24 Dec 1942

    1981 vii. Norman Elton[8] Bedenbaugh, b. 1 March 1944

    1982 viii. Melba Carolyn[8] Bedenbaugh, b. 15 Feb 1952, m. Terry Shull.

1131. George William[7] Conwill (William[6], Jesse[5], John A.[4], Elizabeth[3], Adam[2], Michael[1]) was born 5 March 1909, in Lee County, Mississippi, and died 19 Aug 1977. He married, on 15 May 1927, Eddie Clethus Bethay. Children:

    1983 i. Fay Ellen[8] Conwill, b. 11 Sept 1928, m. 12 Apr 1947, Carl Dallas King, b. 18 Nov 1927, Lee Co., MS; children:

        1984 a. Judy Fay[9] King, b. 17 Feb 1949, m. 19 July 1967 Anthony V. Schilz

        1985 b. Beverly Lynn[9] King, b. 20 Sept 1954

1986 c. Carl Daniel[9] King, b. 27 July 1955, m. 12 May 1978 Fredia Jane
      Bird
1987 ii. Wanell[8] Conwill, b. 26 Sept 1930, m. 21 Dec 1946 Rufus Lafayette Farris;
      children, b. Amory, MS:
      1988 a. Jerry Rufus[9] Farris, b. 27 Aug 1952
      1989 b. Micheal William[9] Farris, b. 19 Dec 1960
1990 iii. Donald Gene[8] Conwill, b. 16 Jan 1946, b. 26 Jan 1946, m. 30 June 1963,
      Mary Kathryn Sloan, b. 12 July 1945; children, b. Amory, MS:
      1991 a. Donna Kay[9] Conwill, b. 4 March 1965
      1992 b. Dena Michelle[9] Conwill, b. 10 July 1967.

1132. Elmer Clay[7] Conwill (William[6], Jesse[5], John A.[4], Elizabeth[3], Adam[2], Michael[1])
was born 6 November 1912 in Shannon, Mississippi, and married, on 2 May 1942,
Dorothy Vernice Coker, who was born 16 May 1920 in Detroit, Alabama. Nine
children, all born in Amory, Mississippi:
1993   i. James Clay[8] Conwill, b. 15 March 1943, m. 20 Feb 1971 Karen Lee
      Dickey
1994   ii. Dorothy Diane[8] Conwill, b. 28 Nov 1944, m. 2 May 1965 Murrel Thomas
      Tubb, b. 23 July 1942; children, b. Amory, MS:
      1995 a. Amber Annette[9] Tubb, b. 14 Sept 1968
      1996 b. Ginger Nicole[9] Tubb, b. 5 March 1975
      1997 c. Eva Margaret[9] Tubb, b. 16 Feb 1977
1998   iii. Zera Pearl[8] Conwill, b. 24 Aug 1947, m. 16 Apr 1965 Larry Alton Ray,
      b. 17 July 1944; children, b. Amory, MS:
      1999 a. Anthony Chad[9] Ray, b. 4 Nov 1965
      2000 b. Cheri Ann[9] Ray, b. 15 Aug 1968
      2001 c. Ali Victoria[9] Ray, b. 1 Aug 1978
2002   iv. Richard Bruce[8] Conwill, b. 10 Sept 1950, m. 18 March 1973 Brenda
      Anne Robinson, b. 10 Sept 1950; children:
      2003 a. Tiffany Anne[9] Conwill, b. 21 Oct 1974, Jackson, MS
      2004 b. Brandon Scott[9] Conwill, b. 20 Dec 1978, Meridian, MS
2005   v. Robert William[8] Conwill, b. 10 Sept 1950, m. 9 June 1972 Karol Elaine
      Pugh, b. 4 Oct 1948, children: b. Amory, MS:
      2006 a. Robert William[9] Conwill, Jr., b. 31 Dec 1972
      2007 b. Joseph Daniel[9] Conwill, b. 25 Dec 1976
2008   vi. Libble Patricia[8] Conwill, b. 11 Sept 1953, m. 3 Apr 1971 Jack Stokes
      Phipps, Jr., b. 7 Dec 1944; children, b. Tupelo, MS:
      2009 a. Philip Anthony[9] Phipps, b. 12 Sept 1971
      2010 b. Nathaniel Cassidy[9] Phipps, b. 19 Oct 1976
2011 vii. Janie Ruth[8] Conwill, b. 23 Apr 1956, m. 20 May 1978 Farris Brent Jones,
      b. 4 Jan 1956
2012 viii. Mary Corinne[8] Conwill, b. 28 June 1960, m. 8 July 1978 Richard Dale
      Aldridge, b. 3 July 1953, Amory, MS.
2013   ix. Peter Gray[8] Conwill, b. 28 June 1960.

1134. John Allen[7] Conwill (William[6], Jesse[5], John A.[4], Elizabeth[3], Adam[2], Michael[1])
was born 12 October 1916 in Itawamba County, Mississippi, and married, on 7
December 1949, Tisha Olene Kerr, who was born 24 May 1927 in Monroe County,
Mississippi. Three children:
2014   i. Ray Allen[8] Conwill, b. 17 Nov 1954, Amory MS
2015 ii. Johnny Lee[8] Conwill, b. 4 Aug 1956, Tupelo, MS, m. 27 Aug 1977 Glenda
      Kellene Burt, b. 7 Oct 1959; child:

2016 a. Jonathan Scott[9] Conwill, b. 15 Feb 1980
2017 iii. Thomas Alvie[8] Conwill, b. 26 July 1963, Amory, MS.

1145. Leonard Eugene[7] Conwill (Ira[6], Yates[5], Yates[4], Elizabeth[3], Adam[2], Michael[1]) was born 8 November 1906 in Itawamba County, Mississippi, and died 22 July 1970, in Tupelo, Mississippi. He married, on 21 January 1949, Effie Christene Rea. Two children, both born Itawamba County, Mississippi:
2018 i. Betty Ruth[8] Conwill, m. Paul Ray Parham
2019 ii. Julia Rea[8] Conwill, m. Corbet B. Bickerstaff, Jr.

1147. Ernest David[7] Conwill (Ira[6], Yates[5], Yates[4], Elizabeth[3], Adam[2], Michael[1]) was born 5 May 1910 in Itawamba County, Mississippi, and died 27 December 1967 in Tupelo, Mississippi. He married, on 7 September 1938, Geneva Perrigen who was born 23 December 1922 in Columbus, Mississippi. Two children, both born in Columbus, Mississippi:
2020 i. Ira Will[8] Conwill, b. 29 July 1942, m. 14 Feb 1962, Barbra Joan Green, b. 10 Nov 1943; children, b. Kankakee, IL:
    2021 a. Dawn Marie[9] Conwill, b. 14 Sept 1964
    2022 b. Jeffery Scott[9] Conwill, b. 11 Dec 1965
2023 ii. Larry Dale[8] Conwill, b. 18 March 1951, m. 5 March 1971 Linda Marie Arseneau, b. 5 March 1953; child:
    2024 a. Kristopher Ashley[9] Conwill, b. 18 Oct 1977, Kankakee, IL.

1151. Paul Rainey[7] Conwill (Ira[6], Yates[5], Yates[4], Elizabeth[3], Adam[2], Michael[1]) was born 11 November 1926 in Itawamba County, Mississippi, and married, on 3 May 1947, Frances Elaine Deason, who was born 29 April 1929, in Lee County, Mississippi. Three children:
2025 i. Paul Eugene[8] Conwill, b. 22 Aug 1949, m. 30 Dec 1972, Debra Gail Burt, b. 30 Aug 1951; child:
    2026 a. Angela Dawn[9] Conwill, b. 14 Aug 1977, Amory, MS
2027 ii. Joseph Lonnie[8] Conwill, b. 22 Dec 1952
2028 iii. James Lee[8] Conwill, b. 23 Dec 1955, Amory, MS, m. 11 Nov 1977, Sylvia J. Smith, b. 10 June 1956.

1166. Edna Geneva[7] Bedenbaugh (Benjamin[6], Wilson[5], Mathias Hare[4], Jacob[3], Adam[2], Michael[1]) was born 2 December 1894 and died 26 September 1971. She married, on 21 Dec 1913, John Haskell O'Neal Bundrick, who was born 15 April 1890 and died 23 April 1983. Both are buried in Newberry Memorial Gardens. Children:
+ 2029 i. Roscoe O'Neal[8] Bundrick, b. 26 Dec 1916
+ 2030 ii. Geneva Ruth[8] Bundrick, b. 28 May 1919
+ 2031 iii. Robert Floyd[8] Bundrick, b. 8 July 1922
+ 2032 iv. Irene[8] Bundrick, b. 16 March 1925 (twin)
+ 2033 v. Pauline[8] Bundrick, b. 16 March 1925 (twin)
+ 2034 vi. Daniel Luther[8] Bundrick, b. 24 July 1927
+ 2035 vii. Earl Mack[8] Bundrick, b. 20 Aug 1929
+ 2036 viii. Dorothy Mae[8] Bundrick, b. 10 Feb 1932
+ 2037 ix. John Henry[8] Bundrick, b. 18 Feb 1940.

1216. Clavis Lorhee[7] Bedenbaugh (Raymond[6], Wilson[5], Mathias Hare[4], Jacob[3], Adam[2], Michael[1]) was born 6 December 1927, and married Ollie Ray Lindler, who was born 12 April 1923. Three children:

2038 i. Michael Ray[8] Lindler, b. 13 Jan 1950, m. 30 May 1970 Linda Faye McLamore, b. 26 Sept 1949; two children:
    2039 a. Wendy Michele[9] Lindler, b. 28 Dec 1973
    2040 b. Michael Ray[9] Lindler, Jr., b. 25 May 1977
2041 ii. Timothy Lee[8] Lindler, b. 30 Oct 1953, m. Gwynn Marie Henry, b. 7 July 1953; children:
    2042 a. Timothy Preston[9] Lindler, b. 31 March 1981
    2043 b. Hillary Janelle[9] Lindler, b. 19 Dec 1984
2044 iii. Jeffrey Keith[8] Linder, b. 23 May 1957, m. Sabara Anne Campbell, b. 4 Nov 1964.

1224. Arlette[7] Bedenbaugh (Martin[6], Mathias Hare Jr.[5], Mathias Hare[4], Jacob[3], Adam[2], Michael[1]) was born 15 December 1899 and died 29 January 1978. She married Maxey Crout. Children:
2045 i. Ruth[8] Crout, b. 8 Dec 1919
2046 ii. Howard[8] Crout, b. 5 Oct 1922
2047 iii. Kenneth[8] Crout, b. 31 Dec 1923.

1225. Annie Grace[7] Bedenbaugh (Martin[6], Mathias Hare Jr.[5], Mathias Hare[4], Jacob[3], Adam[2], Michael[1]) was born 5 December 1902 and died 12 August 1985. She married William Jennings Fulmer, who was born 18 September 1898 and died 11 April 1971. They are buried at St. Mark's Lutheran Church, Saluda County, South Carolina. Children:
2048 i. Gerald Duane[8] Fulmer, b. 11 Dec 1925, m. Gladys Bowers, b. 23 Sept 1920; children:
    2049 a. Mary Ethel[9] Fulmer, b. 3 Oct 1954, m. Donald Lamberton Whiteley, Jr., b. 29 Nov 1952; children:
        2051 (1) Donald Lamberton[10] Whiteley, III, b. 25 Oct 1979
        2052 (2) Michael Christopher[10] Whiteley, b. 29 Dec 1982
    2053 b. Geralyn[9] Fulmer, b. 13 Oct 1956, m. Phillip Michael Brooks. b. 15 June 1950; children:
        2054 (1) Carianna[10] Brooks. b. 21 Jan 1981
        2055 (2) Wesley Michael[10] Brooks, b. 18 Nov 1982
2056 ii. Annie Vernetha[8] Fulmer, b. 1 May 1929, m. Robert Renwick; children:
    2057 a. William Robert[9] Renwick, b. 18 Dec 1952
    2058 b. Martha Grace[9] Renwick, b. 10 Dec 1954
    2059 c. Hugh Fulmer[9] Renwick, b. 6 March 1963
    2060 d. David Marcellus[9] Renwick, b. 31 Oct 1964
2061 iii. Willie Maytrude[8] Fulmer, b. 31 June 1932, m. Larry Katz; children:
    2062 a. Stephen William[9] Katz, b. 28 Oct 1954
    2063 b. Pamela Nancy[9] Katz, b. 14 Feb 1958.

1226. Georgie[7] Bedenbaugh (Martin[6], Mathias Hare Jr.[5], Mathias Hare[4], Jacob[3], Adam[2], Michael[1]) was born 28 November 1905 and died in 1978. She married Noah Calhoun Fulmer, who was born 25 August 1905 and died 5 July 1974. They are buried in Rosemont Cemetery in Newberry, South Carolina. Children:
2064 i. Clarence[8] Fulmer, b. 2 Oct 1927
2065 ii. June[8] Fulmer, b. 7 June 1932.

1227. Brabham[7] Bedenbaugh (Martin[6], Mathias Hare Jr.[5], Mathias Hare[4], Jacob[3], Adam[2], Michael[1]) was born 18 July 1908. He and his wife Lizzie had two children:
2066 i. Wendell[8] Bedenbaugh, b. 26 Nov 1931

THE BEDENBAUGH-BETENBAUGH FAMILY

2067 ii. Keith[8] Bedenbaugh.

1228. Joseph Guy[7] Bedenbaugh (Martin[6], Mathias Hare Jr.[5], Mathias Hare[4], Jacob[3], Adam[2], Michael[1]) was born 28 August 1913 and died 18 December 1965. He married Lorena Warren, and they had one child:
2068 i. Bill[8] Warren.

1229. Roy Leon[7] Bedenbaugh (Thomas U.[6], Mathias Hare Jr.[5], Mathias Hare[4], Jacob[3], Adam[2], Michael[1]) was born 1 January 1916 and died 14 December 1983 at North Augusta, South Carolina. He married, on 3 June 1939, Mary Patricia Stephens, who was born 23 June 1939, and died 8 July 1944 at Augusta Georgia. Both are buried at Sweetwater Baptist Church in Edgefield County. Children:
2069 i. Stephen Thomas[8] Bedenbaugh, b. 3 March 1957
2070 ii. Mary Patricia[8] Bedenbaugh, b. 28 Oct 1961.

1230. Edith Mae[7] Bedenbaugh (Thomas U.[6], Mathias Hare Jr.[5], Mathias Hare[4], Jacob[3], Adam[2], Michael[1]) was born 20 March 1917. She married, first, 6 September 1936, Henry Wilson Metts, and second, 12 October 1979, Leo A. Cook. Children:
2071 i. Gerald Wilson[8] Metts, m. Linda Jean Carter
2072 ii. Marsha Elizabeth[8] Metts, m. Bobby Joe Holman.

1231. Ralph Furman[7] Bedenbaugh (Thomas U.[6], Mathias Hare Jr.[5], Mathias Hare[4], Jacob[3], Adam[2], Michael[1]) was born 3 February 1933 and died 5 November 1990 at Augusta, Georgia. He married, on 4 September 1959 at Clearwater, South Carolina, Eleanor Valerie Owens. She has supplied much of the information on descendants of Mathias Hare Bedenbaugh, Sr. Children:
2073   i. Gregory Owens[8] Bedenbaugh, b. 19 Feb 1961, Augusta, Ga., m 4 Nov 1989 Amy Arlene Samples, b. 11 Feb 1967, Marietta, GA. Children:
2074 a. Megan Alexandria[9] Bedenbaugh, b. 4 Dec 1992, Augusta, GA
2075 b. Stephanie Alexis[9] Bedenbaugh, b. 8 Apr 1994, Augusta, GA
2076 ii. Jeffrey Furman[8] Bedenbaugh, b. 19 Feb 1961, Augusta, GA.
2077 iii. Stuart Thomas[8] Bedenbaugh, b. 14 May 1968 Greenville, S. C., m. 25 Mar 1995, at Aiken, SC, Catherine Hemstreet McManus, b. 29 Nov 1968, Augusta, GA.

1260. Edward Guy[7] Counts (Pearle[6], David Murchison[5], Jacob Asbury[4], Jacob[3], Adam[2], Michael[1]) was born 21 September 1905. He married, on 7 January 1927, Carvilla Long, who was born 29 May 1907. Children:
2078 i. Lorraine[8] Counts, b. 7 Sept 1928, m. 1 May 1949, Herman Charles Shealy, Sr., b. 28 Apr 1928, Laurens Co., SC; children:
2079 a. Herman Charles[9] Shealy, Jr., b. 5 Jan 1953, Abbeville, SC
2080 b. Marcia Lorraine[9] Shealy, b. 15 May 1956, Abbeville, SC, m. 23 Nov 1975, William Heyward Brown, b. 6 Dec 1964, McCormick Co., SC.
2081 c. Bridgette Ann[9] Shealy, b. 2 May 1959, Chester, SC.
2082 ii. Sandra Kaye[8] Counts, b. 25 May 1944, m. 28 Oct 1962, Bobbie Alan Oxner, b. 4 Sept 1941; child:
2083 a. Dawn[9] Oxner, b. 28 July 1970.

1262. Mildred[7] Counts (Pearle[6], David Murchison[5], Jacob Asbury[4], Jacob[3], Adam[2], Michael[1]) was born 8 July 1914 and died 1 May 1982. She married Clarence Lester Werts, who was born 9 December 1914. Children:

THE BEDENBAUGH-BETENBAUGH FAMILY

2084 i. Dorothy Jean[8] Werts, m. 1st Robert Barnes, m. 2nd Bennie Smith; children:
    2085 a. Tony[9] Barnes
    2086 b. Jason[9] Barnes
2087 ii. Jo Anne[8] Werts, m. Wallace Newman.

1266. David Edwin[7] Bedenbaugh (Colon Boyd[6], David Murchison[5], Jacob Asbury[4], Jacob[3], Adam[2], Michael[1]) was born 28 October 1926, and married, on 8 July 1956, Linda Elizabeth Hancock. They live near Prosperity, South Carolina, and have two children:
2088 i. Boyd William[8] Bedenbaugh, b. 16 Jan 1958 (has contributed much information to this work)
2089 ii. Michael Edwin[8] Bedenbaugh, b. 26 June 1961, m. 3 Sept 1989, Doreen Sullivan, b. 17 Nov 1962; children:
    2090 a. Victoria Carson[9] Bedenbaugh, b. 8 Nov 1993
    2091 b. Jacob Warner[9] Bedenbaugh, b. 19 June 1995.

1267. Earle Joiner[7] Bedenbaugh (Colon Boyd[6], David Murchison[5], Jacob Asbury[4], Jacob[3], Adam[2], Michael[1]) was born 7 March 1928 in Prosperity, South Carolina. He married there, on 28 December 1951, Evelyn Jeannine (Jenny) Ballentine, who was born 2 March 1929, at Chapin, South Carolina, the daughter of William Arthur and Clara Armenia (Cumalander) Ballentine. They live in Prosperity, South Carolina, and have four children:
2092 i. Jean[8] Bedenbaugh, b. 22 Nov 1953
2093 ii. Janice Leigh[8] Bedenbaugh, b. 15 May 1956, m. 23 Aug 1980, Larry Wallace Blackwell, b. 14 Dec 1955, Lancaster, SC; children, b. Charlotte, NC:
    2094 a. Heather Nicole[9] Blackwell, b. 23 Mar 1983
    2095 b. Matthew Derek[9] Blackwell, b. 8 Apr 1983
2096 iii. Lisa Ann[8] Bedenbaugh, b. 5 March 1960, m. 31 May 1986, John Louis Sulka, b. 5 May 1959, Wierton, WV; children, b. Hilton Head Island, SC:
    2097 a. Brannon Elizabeth[9] Sulka, b. 4 Dec 1989
    2098 b. Haley Warner[9] Sulka, b. 25 Aug 1991
    2099 c. Michael Louis[9] Sulka, b. 19 June 1994
2100 iv. Charles William[8] Bedenbaugh, b. 30 April 1964, m. 11 July 1987, Sherry Melinda Dill, b. 19 Nov 1963, Dade City, FL; children, b. Columbia, SC:
    2101 a. William Joiner[9] Bedenbaugh, b. 4 Apr 1991
    2102 b. Charles Alexander[9] Bedenbaugh, b. 4 Apr 1991.

1277. Anne[7] Bedenbaugh (Dhent[6], David Murchison[5], Jacob Asbury[4], Jacob[3], Adam[2], Michael[1]) was born 5 August 1932 and married, on 28 July 1957, Heyward Glenn Shealy, who was born 27 October 1928. Children:
2103 i. Laurie Ann[8] Shealy, b. 16 Aug 1959, m. 19 June 1982, Robert Chapman, b. 2 Oct 1959; children:
    2104 a. Anna[9] Chapman, b. 24 Aug 1989
    2105 b. Robert[9] Chapman, b. 20 July 1994
2106 ii. Wanda L.[8] Shealy, b. 26 Nov 1960
2107 iii. Glenn H.[8] Shealy, b. 20 June 1968, m. Megan Donovan.

1278. Jimmy Byrnes[7] Bedenbaugh (Dhent[6], David Murchison[5], Jacob Asbury[4], Jacob[3], Adam[2], Michael[1]) was born 5 September 1936. He married, on 14 June 1959, Alice Faye Koon, who was born 3 September 1937. Children:

THE BEDENBAUGH-BETENBAUGH FAMILY

2108 i. J. Todd[8] Bedenbaugh, b. 11 March 1963, m. 23 May 1987, Susan M. Meetze, b. 24 Oct 1964

2109 ii. Michael Shea[8] Bedenbaugh, b. 28 Oct 1967, m. 10 Sept 1994 Angelia F. Gay, b. 31 Aug 1969.

1279. Merle[7] Bedenbaugh (Dhent[6], David Murchison[5], Jacob Asbury[4], Jacob[3], Adam[2], Michael[1]) was born 18 November 1942 and died 13 October 1990. She married Rodney Farrell Epting, who was born 25 February 1942, the son of Robert F.[7] and Trudie (Bedenbaugh) Epting. Children:

2110 i. Lee Renee[8] Epting, b. 5 Feb 1967, m. Jay Koon

2111 ii. Sheron F.[8] Epting, b. 30 Jan 1969.

1298. Joseph Moody[7] Bedenbaugh (Moody[6], Mack Wilson[5], Jacob Asbury[4], Jacob[3], Adam[2], Michael[1]) was born 15 September 1923. He married, on 5 May 1945, Edna Elizabeth[7] Mills, a daughter of Willie L.[6] (James Burr[5], Rachel[4], Jacob[3], Adam[2], Michael[1]) and Nettie (Barnes) Mills. Two children:

2112 i. Linda[8] Bedenbaugh, b. 18 Apr 1946 m. 9 June 1979 Rev. George Puckett, b. 19 Dec 1952; children:

   2113 a. Caroline Elizabeth[9] Puckett, b. 26 March 1981

   2114 b. Viviana[9] Puckett (adopted), b. 29 June 1981

2115 ii. Mackey Mills[8] Bedenbaugh, b. 21 Nov 1954, m. 5 Jan 1979 Mary Kay Conner, b. 20 Nov 1954; children:

   2116 a. Emily Kay[9] Bedenbaugh, b. 18 March 1986

   2117 b. Matthew Christian[9] Bedenbaugh, b. 2 May 1988.

1313. Mattie Mae[7] Mills (Simon P.[6], David Newton[5], Rachel[4], Jacob[3], Adam[2], Michael[1]) was born 17 February 1899 and died 9 October 1992. She married Willie John Silas McCartha, who was born 28 October 1893 and died 26 November 1977. Children:

2118 i. Lila Mae[8] McCartha, b. 26 Apr 1919, m. Charles Leopard

+ 2119 ii. John Clarence[8] McCartha, b. 28 Oct 1922

+ 2120 iii. Mary Frances[8] McCartha, b. 29 Dec 1932

+ 2121 iv. Ruby[8] McCartha, b. 3 Jan 1935.

1315. Minnie Marie[7] Mills (Simon P.[6], David Newton[5], Rachel[4], Jacob[3], Adam[2], Michael[1]) was born 21 October 1904 and died 26 August 1967. She married, on 5 Aug 1921, Sebern Fred Stockman,[123] who was born 5 June 1901, and died 20 February 1979. Children:

+ 2122 i. Jenell[8] Stockman, b. 11 Sept 1922

+ 2123 ii. Earlene[8] Stockman, b. 7 Nov 1926.

1317. Allene[7] Mills (Willie Lee[6], James Burr[5], Rachel[4], Jacob[3], Adam[2], Michael[1]) married Samuel Carlton Brissie, Lyman, South Carolina. Two children:

2124 i. Robert Mills[8] Brissie (Dr.), lives Birmingham, AL

2125 ii. George Strom[8] Brissie.

1318. William Leslie[7] Mills (Willie Lee[6], James Burr[5], Rachel[4], Jacob[3], Adam[2], Michael[1]) married, first, Elaine Rumph; second, Janice _____; third, Virginia Bouknight Mills. Children:

2126 i. William Leslie[8] Mills, Jr., died at age three.

2127 ii. Virginia Lee[8] Mills, m. Larry Boland

2128 iii. Leslie Renee[8] Mills, m. Buck Stuck.

1320. James Carlysle[7] Mills (Willie Lee[6], James Burr[5], Rachel[4], Jacob[3], Adam[2], Michael[1]) married Joan Claire Boozer. Children:
 2129 i. William Luther[8] (Billy) Mills, m. Dr. Camille Bethea, lives Conway, SC
 2130 ii. Paula Jo[8] Mills, m. James Stuart, lives Lexington, SC.

1392. Alma Zelma[7] Bedenbaugh (Raymond[6], Francis P.[5], James L.[4], John[3], Adam[2], Michael[1]) was born 8 October 1908 and died 27 July 1985 in Lake City, Florida. She married, first, on 12 December 1926, James Adam Witt, Jr., who was born 12 June 1907 and died 23 June 1948. She married, second, on 28 June 1952, George H. Counce and, third, married, on 20 November 1961, Emmitt Cleveland Fortner, who was born 7 November 1910 and died 21 April 1977. She and her first husband, James Adam Witt, Jr., are buried at Bethel Methodist Church in Columbia County, Florida. Children, born Lake City, Florida:
 2131 i. James William[8] (Billy) Witt, b. 3 Aug 1929, m. 24 Dec 1955, Dorothy
  Jeanette Hunter, b. 7 Oct 1952, Bellville, FL. Children:
   2132 a. Robert Langdon[9] Witt, b. 24 Jan 1957
   2133 b. Paula Diane[9] Witt, b. 17 Apr 1958, m. 1st Mickel Alderman, 2nd,
    Jimmie Reed; children:
     2134 (1) April[10] Alderman, b. 28 Apr 1975, Winter Park, FL
     2135 (2) Shane[10] Reed, b. Feb 1983, Orlando, FL
   2136 c. Donald James[9] Witt, b. 22 Aug 1959 (twin)
   2137 d. Ronald James[9] Witt, b. 22 Aug 1959 (twin), d. 19 Apr 1960
   2138 e. Vickie Lynn[9] Witt, b. 3 Sept 1960, m. 7 Sept 1979, John Andrew
    Shipp, b. 7 Sept 1961; children:
     2139 (1) John Andrew[10] Ship, Jr., b. 5 Jan 1980, Lake City ,FL
     2140 (2) Brian Matthew[10] Shipp, b. 2 Feb 1983, Daytona Bch, FL
 2141 ii. Robert Langdon[8] (Bobby) Witt, b. 3 Feb 1935, d. 10 July 1946.

1393. Robert Frank[7] Bedenbaugh (Raymond[6], Francis P.[5], James L.[4], John[3], Adam[2], Michael[1]) was born 18 February 1911, and married, on 15 December 1939, Mamie Irene Watt, who was born 5 May 1916 at Iva, South Carolina. Children, all born Lake City, Florida:
 2142 i. Jane[8] Bedenbaugh, b. 1 Nov 1947, m. 29 March 1969, Rodney Alex North,
  b. 15 Aug 1946, Children, b. Jacksonville, FL:
   2143 a. Drake Alex[9] North, b. 8 May 1973
   2144 b. Daniel William[9] North, b. 5 Dec 1975
 2145 ii. Susan[8] Bedenbaugh, b. 11 Dec 1947, m. 21 June 1969, Francis Ronald
  Mayer, b. 28 May 1937, Boston, MA, d. 10 Aug 1970, Jacksonville, FL; m.
  2nd 16 July 1972, Ronald Elinoff, b. 3 Nov 1942, Brooklyn, NY; children,
  b. Jacksonville, FL:
   2146 a. Michele Mayer[9] Elinoff, b. 25 Nov 1970
   2147 b. Craig Louis[9] Elinoff, b. 4 July 1974
   2148 c. Anna[9] Elinoff, b. 4 March 1976
   2149 d. Jill[9] Elinoff, b. 30 Sept 1977
 2150 iii. Julian Watt[8] Bedenbaugh, b. 24 Sept 1952, d. 30 Oct 1987 m. 15 March
  1980 Sonya Gail Register, b. 20 Apr 1957; child:
   2151 a. Jennifer[9] Bedenbaugh, b. 7 Jan 1984, Jacksonville, FL
 2152 iv. Ann[8] Bedenbaugh, b. 24 June 1954, m. 22 May 1976, Canova Wendell
  Thrasher, b. 14 Feb 1949, Newton, MS; child:
   2153 a. Jordan Neil[9] Thrasher, b. 21 Oct 1981, Gainesville, FL

2154 v. Robert Frank[8] Bedenbaugh, Jr., b. 20 Jun 1956, m. 24 June 1989, Deborah Lynn Suits.

1394. Susan Lee[7] Bedenbaugh (Raymond[6], Francis P.[5], James L.[4], John[3], Adam[2], Michael[1]) was born 12 February 1913. She married, on 17 August 1930, Earnest Wit, who was born 11 March 1905 and died 26 September 1986, Lake City, Florida. They adopted her sister's grandchild:
2155 i. Robert Langdon[8] Witt, b. 24 Jan 1957, m. 1st Frances Huber, b. 9 May 1959, m. 2nd 15 Nov 1980, Susan Harrington; children, b. Lake City, FL:
2156 a. Bobbi Jo[9] Witt, b. 15 Nov 1976
2157 b. Bronson Eli[9] Witt, b. 13 Feb 1983.

1395. Vera Etta[7] Bedenbaugh (Raymond[6], Francis P.[5], James L.[4], John[3], Adam[2], Michael[1]) was born 1 December 1914, and married, on 23 September 1934, Joseph Cullen Wheeler, who was born 29 November 1909 in Watertown, Florida. Children:
2158 i. Mary Joan[8] Wheeler, b. 1 Nov 1935, Lake City, FL, m. John Terris Hagan, Jr., b. 20 Jan 1937. Children:
2159 a. Robert Wheeler[9] Hagan, b. 5 July 1955, m. 3 Dec 1977 Karen DiGirolamo, b. 14 Aug 1955, Plainfield, NJ; children:
2160 (1) Chadwick Scott[10] Hagan, b. 5 May 1980, Atlanta, GA
2161 (2) Kimberly Brooke[10] Hagan, b. 22 Nov 1984, Roswell, GA
2162 b. John Terris[9] Hagan, III, b. 25 Aug 1963, Atlanta, GA, m. 21 Feb 1987 Allison Gant
2163 ii. William Joseph[8] Wheeler, b. 6 Feb 1937, Jacksonville, FL, m. 12 Aug 1961 Janice Ellen Benning, b. 28 Oct 1939, High Point, NC; children, b. Winter Park, FL:
2164 a. Blaine Allan[9] Wheeler, b. 22 Sept 1963
2165 b. Bradley Joseph[9] Wheeler, b. 22 July 1965
2166 iii. Linda Sue[8] Wheeler, b. 2 May 1947, Lake City, FL, m. 24 Nov 1966, Gerald King Conner, b. 15 Jan 1941; children, b. Jacksonville, FL:
2167 a. Michael Sean[9] Conner, b. 6 Feb 1968
2168 b. Chad Christopher[9] Conner, b. 21 June 1972
2169 c. Jason David[9] Conner, b. 11 Nov 1975.

1396. Elizabeth Armada[7] Bedenbaugh (Raymond[6], Francis P.[5], James L.[4], John[3], Adam[2], Michael[1]) was born 14 May 1917. She married, on 9 September 1937, William Ritch Nettles, who was born 11 September 1918 at Lake Butler, Florida, and died 1 August 1983, Franklin, North Carolina. Child:
2170 i. Delores Ann[8] Nettles, b. 11 Feb 1946, m. 1st 29 Aug 1964 Lawrence Wayne Hines, b. 21 Oct 1945; m. 2nd, 7 March 1980 Gene Wayne Hammonds, b. 21 March 1935; children:
2171 a. Lawrence Joe[9] Hines, b. 8 July 1965, St. Petersburg, FL
2172 b. Shannon Wayne[9] Hines, b. 6 Sept 1968, Gainesville, FL.

1397. Tolula Mary Jane[7] Bedenbaugh (Raymond[6], Francis P.[5], James L.[4], John[3], Adam[2], Michael[1]) was born 12 January 1919, and died 14 November 1941 in Rush County, Indiana. She is buried at Bethel Methodist Church, Columbia County, Florida. She married, on 10 June 1936, John William Avery. Two children, born Lake City, Florida:
2173 i. Jacqueline Delores[8] Avery, b. 25 Sept 1938.
2174 ii. Phyllis Ann[8] Avery, b. March 1940.

THE BEDENBAUGH-BETENBAUGH FAMILY

1398. Mansfield Livingston[7] (M. L.) Bedenbaugh (Raymond[6], Francis P.[5], James L.[4], John[3], Adam[2], Michael[1]) was born 24 October 1920. He married, on 14 February 1942, at Live Oak, Florida, Bessie Pearl Thames, who was born 16 January 1922 at Geneva, Alabama. Four children:
 2175 i. Shirley Pearl[8] Bedenbaugh, b. 1 Aug 1944, Miami Beach, FL, m. 14 Apr 1963, Warren William Hollingsworth, b. 12 Sept 1942, Palatka, FL; children:
  2176 a. Scott Warren[9] Hollingsworth, b. 11 Jan 1966, Lake City, FL
  2177 b. Eric William[9] Hollingsworth, b. 11 Oct 1971, Lake City, FL
 2178 ii. Leler Sue[8] Bedenbaugh, b. 13 Dec 1948, Lake City, FL, m. 27 May 1972, Edward Leo Murphy, III, b. 25 Mar 1949.
 2179 iii. Charlotte Ann[8] Bedenbaugh, b. 17 Feb 1951, Lake City, FL, m. 2 July 1977, Albert Ross Talbird, b. 14 Nov 1951; twin children, b. Titusville, FL:
  2180 a. Ann Elizabeth[9] Talbird, b. 27 May 1983
  2181 b. Jill Ross[9] Talbird, b. 27 May 1983
 2182 iv. Cynthia Angela[8] Bedenbaugh, b. 23 Feb 1953, Lake City, FL, d. 25 Feb 1964.

1399. James Edwin[7] Bedenbaugh (Raymond[6], Francis P.[5], James L.[4], John[3], Adam[2], Michael[1]) was born 15 October 1922. He married, on 14 September 1947, Florene Noegel, who was born 5 January 1924, and died 12 March 1989 at Lake City, Florida. He married, second, 8 June 1990, Jeannette Law, who was born 9 October 1928. Five children, all born Lake City, Florida.
 2183 i. Michael James[8] Bedenbaugh, b. 15 June 1951, m. 9 Aug 1973, Betty Hillhouse, b. 4 Sept 1954, Live Oak, FL; children:
  2184 a. Michael Bradford[9] Bedenbaugh, b. 26 Oct 1974
  2185 b. Steven Brent[9] Bedenbaugh, b. 27 July 1976
 2186 ii. Patricia Florene[8] Bedenbaugh, b. 27 Feb 1952, m. 21 Sept 1975, Gary Maxie Thomas, b. 2 July 1950, Lake City, FL; children:
  2187 a. Patrick Gary[9] Thomas, b. 12 July 1977, Lake City, FL
  2188 b. Raga Terri[9] Thomas, b. 18 Apr 1981, Gainesville, FL
 2189 iii. Ronald Edwin[8] Bedenbaugh, b. & d. 15 Dec 1952
 2190 iv. Randi Carol[8] Bedenbaugh, b. 5 July 1955, d. 6 July 1955
 2191 v. Jacquelyn[8] Bedenbaugh, b. 21 Aug 1956, m. 22 Aug 1975, Stanley Calvin Cox, b. 2 Feb 1956; child:
  2192 a. Brooke Leigh[9] Cox, b. 13 Sept 1981, Lake City, FL.

1400. Annie Louise[7] Bedenbaugh (Raymond[6], Francis P.[5], James L.[4], John[3], Adam[2], Michael[1]) was born 5 October 1924, and married on 16 March 1941, Raymond Leonard Colley, who was born 25 November 1921, Waycross, Georgia. Three children, all born in Lake City, Florida:
 2193 i. Carolyn Jane[8] Colley, b. 11 Jan 1944,m. 1 July 1692, Avery Ray Miller, b. 22 March 1940 McMinn Co., TN; children:
  2194 a. Raymond Bart[9] Miller, b. 4 Dec 1963
  2195 b. James Brett[9] Miller, b. 17 July 1968
 2196 ii. Suzanne[8] Colley, b. 16 Oct 1946, m. 2 Dec 1967 Jim Feamster Melton, b. 3 May 1955, Lakeland, FL; children:
  2197 a. Keri Suzanne[9] Melton, b. 1 Oct 1968, Ft. Benning, GA
  2198 b. Jim Alan[9] Melton, b. 12 June 1972, Gainesville, FL
 2199 iii. Cary Leonard[8] Colley, b. 16 Sept 1952, d. 17 Sept 1952.

THE BEDENBAUGH-BETENBAUGH FAMILY

1401. Lena Jeannette[7] Bedenbaugh (Raymond[6], Francis P.[5], James L.[4], John[3], Adam[2], Michael[1]) was born 1 August 1925, and married, on 4 July 1944, Charles Adolphus Burnsed, who was born 21 May 1922 at Macclenny, Florida. Six children:

2200   i. Charles Edwin[8] Burnsed, b. 5 Aug 1945, Lake City, FL, d. 3 Dec 1969, m. 3 June 1967 Rita Godfrey, b. 30 Nov 1948, Chester, SC; child:
> 2201 a. Kelly Denise[9] Burnsed MacDonald, b. 30 Sept 1968, Jacksonville, FL

2202 ii. Mary Jeannette[8] Burnsed, b. 15 Jan 1947, Lake City, FL, m. 10 Dec 1971, m. 2nd 10 Dec 1971, Ronnie Dean Crawford, b. 25 June 1946; children:
> 2203 a. Lance Eric[9] Crawford, b. 1 Apr 1969
>
> 2204 b. Michael Shane[9] Crawford, b. 22 Oct 1972

2205 iii. Margaret Sue[8] Burnsed, b. 30 July 1949, Lake City, FL, m. 2nd 23 Feb 1985, Ralph Sands, b. 13 Aug 1932, Moniac, GA

2206 iv. Betty Jean[8] Burnsed, b. 29 Apr 1952, Glen St. Mary, FL, m. 21 May 1971, Ronald Edward Taylor, b. 6 Apr 1947; children, b. Jacksonville, FL:
> 2207 a. Keri Ann[9] Taylor, b. 9 Sept 1974
>
> 2208 b. Tracy Jean[9] Taylor, b. 2 Jan 1981

2209   v. Kathy Ann[8] Burnsed, b. 14 July 1953, Lake City, FL, m. 14 June 1974 James Franklin Combs, b. 13 Dec 1954; children, b. Jacksonville, FL:
> 2210 a. Deborah Jeanette[9] Combs, b. 16 Dec 1978
>
> 2211 b. Linday Renee[9] Combs, b. 12 Oct 1988

2212 vi. Judy Lee[8] Burnsed, b. 4 July 1955, Jacksonville, FL, m. 16 Jan 1978, Randall Rhoden, b. 12 Jan 1950; child:
> 2213 a. Brandi Nicole[9] Rhoden, b. 16 May 1989, Jacksonville, FL.

1402. Raymond Henry[7] Bedenbaugh (Raymond[6], Francis P.[5], James L.[4], John[3], Adam[2], Michael[1]) was born 22 September 1928. He married, first, on 3 September 1950, Mary Louise Rhoden, who was born 21 November 1928. He married, second, on 3 April 1864, Josephine Lula Law, who was born 16 April 1932. Two children, born in Lake City, Florida:

2214 i. Raymond Marlin[8] Bedenbaugh, b. 15 Oct 1951, m. 11 March 1978 Pamela Gail Cumbie, b. 17 May 1954; children, b. Jacksonville:
> 2215 a. Shelley Nicole[9] Bedenbaugh, b. 23 Jan 1979
>
> 2216 b. Stacey Amanda[9] Bedenbaugh, b. 3 Feb 1983

2217 ii. Deborah Lynn[8] Bedenbaugh, b. 22 Apr 1967, m. 15 June 1974, Sherwin Trent Bennett, b. 8 Oct 1951; child:
> 2218 a. Adam Trent[9] Bennett, b. 31 Aug 1977, Palatka, FL.

1403. Roy Bishop[7] Bedenbaugh (Raymond[6], Francis P.[5], James L.[4], John[3], Adam[2], Michael[1]) was born 14 November 1930, and married, on 16 September 1956, Esta Mae Taylor, who was born 8 November 1934. Three children, born in Lake City, Florida:

2219   i. Jeanne Marie[8] Bedenbaugh, b. & d. 10 March 1964

2220 ii. David Roy[8] Bedenbaugh, b. 13 June 1965

2221 iii. Steve Bishop[8] Bedenbaugh, b. 16 Apr 1967, m. 16 June 1990, Marilyn Janette McCullers, b. 30 Dec 1964.

1404. Jerry Hugh[7] Bedenbaugh (Raymond[6], Francis P.[5], James L.[4], John[3], Adam[2], Michael[1]) was born 12 May 1933, and married, on 8 September 1957, Toby Faye Stevens, who was born 4 February 1937, Jacksonville, Florida. Three children, all born in Jacksonville:

2222   i. John Hugh[8] Bedenbaugh, b. 19 Jan 1959, m. 20 March 1982 Deborah Lynn Lounsbury, b. 21 Nov 1960, Homestead, FL; children:
      2223 a. Justin Hugh[9] Bedenbaugh, b. 18 Aug 1986, Orange Park, FL
      2224 b. Jennifer Lynn[9] Bedenbaugh, b. 27 June 1988
2225 ii. Jeffrey Artemas[8] Bedenbaugh, b. 19 Aug 1960, m. 23 June 1984 Pamela Dian Griffis, b. 28 Jan 1962, child:
      2226 a. Jeffrey Austen[9] Bedenbaugh, b. 12 Sept 1988
2227 iii. Jed Willoughby[8] Bedenbaugh, b. 18 Jan 1964, m. Lorrilee Gay Gill, b. 3 Nov 1957. child:
      2228 a. Lyndsey Rachel[9] Bedenbaugh, b. 19 July 1989, Palatka, FL.

1406. Armada[7] Hunter (Sallie[6], Francis P.[5], James L.[4], John[3], Adam[2], Michael[1]) was born 23 December 1917. She married, first, on 30 March 1935, Joe William Hagans, who as born 26 March 1911 in Hosford, Florida. She married, second, on 21 July 1943, in Sparta, Wisconsin, Waver Preston Williams, who was born 18 October 1912 in Statenville, Georgia. Five children:
2229   i. Joe William[8] Hagans, b. 7 March 1936, Lake City, FL; m. 4 June 1961, Marjean Joyce, b. 23 Dec 1933, widow of Marvin Bailey McCullough, Jr.; children:
      2230 a. Joe William[9] Hagans, III, b. 7 March 1962, Jacksonville, FL, m. 1 Aug 1980, Marlene Derryl Glisson, b. 26 Apr 1962; children:
         2231 (1) Jessica Leigh[10] Hagans, b. 10 Mar 1987, Gainesville, FL
         2232 (2) Joe William[10] Hagans, IV, b. 17 Jan 1990, Gainesville,FL
      2233 b. Jonathan Edward[9] Hagans, b. 3 May 1965, Tampa, FL
      2234 c. Julie Marabeth[9] Hagans, b. 20 May 1967, Jacksonville, FL
      2235 d. Joel Matthew[9] Hagans, b. 24 Apr 1972, Jacksonville, FL
2236 ii. Jack Dempsey[8] Hagans, b. 26 June 1938, Lake City, FL, m. 13 Sept 1961 Grace Carolyn Neeley, b. 8 March 1938, Appalachia, VA; children:
      2237 a. Jeffrey S.[9] Hagans, b. 9 Nov 1965, Montgomery, AL
      2238 b. Kenneth W.[9] Hagans, b. 16 Dec 1969, Charleston, SC
2239 iii. Jerry Preston[8] Williams, b. 29 Apr 1944, Fayetteville, NC, m. 28 Feb 1970, Diane Cheshier, b. 13 Dec 1905, Anderson, SC; children, b. Lake City, FL:
      2240 a. Phyllis Ann[9] Williams, b. 4 March 1971
      2241 b. Brandy Nichole[9] Williams, b. 6 Jan 1976
      2242 c. Jerry Mikeal[9] Williams, b. 19 Feb 1980
2243 iv. Larry Waver[8] Williams, b. 22 June 1947, Lake City, FL, m. 1st 31 July 1972, Diana L. Anderson, m. 2nd 14 July 1985 Robin Ann Gauthier, b. 3 Jan 1952, Ludlow, MA
2244 v. Alice Armada[8] Williams, b. 8 Oct 1952, Lake City, FL, m. 8 Aug 1970 Mitchell Frederick Sander, b. 14 May 1949, Hamilton, OH; children:
      2245 a. Travis Aaron[9] Sander, b. 17 Apr 1974, Tallahassee, FL
      2246 b. Rebecca Ann[9] Sander, b. 9 May 1979, Tallahassee, FL.

1407. Amon Lyttleton[7] Bedenbaugh, Jr. (Amon[6], Francis P.[5], James L.[4], John[3], Adam[2], Michael[1]) was born 16 January 1919 and died 8 December 1985 in Orlando, Florida. He married, on 11 August 1940, Mary Kathleen Atkinson, b. 5 July 1919. One child:
2247 i. Kirk Lyttleton[8] Bedenbaugh, b. 11 March 1960, m. 1st Shelley Diane Strange; m. 2nd 9 Nov 1985 Tamara Lynne Harmon, b. 1 June 1958, Camden, NJ; child:
      2248 a. Allison Diane[9] Bedenbaugh, b. 12 Feb 1981, Ocala, FL.

1408. Claude Julian[7] Bedenbaugh (Julian[6], Francis P.[5], James L.[4], John[3], Adam[2], Michael[1]) was born 27 November 1915 in Lake City, Florida, and died there 23 February 1973. He married, first, on 10 September 1939, Nell Elizabeth Mears, who was born 6 February 1918. He married, second, on 10 April 1956, at Statenville, Georgia, Marcelle Tyre, who was born 17 November 1936 in Lake City. Children:

2249   i. Sharon Ruth[8] Bedenbaugh, b. 19 Nov 1940, Willacoochee, GA, m. 1st 24 Aug 1957, Robert Lee Wester, Jr., b. 17 Feb 1938; m. 2nd 12 Jun 1971, Dewey Wayne Wester; children, b. Jacksonville, FL:
2250 a. Daniel Lee[9] Wester, b. 11 July 1959, d. 3 Apr 1987
2251 b. Timothy Scott[9] Wester, b. 17 Nov 1964 m. Nicole Liester
2252 ii. Claudia Renee[8] Bedenbaugh, b. 8 March 1957, Lake City, FL, m. 1st 10 March 1974, Deryck Laverne Pyles, b. 28 Dec 1952; m. 2nd Terry Lee Miller, b. 27 Dec 1959
2253 a. Deryck Laverne[9] Pyles, Jr. b 21 Feb 1977, Thomasville, GA
2254 b. Shawn Lee[9] Miller, b. 27 May 1989, Jacksonville, FL
2255 iii. Alvin Lewis[8] Bedenbaugh, b. 1 Feb 1959, Lake City, FL, m. 14 Sept 1979, Teri Tuggle, b. 22 March 1961, Lake City, FL; children:
2256 a. Daran Cole[9] Bedenbaugh, b. 22 Jan 1984, b. Gainesville, FL
2257 b. Gabriel Lewis[9] Bedenbaugh, b. 13 Aug 1986, b. Gainesville, FL
2258 c. Mallory[9] Bedenbaugh, b. 23 Dec 1988, b. Gainesville, FL
2259 iv. Ruby LaDell[8] Bedenbaugh, b. 13 Sept 1965.

1409. Minnie Lee[7] Bedenbaugh (Julian[6], Francis P.[5], James L.[4], John[3], Adam[2], Michael[1]) was born 23 April 1917 in Lake City, Florida. She married, first, on 12 September 1937, in Savannah, Georgia, Curtis Henley Woodcock, of Statesboro, Georgia, who was born 26 December 1906. She married, third, in 1962, Joe D. Buck. Children:

2260   i. Curtis Wayne[8] Woodcock, b. 5 Aug 1938, m. Deanna Miller
2261 ii. Nina Lee[8] Woodcock, b. 16 Sept 1940, Lake City, FL, d. 3 Aug 1985, Mobile, AL, m. 24 Apr 1976 Bryan Quarles
2262 iii. Janet[8] Woodcock, b. 14 Oct 1944, Savannah, GA.

1410. Earl George[7] Bedenbaugh (Julian[6], Francis P.[5], James L.[4], John[3], Adam[2], Michael[1]) was born 29 October 1919 in Lake City, Florida. He married, first, on 15 October 1941, Charity Mills Bullard, who was born 12 February 1923 in White Springs, Florida. He married, second, on 5 November 1949, at Garden City, New York, Frances Soffie Marks, who was born 15 May 1918 in Passaic, New Jersey. Child:

2263 i. Mary Elaine[8] Bedenbaugh, b. 15 Nov 1942, Lake City, FL., m. 1st 17 Sept 1960 Robert Dion Keen, b. 7 Aug 1939; m. 2nd 8 Oct 1976, Charles Edward Willis, b. 15 Feb 1942; children, b. Lake City, FL:
2265 a. Charity Alisa[9] Keen, b. 31 Oct 1961, m. 1st 18 Apr 1978 Wyndell Mathis; m. 2nd 1 May 1984, Palmer Gene Smith, Jr., b. 20 Mar 1958; children:
2265 (1) Charity Michelle[10] Mathis, b. 19 June 1980, Jasper, FL
2266 (2) Addie Elaine[10] Smith, b. 17 Feb 1985, Jasper, FL
2267 (3) Marsha Diane[10] Smith, b. 8 Feb 1987, Jasper, FL
2268 b. Robert Dion[9] Keen, Jr., b. 10 Oct 1962.

1411. Catherine Elizabeth[7] Bedenbaugh (Julian[6], Francis P.[5], James L.[4], John[3], Adam[2], Michael[1]) was born 5 March 1922 in Lake City, Florida. She married, on 17

March 1945, in Hinesville, Georgia, Dupree Lavanda Moody, who was born 11 December 1920 in Hinesville. Children:

2269   i. Donald George[8] Moody, b. 9 Dec 1945, Savannah, GA
2270 ii. Julian Mark[8] Moody, b. 19 May 1947, Lake City, FL
2271 iii. Alan Dupree[8] Moody, b. 22 Apr 1951, Lake City, FL
2272 iv. Kathryn Elizabeth[8] Moody, b. 4 Dec 1952, Lake City, FL, m. 29 Nov 1985 William Lewis
2273   v. Teresa Jayne[8] Moody, b. 15 Nov 1970, Lake City, FL, m. 8 Dec 1989 James Anthony Rountree.

1412. Arthur Nelson[7] Bedenbaugh (Frank[6], Francis P.[5], James L.[4], John[3], Adam[2], Michael[1]) was born 3 August 1922 in Lake City, Florida. He married, first, on 16 August 1947, in Valdosta, Georgia, Helen Louise Frier, who was born 30 December 1928 in Jacksonville, Florida. He married, second, on 2 October 1953, Janie Louise Raulerson, who was born 1 May 1935 in Lake City. Children:

2274   i. Elleene Ann[8] Bedenbaugh, b. 28 May 1948, Jacksonville, FL, m. 1st 19 Dec 1967, James Franklin Hilton,; m. 2nd 1 May 1971, Michael Francis Wilson; children, b. Jacksonville, FL:
     2275 a. James Franklin[9] Hilton, b. 14 July 1968
     2276 b. Michael Aaron[9] Wilson, b. 28 Sept 1971
     2277 c. Selina Nicole[9] Wilson, b. 20 Sept 1972
2278 ii. Arthur Nelson[8] Bedenbaugh, Jr., b. 17 Oct 1954, Lake City, FL, m. 22 Jan 1979, Barbara Diann Durham, b. 25 Nov 1960, Las Vegas, NV; children:
     2279 a. Arthur Nelson[9] Bedenbaugh, III, b. 6 Sept 1979 Lake City, FL
     2280 b. Daniel Travis[9] Bedenbaugh, b. 13 March 1982
2281 iii. Gregory Alvin[8] Bedenbaugh, b. 23 Oct 1955, Lake City, FL, m. 18 Dec 1972, Judith Ann Milton, b. 12 Oct 1956; children, b. Lake City:
     2282 a. Gregory Adam[9] Bedenbaugh, b. 16 Nov 1975
     2283 b. Brooke[9] Bedenbaugh, b. 12 March 1978
     2284 c. Matthew Clay[9] Bedenbaugh, b. 20 Dec 1983
2285 iv. Kevin Lyttleton[8] Bedenbaugh, b. 19 Feb 1957, Lake City, FL, m. 1st 8 Sept 1978 Marcia Lynn Deas, b. 14 Oct 1959; m. 2nd 25 Aug 1989, Marla Belinda Hall; children, all b. Lake City:
     2286 a. Brandi Lynn[9] Bedenbaugh, b. 10 July 1979
     2287 b. Kevin Lyttleton[9] Bedenbaugh, Jr., b. 17 Apr 1981
     2288 c. Halie Ann[9] Bedenbaugh, b. 14 Jan 1987
     2289 d. Kaleb Wilson[9] Bedenbaugh, b. 21 Oct 1990
2290   v. Terri Louise[8] Bedenbaugh, b. 8 July 1959, Jacksonville, FL, m. 1st Robert Leslie Lee, b. 26 Aug 1958; m. 2nd 12 May 1990, Richard Allen Rose, b. 2 May 1964; children:
     2291 a. Destiny Louise[9] Lee, b. 12 June 1977 Gainesville, FL
     2292 b. Tabatha Leslie[9] Lee, b. 23 Oct 1980, Lake City, FL
2293 vi. Cheryl Emma[8] Bedenbaugh, b. 3 Nov 1960, Jacksonville, FL
2294 vii. Paul Edward[8] Bedenbaugh, b. 24 Dec 1962, Lake City, FL, m. 2 Oct 1986, Pamela Alynn Martin, b. 10 July 1963; children:
     2295 a. Briham Edward[9] Bedenbaugh, b. 8 Feb 1989, Gainesville, FL
     2296 b. Dylan Ezra[9] Bedenbaugh, b. 1 Aug 1990, Lake City, FL.

1413. Frank Pickens[7] Bedenbaugh (Frank[6], Francis P.[5], James L.[4], John[3], Adam[2], Michael[1]) was born 11 May 1924 in Lake City, Florida. He married, on 8 April 1950, Lillian Eunice Brown, who was born 24 January 1923, in Archer, Florida. Child:

THE BEDENBAUGH-BETENBAUGH FAMILY

2297 i. Frank Pickens[8] Bedenbaugh, Jr., b. 15 July 1951, Lake City. FL, m. Toleoa Boland, b. 17 Jan 1948 (div).

1414. Joyce[7] Bedenbaugh (Frank[6], Francis P.[5], James L.[4], John[3], Adam[2], Michael[1]) was born 2 April 1930 in Jacksonville, Florida. She married, on 4 June 1952, in Salt Lake City, Utah, Louis Blaine Vorwaller, who was born 17 January 1932, in Tooele, Utah. Joyce B. Vorwaller has compiled a volume on the descendants of Frank P. and Catha Lee Bedenbaugh from which much of this information has been supplied. Children:

  2298 i. Gaylon Blaine[8] Vorwaller, b. 6 Jan 1954, Provo, UT, m. 30 July 1976, Madonna Lynn Clark, b. 21 nov 1954, Jacksonville, FL; Children:

      2299 a. Marcus Gaylon[9] Vorwaller, b. 5 June 1977, Provo, UT

      2300 b. Michael Blaine[9] Vorwaller, 16 July 1978, Provo, UT

      2301 c. Elizabeth Ann[9] Vorwaller, b. 26 Dec 1980, Jacksonville, FL

      2302 d. Caleb Clark[9] Vorwaller, b. 2 Feb 1982, Jacksonville, FL

      2303 e. Rebekah Lynn[9] Vorwaller, b. 18 Apr 1985, Salt Lake City, UT

      2304 f. Benjamin Louise[9] Vorwaller, b. 6 May 1987, Jacksonville, FL

      2305 g. Ruth Emily Vorwaller, b. 19 Dec 1989, Jacksonville, FL

  2306 ii. Dana[8] Vorwaller, b.9 March 1957, Udine, Italy, m. 20 May 1976, Brent Richins Holladay, b. 17 July 1754, Denver, CO; children:

      2307 a. Nathan Brent[9] Holladay, b. 30 March 1977, Provo, UT

      2308 b. Seth Richins[9] Holladay, b. 18 Sept 1978, Provo, UT

      2309 c. Sara Lyn[9] Holladay, b. 9 Nov 1981, Orlando, FL

      2310 d. Daniel Thomson[9] Holladay, b. 12 Aug 1984, Orlando, FL

      2311 e. David Benjamin[9] Holladay, b. 12 Oct 1986, Orlando, FL

      2312 f. Karie LaVon[9] Holladay, b. 15 July 1990, Altamonte Springs, FL

  2313 iii. Rhonda[8] Vorwaller, b. 27 July 1958, Jacksonville, FL, m. 28 Sept 198, Alan George Williamson, b. Tooele, UT; children, all born Salt Lake City:

      2314 a. Paul Alan[9] Williamson, b. 22 July 1979

      2315 b. Sarah[9] Williamson, b. 16 June 1981

      2316 c. Elaine[9] Williamson, b. 2 Feb 1984

      2317 d. Emalie[9] Williamson, b. 8 Jan 1987

      2318 e. Matthew Louis[9] Williamson, 23 March 1990

  2319 iv. Mark Louis[8] Vorwaller, b. 3 Sept 1959, Jacksonville, FL, m. 23 Aug 1984, Kristi Kay Davis, b. 14 Oct 1962, Jacksonville, FL; children:

      2320 a. Mark Ryan[9] Vorwaller, b. 28 Dec 1985, Gainesville, FL

      2321 b. Leslie Ann[9] Vorwaller, b. 17 July 1990, Melbourne, FL

  2322 v. Carmen[8] Vorwaller, b. 9 Oct 1962, Jacksonville, FL, m. 22 July 1989, Mark Louis Jones, b. 5 June 1958, Jacksonville, FL; child:

      2323 a. Catherine[9] Jones, b. 13 May 1990, Orlando, FL.

1643. Katherine Jane[8] Shealy (Ethan[7], Nancy[6], Hawkins[5], Simeon[4], Henry[3], Adam[2], Michael[1]) was born 31 November 1931 and married Berlie Edwin Wicker, who was born 13 March 1927. Children:
  2324   i. Anna[9] Wicker, b. 14 Jan 1951, m. William Lee Sease, b. 4 Aug 1950; children:
      2325 a. Naomi Shealy[9] Sease, b. 13 Mar 1979
      2326 b. Arden Cathey[9] Sease, b. 17 Apr 1985
  2327   ii. Emmett Edwin[9] Wicker, b. 6 Mar 1955
  2328 iii. Kevin Shealy[9] Wicker, b. 31 July 1960, m. Sallie Diane Dorrah, b. 6 June 1960; children:
      2329 a. Benjamin Lee[10] Wicker, b. 25 Nov 1986
      2330 b. Rebecca Grace[10] Wicker, b. 1 May 1990
  2331   iv. Edwina[9] Wicker, b. 5 Apr 1962.

1644. Keith Wayne[8] Shealy (Ethan[7], Nancy[6], Hawkins[5], Simeon[4], Henry[3], Adam[2], Michael[1]) was born 28 April 1935 and married Patsy Ruth King, who was born 29 January 1934. Children:
  2332   i. Denise[9] Shealy, b. 16 Sept 1958, m. Toy Randal Lybrand, b. 14 Oct 1954; children:
      2333 a. Casey Shealy[10] Lybrand, b. 5 Dec 1979
      2334 b. Erika Dawn[10] Lybrand, b. 1 Sept 1981
  2335   ii. Dalton Wayne[9] Shealy, b. 16 Sept 1959, m. Kathy Jo Riley, b. 3 Oct 1963; children:
      2336 a. Nicholas Dalton[10] Shealy, b. 4 July 1983
      2337 b. Kristopher Neal[10] Shealy, b. 22 May 1986
  2338 iii. Anthony Keith[9] Shealy, b. 21 Apr 1970, m. Tina Michelle Leitsey, b. 14 Feb 1967; children:
      2339 a. Ashley Theodore[10] Mendenhall, b. 2 May 1986
      2340 b. Anthony Bryant[10] Shealy, b. 28 Apr 1988
      2341 c. Christen Michelle[10] Shealy, b. 26 July 1989.

1645. Ethan Wise[8] Shealy (Ethan[7], Nancy[6], Hawkins[5], Simeon[4], Henry[3], Adam[2], Michael[1]) was born 6 July 1938 and married Zeita Marie Cannon, who was born 7 September 1938. Children:
  2342   i. Janice Marie[9] Shealy, b. 4 Oct 1964, m. Robert Allen Wells, b. 20 Mar 1965
  2343   ii. Diane Elizabeth[9] Shealy, b. 29 Jan 1969, m. Timothy Hugh Howard, b. 8 June 1962; child:
      2344 a. Joshua Gracen[10] Howard, b. 19 March 1995
  2345 iii. Laura Wise[9] Shealy, b. 16 June 1975.

1646. Ina Sandra[8] Shealy (Ethan[7], Nancy[6], Hawkins[5], Simeon[4], Henry[3], Adam[2], Michael[1]) was born 13 July 1944 and married Arnold Moore Gilliam, who was born 1 September 1944. Children:
  2346   i. Ina Celeste[9] Gilliam, b. 9 Nov 1966, m. Bradley Morgan
  2347   ii. Sanford Moore[9] Gilliam, b. 20 Feb 1968, m. Lauren Ann Collins, b. 22 Jan 1967 (div); child:
      2348 a. Lacee Devin[10] Gilliam, b. 23 May 1987
  2349 iii. Alyce[9] Gilliam, b. 29 June 1973, m. John Wayne McIver.

THE BEDENBAUGH-BETENBAUGH FAMILY

2029. Roscoe O'Neal[8] Bundrick (Edna Geneva[7], Benjamin[6], Wilson[5], Mathias Hare[4], Jacob[3], Adam[2], Michael[1]) was born 26 December 1916 and died 12 February 1987 and is buried at Little River Dominick Presbyterian Church in Newberry County, South Carolina.. He married, on 24 December 1937, Halen Mables Moates, who was born 9 October 1917. Children:

2350　i. Sylvia O'Nelia[9] Bundrick, b. 28 Feb 1941, m. 2 Dec 1962 Jacob Dewey Epting, Jr. Children:
　　　2351 a. Jacob Dewey[10] Epting, III, b. 27 May 1964
　　　2352 b. Rodney O'Nelia[10] Epting, b. 23 Feb 1966
　　　2353 c. Timothy James[10] Epting, b. 13 May 1969
　　　2354 d. Kimberly Tina Lilie[10] Epting, b. 1 July 1976
2355 ii. Rebecca Lee[9] Bundrick, b. 17 March 1943, m. James L. Stewart. Child:
　　　2356 a. Sandy Michele[10] Stewart, b. 10 Oct 1967
2357 iii. Jerome O'Neal[9] Bundrick, b. 15 July 1953, m. 19 Jan 1973 Lana Sue Stephens. b. 4 June 1956. Children:
　　　2358 a. Jason Jerome[10] Bundrick, b. 4 Aug 1974, Greenwood, SC
　　　2359 b. Brantlee Suzanne[10] Bundrick, b. 16 May 1980, Greenville, SC
2360 iv. Joanne Helen[9] Bundrick, b. 15 Oct 1954, m. 11 May 1975, John Aubrey Smitherman, Jr., b. 18 May 1954. Child:
　　　2361 a. Ruthston[10] Smitherman, b. 11 July 1978, Greenwood, SC.

2030. Geneva Ruth[8] Bundrick (Edna Geneva[7], Benjamin[6], Wilson[5], Mathias Hare[4], Jacob[3], Adam[2], Michael[1]) was born 28 May 1919 in Newberry County, South Carolina, and married, on 21 December 1935, James Norman Floyd, who was born 8 November 1913. Children:

2362　i. Gene Gordon[9] Floyd
2363　ii. Elvin[9] Floyd
2364 iii. Leonard[9] Floyd
2365 iv. Collette[9] Floyd.

2031. Robert Floyd[8] Bundrick (Edna Geneva[7], Benjamin[6], Wilson[5], Mathias Hare[4], Jacob[3], Adam[2], Michael[1]) was born 8 July 1922 in Newberry County, South Carolina, and died 8 January 1986. He married, on 23 November 1946, Velma Emma Louise[8] Bedenbaugh (Leon[7] Bedenbaugh, Ernest W.[6], Jacob C.[5], John Adam[4], Adam Jr.[3], Adam[2], Michael[1]) who was born 28 June 1929 in Lexington County, South Carolina. Three children.

2366　i. Gwendol Floyd[9] Bundrick, b. 28 Jan 1950, Richland Co., SC, m. 15 Oct 1977, Ruth M. Price, b. 9 Aug 1955, live Clinton, SC (1995); children:
　　　2367 a. Ashley Elizabeth[10] Bundrick, b. 9 March 1981
　　　2368 b. Floyd Blane[10] Bundrick, b. 6 July 1988
2369 ii. Derry Julian[9] Bundrick, b. 5 June 1951, m. 12 Feb 1971 Melissa Ann Darnell, b. 14 Jan 1954; child:
　　　2370 a. Jonathan Isaac[10] Bundrick, b. 31 May 1980, Greenwood, SC
2371 iii. Robert Dwight[9] Bundrick, b. 6 Sept 1952, m. 27 June 1981 Jennifer A. Wetherell; child:
　　　2372 a. Matthew Jason[10] Bundrick, b. 21 Sept 1983
　　　2373 b. Brittany Ann[10] Bundrick, b. 16 Feb 1989.

2032. Irene[8] Bundrick (Edna Geneva[7], Benjamin[6], Wilson[5], Mathias Hare[4], Jacob[3], Adam[2], Michael[1]) was born 16 March 1925 and married Isom Demerest Ward, Jr., who was born 11 April 1920. They live in West Columbia, South Carolina (1995). Children, all born in Richland County, South Carolina:

2374   i. Michael Demerest[9] Ward, b. 7 Oct 1948, m. 22 Aug 1970 Lorraine
       Hollowell, b. 29 Sept 1950; child:
          2375 a. Jeremy D.[10] Ward, b. 23 Oct 1979
2376 ii. Carol Marie[9] Ward, b. 6 March 1952
2377 iii. Janice Irene[9] Ward, b. 8 Nov 1955.

2033. Pauline[8] Bundrick (Edna Geneva[7], Benjamin[6], Wilson[5], Mathias Hare[4], Jacob[3],
Adam[2], Michael[1]) was born 16 March 1925, and married in Lexington County, South
Carolina, Earl Watson Burkett, who was born 15 April 1917. Children:
2378   i. Patricia Ann[9] Burkett, b. 16 Aug 1947
2379 ii. Anthony Earl[9] Burkett, b. 14 Jan 1950
2380 iii. John Frederick[9] Burkett, b. 11 Aug 1951.

2034. Daniel Luther[8] Bundrick (Edna Geneva[7], Benjamin[6], Wilson[5], Mathias Hare[4],
Jacob[3], Adam[2], Michael[1]) was born 24 July 1927, and married in Woodruff, South
Carolina, Mozelle Taylor, who was born 21 September 1928. Two children:
2381   i. Martha[9] Bundrick, b. 16 Dec 1948, Newberry Co., SC,, m. George
       Franklin Lemond, b. 23 Jan 1946; two children:
          2382 a. George Franklin[10] Lemond, Jr., b. 25 Aug 1974
          2383 b. Brian Daniel[10] Lemond, b. 27 Aug 1977
2384 ii. Mary Edna[9] Bundrick b. 16 June 1950, Joanna, SC.

2035. Earl Mack[8] Bundrick (Edna Geneva[7], Benjamin[6], Wilson[5], Mathias Hare[4],
Jacob[3], Adam[2], Michael[1]) was born 20 August 1929, and married, in Lexington
County, South Carolina, on 20 November 1947, Mary Lou Oswald, who was born
30 March 1929, and died 1 September 1962. Children:
2385   i. Danny Earl[9] Bundrick, b. 11 March 1949, m. 15 July 1968 Linda Ann Shull,
       b. 26 May 1947, d. 17 Apr 1984. Children:
          2386 a. Kevin O'Neal[10] Bundrick, b. 2 Sept 1969
          2387 b. Dennis Patrick[10] Bundrick, b. 24 Sept 1976
2388 ii. Karen Dianne[9] Bundrick, b. 16 May 1951, m. in Brevard, NC, 26 Apr 1969,
       William Dewey Holden, b. 14 Oct 1947.

2036. Dorothy Mae[8] Bundrick (Edna Geneva[7], Benjamin[6], Wilson[5], Mathias Hare[4],
Jacob[3], Adam[2], Michael[1]) was born 10 February 1932, and died 13 August 1963,
buried in Newberry Memorial Gardens. She married, on 12 May 1949, William Boyd
Morris. Two children:
2389   i. Debbie[9] Morris
2390 ii. Neal[9] Morris.

2037. John Henry[8] Bundrick (Edna Geneva[7], Benjamin[6], Wilson[5], Mathias Hare[4],
Jacob[3], Adam[2], Michael[1]) was born 18 February 1940 at Cross Anchor, South
Carolina. He married in Gilbert, South Carolina, on 4 September 1960, Sara
Hampton Keisler. Children:
2391   i. John Daniel[9] Bundrick, b. 29 May 1962
2392 ii. David Hampton[9] Bundrick, b. 7 March 1964
2393 iii. Sara Denise[9] Bundrick, b. 14 Apr 1966.

2119. John Clarence[8] McCartha (Mattie[7], Simon P.[6], David Newton[5], Rachel[4],
Jacob[3], Adam[2], Michael[1]) was born 28 October 1922. He married, first, Helen
Doneria Bledsoe, who was born 8 May 1929. (She married, second, George Luther

Carver, Sr., who was born 21 December 1929.) He married, second, Lucy Bradley, who was born 10 January 1927. Children:
  2394 i. James Bernard[9] McCartha, b. 18 Aug 1945, m. Edith Whiteman
  2395 ii. Gerald Louis[9] Carver (was born a McCartha but adopted by his step-father), b. 6 Oct 1946, m. Carolyn Sue Cox; child:
      2396 a. Diana C.[10] Carver, b. 8 Nov 1969
  2397 iii. Brenda Diane[9] McCartha, b. 5 Aug 1946, m. 9 Sept 1986 Olin Coppock, b. 16 June 1936; children:
      2398 a. Christopher Olin[10] Coppock, b. 29 March 1971
      2399 b. Chad Patrick[10] Coppock. b. 28 Apr 1974
  2400 iv. Clarence Wayne[9] McCartha, b. 18 Sept 1948
  2401 v. Randy Lee[9] McCartha, b. 20 Aug 1956, m. Joyce Hutchinson; child:
      2402 a. Angelina Elisha[10] McCartha.

2120. Martha Frances[8] McCartha (Mattie[7], Simon P.[6], David Newton[5], Rachel[4], Jacob[3], Adam[2], Michael[1]) was born 29 December 1932 and married Dan Eugene Hembree, who was born 21 May 1930. Children:
  2403 i. Judy Ann[9] Hembree, b. 8 June 1955, m. Charles Holwell, Jr.; children:
      2404 a. Adria[10] Holwell, b. 22 July 1977
      2405 b. Bryan[10] Holwell, b. 15 Oct 1978
      2406 c. Christa[10] Holwell, b. 27 Feb 1980
  2407 ii. Gail[9] Hembree, b. 20 Dec 1957, m. Richard Moose; children:
      2408 a. Melissa[10] Moose, b. 26 March 1982
      2409 b. Alicia[10] Moose, b. 3 Nov 1983
      2410 c. Brandon[10] Moose, b. 17 May 1988
      2411 d. Kaitlin[10] Moose, b. 27 Feb 1990.

2121. Ruby[8] McCartha (Mattie[7], Simon P.[6], David Newton[5], Rachel[4], Jacob[3], Adam[2], Michael[1]) was born 3 January 1935 and married Alton Lake, who was born 18 October 1930. Children:
  2412 i. Janie Marie[9] Lake, b. 6 May 1957, m. Benny Hallman, b. 29 June 1950; children:
      2413 a. Deena Marie[10] Hallman, b. 27 May 1981
      2414 b. Kenneth Everett[10] Hallman, b. 13 Dec 1982
  2415 ii. Tony Eugene[9] Lake, b. 6 June 1961, m. Doris Hipp, b. 19 May 1963; child:
      2416 a. Courtney Alison[10] Lake, b. 23 June 1990
  2417 iii. Kevin Dean[9] Lake, b. 18 Nov 1961, m. Connie Nichols, b. 27 July 1961; child:
      2418 a. Brent Daniel[10] Lake, b. 17 Oct 1991.

2122. Jenell[8] Stockman (Minnie[7], Simon P.[6], David Newton[5], Rachel[4], Jacob[3], Adam[2], Michael[1]) was born 11 September 1922 and married James William King who was born 21 November 1927. Children:
  2419 i. Stephen E.[9] King, m. Lynda Lynch; child:
      2420 a. Stephen Michael[10] King, b. 21 Mar 1972
  2421 ii. James Ray[9] King, b. 27 June 1945, m. Ann Smith, b. 22 May 1948
  2422 iii. Joyce Ann[9] King, b. 22 May 1948
  2423 iv. Fred William[9] King, b. 5 March 1951, m. 21 May 1977 Debbie Wise
  2424 v. Michael Gene[9] King, b. 25 Apr 1954.

2123. Earlene[8] Stockman (Minnie[7], Simon P.[6], David Newton[5], Rachel[4], Jacob[3], Adam[2], Michael[1]) was born 7 November 1926 and married Bertrum Cotney, who was born 30 August 1920. Children:

  2425   i. Retha Cheryl[9] Cotney, b. 5 Aug 1946, m. Clifton Samuel Baker, Jr.

  2426 ii. Kathy Lynn[9] Cotney, b. 1 Dec 1949, m. Frank James Rish, b. 28 June 1950; children:

      2427 a. Frank James[10] Rish, Jr., b. 10 Aug 1974

      2428 b. Michael Paul[10] Rish, b. 16 Dec 1978

  2429 iii. Sandra Jane[9] Cotney, b. 28 July 1953, m. 1st Albert Boland, b. 11 March 1955; m. 2nd Tommy J. Worley, b. 20 Feb 1950; children:

      2430 a. Stacy Allen[10] Boland, b. 31 Dec 1973

      2431 b. Regina Marie[10] Boland, b. 1 Oct 1977

  2432 iv. Charles Lanier[9] Cotney, b. 14 June 1959, m. 21 Dec 1992 Wendy Jones.

THE BEDENBAUGH-BETENBAUGH FAMILY

NOTES AND REFERENCES

1. "Records of St. Luke's Lutheran Church Newberry County, South Carolina," *The South Carolina Magazine of Ancestral Research*, II (Spring, 1974), p. 59.

2. *Heads of Families First Census of the United States 1790 South Carolina*, p. 79

3. John Belton O'Neall and John A. Chapman, *The Annals of Newberry* (Baltimore: Genealogical Publishing Co., reprinted 1974), pp. 636-637. This account states that Adam Bedenbaugh married a Miss Wertz. The will of Adam Bedenbaugh names wife Barbary, and she is referred to in the records of St. Luke's Lutheran Church.

4. Audited Account #7526, original at South Carolina Archives.

5. State Land Grants, Vol. 26, p. 152.

6. Lexington County Deed Book S, pp. 197-198, microfilm at South Carolina Archives.

7. Newberry County Deed Book D, p. 555, original in Office of Clerk of Court, Newberry County Court House, Newberry, South Carolina.

8. The deed was dated 4 May 1816 and is recorded in Newberry County Deed Book M, page 433.

9. Newberry County Estates, Box 36, Package 1.

10. John Belton O'Neall and John A. Chapman, *The Annals of Newberry* (Baltimore: Genealogical Publishing Company, reprinted 1974).

11. Newberry County, S. C., Guardianships, Box 23 package 16, original in the Office of the Probate Judge, Newberry County Court House.

12. "Records of St. Luke's Lutheran Church," *Ibid.*, p. 59. Some relationships are stated in these church records. Others of these children are proved from 1850 U. S. Census, Newberry District, p. 208.

13. Obituary notice in the *Lutheran Visitor*, issue of 24 March 1880, microfilm at the Lineberger Library, Lutheran Southern Theological Seminary, Columbia, South Carolina.

14. Newberry County Estates, Box 48, Package 1.

15. Newberry County Estates, Box 62, package 20.

16. Newberry Equity Bills, 1858 #20, original at SC Archives, gives the names of the legatees and a division of the land holdings.

17. This marker was seen by the writer on 10 June 1995, guided by Mr. Ira Bedenbaugh. There are no other marked graves in the cemetery, which is on property on Mother Goose Road, off Highway 391 near Prosperity, owned by Mr. James Earl Morris. It is probably the site where Adam Bedenbaugh, Sr., is also buried.

THE BEDENBAUGH-BETENBAUGH FAMILY

18. Brent H. Holcomb, *Memorialized Records of Lexington District, S. C. 1814-1825* (Easley, S. C.: Southern Historical Press), p. 74.

19. Newberry County Estates, Box 83, Package 1.

20. Newberry County Estates, Box 113, Package 2.

21. Newberry County Estates, Box 29, Estate 22, original in the Office of Probate Judge, Newberry County Court House, Newberry, South Carolina.

22. Office of Chancery Court, Inventory Book 17, p. 398.

23. Office of Chancery Court, packet #2362.

24. Data on the descendants of Daniel G. and Elizabeth (Bedenbaugh) Conwill was supplied to the writer by Dr. David E. Conwill.

25. 1850 U. S. Census, Monroe County, Alabama, page 114; 1860 U. S. Census, Monroe County, Mississippi, Western Division, page 2.

26. Death dates of Jacob and Rebecca Bedenbaugh recorded in family Bible of their son Levi Bedenbaugh, which was in possession of Mrs. Susie B. Sullivan, Senioa, Georgia, in 1966. The birth date of Levi Bedenbaugh is also from this source.

27. Newberry Probate, Box 121, Estate #1, original in Office of Probate Judge, Newberry County Court House.

28. Newberry County Estates, Box 150, Estate #2, original in Newberry County Court House.

29. John Belton O'Neall and John A. Chapman, *The Annals of Newberry*.

30. 1850 U. S. Census, Newberry District, South Carolina, p. 207.

31. Newberry County Estates, Box 76, Estate 2.

32. Newberry County Estates, Box 55, Package 20, original in the Office of Probate Judge, Newberry County Court House, Newberry, South Carolina.

33. 1850 U. S. Census, Newberry District, South Carolina, page 205; 1860 U. S. Census, Newberry District, page 221.

34. Carlee McClendon, *Edgefield Marriage Records*, page 94.

35. Much of the information on these descendants is from *The Boozer Family of South Carolina* by Mary E. Boozer.

36. Newberry County Estates, Box 76, Package 2.

37. Typescript of the diary of Thaddeus S. Boinest, 1851-1875, copy in South Caroliniana Library.

38. Chapman and O'Neal, *Annals of Newberry*, pp. 636-637.

39. Bethlehem Lutheran Church records.

40. An obituary notice for Caty Bedenbaugh is found in *Lutheran Church Visitor*, issue of 26 January 1905, page 20.

41. St. Luke's Lutheran Church Records, her name is indicated as M. P. J. Bedenbaugh, perhaps Mary Permelia (instead of Amelia) J.

42. Marriage notice in *Lutheran Visitor*, issue of 22 March 1888.

43. Death Certificate of Thompson L. Morris, 1920 #5979, DHEC microfilm at SC Archives.

44. Newberry County Estates, Box 397, Package 124.

45. Additional data on these children from *Our Wicker Family* by Eleanor Clyburn Wicker (1993), pages 80-81.

46. The obituary notice of John Adam Bedenbaugh is found in the *Lutheran Church Visitor*, issue of 2 March 1905, page 16.

47. This surname is usually spelled Buzhardt today, but it was spelled and pronounced Buzzard in the nineteenth century.

48. Death Certificate of Jacob C. Singley, 1931 #13760, DHEC microfilm at SC Archives.

49. Marriage date from Bible in possession of his granddaughter, Miss Eleanor Bedenbaugh, Prosperity, SC.

50. For a detailed biographical sketch, see D. D. Wallace, *History of South Carolina*, Volume IV, page 933.

51. The estates papers of Michael and Magdalene Bedenbaugh name Cutter grandchild still living.

52. 1860 Census, Newberry District, South Carolina, household number 150.

53. Confederate Pension Application of Nancy Caroline Bedenbaugh, widow of Frank S. Bedenbaugh, #9867, at South Carolina Archives.

54. Obituary notice in the *Lutheran Visitor*, issue of 14 January 1880, microfilm at Lineberger Library, Lutheran Theological Southern Seminary, Columbia, South Carolina.

55. Brent H. Holcomb, *Marriage and Death Notices from the Lutheran Observer 1831-1861 and the Southern Lutheran 1861-1865*, page 231.

56. 1850 Federal Census, Mortality Schedule, Edgefield District, SC, page 19, SC Archives microfilm AD281.

57. Estates papers of Mathias H. Bedenbaugh, Edgefield County Estates, Box 63, Package 2593.

58. Brent H. Holcomb, *Death and Obituary Notices from the Southern Christian Advocate, 1867-1878*, page 210.

59. Brent H. Holcomb, *Marriage and Death Notices from Baptist newspapers of South Carolina*, p. 62, notice in *Southern Baptist*, issue of 22 July 1856.

60. St. Luke's Lutheran Church Records indicate his date of death as stated, and that he was "in his 60th year."

61. Death Certificate of Sarah J. Bedenbaugh, 1917 #5184, DHEC microfilm at SC Archives.

62. *Walsh's Columbia, S. C. Directory 1916*, page 182, copy at the South Caroliniana Library, Columbia, SC.

63. 1870 Census, Newberry County, SC, page 722-B; 1880 Census, Newberry County, SC, page 219; 1900 Census, Richland County, SC, page 70-A.

64. 1910 Census, Richland County, Columbia Township, page 255.

65. A list of these children is included in the "Summer" article in *Newberry County, Historical and Genealogical Annals* by G. L. Summer.

66. Death Certificate 1920 #12343, DHEC microfilm at SC Archives.

67. Death Certificate, 1931 #4735, DHEC microfilm at SC Archives.

68. Death Certificate of Frank S. Bedenbaugh, 1916 #31179, DHEC microfilm at SC Archives.

69. Confederate Pension Application #9867 at SC Archives.

70. Death Certificate of Nancy Caroline Bedenbaugh, 1921 #5716, DHEC microfilm at SC Archives.

71. The marriage (same date) was also reported in the *Lutheran Visitor*, issue of 4 January 1871.

72. Confederate Pension Application #8414, original at South Carolina Archives.

73. O'Neal and Chapman, *Annals of Newberry*, page 428.

74. 1900 Census, Saluda County, South Carolina, page 12-B.

75. Obituary notice in the *Southern Christian Advocate*, issue of 15 December 1898.

76. A biographical sketch of James Ira Bedenbaugh is found in D. D. Wallace's *History of South Carolina*, Volume IV, pages 908-909.

77. Newberry County Marriage Book A, page 202.

78. St. Luke's Lutheran Church Records.

79. Joseph Ira Cronk Bedenbaugh supplied most of the information on this family group.

80. Marriage notice in the *Lutheran Visitor*, issue of 24 September 1879, microfilm at the Lineberger Library, Lutheran Southern Theological Seminary, Columbia, South Carolina. The marriage was performed by Rev. J. D. Bowles.

81. Bible record published in the *Lexington Genealogical Exchange*, Volume III, Book II, pages 113-114.

82. Death Certificate of Mrs. Ellen R. Moore, 1933 #10094, DHEC microfilm at SC Archives.

83. Marriage notice in the *Lutheran Visitor*, issue of 14 January 1880, microfilm at Lineberger Library, Lutheran Theological Southern Seminary, Columbia, South Carolina.

84. Bethlehem Lutheran Church records.

85. Marriage Notice in the Union *Progress*, issue of 28 February 1911.

86. Mrs. Susie B. Sullivan supplied most of the information on this branch of the family in the 1970s.

87. Obituary notice of Margaret Angelina Bedenbaugh, *Southern Christian Advocate*, issue of 6 May 1920, page 11, col. 2. It names her children, as follows: Angelina Rhinehart, Birdie B. Mills, Corria J. Matthews, Rev. L. L. Bedenbaugh, A. A. Bedenbaugh, B. A. Bedenbaugh, and C. G. Bedenbaugh.

88. Comptroller Generals Records, Claims for Disabilities, Box 1, Folder 1, original in the South Carolina Archives.

89. 1900 Census, Saluda County, South Carolina, page 17-B, gives names and ages of Alvin A., Barnoe, Carrie J., and Calhoun.

90. Death Certificate of Angella Rinehart, 1937 #15937, original at DHEC in Columbia.

91. Marriage notice in the *Southern Christian Advocate*, issue of 28 February 1889.

92. Geroge K. Way and C. E. Peele, *Methodist Ministers in South Carolina 1942*, page 176.

93. Edgefield County, SC, Equity Bills #1413 and #2097.

94. 1900 Federal Census, Saluda County, South Carolina, page 82-A, Hewit Township.

95. 1900 Census, Saluda County, South Carolina, page 14-B, Germanville.

96. Saluda County Probate Records, Box 63, Package 3, original in Saluda County Court House, Saluda, South Carolina.

97. Estate papers of Ross Bedenbaugh, Saluda County Probate Records, File 17, Package 5.

98. Death certificate of Mary E. Thurmond, 1917 #15109, DHEC microfilm at SC Archives.

99. 1900 Census, Fayettte County, Georgia, ED 45, Sheet 6.

100. 1910 Census, Greenwood County, SC, page 300-B.

101. St. Luke's Lutheran Church Records.

102. Death Certificate of Mark B. Bedenbaugh, 1938 #7700, DHEC microfilm at SC Archives.

103. Obituary of Mrs. M. B. Bedenbaugh, *The State*, issue of 22 September 1936, page 6-A.

104. The birth year on his tombstone is 1876 but is incorrect. The 1900 census of Lexington County, Hollow Creek Township, page 205, indicates that he was born October 1870. Living in his household were also his wife Leila, his son Dow, and his brother Miles B. Bedenbaugh.

105. Obituary notice of W. P. Bedenbaugh in the (Newberry) *Herald and News*, issue of 8 April 1913, page 8.

106. 1900 Census, Newberry County, SC, page 29; 1910 Census, Newberry County, SC, page 287.

107. Much of the information on the descendants of this family has been supplied by Mr. and Mrs. James R. Logan, Stockton, California.

108. 1910 Census, Richland County, Columbia Township, page 255.

109. Newberry County Marriage Book A, page 438.

110. Death Certificate of Ben W. Bedenbaugh, 1939 #7157, DHEC microfilm at SC Archives.

111. Obituary notice of James W. Bedenbaugh, *Southern Christian Advocate*, issue of 16 October 1930, page 7, col. 3-4. It names his children, as follows: George W. Bedenbaugh, Alton Bedenbaugh, Mrs. J. A. Howard, and Helen Bedenbaugh.

112. Death Certificate of America Bedenbough, 1937, #15606, DHEC microfilm at SC Archives.

113. 1900 Census, Saluda County, South Carolina, page 7; 1910 Census, Lexington County, South Carolina, page 110.

114. Death Certificate of Ella Bedenbough, 1943 #16108, DHEC microfilm at SC Archives.

115. 1900 Census, Lexington County, SC, page 167.

116. Obituary notice of Dove Taylor, Newberry *Herald & News*, issue of 8 February 1918, page 5.

117. Newberry County Marriage Book A, page 485.

118. Newberry County Marriage Book A, page 69.

119. Newberry County Marriage Book C, page 360.

120. Newberry County Marriage Book B, page 466.

121. Newberry County Marriage Book B, page 77.

122. Death Certificate of Velma Bedenbaugh, 1929 #12534, DHEC microfilm at SC Archives.

123. Newberry County Marriage Book C, page 209.

THE BEDENBAUGH-BETENBAUGH FAMILY

SECOND GENERATION

2. John Uriah[2] Beatenbaugh or Ulrich Bidenbach (Michael[1]) was born c1770 and died 17 September 1835. He proved to be almost as difficult to trace as Michael Pitebag. Obviously, he was too young to have served in the Revolution. The name of his wife Mary was revealed in a general sessions court case in Union District, South Carolina, in 1819.[1] The name of John Uriah appears on the 1790 census of Newberry County as Uriah Pitinboa (several households away from Adam Pitingboa), and on the 1800 census (still in Newberry District), as Uriah Pedembox.[2] On the 1810 census of Lexington District, his name appears as Uriah Peterboch. He, with Adam, signed a petition 5 December 1792 against abolishing the County Court of Newberry, on which petition their names appear as Adam Beatenbock and Olrick Peterpock.[3] These are probably not actual signatures. Ulrich signed the petition for incorporation of St. John's Lutheran Church in 1794 where he signed as Ulrich Bidenbach, the only signature yet found for him in German script.[4] He witnessed a deed from Adam and Mary Summer to Jacob Cromer, 28 March 1798, as Uriah Beatenbauh, where he made a mark "B."[5] Many Germans appear to have been embarrassed by their signatures in German and began to use English letters as marks; some of them eventually learned to write their names using the English alphabet. As evidenced by an equity suit, John Uriah Betenbaugh purchased land from Col. John Hampton in 1808.[6] He conveyed 100 acres of land to Lewis George on 23 April 1807 in what was then Lexington District.[7] He purchased 100 acres on Swift Creek in Union District from Alvah Burns, 9 Sept 1817.[8] He was involved in a common pleas suit in that district in 1817 with one Michael Dickert of Newberry District.[9] His name appears on the 1820 and 1830 census reports of Union District. We have an exact date of death for him from a coroner's inquisition, which states that the body of John Uriah Bedenbaugh was found on the plantation of Thomas Salter in Union District, 17 September 1835.[10]

There is no document which proves the children of John Uriah Beatenbaugh. However, there is no other person who appears on Union District who could have been their father. As previously stated, his name appears on the 1810 census of Lexington District as Uriah Peterbock. In that household are two males 0-10, 1 male 26-45, two females 0-10, and one female 26-45.[11] In 1820 his name appears in the census of Union District, as Jno U Bedenbaugh with four males 0-10, one male 16-18, one male over 45, one female 10-16, one female 26-45.[12] In the same district in 1830, appears John U. Beatenbough with one male 50-60, one female 5-10, one female 40-50.[13]

The children of John Uriah[2] Beatenbaugh and his wife Mary:

+ 2433   i. David[3] Betenbaugh, b. 1799
+ 2434　 ii. Michael[3] Beatenbaugh, b. c1802
+ 2435　 iii. Elizabeth[3] Betenbaugh, b. c1807
+ 2436　 iv. Adam[3] Betenbaugh, b. c1810
+ 2437   v. John[3] Betenbaugh, b. c1812
+ 2438　 vi. Joseph[3] Betenbaugh, b. 4 March 1814
+ 2439 vii. Mary Ann[3] Betenbaugh, b. c1822

THIRD GENERATION

2433. David[3] Betenbaugh (John Uriah[2], Michael[1]) was born in Newberry County, South Carolina, in 1799 and came to Union District with his father by 1817. He married Freelove Trammell and died in 1854. She was born about 1807 and apparently survived until about 1881. Both died in Union County, South Carolina, and are buried at Sardis United Methodist Church, near Union.

No probate record has been located for either of them. However, a settlement of the land of David Betenbaugh was made by way of deeds naming the children (or grandchildren, children of a deceased child) and stating the relationships, also that David Betenbaugh "departed this life _____ 1854."[14] All of these deeds are dated 28 Feb 1882, except for on dated 23 Dec 1881. We, therefore, assume that Freelove held a life estate on the property, and it was sold after her death.

The children of David[3] Betenbaugh and wife Freelove:[15]

+ 2440   i. George W.[4] Betenbaugh, b. 1824
+ 2441   ii. Micheal Robert[4] Betenbaugh, b. 22 Nov 1827
  2442   iii. Thomas[4] Betenbaugh, b. 1830, probably died young
+ 2443   iv. Elizabeth[4] (Betsy) Betenbaugh, b. 20 Jan 1832
+ 2444   v. John J.[4] Betenbaugh, b. 1834
  2445   vi. Sarah[4] Betenbaugh, b. 1837, d. after 1880, unm.
  2446   vii. Mary[4] Betenbaugh, b. 1840, probably died young.

2434. Michael[3] Betenbaugh (John Uriah[2], Michael[1]) was born c1802, in Newberry District, South Carolina, moved with his father to Union District by 1817, removed to Franklin County, Georgia, by 1834, where he married Caroline Hemphill. He died 25 January 1888 and is buried in Franklin County, Georgia, near Carnesville, in the Hemphill Cemetery. His Bible (now in possession of a descendant Mr. Ron Betenbough, Lubbock, Texas) published by the American Bible Society, in 1853, names the children and gives their birthdates. The children are also named in the will of Michael Beatenbough (signed by mark).[16]

The following obituary notices were found in the Bible of Carl Betenbaugh, which was in possession of Tollie Star of Atlanta, Georgia, and is now in the possession of Ron Betenbough.

> Michael Beatenbaugh died suddenly one morning last week. He was upwards of ninety years old and had been a citizen of this county ever since he was a young man. He was a man of stirling [sic] qualities, though somewhat eccentric. We have heard it said that he once rode to Athens to buy an axe because he thought the merchants at Carnesville demanded an unreasonable price, and for the same reason made the same journey after a bushel of salt. It is also said that he once built a saw mill to saw lumber for a house and when the lumber was sawed the mill was torn down. Since writing the above we have received a short obituary notice of Mr. Beatenbaugh which will be found elsewhere.

THE BEDENBAUGH-BETENBAUGH FAMILY

Death of Michael Beatenbaugh

We are pained to announce the death of Uncle Mike Beatenbaugh, which occured on 25th January 1888, at his home on North river, where he had lived for upwards of fifty. His death was very sudden as he was sick only a few hours previous to his death. Uncle Mike as he was commonly called, was an industrious man and esteemed by all who knew him. He was 88 years old when he died. The relatives have our heartfelt sympathies and can assure them "that he is not dead but sleepeth." He was carried to his final resting place on 26 inst., where he was intered in the family burying ground on North River.

The children of Michael[3] Betenbaugh, and wife Caroline Hemphill:

    2447 i. John U. or W. (Al)[4] Beatenbough, b. 12 Dec 1835, d. 4 Nov 1863, private Co. G, 34th Ga. Infantry
    2448 ii. Unetta (Nettie)[4] Beatenbough, b. 12 Oct 1837, d. 7 Nov 1913, m. _____ Corry.
    2449 iii. Robert B.[4] Beatenbough born 25 Dec 1839, d. 11 April 1862
+ 2450 iv. Trisvan Reeder[4] Betenbough (note change in spelling), b. 7 Nov 1841
    2451 v. James D.[4] Beatenbough, b. 5 Dec 1843, d. 8 June 1862, private in Co. G, 34th Ga. Infantry
    2452 vi. Henry T. or F.[4] Beatenbough, b. 31 Nov 1845
    2453 vii. Jane J.[4] Beatenbough born 7 Oct 1849, m. _____ Fowler
+ 2454 viii. Nicholas Glen[4] Beatenbough, born 13 Dec 1851
    2455 ix. Americus H.[4] Beatenbough, b. 14 Oct 1854, d. 11 Nov 1918 (did not marry) bur. Carroll's Methodist Church, Franklin Co.. Ga.
+ 2456 x. Henry Boston[4] Beatenbough, b. 29 Aug 1857.

2435. Elizabeth[3] Betenbaugh (John Uriah[2], Michael[1]) was born c1807 and died 1850-60. She married William Koon. In the estate settlement of Joseph Betenbaugh (1881), she is listed as a predeceased sister, having two surviving children Viny and Frances. However, her name appears on the 1850 census with one John Koon, presumably her son.[17] Her name is not found in the 1860 census, but the name of the son John is found listed in the household of James B. Jeter, listed as a farm manager.[18] No further record has been found of John Koon.

Children of William and Elizabeth[3] (Betenbaugh) Koon:

+ 2457 i. Lavinia[4] (Viny) Koon, b. 20 May 1826
    2458 ii. John Koon, b. 1829
+ 2459 iii. Frances Koon, b. 1831.

2436. Adam[3] Beatenbaugh (John Uriah[2], Michael[1]) was born c1810, probably in Lexington District, South Carolina, and moved with his father to Union District by 1817. He was living in DeKalb County, Georgia, at the taking of the 1850 census[19] and in Campbell County, Georgia, by the taking of the 1860 census[20] with wife Nancy, aged 30. He was living in Campbell County in 1870[21] and probably died before 1880, as the widow Nancy was living in the household of her son Joseph in that year. The census is not consistent in stating the state of birth of Nancy. The 1850 and 1880 census indicate that she was born in South Carolina. The 1860 and 1870 census indicate that she was born in Georgia. She is probably the Nancy "Bedenbeau" named as a daughter of Ellender McGlothen in the will of Nancy Lathers dated 7 November 1855.[22] In 1881 when the estate of Joseph Betenbaugh was settled, the whereabouts of his children were unknown to the family who had remained in Union County, South Carolina. His name appears as Adam Peterpaw where he signed (by mark) 27 September 1837 as security for the appearance of Thomas Tramel as a witness in a case against M. D. Sims brought by R. C. Jeter.[23] Children of Adam[3] Beatenbaugh and wife Nancy (all born in Georgia):

+ 2460   i. Joseph Jackson[4] Beatenbaugh, b. June 1847
  2461   ii. Caroline[4] Beatenbaugh, b. c1850, did not marry
  2462   iii. John[4] Beatenbaugh, b. 1852, died young, probably before 1870
+ 2463   iv. George Washington[4] Beatenbaugh, b. c1856.

2437. John[3] Betenbaugh (John Uriah[2], Michael[1]) was born c1812 and died after 1850. He married the widow Theressa Nance. The 1850 census shows him with wife "Rezia" and a large family of children. Theressa (as stated) was a widow Nance, and most of the children were hers by a former marriage. A court case from 1859 proves that "Mrs. John Beadenbaugh," also referred to as "Reesy" had a son Jefferson Nance still living with her at that time.[24] In the estate settlement of Joseph Betenbaugh in 1881, only two children were named for John Betenbaugh deceased: Cynthia and Christopher C. Betenbaugh. John Betenbaugh signed by mark as an appraiser, with George Betenbaugh and John Willard, on an estray item 7 September 1857.[25] He died between that date and 16 October 1858, the date that Theressa Betenbaugh bound out her son Christopher C. Y. Betenbaugh as an apprentice to Sims McDaniel.[26] John and Theressa Betenbaugh are buried at Mt. Vernon Presbyterian Church in Union County, but no gravestones have been located for them.

Children of John[3] Betenbaugh and wife Theressa:
  2464   i. Cynthia[4] Betenbaugh, b. 1847, did not marry
+ 2465   ii. Christopher Columbus Young[4] Betenbaugh, b. 15 Oct 1849.

2438. Joseph[3] Betenbaugh (John Uriah[2], Michael[1]) was born 4 March 1814, and died 5 February 1881 in Union County, South Carolina. He is buried at Sardis United Methodist Church, Union County. He was never married. A daguerreotype of him is reproduced on page 129. The probate papers of his estate are the most revealing documents establishing relationships in this family.[27] One document bears quoting:

> The Petition of M. Betenbaugh respectfully shews-- Joseph Betenbaugh late of Union County died intestate on the 5th day of February 1881 leaving him surviving as his heirs at law and distributees His sister Mrs. Mary Ann McCreight. His brother Michael Betenbaugh who resides at or near Carnsville in the State of Georgia and the following nephews and neices-- Christopher Betenbaugh and Cinthia Betenbaugh children of John Betenbaugh a predeceased brother of the said intestate.
> Frances Davis, wife of Hiram Davis, and Viny Gregory, wife of Tresvan Gregory, children of Elizabeth Koon a predeceased sister of the said intestate.
> And the children of Adam Betenbaugh names and residences unknown by your Petitioner.
> That the said Jos. Betenbaugh was the owner of a personal estate of about the value of four hundred dollars. That the said personal estate consists of two mules of the value of about two hundred and fifty dollars and of one half interest in eight or nine bales of cotton, some

farming tools which said cotton and farming tools are owned jointly by your Petitioner and the said intestate....

14th February 1881   M. Betenbaugh

He served as a private in Company F, 15th South Carolina Infantry. The obituary of Joseph Betenbaugh is found in the *Weekly Union Times*, issue of Friday, February 11, 1881, and follows:

Death of Joseph Betenbaugh.
Information reach this town on Sunday morning last that Mr. Joseph Betenbaugh, a man well known all over this County, died very suddenly the evening before. He was one of the most industrious men in the County, and had been working hard all day ginning cotton, and going from the gin house to his dwelling about 6 o'clock, was stricken down with paralysis. He was taken to the dwelling and died between 9 and 10 o'clock that night.

2439. Mary Ann[3] Betenbaugh (John Uriah[2], Michael[1]) was born c1822, died 5 April 1889,[28] at Glendale Factory, Spartanburg County, South Carolina. She married William McCreight, who was born c1822. Her photograph is reproduced on page 131.

The obituary notice of Mrs. William McCreight states that she was born in Union District and that she left seven children. This statement of her birthplace is supported by the presence of John Uriah Beatenbeaugh on the 1820 census there. This family has not been located on the 1850 or 1860 census returns. We do find their names (with seven children) appearing on the 1870 census in York County, South Carolina.[29] We find their names on the 1880 census in Union County as well.[30] There were three children (David, Mary, and Cornelia) living with them at that time, all indicated as having been born in South Carolina.

Children of Mary Ann[3] Betenbaugh, and her husband William McCreight:

+ 2466   i. James P. W.[4] McCreight, b. c1849
+ 2467   ii. John Robert[4] McCreight, b. c1850
+ 2468   iii. Nancy Ann[4] McCreight, born 6 Oct 1851
+ 2469   iv. Thomas Herndon[4] McCreight, b. Jan 1854
+ 2470   v. David Andrew[4] McCreight, b. 4 Nov 1857
    2471   vi. Mary E.[4] McCreight, b. c1860
+ 2472   vii. Cornelia (Neely)[4] McCreight, b. 1863.

THE BEDENBAUGH-BETENBAUGH FAMILY

Joseph Betenbaugh

Mary Ann (Betenbaugh) McCreight

THE BEDENBAUGH-BETENBAUGH FAMILY

FOURTH GENERATION

2440. George W. Betenbaugh (David[3], John Uriah[2], Michael[1]) was born c1824 and died 4 July 1899 in the Sardis Community near Union, South Carolina,[31] and is buried at Sardis United Methodist Church. He married Mrs. Nancy Frazier Keisler, but there were no children of this marriage. George Betenbaugh was in Confederate service in Company M, 5th South Carolina State Troops. His signature appears an appraiser on an estray item 7 September 1857.[32]

2441. Micheal Robert[4] Betenbaugh (David[3], John Uriah[2], Michael[1]) was born 22 November 1827, and died 19 November 1906, married 1860-61 (per 1900 census) to Martha Ellen Young, who was born 24 January 1841, and died 6 May 1918, a daughter of Rev. Thomas and Elizabeth (Skelton) Young. Tradition states that she ran away from school at Salem, North Carolina, to marry him. The records at Salem College show that she attended there 1858-1860. Both are buried at Sardis United Methodist Church, Union County, South Carolina. Their photograph is reproduced on page 132. Mike Betenbaugh (sometimes spelled Batenbaugh in the record) served in Company E, 1st South Carolina, enlisting for six months in January 1861. Children of Micheal Robert[4] and Martha E. Young Betenbaugh:

+ 2473   i. Thomas Joseph[5] Betenbaugh, b. 28 Aug 1862.
+ 2474 ii. John Calhoun[5] Betenbaugh, b. 16 Oct 1864.
+ 2475 iii. Elizabeth Ann Freelove[5] Betenbaugh, b. 20 July 1867
+ 2476 iv. Micheal Robert[5] Betenbaugh, Jr., b. 15 Feb 1870
   2477 v. William David[5] Betenbaugh, b. 11 Nov 1872, d. 10 Feb 1895, unm., bur. Sardis United Methodist Church
+ 2478 vi. James Claude[5] Betenbaugh, b. 24 June 1875
+ 2479 vii. Powell Higgerson[5] Betenbaugh, b. 27 Dec 1877
+ 2480 viii. Sallie E.[5] Betenbaugh, b. 4 July 1881
+ 2481 ix. Beaty Harden[5] Betenbaugh, b. 28 Nov 1884.

2443. Elizabeth (Betsy)[4] Betenbaugh (David[3], John Uriah[2], Michael[1]) was born 20 January 1832, and died 3 June 1910.[33] She married, in 1855,[34] John T. (Cap) Willard, who was born 28 November 1834 and died 24 June 1901. Her obituary notice, written by Rev. Albert D. Betts, states that she had been a member of Sardis Methodist Church for over forty years. Both are buried at Sardis United Methodist Church, Union County, South Carolina. A photograph of Elizabeth Betenbaugh Willard is reproduced on page 133. John Willard took up an estray mare "found wandering about on his plantation" on which his brother-in-law George Betenbaugh and his wife's uncle John Betenbaugh, signed with him as appraisers on 7 September 1857.[35] Children:

+ 2482 i. Thomas[5] Willard, b. c1859
+ 2483 ii. Mary[5] Willard, b. 30 August 1856
+ 2484 iii. David Jefferson[5] Willard, b. 18 Feb 1863
+ 2485 iv. Martha[5] Willard, b. 22 Sept 1865, d. 8 Jan 1940, m. Glenn P. Adams, bur. Sardis United Methodist Church
+ 2486 v. Joseph J.[5] Willard, b. 7 Nov 1872.

Micheal R. and Martha E. (Young) Betenbaugh

Elizabeth (Betenbaugh) Willard

THE BEDENBAUGH-BETENBAUGH FAMILY

2444. John J.[4] Betenbaugh (David[3], John Uriah[2], Michael[1]) was born c1834 and died 14 March 1865 while a prisoner of war in Confederate service at Point Lookout, Maryland.[36] He married Adelade Humphries, who was born 10 November 1841 and died 16 May 1900, a daughter of John Thomas and Louisa (Pressley) Humphries. Adelade (Humphries) Betenbaugh married, second, Carey W. Willard. John J. Betenbaugh served as a private in Company F, 15th South Carolina infantry. Two children:

+ 2487   i. Sarah Ellen[5] Betenbaugh, b. 16 May 1859
+ 2488   ii. James Beauregard[5] Betenbaugh, b. 15 Apr 1860.

2450. Trisvan Reeder[4] (T. R.) Beatenbough (Michael[3], John Uriah[2], Michael[1]) was born on 7 Nov 1841 in Franklin County, Georgia, and died there 23 March 1921. He married, on 4 September 1867, Mary Vastine Bond, who was born on 19 January 1851 in Georgia and died 19 October 1907 in Franklin County, Georgia. Both are buried at Zidon Baptist Church, Franklin County, GA. Trisvan Reeder Beatenbough married, second, after 1907, a widow, Armedow Stribling. Armedow Stribling was also buried in Zidon Baptist Church, Franklin County, Georgia. She was called "Aunt Metter," and she had at least one Stribling child.

Usually called "T. R.," or sometimes "Reeder," he enlisted on 12 May 1862, in Captain Russell A. Jones' Company G, of the 34th Regiment, Georgia Volunteer Infantry, Army of Tennessee. He later transferred to Company K, 52nd Regiment, Georgia Infantry. He was captured at Bakers Creek, Mississippi, on 16 May 1863, and held prisoner at Memphis, Tennessee; Camp Morton, Indiana; and at Fort Delaware where he was paroled for exchange on 4 July 1863. A record of 1 August 1863 lists him as a deserter and shows that Thomas Craft, jailor, of Franklin County, Virginia, was paid $6.25 for his apprension and keep for five days. A muster roll for November and December 1863 shows T. R. present, and pension records show that he was on detail with a wagon train at the end of the war. He and his wife Mary V. Bond had the following children, all born in Franklin County, Georgia:[37]

   2489   i. Mary C.[5] Beatenbough, b. 4 July 1868, d. 25 Oct 1874 Franklin County, GA
+ 2490   ii. Fannie McNelie[5] Beatenbough, b. 27 Nov 1870
+ 2491   iii. Henry Estee[5] Beatenbough, b. 7 Apr 1873
+ 2492   iv. Hanna Lou[5] "Nettie" Beatenbough, b. 15 July 1876
   2493   v. Doctor Wylie[5] "Dee" Beatenbough, b. 7 Sept 1880, d. in 1949 in GA, bur. Jones Chapel, Madison County, GA, m. Callie Tyner
   2494   vi. Matthew Michael[5] Beatenbough, b. 21 Feb 1883, d. 30 Nov 1885 in Franklin Co., GA, bur. Zidon Bapt Church, Franklin County, GA
+ 2495   vii. Charlie Amos[5] Beatenbough, b. 7 Sept 1885
   2496   viii. Ralph[5] Beatenbough, b. 6 Nov 1886, d. 2 May 1888, bur. Carrolls Meth Church, Franklin County, GA.
+ 2497   ix. Nancy Jane[5] "Jennie" Beatenbough, b. 19 Oct 1888
+ 2498   x. Freddy Glen[5] "Fred" Beatenbough, b. 3 Jan 1892, d. 20 Feb 1946 in GA, bur. Shiloh Bapt Church, Madison County, GA, m. Pearl Bray.

2454. Nicholas Glen[4] (Nick) Betenbough (Michael[3], John Uriah[2], Michael[1]) was born 13 December 1851 and died _____ in Andrews, Texas. He married Matilda Sewell, who was born 1855 or 1856 and died _____ at Shamrock, Texas. Children:

   2499   i. Alice E.[5] Betenbough, b. c1874, m. 1st Buford R. Horton; m. 2nd in 1916, Lovington, NM, H. Elic Whitmire

2500 ii. Robert E.[5] Betenbough, b. c1876, Franklin Co., GA, m. Mattie

2501 iii. Dennis J.[5] Betenbough, b. 3 Oct 1880, Franklin Co., GA, d. 20 March 1969 Shamrock, TX, m. Mae _____; children:

    2502 a. Bert[6] Betenbough

    2503 b. Opal[6] Betenbough

+ 2504 iv. Toomy[5] Betenbough, b. 7 May 1884

+ 2505 v. Cnitgrouss George[5] Betenbough, b. 7 Oct 1886

+ 2506 vi. Carl Betenbough[5] born 19 Jan 1888

2507 vii. Isa Belle[5] Betenbough, b. 6 March 1890, Nocona, TX, m. 31 Oct 1909, O'Donnel TX, Lloyd Edisto McClish; children:

    2508 a. R. E.[6] McClish (d. inf.)

    2509 b. Velma Lee[6] McClish, b. 20 Jan 1913, m. Robert Louis Little

    2510 c. Martha[6] McClish, m, 1st Clinton Woodside, m. 2nd Wayne Hogan.

2456. Henry Boston[4] Beatenbough (Michael[3], John Uriah[2], Michael[1]) was born 29 August 1857 and died 9 July 1925. He married Annie Ruth Douthit. (He changed the spelling of his name to Bedenbaugh.) Children:

2511 i. Carl[5] Bedenbaugh, b. 27 Oct 1888, d. 17 Oct 1960, m. 20 Feb 1920 Leola Gilbert; child:

    2512 a. Tollie Star[6] Bedenbaugh, b. 11 Sept 1922 m. 1st Dan Tolan; m. 2nd Wm Berry Hartsfield; child:

        2513 (1) Carl Siefgrief[7] Tolan, b. 20 Nov 1954

2514 ii. Robert Mack[5] (Bob) Bedenbaugh, b. 31 Dec 1890 Franklin Co., GA, m. Olive Gertrude Cole; children:

    2515 a. Annie Ruth[6] Bedenbaugh, b. 16 Oct 1918, m. Buster Reece; child:

        2516 (1) Terry Lou[7] Reece

    2517 b. Robert Hudson[6] Beatenbough, b. 27 Nov 1919 Franklin Co., GA, m. 1st Thelma Gintz; m. 2nd Marilyn Miller; children:

        2518 (1) Robert[7] Beatenbough

        2519 (2) Eric Neal[7] Beatenbough

        2520 (3) Michelle[7] Beatenbough

    2521 c. Bernice Beatrice[6] Bedenbaugh, b. 12 Aug 1921 Franklin Co., GA, m. Ernest Massey; children:

        2522 (1) Claudia Ann[7] Massey, m. Tommy King

        2523 (2) Rosilend Paulette[7] Massey, m. Larry Mayo

        2524 (3) Pamela Ernestine[7] Massey

    2525 d. Bertie Sue[6] Bedenbaugh, b. 20 Feb 1925 Franklin Co., GA, m. James Gay

    2526 e. Myrtle Douthit[6] Bedenbaugh, b. 5 May 1927 Franklin Co., GA, m. Grady Moon.

2457. Lavinia[4] (Viny) Koon (Elizabeth[3], John Uriah[2], Michael[1]) was born 20 May 1826 and died 12 October 1889. She married Tresvan Gregory, who was born 13 August 1822 and died 30 June 1899. Both are buried at Beulah Baptist Church, Union County, South Carolina. Children[38]:

2527 i. John Henderson[5] Gregory, b. 3 March 1852, d. 16 October 1924,[39] Columbia, SC; married Emma Eubanks, b. 1 March 1858, d. 5 Nov 1938. Both are buried at Beulah Baptist Church, Union Co., SC

2528 ii. Robert[5] Gregory, b. c1856

2529 iii. Mary[5] Gregory, b. c1858.

C. C. Y. (Kit) Betenbaugh

2459. Frances[4] Koon (Elizabeth[3], John Uriah[2], Michael[1]) was born about 1831 and died in March or April of 1890. She married Hiram Davis, who was born c1823 and died 27 September 1889.[40] Children, all born in Union District, South Carolina:

   2530 i. Sarah Elizabeth[5] Davis, b. 31 March 1848, m. ___ Goforth
   2531 ii. Mary Ann[5] Davis, b. 23 March 1851
   2532 iii. William Gist[5] Davis, b. 5 March 1853, d. 5 Aug 1855
   2534 iv. Nancy Thompson[5] Davis, b. 31 Aug 1854
   2535 v. John Beaty[5] Davis, b. 18 Dec 1856
+ 2536 vi. Frank Edward[5] Davis, b. 28 March 1859
+ 2537 vii. Caroline Virginia[5] (Virgie) Davis, b. 11 Sept 1861
   2538 viii. Jeff[5] Davis, b. 24 Apr 1864, d. 9 March 1887
   2539 ix. Josephine Farr[5] Davis, b. 26 June 1867.

2460. Joseph Jackson[4] Beatenbaugh (Adam[3], John Uriah[2], Michael[1]) was born June 1847 and died in 1912. He married, on 7 December 1876, Sarah F. Carter who as born c1856 and died in 1925. Children:

   2540 i. Josie[6] Beatenbaugh, b. c1875 Campbell Co., Ga., m. 2 March 1890 to Tandy Bennett
   2541 ii. William Pinckney Jesse Jackson[5] Beatenbaugh, b. Red Oak, Campbell (now Fulton) Co., Ga., 26 Sept 1886, d. 29 Jan 1969; m. 18 Sept 1910 Minnie Lee Ledbetter b. 3 March 1894 [she supplied a large portion of information on descendants of Adam Betenbaugh]. Children:
       2542 a. Inez[6] Beatenbaugh, b. 12 Nov 1913 Atlanta, Ga., m. John A. Parlier
       2543 b. William Pinckney[6] Beatenbaugh, Jr., b. & d. 1918
       2544 c. R. A.[6] Beatenbaugh, b. 11 Sept 1919
       2545 d. Irene[6] Beatenbaugh, b. 12 Feb 1922, m. Hubert Holbrook
       2546 e. Elizabeth[6] Beatenbaugh, b. 19 Sept 1925, m. Lawrence Anderson
   2547 iii. Ida[6] Beatenbaugh, m. 17 March 1912 to Virgil Haney
   (possibly other children of Joseph J. Beatenbaugh).

2463. George Washington[4] Beatenbaugh (Adam[3], John Uriah[2], Michael[1]) was born c1857 in Campbell County, Georgia, and died 24 December 1924 in Cedartown, Polk County, Georgia. He married, on 25 September 1878 in Fulton County, Georgia, to Annie Miller. [His name is listed as Green on the 1860 census.] (There is the possibility of a second marriage.) Children:

   2548 i. George[5] Beatenbaugh, b. 1879
   2549 ii. Lilla Mae[5] Beatenbaugh, b. 20 May 1888
   (there may have been other children).

2465. Christopher Columbus Young[4] (Kit) Betenbaugh (John[3], John Uriah[2], Michael[1]) was born 15 October 1849 died 9 September 1911 in Union County, South Carolina. He married Sarah Jane (Sallie) Jolly, who was born 30 October 1849 and died 23 September 1925 in Union.[41] They are buried Hebron Baptist Church. A tintype of Kit Betenbaugh is reproduced on page 136. Kit Betenbaugh was named for a neighbor, Christopher Columbus Young, Sr., who died 28 February 1849. Children, born in Union, South Carolina:

   2550 i. Aurie[5] Betenbaugh, b. 28 Jan 1882, d. 22 Oct 1918, m. 24 June 1900, J. Ed Helton
+ 2551 ii. Eva[5] Betenbaugh, b. 5 July 1883
   2552 iii. Mamie Betenbaugh, b. 6 Oct 1883, d. 12 July 1907 of consumption, bur. Hebron Bapt. Church[42]

2553 iv. Hattie Belle[5] Betenbaugh, b. 5 March 1886, d. 12 Feb 1911
2554 v. Effie L.[5] Betenbaugh, b. 26 May 1887, d. 30 Apr 1913
2555 vi. Wallace[5] Betenbaugh b. 5 May 1889, d. 19 Nov 1892
2556 vii. States[5] Betenbaugh, b. 15 Sept 1890, d. 26 Nov 1892
+ 2557 viii. Cynthia Pearl[5] Betenbaugh, b. 5 May 1892.

2466. James P. W.[4] McCreight (Mary Ann[3], John Uriah[2], Michael[1]) was born c1849 and married, on 26 December 1878,[43] Victoria (Victory) Faucett, who was born c1846.[44] Child:
2558 i. Albertha[5] McCreight, b. Aug 1879.

2467. John Robert[4] McCreight (Mary Ann[3], John Uriah[2], Michael[1]) was born c1850 in South Carolina and died in 1920 at Houlka, Chickasaw County, Mississippi. He married, first, Eleanor (Ellie) Halsell, who was born 20 October 1856 in Houlka, Mississippi, and died there 21 January 1897. She is buried in the Holladay Cemetery, on Highway 15 North in Pontotoc County, Mississippi.[45] He married, second, in Pontotoc County, Mississippi, on 3 October 1897, Fannie Savely.[46]
Children by Eleanor Halsell:
2559 i. Robert White[5] McCreight, b. 19 Dec 1888, d. 5 July 1916, bur. in Holladay Cem.
2560 ii. Samuel Walker[5] McCreight, b. 1892 Van Fleet, MS, m. 1 July 1914 at Buffalo, Union Co., SC, Maggie Elizabeth[5] McCreight (1st cousin), b. 1896, d. 15 Dec 1970 Ninety Six, Greenwood Co., SC. (Samuel Walker McCreight supplied some of this information in 1972.) Children:
2561 a. Herndon Walker[6] McCreight, b. 9 Dec 1915, Buffalo, SC, d. 25 Mar 1983, Columbia, SC, (bur Greenwood Mem. Gardens) m. Nelle Griffin; three children:
2562 (1) Robert W.[7] McCreight
2563 (2) Tony Ryan[7] McCreight
2564 (3) Donna[7] McCreight
2565 b. Vera Eloise[6] McCreight, b. 12 Sept 1917, Buffalo, SC, m. S. E. Hendrick
2566 c. Myra Lee[6] McCreight, b. 1 July 1923, Buffalo, SC (d. inf.)
2567 d. Ellie Mae[6] McCreight, b. 6 Dec 1926, Greer, SC, m. Charlie Skelton
2568 iii. Will Shelton (W. S.) McCreight.

Children by Fannie Savely, all born in Chickasaw County, Mississippi:
2569 iv. Roberta[5] McCreight, b. c1899
2570 v. Katie Lee[5] McCreight, b. c1900
2571 vi. Ora[5] McCreight, b. c1902
2572 vii. Cornelia[5] McCreight, b. c1904
2573 viii. Jimmie[5] McCreight, b. c1906
2574 ix. Mollie[5] McCreight, b. c1907.

2468. Nancy Ann[4] McCreight (Mary Ann[3], John Uriah[2], Michael[1]) was born 6 October 1851 and died 12 February 1930 in Greenville County, South Carolina, and is buried at Paris Mountain Holiness Baptist Cemetery.[47] She married Dr. Ira Keenan. Children:
+ 2575 i. William Decater[5] (Bud) Keenan, b. 1876 Union Co., SC
+ 2576 ii. James Webster[5] (Jimmy) Keenan, b. 10 June 1878, Union Co., SC
+ 2577 iii. Bernice Arminta[5] Keenan, b. 7 Sept 1881

+ 2578 iv. Ira Henry[5] Keenan, b. 3 Sept 1883, Spartanburg Co., SC
+ 2579 v. Beulah[5] Keenan, b. 27 May 1887.

2469. Thomas Herndon[4] McCreight (Mary Ann[3], John Uriah[2], Michael[1]) was born in January of 1854 and died after 1900. The name of his first wife, by whom he had one child, has not been discovered. It is not included on the death certificate of her child, John Robert McCreight (spelled McCright on the certificate). Thomas Herndon McCreight, married, second, about 1878, Mary Dunn, who was born about 1862. They were living in Union County in 1880, and lived in Spartanburg County before removing to Greenville County (by 1900). Children:
+ 2580   i. John Robert Levi[5] McCreight, b. 4 July 1873, Union Co., SC
+ 2581 ii. Alice Gertrude[5] McCreight, b. 1 Jan 1883, Greenville, SC
+ 2582 iii. Sudie Agness[5] McCreight, b. 6 Aug 1886, Spartanburg, SC
   2583 iv. James C.[5] McCreight, b. 1889
+ 2584 v. Hassie[5] McCreight, b. Oct 1897
+ 2585 vi. Lillie Mae[5] McCreight, b. 1 Feb 1902.

2470. David Andrew[4] McCreight (Mary Ann[3], John Uriah[2], Michael[1]) was born 4 November 1857 and died 20 November 1940 at Ninety Six, Greenwood County, South Carolina.[48] He married Nannie Gregory (1867-1932). Both are buried Church of the Nativity (Episcopal) in Union, South Carolina. Children:
   2586   i. Evangeline[5] McCreight, b. 15 March 1886, d. 6 Feb 1889, bur. Nativity.
   2587 ii. Paul G.[5] McCreight, b. 8 July 1888, d. 19 Apr 1897, bur. Nativity.
   2588 iii. Rosa Lee[5] McCreight married _____ Ochiltree (lived Startex, SC)
   2589 iv. John Gary[5] McCreight, b. 17 Feb 1894, d. 1 March 1910, bur. Nativity
   2590 v. Maggie Elizabeth[5] McCreight, b. 1896, d. 15 Dec 1970, m. 1 July 1914 Samuel Walker[5] McCreight (see under him for children).

2472. Cornelia (Neely)[4] McCreight (Mary Ann[3], John Uriah[2], Michael[1]) was born in December 1863 and died 11 November 1933 at Glendale, Spartanburg County, South Carolina.[49] She married Calhoun Humphries, son of John Thomas and Louise (Pressley) Humphries. She is buried Sardis Methodist Church, Union County, South Carolina. Children:
   2591   i. Edward[5] Humphries, b. Nov 1885, m. Florence Holder
   2592 ii. Annie[5] Humphries, b. Aug 1888, m. Herbert Branch
   2593 iii. John[5] Humphries, b. Apr 1890, m. Inez Fowler
   2594 iv. George[5] Humphries, b. Jan 1895
   2595 v. Eva[5] Humphries, b. Aug 1899, m. Wallace Fowler.

2473. Thomas Joseph[5] Betenbaugh (Micheal R.[4], David[3], John Uriah[2], Michael[1]) was born 28 August 1862 and died 16 October 1915 in Union County, South Carolina. He married, on 15 January 1880,[50] Susan Fair Sanders who born 25 December 1862 and died 23 June 1934, a daughter of William and Katherine (Humphries) Sanders. Both buried at Sardis United Methodist Church in Union County. A photograph of Thomas J. Betenbaugh is reproduced on page 141. He was county auditor in Union and took office 28 April 1911.[51] Upon his death, his son James Sanders Betenbaugh was appointed to fill the unexpired term and was later elected to that office. Fourteen children:

+ 2596   i. Della Young[6] Betenbaugh, b. 14 Oct 1880
  2597 ii. William Glover[6] Betenbaugh, b. 24 Feb 1886, d. 18 Apr 1905, bur. Sardis United Methodist Church
  2598 iii. Michael[6] Betenbaugh, b. 24 Feb 1886
+ 2599 iv. James Sanders[6] Betenbaugh, b. 22 Aug 1882
+ 2600   v. Madge Cleora[6] Betenbaugh, b. 26 June 1884
+ 2601 vi. Walter Russell[6] Betenbaugh, b. 13 Sept 1889
  2602 vii. Thomas Boyd[6] Betenbaugh, b. 24 Apr 1888, d. 1 Apr 1941 m. 5 July 1911[52] Bertha Bentley
  2603 viii. Pearl[6] Betenbaugh, b. 30 May 1890, d. 7 June 1914, m. 27 Oct 1909[53] John Andy Hollingsworth
+ 2604 ix. Annie Lou[6] Betenbaugh, b. 27 Sept 1892
+ 2605   x. Morris Douglas[6] Betenbaugh, b. 23 Mar 1895
  2606 xi. John Roper[6] Betenbaugh, b. 2 Aug 1897, d. 27 Aug 1927, bur. Sardis United Methodist Church
+ 2607 xii. Charlie Norman[6] Betenbaugh, b. 27 Apr 1902
  2608 xiii. Sudie Ruby[6] Betenbaugh, b. 10 July 1904, d. 13 Feb 1988, m. Perry Ralph Smith, b. 9 March 1894, d. 9 Sept 1940, both bur. Sardis United Methodist Church
+ 2609 xiv. Nina Coline[6] Betenbaugh, b. 8 Dec 1906.

2474. John Calhoun[5] Betenbaugh (Micheal R.[4], David[3], John Uriah[2], Michael[1]) was born 16 October 1864 in Union County, South Carolina, and died 23 August 1911, at Glendale, Spartanburg County, South Carolina.[54] He married, on 21 February 1889,[55] Aurelia Adell Greer, who was born 27 February 1868 in Union County and died 3 December 1931 at High Point, North Carolina, the daughter of Charner Sanders and Mary Ann (Malone) Greer. Both are buried at Sardis United Methodist Church, Union County. A photograph of this family group is reproduced on page 142. Children:

+ 2610   i. Martha Ann (Mattie)[6] Betenbaugh, b. 18 Nov 1889
+ 2611 ii. William David[6] Betenbaugh, b. 16 May 1894
+ 2612 iii. Mary Morris[6] Betenbaugh, b. 29 Jan 1897
  2613 iv. Margaret Aurelia[6] (Maggie) Betenbaugh, b. 22 Jan 1900, d. 20 Jan 1969, Butner, NC, married Clyde Everhart
  2614   v. Gordan[6] Betenbaugh, b. 21 Jan 1904, Spartanburg Co., d. 13 March 1913, Union, SC[56]
+ 2615 vi. Charner Michael[6] Betenbaugh, b. 14 Aug 1907.

THE BEDENBAUGH-BETENBAUGH FAMILY

Thomas J. Betenbaugh

The Family of John C. Betenbaugh, c1910

[back row]: William David Betenbaugh, Mattie Betenbaugh
[second row]: John C. Betenbaugh, Mike Betenbaugh, Aurelia (Greer) Betenbaugh, Mary Betenbaugh
[front row]: Maggie Betenbaugh, Gordan Betenbaugh

THE BEDENBAUGH-BETENBAUGH FAMILY

2475. Elizabeth Ann Freelove (Annie Elizabeth)[5] Betenbaugh (Micheal[4], David[3], John Uriah[2], Michael[1]) was born 30 July 1867 and died 10 October 1938 in Union, South Carolina. She married, on 25 December 1884, Thomas Calhoun (Cal) Jolly, who was born 8 June 1863 and died 30 October 1946. Both are buried at Sardis United Methodist Church. Children:
+ 2616   i. Alvin S.[6] Jolly, b. 12 April 1886
   2617 ii. Bertran (Bertie)[6] Jolly, b. 21 Jan 1889, died 7 Apr 1976, Union, SC, unm.
+ 2618 iii. Thomas Claude[6] Jolly, b. 11 Nov 1892, m. Mary Spears
   2619 iv. Herbert M.[6] Jolly, b. 27 Dec 1896
   2620   v. Floretta[6] Jolly, b. 6 June 1899, d. 18 July 1902
+ 2621 vi. Leila Pearl[6] Jolly, b. 17 Aug 1903.

2476. Micheal Robert[5] Betenbaugh Jr. (Micheal[4], David[3], John Uriah[2], Michael[1]) was born 15 February 1870 and died 10 November 1895. He married Nannie Barnett. She married, second, David Johnson. Two daughters:
   2622 i. Blanche[6] Betenbaugh married _____ Shirley
   2623 ii. Willie[6] Betenbaugh.

2478. James Claude[5] Betenbaugh (Micheal[4], David[3], John Uriah[2], Michael[1]) was born 24 June 1875, died 10 October 1964 in Decatur, Georgia. He married Dovie Fuller, who was born 11 September 1891 and died 16 December 1967. Children:
   2624   i. Dovie Marie[6] Betenbaugh m. Willis Andrew Bailey
   2625   ii. James Raymond[6] Betenbaugh
   2626 iii. William Hubert[6] (Bill) Betenbaugh
   2627   iv. Thomas Alvin[6] Betenbaugh
   2628   v. Cecil Robert[6] Betenbaugh
   2629   vi. George Carlton[6] Betenbaugh
   2630 vii. Annie Cornelia[6] Betenbaugh.

2479. Powell Higgerson[5] Betenbaugh (Micheal[4], David[3], John Uriah[2], Michael[1]) was born 27 December 1877 in Union County, South Carolina, and died there 25 July 1961. He married, on 26 December 1901, Corrie Letha Hodge, who was born 19 January 1879 and died 25 December 1961 in Union. Both are buried at Sardis United Methodist Church in Union County. Children, all born in Union, South Carolina:
   2631   i. Alma[6] Betenbaugh, b. 11 Jan 1903, d. 7 March 1991, bur. Sardis
   2632   ii. Myrtle[6] Betenbaugh, b. 19 Jan 1905, d. 6 Apr 1988, bur. Sardis
   2633 iii. Lunette[6] Betenbaugh, b. 11 May 1911, d. 13 Nov 1992, bur. Sardis
+ 2634 iv. Margaret[6] Betenbaugh, b. 15 Jan 1916
   2635   v. Ruth[6] Betenbaugh, b. 24 Nov 1919, d. 16 Apr 1976, bur. Sardis.

2480. Sallie E.[5] Betenbaugh (Micheal[4], David[3], John Uriah[2], Michael[1]) was born 4 July 1881 and died 27 November 1909. She married, first, Sam O'Shields who was born 22 December 1876 and died 8 February 1905. She married, second, John Sanders.
Children:
   2636   i. James Wesley[6] O'Shields
   2637   ii. Eunice Mae[6] O'Shields
   2638 iii. Lewis Willis[6] O'Shields
   2639   iv. Sarah Elizabeth[6] Sanders, b. 8 Nov 1909, d. 27 Dec 1910.

2481. Beaty Harden[5] Betenbaugh (Micheal[4], David[3], John Uriah[2], Michael[1]) was born 28 November 1884 and died 14 August 1957. He married, on 6 September 1914, Maude Cunningham, who was born 8 May 1896 and died 23 December 1977 in California while on a visit. Children:
  2640 i. Cyril Charles[6] (Mike) Betenbaugh, b. 24 Sept 1915, d. 12 July 1983
        m. 12 Sept 1945 Sara Strange; children:
        2641 a. Charles Michael[7] Betenbaugh, b. 19 May 1953, m. Laura Frazier
        2642 b. Thomas Stanley[7] Betenbaugh born 11 Sept 1954, m. 7 June 1986
            Mary Ann Boggs, b. 20 July 1961. They live in Columbia, SC;
            children:
            2643 (1) Amy Marie[8] Betenbaugh, b. 11 Apr 1989
            2644 (2) Sara Ann[8] Betenbaugh, b. 22 Sept 1992
  2645 ii. Neal Harden[6] Betenbaugh, m. Peggy Ida McGeachen (live San Francisco, CA); children:
        2646 a. Carol Wendy[7] Betenbaugh m. Jerry Allen Watson
        2647 b. Jill Ann[7] Betenbaugh m. Philip James Conner
        2648 c. Sherry Lynn Betenbaugh m. Theodore Charles Czuprynski
  2649 iii. Hubert Stanley[6] Betenbaugh m. Bernadette Burnet (live Bakersfield, CA); children:
        2650 a. Christina Marie[7] Betenbaugh
        2651 b. Paul Martin[7] Betenbaugh
        2652 c. Rita Ann[7] Betenbaugh
        2653 d. Susan[7] Betenbaugh
        2654 e. Antoinette[7] Betenbaugh.

2482. Thomas[5] Willard (Elizabeth[4], David[3], John Uriah[2], Michael[1]) was born c1859 and died before 1900. He married Sallie T. Faucett,[57] who was born 15 April 1867 and died 2 September 1946. After the death of Thomas Willard, she married W. T. (Will) Wilburn. Child:
  2655 i. Thomas[6] Willard, b. 15 June 1882, d. 9 Oct 1932, bur. Hebron Bapt Ch., Union Co., SC.

2483. Mary[5] Willard (Elizabeth[4], David[3], John Uriah[2], Michael[1]) was born 30 August 1856, died 4 February 1926. She married, about 1875,[58] Leonard Keisler, who was born 21 January 1852 and died 12 February 1925. Both are buried at Mt. Vernon Presbyterian Church in Union County, South Carolina. Seven children:
  2656 i. John D.[6] Keisler, b. 10 March 1878, d. 11 Nov 1950, m. Mamie McGowan, b. 3 Nov 1871, d. 12 Nov 1957, buried Union Mem. Garden.
  2657 ii. Ruth[6] Keisler
  2658 iii. Frances[6] Keisler, b. Nov 1885
  2659 iv. Robert Murphy[6] Keisler, b. 29 Aug 1888, d. 3 Dec 1955, wife Lorena b. 13 Feb 1884, d. 10 July 1964, bur. Rosemont Cem.
  2660 v. Anna Pearl[6] Keisler, b. 16 July 1891, d. 1 July 1974, m. George S. Noland, b. 17 July 1889, d. 19 May 1957, both bur. Rosemont Cem, Union, SC.
  2661 vi. Wallace[6] Keisler, b. 14 Nov 1893, d. 28 Sept 1967, bur. Union Memorial Garden
  2662 vii. Russell[6] Keisler, b. 1 Aug 1896, d. 11 Apr 1926, bur. Mt. Vernon Pres. Church.

2484. David Jefferson[5] Willard (Elizabeth[4], David[3], John Uriah[2], Michael[1]) was born 18 February 1863 and died 5 October 1934. He married, c1883, Janie Sanders, who was born 25 September 1865 and died 10 January 1901, the daughter of William and

THE BEDENBAUGH-BETENBAUGH FAMILY

Katherine (Humphries) Sanders. Both are buried at Sardis United Methodist Church. Six children:
+ 2663 i. Humphries Henry[6] Willard, b. 15 Feb 1884
  2664 ii. Glover E.[6] Willard, b. 15 Jan 1886, d. 17 July 1947, unm.
+ 2665 iii. Kate[6] Willard, b. 11 Aug 1888 married Robert Jenkins
+ 2666 iv. Mattie Louise[6] Willard, b. 23 July 1892 married Preston Bailey
  2667 v. Bessie[6] Willard, b. 20 Sept 1895, m. 18 Jan 1930, Sam Sherbert. They had an infant son, b. 31 Jan & d. 1 Feb 1922
  2668 vi. Janie S.[6] Willard, b. 5 Jan 1901, d. 29 Jan 1901.

2485. Martha[5] Willard (Elizabeth[4], David[3], John Uriah[2], Michael[1]) was born 22 September 1865 and died 8 January 1940. She married Glenn P. Adams, who was born 6 October 1853, and died 24 July 1909. They are buried at Sardis United Methodist Church, Union County, South Carolina. There were thirteen children, several of whom died in infancy. The surviving children were, as follows:
  2669 i. Annie[6] Adams, b. 16 Oct 1881, d. 25 Sept 1946
  2670 ii. Betty[6] Adams, b. 29 Sept 1883, d. 4 Dec 1954, m. 1909 Thomas McManus, b. 18 Sept 1874, d. 3 March 1953, both bur. Sardis United Meth. Ch.
  2671 iii. Ethel[6] Adams, b. 26 Nov 1886, d. 5 March 1942
  2672 iv. Leathea[6] Adams, b. 19 May 1887, d. 25 Feb 1955
  2673 v. Martha[6] (Mattie) Adams, b. 15 Oct 1890, d. 22 Sept 1935, m. J. F. Queen
  2674 vi. Carrie[6] Adams, b. 12 Aug 1898, d. 6 Dec 1969
  2675 vii. Ethel[6] Adams, b. 1896
  2676 viii. Irene[6] Adams, b. 1899
  2677 ix. Mamie[6] Adams, b. 1902, m. John Tessier
  2678 x. James M.[6] Adams, b. 1907.

2486. Joseph J.[5] Willard (Elizabeth[4], David[3], John Uriah[2], Michael[1]) was born 7 November 1872, died 27 April 1938. He married, about 1899,[59] Sallie J. Baldwin, who was born 22 February 1879, and died 28 May 1959. Both are buried at Sardis United Methodist Church in Union County. Children:
+ 2679 i. Lois[6] Willard, b. 19 Apr 1900.
  2680 ii. John D.[6] Willard, b. & d. 1902, bur. Sardis United Meth. Ch.
+ 2681 iii. Joe Barth[6] Willard, b. 17 Sept 1904
+ 2682 iv. Harry Baldwin[6] Willard, b. 30 Oct 1912.

2487. Sarah Ellen[5] Betenbaugh (John J.[4], David[3], John Uriah[2], Michael[1]) was born 16 May 1859 died 20 February 1934. She married, in 1875, Gilliam Gregory who was born 1 January 1854 and died 20 January 1926. Both are buried Hebron Baptist Church in Union County, South Carolina. Children:
+ 2683 i. John Clarence[6] Gregory, b. 4 Sept 1876
  2684 ii. Mamie[6] Gregory, b. 25 Jan 1878, d., 3 Jan 1963, m. Rev. Jesse C. Lawson
  2685 iii. Theodore Monroe[6] Gregory, b. 12 Dec 1879, d. 12 Nov 1954, m. Della Foster, b. 15 June 1882
  2686 iv. Leila Pearl[6] Gregory, b. 12 Dec 1879, d. 25 Dec 1883
+ 2687 v. Grover Cleveland[6] Gregory, b. 13 Nov 1884
  2688 vi. Nelle[6] Gregory, b. 20 Jan 1887, d. 15 Oct 1977, m. 15 Aug 1909[60] J. Hunter Finney
+ 2689 vii. Eugene[6] Gregory, b. 2 May 1889 (twin)

2690 viii. Colene[6] Gregory, b. 2 May 1889 (twin), m. Luke Scott
2691 ix. Sarah Louise[6] Gregory, b. 23 June 1892, d. 1971, m. Fletcher Clark
2692 x. Gilliam Maurice[6] Gregory, b. 25 Oct 1896, d. 16 May 1946, m. Helen
      Sweeney
+ 2693 xi. Ida[6] Gregory, b. 20 Apr 1902.

2488. James Beauregard[5] Betenbaugh (John J.[4], David[3], John Uriah[2], Michael[1]) was born in 1860 and died 10 January 1937,[61] Union County, South Carolina. He married, first, c1883, Sarah Ann (Sallie) Greer, who was born 4 April 1844, and died 28 May 1924,[62] a daughter of Jason Martin, Sr., and Sarah (Sanders) Greer. He married, second, on 30 December 1924, Sarah (Sallie) Goforth,[63] who was born 28 September 1876 and died 16 January 1967. There were no children by either marriage. Sallie (Goforth) Betenbaugh married, second, on 12 November 1947, Robert Lee Young. All are buried at Sardis United Methodist Church.

2490. Fannie McNelie[5] Beatenbough (T. R.[4], Michael[3], John Uriah[2], Michael[1]) was born 27 November 1870 and died 26 December 1952. She married, on 8 August 1887, John Walton Jordan. They are buried at Zidon Baptist Church, Franklin County, Georgia. Children:
2694 i. Estee[6] Jordan m. Lee Fowler
2695 ii. Millie B.[6] Jordan m. Lude Bishop
2696 iii. Revie[6] Jordan m. 1st Tom Dudley; m. 2nd Curt Whiten; m. 3rd Claude
      Addison
2697 iv. Carrie Sue[6] (Peggy) Jordan m. Repard James
2698 v. Vassie Lou[6] (Casey) Jordan m. 1st Paul Chastain; m. 2nd Hall Roach
2699 vi. Sammie[6] Jordan m. Vera Berryman
2700 vii. Hamilton[6] Jordan
2701 viii. Wade[6] Jordan m. Lilly Smith
2702 ix. Brooks[6] Jordan m. Eva Hanley
2703 x. Harvey[6] Jordan m. Verba Chastain.

2491. Henry Estee[5] Beatenbough (T. R.[4], Michael[3], John Uriah[2], Michael[1]) was born on 7 Apr 1873 in Franklin County, Georgia, and died 26 December 1959. Buried in Dec 1959 at Shiloh Baptist Church, Madison County, GA. He married, on 16 February 1896, Martha Williford "Mattie" Carruth, who was born on 26 March 1875 in Madison County, Georgia, and died 13 December 1959. Both are buried at Shiloh Baptist Church in Madison County. They had the following children, all born in Madison County, Georgia:

2704 i. Johnnie Ralph[6] Beatenbough, b. 16 Feb 1897, d. 18 May 1899, bur.
      Liberty Meth. Ch., Madison Co., GA
+ 2705 ii. Horace Hughey[6] Beatenbough, b. 23 March 1899
+ 2706 iii. Charles Edwin[6] Beatenbough, b. 30 Oct 1901
+ 2707 iv. William Clifford[6] Beatenbough, b. 27 Dec 1905
+ 2708 v. Clara Elizabeth[6] Beatenbough, b. 27 Dec 1905
+ 2709 vi. Robert King[5] Beatenbough. b. 23 Jul 1908
2710 vii. Michael[6] Beatenbough, b. 25 Jun 1910, d. 15 Nov 1914, bur. Liberty
      Meth Ch., Madison Co., GA
+ 2711 viii. Thomas Reeder[6] Beatenbough, b. 21 Sep 1912.

2492. Hanna Lou[5] "Nettie" Beatenbough (T. R.[4], Michael[3], John Uriah[2], Michael[1]) was born 15 July 1876 in Franklin County, Georgia, and died 14 May 1923. She married John Morgan Phillips and is buried at Zidon Bapt Church, Franklin County, Georgia. Children:

2712   i. T. R.[6] Phillips
2713 ii. May Phillips[6] m. Plumer Mealor
2714 iii. Callie[6] Phillips
2715 iv. Mattie Lee[6] Phillips, m. Odis Cromer
2716   v. Howard[6] Phillips, m. Bevie Smith
2717 vi. Lafayette[6] Phillips
2718 vii. Hoyt[6] Phillips
2719 viii. Grady[6] Phillips.

2495. Charlie Amos[5] Beatenbough (T. R.[4], Michael[3], John Uriah[2], Michael[1]) was born 7 September 1885 in Franklin County, Georgia, and died 8 July 1929. He married Mamie Cape and is buried at Zidon Baptist Church, Franklin County, Georgia.
Children:

2720   i. Virgil[6] (Fudge) Beatenbo m. Bertie Guess; children:
       2721 a. Charlie Eldon[7] Beatenbo m. Ethel Overcash; children:
             2722 (1) Charlie Eldon[8] Beatenbo, Jr., m. Linda Forrester
             2723 (2) Joyce Elaine[8] Beatenbo m. Danny Hamilton
             2724 (3) Judy Anne[8] Beatenbo m. Carl Helton, Jr.
             2725 (4) Virgil Wayne[8] Beatenbo
             2726 (5) Joan[8] Beatenbo m. Clayton Christopher
       2727 b. Lettie Mae[7] Beatenbo m. Junior Lewis; children:
             2728 (1) Linda Faye[8] Lewis m. Eddie Klein
             2729 (2) Danny[8] Lewis
             2730 (3) Ricky[8] Lewis
       2731 c. Louise[7] Beatenbo m. Homer Lee Clay; children:
             2732 (1) Homer Lee[8] Clay, Jr.
             2733 (2) Tommy[8] Clay
             2734 (3) Deanie[8] Clay
2735 ii. R. V.[6] Beatenbough m. Sis James
2736 iii. Idis[6] Beatenbough m. Azalea ____; children:
       2737 a. Rodney[7] Beatenbough
       2738 b. Annie Louise[7] Beatenbough
       2739 c. Stewart[7] Beatenbough
       2740 d. David[7] Beatenbough
2741 iv. Odis[6] Beatenbough
2742   v. Grace[6] Beatenbough m. Bill Overcash
2743 vi. Watson[6] Beatenbough m. Louise ____.

2497. Nancy Jane[5] "Jennie" Beatenbough (T. R.[4], Michael[3], John Uriah[2], Michael[1]) was born 19 October 1888 and died 8 December 1973 in Georgia. She is buried at Shiloh Baptist Church, Madison County, Georgia. She married Edgar Hamilton Carey. Children:

2744   i. Albert Worley[6] Carey, b. 17 November 1911, m. 17 Nov 1934 Edna Ward
2745 ii. Comi Castine[6] Carey, b. 2 Jan 1914, m. Grady Fortson
2746 iii. Mary Modie[6] Carey, b. 13 Apr 1915, m. Eldridge Crowe
2747 iv. Candler Thurman[6] Carey, b. 10 Oct 1919, m. 23 Dec 1938 Dorcas Fitzpatrick
2748   v. Trammel Alton[6] Carey, b. 12 Sept 1924, m. Betty Jean Folson

2749   vi. Jimmy Mitchell[6] Carey, b. 24 Nov 1930, m. Faye Dora Hill; children:
    2750 a. Wanda Dianne[7] Carey, b. 9 April 1956
    2751 b. Dana Leanne[7] Carey, b. 20 Sept 1972
2752   vii. Ila Mae[6] Carey, b. 11 Oct 1917, d. 3 June 1919
2753   viii. Hershell M.[6] Carey, b. 14 Nov 1922, d. 8 June 1923.

2498. Freddy Glen[5] "Fred" Beatenbough (T. R.[4], Michael[3], John Uriah[2], Michael[1]) was born 3 January 1892 in Franklin County, Georgia, and died 20 February 1946 in Georgia. He married Pearl Bray and is buried at Shiloh Baptist Church, Madison County, Georgia. Children:
2754   i. Woodrow Isaiah[6] Beatenbo, b. 8 Aug 1914, m. Georgia Willie Fitts. Child:
    2755 a. Anthony Wayne[7] Beatenbo m. Linda White; child:
        2756 (1) Joseph Scott[8] Beatenbo born 28 August 1968
2757   ii. Gaston G.[6] Beatenbo, b. 20 Apr 1921, m. 26 June 1938 Kathryn Bird; child:
    2758 a. Barbara Elizabeth[7] Beatenbo, b. 24 Feb 1942, Field Ave, Va., m. 13 Nov 1959 James F. McGee, Jr.; children:
        2759 (1) James Darwin[8] McGee, b. 2 Feb 1962 Clark Co., Ga.
        2760 (2) Janet Delores[8] McGee, b. 27 Oct 1964 Jackson Co., Ga.
    2761 b. Sarah Althea[8] Beatenbough, m. Homer Lee Bond; children:
        2762 (1) Pascal[9] Bond
        2763 (2) Jerry[9] Bond
        2764 (3) Sarah[9] Bond
2765   iii. Henry Elmo[6] Beatenbo, b. 27 May 1926, m. 21 Jan 1947 Johnnie Mell Fitts; children:
    2766 a. Carol Ann Beatenbo, b. & d. 17 May 1948
    2767 b. Dennis F.[7] Beatenbo, b. 15 Feb 1950 Royston, GA
    2768 c. Deborah Leigh[7] Beatenbo, b. 19 July 1952.

2504. Toomy[5] Betenbough (Nicholas[4], Michael[3], John Uriah[2], Michael[1]) was born 7 May 1884 in Franklin County, Georgia and died 25 October 1952. He is buried in Tatum, New Mexico. He married, on 11 September 1918, Lena Estella Gentry who was born 4 August 1900 at Lone Wolf, Indian Territory (now Oklahoma). Children:
2769   i. Ronald Toomy[6] Betenbough, b. 8 Jan 1941, Lubbock, TX, m. 3 Aug 1963 Mildred Joy Sanders, b. 25 Jan 1945 Dumas, TX. He supplied information on the descendants of Nicholas Glen[4] Betenbough). Children:
    2770 a. Richard Toomy[7] Betenbough, b. 5 July 1964, Lubbock, TX
    2771 b. Arlan Sean[7] Betenbough, b. 1 Sept 1965 Lubbock, TX
    2772 c. Tohi Dawn[7] Betenbough, b. 18 June 1967 Lubbock, TX
    2773 d. Huni Renee[7] Betenbough, b. 4 Aug 1972 El Paso, TX
2774   ii. Wayne Lamar[6] Betenbough, b 14 May 1928, Amarillo, TX, m. 1st Maxine Collier; m. 2nd Shirley Ann Henry; m. 3rd Mary _____ ; children:
    2775 a. Wayne Lamar[7] Betenbough, Jr., b. 18 July 1954
    2776 b. Sheryl Ann[7] Betenbough, b. 9 Aug 1955, m. 15 Aug 1975 James Paul Dennis
    2777 c. Bryan Keith[7] Betenbough, b. 15 June 1967
    2778 d. Ronald Wayne[7] Betenbough, b. 15 Jan 1965
    2779 d. Donald Eugene[7] Betenbough, b. 15 Jan 1965.

2505. Cnitgrouss George[5] Betenbough (Nicholas[4], Michael[3], John Uriah[2], Michael[1]) was born 7 October 1886 in Franklin County, Georgia. He married, on 4 August 1920 in Roswell, New Mexico, Maudie Johnson. Children:

2780　i. Clinton George[6] Betenbough, b. 9 May 1922 Kenna, NM, m. 12 Jan 1946
　　　Bernice Waldrop; children:
　　　2781 a. Trudy Jean[7] Betenbough, b. 23 Oct 1948 Poncho Pass, CO, m.
　　　　　Jack Jordan
　　　2782 b. Karen Lee[7] Betenbough, b. 26 Feb 1950 Alamosa, CO
　　　2783 c. Vick Jan[7] Betenbough, b. 26 July 1951, Del Norte, CO
　　　2784 d. Edna Jo[7] Betenbough, b. 19 Oct 1954 Del Norte, CO.
　　　2785 e. Clinton Glen[7] Betenbough, born 13 June 1958 Del Norte, CO
2786　ii. D. J.[7] Betenbough, b. 2 March 1925, Tatum, NM, m. Anna Marie Martin;
　　　children:
　　　2787 a. Donald James Lee[8] Betenbough, b. 26 May 1946, Lovington, NM
　　　2788 b. Thelma Jean[8] Betenbough, b. 23 Oct 1948, Lovington, NM
　　　2789 c. Damon Martin[8] Betenbough, b. 21 Jan 1949, Lovington, NM
2790 iii. Dorthy Jean[7] Betenbough, b. 15 Dec 1928, Tatum, NM, m. 17 June 1947
　　　at Roswell, NM, James Thomas Bess; children:
　　　2791 a. Gayla Joyce[8] Bess, b. 8 Apr 1949, m. Michael Smith
　　　2792 b. Sherry Jean[8] Bess, b. 2 March 1952, m. Devoe Taylor.

2506. Carl[5] Betenbough (Nicholas[4], Michael[3], John Uriah[2], Michael[1]) was born 19 January 1888 in Bowie, Texas, and died 28 June 1968 in Ruidoso, New Mexico. He married, on 15 March 1915, Ona Marie Braswell, who born 20 August 1894 in Ironton, Missouri. One child:
　　　2793 i. Lilburn Glenn[6] Betenbough, b. 25 March 1916, O'Donnel, TX, m. Helen Marie Cox; children:
　　　　　2794 a. Terry Glen[7] Betenbough, b 23 Nov 1941, Andrew, TX, m. Sandra Kay Brice
　　　　　2795 b. Carl Vin[7] Betenbough, b. 9 July 1947 Andrews, TX, m. Barbara Kay Clay.

2536. Frank Edward[5] Davis (Frances[4], Elizabeth[3], John Uriah[2], Michael[1]) was born 28 March 1859 and died 23 March 1939. He married, on 4 April 1889, Caroline Virginia (Carrie) Sartor, who was born 10 February 1861 and died 24 July 1959, the daughter of William Henry and Catherine Brandon (Young) Sartor. Children, born Union County, South Carolina:
　　　2796　i. Annie Belle[6] Davis, b. 3 Oct 1891, d. 11 May 1993 (aged 101), m. 1st 5 Apr 1911, William Thaddeus Holcomb, b. 9 July 1974, d. 24 Feb 1932; m. 2nd 10 Nov 1936, Jefferson Bennette Stone, b. 27 Jan 1985, d. 20 June 1973
　　　2797 ii. Kathleen[6] Davis, b. 18 June 1892, d. 1 May 1893
　　　2798 iii. Jack Hiram[6] Davis, b. 13 Apr 1894, d. 8 Nov 1895
　　　2799 iv. Ethelind Lucille[6] Davis, b. 7 June 1896, d. 23 Sept 1951, m. William Matthews Butler, b. 23 Feb 1870, d. 8 May 1945. Both bur. at Cane Creek Pres. Ch., Union Co., SC.
+ 2800　v. Carrie Sartor[6] Davis, b. 1 July 1903.

2537. Caroline Virginia[5] (Virgie) Davis (Frances[4], Elizabeth[3], John Uriah[2], Michael[1]) was born 11 September 1861 in Union District, South Carolina, and died 7 January 1932 in Union County. She married, on 1 November 1882, John Fletcher Brandon, who was born 25 January 1860 in Union District and died 18 October 1915. Both are buried at Sardis United Methodist Church in Union County. The journals of John Fletcher Brandon have provided much data on this family group. Children:
　　　2801　i. Obry Davis[6] Brandon, b. 13 Aug 1883, d. same year.

2802 ii. Frank Kenneth[6] Brandon, b. 1 Nov 1884, d. 4 Sept 1940
+ 2803 iii. Sarah Francis Elizabeth[6] Brandon, b. 1 Sept 1887
2804 iv. Hardie Stroud[6] Brandon, b. 11 July 1889, d. 31 Nov 1954, m. Sallie
       Sligh; children:
          2805 a. William Wallace[7] Brandon, d. 31 Aug 1914
          2806 b. Cleo[7] Brandon
+ 2807 v. Lovick Pierce[6] Brandon, b. 16 Aug 1891
2808 vi. John Herbert[6] Brandon, b. 25 Aug 1893
2809 vii. Paul David[6] Brandon, b. 6 July 1895
+ 2810 viii. Janie Musgrove[6] Brandon, b. 1 Nov 1899
2811 ix. Cleopatra Virginia[6] Brandon, b. 2 Sept 1904, d. 19 June 1905.

2551. Eva[5] Betenbaugh (Christopher[4], John[3], John Uriah[2], Michael[1]) was born 5 July 1883 and died 1 April 1943. She married Vernon Gault, who was born 18 October 1872 and died 1 February 1930. Children:
2812 i. Marie[6] Gault, b. 14 Nov 1901, d. 20 May 1975, m. Thomas Edgar
       Hollingsworth, b. 29 Nov 1899, d. 8 March 1924; two children:
          2813 a. Helen[7] Hollingsworth, b. 8 June 1921, m. Reese Beckham
          2814 b. Thomas E.[7] Hollingsworth, b. 3 June 1923, d. 14 June 1966
2815 ii. Mable[6] Gault, b. 25 Aug 1905, d. 3 Nov 1988, Union, SC, unm.
2816 iii. Mamie[6] Gault m. Guy Hughes, no ch.

2557. Cynthia Pearl[5] Betenbaugh (Christopher[4], John[3], John Uriah[2], Michael[1]) was born 5 May 1892 and died 29 March 1982. She married, on 17 April 1912, Charles D. Blalock,[64] who was born 29 March 1892 and died 27 December 1942. They are buried at Forest Lawn Cemetery in Union, South Carolina Mrs. Pearl B. Blalock supplied information on descendants of John Betenbaugh. Children:
2817 i. Charles D.[6] Blalock, Jr., b. 28 May 1913, m. 18 July 1987, Greenwood, SC,
       m. 30 Aug 1953, Dorothy Hart, no ch.
2818 ii. James Clyde[6] Blalock, b. 19 May 1915, d. 20 Aug 1982 in Union, SC, bur.
       Forest Lawn Cem.
2819 iii. Ruby[6] Blalock, b. 17 Nov 1919, m. 26 Dec 1949 Ray Singleton, reside
       Monroe, NC; children:
          2820 a. Ray[7] Singleton, Jr., b. 20 Oct 1950
          2821 b. Sarah Jane[7] Singleton, b. 8 May 1954
2922 iv. Frances[6] Blalock, b. 1 June 1921, m. 4 May 1944 Dwight Wesley Bowling,
       resides Columbia, SC; children:
          2923 a. Dwight Wesley[7] Bowling, Jr., b. 14 Nov 1949, m. Thomasine
             Rodgers; children:
                2924 (1) Emily Rodgers[8] Bowling, b. 26 June 1979
                2925 (2) Dwight Wesley[8] Bowling, III, b. 23 Jan 1983
          2926 b. Susan[7] Bowling, b. 11 Sept 1953, m. 25 Sept 1976 Don Reeves;
             children:
                2927 (1) Don Allen[8] Reeves, Jr., b. 10 Jan 1978
                2928 (2) Amy Frances[8] Reeves, b. 8 May 1979
                2929 (3) Sarah Kathryn[8] Reeves, b. 16 June 1988
          2930 c. James[7] Bowling, b. 3 Nov 1955
2931 v. John[6] Blalock, 28 Jan 1923, resides Union, SC.

2575. William Decater[5] (Bud) Keenan (Nancy[4], Mary Ann[3], John Uriah[2], Michael[1]) was born 1876 in Union County, South Carolina, and died 1951 in Cherokee

County, South Carolina. He married, about 1899, Ida Mae Bridges (1880-1933).
Both are buried at Macedonia Baptist Church in Cherokee County. Children:
    2932 i. Cora Lee[6] Keenan, d. young.
    2933 ii. Lillie Belle[6] Keenan, m. John E. Clary; children:
            2934 a. Margaret[7] Clary, m. Wilson Johnson
            2935 b. Libbie[7] Clary, m. Nick Cumom
            2936 c. J. Raymond[7] Clary
+ 2937 iii. Ira Lee[6] Keenan, b. 28 Dec 1900
    2938 iv. William Baxter[6] Keenan, b. 14 July 1902., d. 10 Mar 1980, bur. Sunset
        Mem. Gardens, Tampa, FL. He m. 1st Lillie Dial, 2nd Juanita ____. One
        child:
            2939 a. William[7] Keenan
    2940 v. Mamie Catherine[6] Keenan m. Odis Huskey
+ 2941 vi. Ida Mae[6] Keenan, b. 24 Aug 1908, m. W. Harold Friddle, b. 19 Aug
        1910, d. 1946
+ 2942 vii. Coleman Blease[6] Keenan, b. 1 July 1912, m. 8 Feb 1936 Gaynell Hall,
        b. 18 Feb 1916
    2943 viii. Paul Herman[6] Keenan, m. Edith McCraw; child:
            2944 a. Ida Mae[7] Keenan, m. Horace Whelchel
+ 2945 ix. James Talmadge[6] Keenan, b. 3 Nov 1916, m. 23 Dec 1923, Louise Cook,,
        b. 5 Nov 1917.

2576. James Webster[5] (Jimmy) Keenan (Nancy[4], Mary Ann[3], John Uriah[2], Michael[1])
was born 10 June 1878 in Union County, South Carolina, and died 6 October 1940
in Cherokee County, South Carolina. He married, in 1898, Nancy Stella Jenkins,
who was born 2 February 1884, and died 11 May 1941. Both are buried at State Line
Baptist Church in Cherokee County. Children:
    2946 i. Clara[6] Keenan, m. Homer Alexander; children:
            2947 a. Kelly[7] Alexander
            2948 b. Ralph[7] Alexander
            (two other children)
    2949 ii. Nannie Emma[6] Keenan, m. Bailey Cromer, and they had four children
    2950 iii. Marie[6] Keenan, m. Arthur Tabor.
+ 2951 iv. Clyde Webster[6] Keenan, b. 6 Nov 1904
    2952 v. Rosa Lee[6] Keenen, m. Reece Hayes
    2953 vi. William[6] Keenan, m. 1st Mary Lou Wiles, 2nd ____ Drister
+ 2954 vii. Mazie[6] Keenan
    2955 viii. Hattie[6] Keenan, m. Ramsey Spencer
    2956 ix. Mae[6] Keenan m. Sam Hoover
    2957 x. Thomas Lonzo[6] Keenan, m. Janette Fowler
    2958 xi. Howard[6] Keenen
    2959 xii. Ella[6] Keenan, m. Elma Henderson
+ 2960 xiii. Paul Edward[6] Keenan, b. 3 Dec 1923.

2577. Bernice Arminta[5] Keenan (Nancy[4], Mary Ann[3], John Uriah[2], Michael[1]) was
born 7 September 1881 and died 30 August 1927. She married William Alexander
White who was born 31 May 1867 in North Carolina and died 10 November 1921
in Central, Pickens County, South Carolina. He is buried at Mt. Zion United
Methodist Church.[65] Children:
    2961 i. Noah I.[6] White m. Essie Turner; child:
            2962 a. James[7] White
    2963 ii. Arminta[6] White (d. 8 Mar 1972), m. Forest Byrd Newsome; children:

2964 a. Forest Byrd[7] Newsome, Jr.
2965 b. Margaret[7] Newsome
2966 c. Bobbie[7] Newsome
2967 d. Opal[7] Newsome
2968 iii. Willie Mae[6] White, m. Guy C. Landrum
2969 iv. Bernice[6] White, m. Oral Duke Dyer; children:
    2970 a. Doris[7] Dyer m. John Ayers
    2971 b. Oral Doyle[7] Dyer, m. Marie Lynn
    2972 c. Teddy[7] Dyer, m. John Decarlis; children:
        2973 (1) John[8] Decarlis, Jr.
        2974 (2) David[8] Decarlis
2975 v. Webster M.[6] White m. Ruby Hopkins
2976 vi. Elbert B.[6] White, m. Ruth McGriff
2977 vii. Lorene[6] White m. Ernest C. Devenport.

2578. Ira Henry[5] Keenan (Nancy[4], Mary Ann[3], John Uriah[2], Michael[1]) was born 3 September 1883 in Spartanburg County, South Carolina, and died 17 November 1945. He married Olly Ann Williams, who was born 30 June 1893 in Cocke County, Tennessee, and died 15 April 1985. They are buried in Woodlawn Memorial Cemetery in Greenville, South Carolina. Children:
+ 2978 i. Ira Kenith[6] Keenan, b. 23 Aug 1917
+ 2979 ii. Alvin Decatur[6] Keenan, b. 14 Oct 1919
+ 2980 iii. Duran Garrett[6] Keenan, b. 22 Feb 1922
+ 2981 iv. Evelyn Inez[6] Keenan, b. 4 Aug 1925
+ 2982 v. Theodore Roosevelt[6] Keenan, b. 23 July 1927
+ 2983 vi. Henry Junior[6] Kennan, b. 19 Nov 1928
+ 2984 vii. James Douglas Keenan, b. 4 May 1933.

2579. Beulah[5] Keenan (Nancy[4], Mary Ann[3], John Uriah[2], Michael[1]) was born 27 May 1887 in Spartanburg County, South Carolina, and died 2 October 1951. She married Newton A. Quinn, who was born 5 April 1884 and died 3 November 1965. Both are buried Paris Mountain Holiness Baptist Cemetery in Greenville County, South Carolina. Children:
+ 2985 i. Dewey William[6] Quinn, b. 3 Feb 1904
  2986 ii. Mae Irene[6] Quinn, b. 21 Feb 1909, m. 1st Fred Boling, b. 1912, d. 15 Oct 1933; m. 2nd Powers. children:
    2987 a. Nettie Sue[7] Powers, m. ____ Moore
    2988 b. Juanita[7] Powers, m. Lowell Cross
    2989 c. Emily Jeannelle[7] Powers, b. 9 Sept 1937, d. 25 Oct 1962
  2990 iii. Clara Ethel[6] Quinn, b. 28 Aug 1911, m. William T. Duncan; children:
    2991 a. Randy[7] Duncan
    2992 b. Sandra[7] Duncan, m. Nick Grillo; child:
        2993 (1) Nick[8] Grillo
  2994 iv. Ibera Beatrice[6] Quinn, b. 1 Apr 1913, m. John Sam Smith, b. 25 Dec 1912; one child:
    2995 a. Nancy Jennette[7] Smith
  2996 v. Houston Herbert[6] Quinn (1920-1976), m. 1st Lila Lunsford; m. 2nd Nona Lee Carpenter; children:
    2997 a. Stanley[7] Quinn
    2998 b. Ronnie[7] Quinn
  2999 vi. Harold Newton[6] Quinn, b. 1921, m. 1st Janie Vaughan; m 2nd Flossie Alexander

+ 3000 vii. Frances Elizabeth[6] Quinn, b. 19 July 1926.

2580. John Robert Levi[5] McCreight (Herndon[4], Mary Ann[3], John Uriah[2], Michael[1]) was born 4 July 1873 in Union County, South Carolina, and died 1 August 1935, in Greenville, South Carolina. He married Nannie Jane Miller, who was born 15 December 1882, and died 1 April 1928. Both are buried in the Gramling Methodist Church Cemetery. Children:
   3001   i. Luther[6] McCreight, b. c1903, d. 1923, unm.
   3002   ii. John[6] McCreight, b. c1905, m. Annie Belle Harris; child:
        3003 a. Sarah Alice[7] McCreight, d. unm.
   3004   iii. Clarence[6] McCreight, b. c1907, m. Nora Lloyd; children:
        3005 a. Jacky[7] McCreight
        3006 b. Margaret[7] McCreight
        3007 c. Ruby[7] McCreight
+ 3008   iv. Paul Levi[6] McCreight, b. 17 Apr 1909
+ 3009   v. Elsie Mary Lee[6] McCreight, b. 30 Sept 1911
   3010   vi. Virginia[6] McCreight, b. 20 Jan 1916, m. 1st ___ Dewbery, m. 2nd Tom Newton Broome
   3011   vii. Michael Harry[6] McCreight, b. 1918, m. Bernice Yokum; children:
        3012 a. Larry[7] McCreight, m. Ann Brown
        3013 b. Michael Harry[7] McCreight
        3014 c. (dau)
        3015 d. (dau)
   3016   viii. Mildred[6] McCreight, b. c1921, m. Arthur Odlum; child:
        Ronald Odlum
+ 3017   ix. George Edward[6] McCreight, b. 14 Sept 1923.

2581. Alice Gertrude[5] McCreight (Herndon[4], Mary Ann[3], John Uriah[2], Michael[1]) was born 1 January 1883, Greenville, South Carolina, and died 21 July 1974. She married Rev. Emmerize Bozman Dock Foister, who was born 11 May 1882, and died 31 August 1940.[66] They are buried at Paris Mt. Holiness Baptist Church in Greenville county. Children:
   3018   i. Jethro[6] Foister, b. Mar 1909, m. Grace Nalley, b. 12 June 1912; child:
        3019 a. Betty Sue[7] Foister, m. Roy Hendrix; child:
           3020 (1) Mark[8] Hendrix
        3021 b. Bobby Earl[7] Foister, m. Faye ____; children:
           3022 (1) Bobby Earl[8] Foister, Jr.
           3023 (2) Jody[8] Foister
           3024 (3) Susan[8] Foister
   3025   ii. George[6] Foister, b. 31 March 1911, m. 1st Annie Lester, 2nd Esther Jones; children:
        3026 a. Larry[7] Foister, b. 27 June 1967, m. 1st Dianne Shaw, 2nd Sally Swart; children:
           3027 (1) Brandon[8] Foister, b. 10 Aug 1984
           3028 (2) Samuel Logan[8] Foister, b. 22 March 1992
        3029 b. Martha[7] Foister, b. 18 Oct 1954, m. Samuel Delton Nelly
+ 3030   iii. Clarence[6] Foister, b. c1912
   3031   iv. Raymond[6] Foister, b. 27 Nov 1913, d. 29 Dec 1987, m. 1st, Myrtle Foister; m. 2nd, Grace Parker; child:
        3032 a. Mickey[7] Foister, b. 31 March 1944, m. Wilda Vaughan, b. 28 Dec 1945; child:

3033 (1) Angelia[8] Foister, b. 22 Oct 1968, m. Kyle Greer, b.
    25 Jan 1968
3034 v. Lucian[6] Foister, b. c1915, killed in WWII, m. Frances Turner
3035 vi. William[6] Foister, b. c1917, m. Ruby Keith; child
    3036 a. Judy[7] Foister
3037 vii. Zula[6] Foister, b, c1919, m. Claude Thomas; children:
    3038 a. Joe[7] Thomas, killed in Korean War
    3039 b. Jack[7] Thomas
    3040 c. Jimmy[7] Thomas, m. Barbara Brown
3041 viii. Mildred[6] Foister, b. 24 May 1921, m. Arnold Manueal Buckner, b. 12
    June 1920; child:
    3042 a. Glenda[7] Buckner, m. Robert Echols; children:
        3043 (1) Eric[8] Echols, m. Angie Holland
        3044 (2) Carla[8] Echols
3045 ix. Naomi[6] Foister, b. 30 March 1923, m. Robert L. Lister, b. 22 Oct 1917;
    children:
    3046 a. Bobby Joe[7] Lister, b. 25 Oct 1942, m. Louise Steel, b. 9 Feb
        1943; children:
        3047 (1) Alliston[8] Lister
        3048 (2) Ashley[8] Lister
    3049 b. Debbie[7] Lister, b. 4 Sept 194-, d. 1984, m. Steve Hall; children:
        3050 (1) Ginger[8] Hall
        3051 (2) Eric[8] Hall
    3052 c. Beverly[7] Lister, b. 5 Nov 1954, m. Dwight Reid; child:
        3053 (1) Kevin[8] Reid, b. 14 Dec 1975
3054 x. Evelyn[6] Foister, b. 4 Sept 1924, m. !951 Alton L. Arms, b. 23 July 1924;
    child:
    3055 a. Rhonda[7] Arms, b. 28 Jan 1962, m. David Altman; child:
        3056 (1) Madelaine[8] Altman, b. 23 Aug 1990
3057 xi. Dovie[6] Foister, b. 25 March 1926, m. Frank Milton Hopkins, b. 29 Aug
    1921; children:
    3058 a. Donnie Milton[7] Hopkins, b. 22 Aug 1946, m. Brenda Ranson
    3059 b. Frankie Dianne[7] Hopkins, m. 1st Jack Green, m. 2nd Bill
        Welford; children:
        3060 (1) Michelle[8] Green, m. Ricky Guinn; children:
            3061 Todd[9] Guinn
            3062 Tayler[9] Guinn
            3063 Tyler[9] Guinn
        3064 (2) Scott[8] Green, b. c1971.

2582. Sudie Agness[5] McCreight (Herndon[4], Mary Ann[3], John Uriah[2], Michael[1]) was
born 6 August 1886 and died 3 March 1974 at Inman, South Carolina. She married
William Calvin Cartee, who was born 13 September 1880 and died 11 June 1957, in
Spartanburg, South Carolina. They are buried at Holly Springs Baptist Church, near
Inman. Six children:[67]
3065 i. Boyce Lee[6] Cartee, b. 13 Apr 1907, d. 12 Nov 1967, bur. Holly Springs
    Bapt. Ch., m. 26 Jan 1925 Myrtle Roper
3066 ii. James Broadus[6] Cartee, b. 28 May 1910, d. 18 Nov 1982, bur. Wood
    Memorial, Spartanburg, SC, m. 17 Mar 1934, Minnie Roper
3067 iii. Roy Talmadge[6] Cartee, b. 24 Nov 1912, d. Apr 1970, bur. Wood
    Memorial, Spartanburg, m. Minnie Lee Crow
3068 iv. Hassie Louise[6] Cartee, b. c1916, m. Julive J. Chandler

3069 v. Georgia Mae[6] Cartee, b. 6 Jun 1919, m. 25 Aug 1939, Carl Vaughan Wyatt
3070 vi. Huey Amber[6] Cartee, b. 21 Aug 1922, d. 28 Dec 1986, bur. Roselawn Gardens, Spartanburg, SC, m. 19 Nov 1943 Frances M. Tucker.

2584. Hassie[5] McCreight (Herndon[4], Mary Ann[3], John Uriah[2], Michael[1]) was born in October 1897. She married Edward Rollins and was living in Greer, South Carolina, in 1974. Children:
3071 i. William[6] Rollins
3072 ii. Paul[6] Rollins
3073 iii. Vivian[6] Rollins
3074 iv. Myrtle[6] Rollins.

2585. Lillie Mae[5] McCreight (Herndon[4], Mary Ann[3], John Uriah[2], Michael[1]) was born 1 February 1902 and died 20 May 1984. She married James Curtis Cartee, who was born 25 November 1895 in Polk County, North Carolina, and died 1 March 1958 in Spartanburg. They are buried at Holly Springs Baptist Church near Inman, South Carolina. Eight children, all born Spartanburg, South Carolina:[68]
3075   i. Alma[6] Cartee, b. 30 July 1923, m. 10 Oct 1940, Floyd David Cudd
3076 ii. James Earle[6] Cartee, b. 6 June 1925, d. 5 Dec 1926, bur. Holly Springs Bapt. Ch., near Inman, SC
3077 iii. Ruby[6] Cartee, b. 29 Nov 1927, d. 23 Jan 1977, m. 1st Jerome Tapp, 2nd George Carpenter
3078 iv. Ethel Lorene[6] Cartee, b. 23 Feb 1930, d. 3 March 1930, bur. Holly Springs Bapt. Ch.
3079 v. Claude Edward[6] Cartee, b. 12 May 1932, d. 25 Dec 1987, bur. Hillcrest Garden, Spartanburg, SC, m. 31 Aug 1953 Vivian Annalle Mace
3080 vi. James Curtis[6] Cartee, Jr., b. 13 Apr 1938, m. Peggy Foster
3081 vii. Marvin Lewis[6] Cartee, b. 1 Feb 1970, m. 1st Helga Stegmann, 2nd 14 Aug 1964 Janet Charlene Ponder
3082 viii. Margie Faye[6] Cartee, b. 4 July 1944, m. Gordon Powell.

SIXTH GENERATION

2596. Della Young[6] Betenbaugh (Thomas J.[5], Micheal R.[4], David[3], John Uriah[2], Michael[1]) was born 14 October 1880 and died 29 June 1911. She married A. Nesbitt Vise, who was born 17 October 1861 and died 17 August 1911. They had four children.

   i. (infant), b. Nov 1898
+ 3083 ii. Boyce Malcolm[7] Vise, b. 4 Aug 1900
+ 3084 iii. Jeanette[7] Vise, b. 22 Aug 1905
 3085 iv. Ethel Cleora[7] Vise, b. 22 Feb 1908, d. 13 Nov 1983, Columbia, SC. bur. Dutch Fork Bapt. Church, Ballentine, SC, unm.

2599. James Sanders[6] Betenbaugh (Thomas J.[5], Micheal R.[4], David[3], John Uriah[2], Michael[1]) was born 22 August 1882 in Union County, South Carolina and died 6 November 1951. He married, on 9 July 1905,[69] Tillie Goodman, who was born 8 October 1886 and died 2 April 1964. James Sanders Betenbaugh became Union County Auditor upon the death of his father Thomas Joseph Betenbaugh. A photograph of him and his brother Roper is reproduced on page 157. James S. and Tillie G. Betenbaugh are buried at Sardis United Methodist Church. Seven children:
+ 3086 i. Herman Douglas[7] Betenbaugh, b. 27 Dec 1905
 3087 ii. Carl Alvin[7] Betenbaugh, b. 15 Sept 1907, d. 29 May 1933
   iii. (infant son), b. 7 Dec 1909
   iv. (infant son)
   v. (infant dau), d. Sept 1916
   vi. (infant son), d. 28 May 1919
 3088 vii. Patricia Ann[7] Betenbaugh, b. 27 Oct 1931, d. 15 July 1938.

2600. Madge Cleora[6] Betenbaugh (Thomas J.[5], Micheal R.[4], David[3], John Uriah[2], Michael[1]) was born 26 June 1884 and died 25 June 1938. She married Lawrence Burgess, who was born 3 October 1875 and died 26 May 1913. Both are buried at Sardis United Methodist Church in Union County. Two children:
 3089 i. Lewis Manley[7] Burgess
 3090 ii. Paul Heyward[7] Burgess, d. 20 Apr 1990, m. Rose Finger. Child:
   3091 a. Paul Heyward Burgess, Jr., m. Phyllis Kelly. child:
     3092 (1) Paul Heyward Burgess, III.

2601. Walter Russell[6] Betenbaugh (Thomas J.[5], Micheal R.[4], David[3], John Uriah[2], Michael[1]) was born 13 September 1899 in Union County, South Carolina, and died in Union, 5 January 1985. He married Kathleen Smith, who was born 30 April 1903 and died 18 December 1986. Child:
 3093 i. Walter Russell[7] Betenbaugh, Jr, m. 1st Frank Eline, m. 2nd, Susan ____; children:
   3094 a. Linda[8] Betenbaugh
   3095 b. David[8] Betenbaugh.

2604. Annie Lou[6] Betenbaugh (Thomas J.[5], Micheal R.[4], David[3], John Uriah[2], Michael[1]) was born 27 September 1892 and died 21 July 1984. She married, on 25 December 1913, in Union County, George Ernest Young, who was born 17 May 1890 in Union County and died there 12 October 1926. Two children:
+ 3096 i. Leila Mae[7] Young, b. 17 March 1920
 3097 ii. Frances Thomas[7] Young, b. 14 Feb 1926, m. Isaac Smith Vaughan, b. 10 May 1918, d. 4 Apr 1975.

James Sanders Betenbaugh and Roper Betenbaugh, Union County Auditor's Office

1918

2605. Morris Douglas[6] Betenbaugh (Thomas J.[5], Micheal R.[4], David[3], John Uriah[2], Michael[1]) was born 23 March 1895 in Union County, South Carolina, and died there 20 November 1977. He married, on 31 March 1918, Lola Lawson[7] Gregory (a second cousin once removed), who was born 27 October 1897 and died 27 June 1990. They are buried at Hebron Baptist Church in Union County. Children:

3098 i. Hazel[7] Betenbaugh, b. 18 Feb 1922, d. 1 Feb 1972, m. Ralph Robinson; children:

3099 a. Janet Sue[8] Robinson, b. 6 May 1948
3100 b. Ralph Douglas[8] Robinson, b. 1 Nov 1952
3101 ii. Nellie Sue[7] Betenbaugh, b. 6 Mar 1924, m. Thomas Davis.

2607. Charlie Norman[6] Betenbaugh (Thomas J.[5], Micheal R.[4], David[3], John Uriah[2], Michael[1]) was born 27 April 1902 and died 26 June 1965. He married, on 26 October 1936, Margaret Ruth Parks, who was born 21 May 1917 and died 14 June 1995 in Union, South Carolina. Six children:

3102 i. Helen Sue[7] Betenbaugh, m. Wilbur Lawson
3103 ii. Carl Roper[7] Betenbaugh
3104 iii. Bruce[7] Betenbaugh, m. 1st Linda Trantham; m. 2nd Linda Wells
3105 iv. Joyce[7] Betenbaugh, m. Bruce Carson
3106 v. Charlie[7] Betenbaugh, Jr., m. Gail Lewis
3107 vi. Robert[7] Betenbaugh, m. 1st Susan Hart; m. 2nd Patricia Dianne Holcombe.

2609. Nina Coline[6] Betenbaugh (Thomas J.[5], Micheal R.[4], David[3], John Uriah[2], Michael[1]) was born 8 December 1906. She married, on 12 February 1938, Henry E. Strahley, who was born 30 September 1905 and died 15 May 1978. Nine B. Strahley currently (1995) resides in Union, South Carolina. Children:

3108 i. Susan Earle[7] Strahley, b. 19 Sept 1941, m. 24 June 1962 Charlie Glaser, b. 8 June 1939 (live Union, SC); child:

3109 a. Susan Fair[8] Glaser, b. 5 Aug 1963 m. 17 Dec 1994 Ralph Lee Moss, Jr.
3110 ii. Rebecca Ann[7] Strahley (twin), b. 18 July 1944 m. 21 Dec 1965 Grover Mac Vinson, b. 19 Jan 1942 (live Greenville, SC); two children:

3111 a. David Mac[8] Vinson, b. 29 Sept 1969 Charlotte, NC
3112 b. Eric Earl[8] Vinson, b. 1 Nov 1972, Greenville, SC
3113 iii. William Michael[7] Strahley (twin), b. 18 July 1944 (lives Union, SC).

2610. Martha Ann[6] (Mattie) Betenbaugh (John C.[5], Micheal R.[4], David[3], John Uriah[2], Michael[1]) was born 18 November 1889 and died 10 March 1978 in Spartanburg, South Carolina. She married, on 16 January 1910, Lonnie Marcellous Littlejohn, who was born 15 February 1887 and died 19 December 1957. They are buried at Corinth Baptist Church, near Gaffney, South Carolina. Children:

+ 3114 i. Era Virginia[7] Littlejohn, b. 26 Sept 1912
+ 3115 ii. Lavare Verbena[7] Littlejohn, b. 15 July 1916
+ 3116 iii. Lonnie Vernon[7] Littlejohn, b. 5 May 1919
+ 3117 iv. Edisto Edith[7] Littlejohn, b. 10 Aug 1921
3118 v. Alvin Pittman[7] Littlejohn, b. 15 July 1924
3119 vi. Ruth Devinnie[7] Littlejohn, b. 1 May 1915, d. 8 Sept 1915
3120 vii. Helen Louise[7] Littlejohn, b. & d. 6 Apr 1931.

2611. William David[6] Betenbaugh (John C.[5], Micheal R.[4], David[3], John Uriah[2], Michael[1]) was born 16 May 1894 and died 11 September 1990 in High Point, North

Carolina. He married, on 20 February 1926, Mamie Foster, who was born 15 May 1904 and died 4 May 1989 in High Point. Children:

3121 i. William David[7] (Bill) Betenbaugh, Jr., b. 30 Jan 1927 in High Point, NC, m. Donna Belle Klamen; children:

    3122 a. Sheryl[8] Betenbaugh, b. 14 Feb 1963

    3123 b. Timothy Shawn[8] Betenbaugh, b. 5 May 1965

3124 ii. Betty[7] Betenbaugh, b. 16 Nov 1930, m. Delmar Burch Auman; children:

    3125 a. Richard Curtis[8] Auman, b. 26 Oct 1951, m. Kathy Ackers

    3126 b. Robin Marie[8] Auman, b. 20 Nov 1956, m. Fred Clement; child:

        3127 (1) Bradley[9] Clement

    3128 c. John Andrew[8] Auman, b. 17 Jan 1965, m. 19 Sept 1987 Tamara Lynn Siler, High Point, NC.

2612. Mary Morris[6] Betenbaugh (John C.[5], Micheal R.[4], David[3], John Uriah[2], Michael[1]) was born 29 January 1897 at White Stone in Spartanburg County, South Carolina, and died 11 October 1987 in Memphis, Tennessee. She married, on 24 December 1915, in Union, South Carolina, Rufus Thompson Holcomb, who was born 29 September 1893 and died 11 January 1952, the son of Jesse President and Rachael Ann (Young) Holcombe. Both are buried at Sardis United Methodist Church, Union County.

+ 3129 i. Gary Hope[7] Holcomb, b. 30 November 1916, Union, SC

  3130 ii. Mary Ruth[7] Holcombe, b. 6 May 1919, Union, SC

+ 3131 iii. Rufus T.[7] Holcomb, Jr., b. 31 December 1924, Union, SC

+ 3132 iv. Jessie Marie[7] Holcomb, b. 10 July 1932, High Point, NC

  3133 v. Nancy Janet[7] Holcomb, b. 17 April 1937, d. 23 May 1961, m. 8 March 1958 to Ben Nix, Jr. (no children).

2615. Charner Michael[6] Betenbaugh (John C.[5], Micheal R.[4], David[3], John Uriah[2], Michael[1]) was born 14 August 1907, in Union, South Carolina. He married, first, on 27 March 1937, Gladys Lucille Totten, who was born 28 January 1910 and died 12 February 1987 in High Point, North Carolina. He married, second, 4 April 1988, Gladys (Nunn) Bowman, in High Point, where they reside (1995). One child:

3134 i. Gordon Murray[7] Betenbaugh, b. 30 June 1941, m. 5 June 1965, Helen Reckenzaun. Gordon lives in Beaumont, Texas; two children:

    3135 a. Melanie Louise[8] Betenbaugh, b. 7 July 1970

    3136 b. Jennifer Elaine[8] Betenbaugh, b. 19 Dec 1972.

2616. Alvin S.[6] Jolly (Annie Elizabeth[5], Micheal[4], David[3], John Uriah[2], Michael[1]) was born 12 April 1886 and died 25 October 1964. He married Nina Belcher. Children:

3137 i. Alvin S.[7] Jolly, Jr., m. Dorothy Harlan; child:

    3138 a. Alvin S.[8] Jolly III

3139 ii. Edward K.[7] Jolly, b. 9 Aug 1923, m. Dorothy Harrilson; children:

    3140 a. Deborah[8] Jolly, b. 5 Nov 1953

    3141 b. Edward K.[8] Jolly, Jr., 17 Jan 1957

    3142 c. Benjamin[8] Jolly, b. 15 May 1968

3143 iii. Christine[7] Jolly, b. 18 Jan 1928 m. Paul Anderson.

2618. Thomas Claude[6] Jolly (Annie Elizabeth[5], Micheal[4], David[3], John Uriah[2], Michael[1]) was born 11 November 1892 and died 13 November 1971. He married Mary Spears and had three children:

3144 i. Thomas C.[7] Jolly III, d. 23 Oct 1994, m. Mollie Heath; children:

3145 a. Thomas C.[8] Jolly, IV

3146 b. Christopher[8] Jolly

3147 ii. Mary Ann[7] Jolly, m. Thomas Mack

3148 iii. Michael Spears[7] Jolly, b. 17 June 1925, d. 1 Dec 1984, m. 18 Dec 1948 Betty Pope, b. 6 Aug 1925. Mike Spears Jolly was city attorney of Union and solicitor in the 16th Judicial Circuit.

 3149 a. Michael S.[8] Jolly, Jr., b. 21 Nov 1950, m. Helen Free

 3150 b. Robert Ross[8] Jolly, b. 26 June 1952, m. Judy Martin

 3151 c. Lynn[8] Jolly, b. 29 July 1957, m. Stan Sewell.

2621. Leila Pearl[6] Jolly (Annie Elizabeth[5], Micheal[4], David[3], John Uriah[2], Michael[1]) was born 17 August 1903. She married, on 14 December 1936, Thomas J. Hannon. They lived near Inman, South Carolina. Child:

3152 i. Suzanne[7] Hannon m. Dean Cochran; children:

 3153 a. Marc[8] Cochran

 3154 b. James[8] Cochran.

2634. Margaret[6] Betenbaugh (Powell[5], Micheal[4], David[3], John Uriah[2], Michael[1]) was born 15 January 1916 in Union, South Carolina, and died there 25 August 1995. She married, first, on 3 May 1942, Ralph Phillips, who was born 18 April 1914 and died 24 June 1968. She married, second, on 6 November 1971, George W. Brown, who was born 11 January 1912. One child:

+ 3155 i. Ralph[7] Phillips, Jr., b. 9 June 1942.

2663. Humphries Henry[6] Willard (David[5], Elizabeth[4], David[3], John Uriah[2], Michael[1]) was born 15 February 1884 in Union County, South Carolina, and died there 9 September 1960. He married, on 28 February 1906, Carrie Burgess, who was born 29 May 1891 and died 30 July 1977. Both are buried at Forest Lawn Cemetery in Union. Six children:

3156 i. Ezell Manly[7] Willard, b. 10 Nov 1910, d. 3 June 1962, m. Grace Godshall 8 Feb 1942; children:

 3157 a. Ezell Manly[8] Willard, Jr., b. 2 Mar 1943

 3158 b. Humphries Eugene[8] Willard, b. 4 Oct 1946

3159 ii. Mary Louise[7] Willard, b. 2 Oct 1912, d. 8 Jan 1942, unm.

3160 iii. Nina Lee[7] Willard, b. 29 Apr 1916, m. 6 Aug 1943 Ned Woodrow Skelton, b. 15 Jan 1912.

3161 iv. Helen Ruth[7] Willard, b. 9 Oct 1918, m. 26 Aug 1945, John Tatom Bradley, d. 29 Oct 1980; children:

 3162 a. Helen Tate[8] Bradley, b. 3 Dec 1946, m. 4 Aug 1972, Dr. Louis Dean Majette; children:

  3163 (1) Bradley Lynn[9] Majette, b. 26 July 1975

  3164 (2) Helen Claire[9] Majette, b. 24 Apr 1980

  3165 (3) John Fox[9] Majette, b. 28 June 1983

 3166 b. Caroline Lad[8] Bradley, b. 24 Jul 1955, m. 4 June 1977, Dr. Larry Herm Smith

3167 v. Humphries Henry[7] Willard, Jr., b. 3 Nov 1920, m. 8 Jan 1942, Kathryn Howell

3168 vi. Dorothy Sanders[7] Willard, b. 26 Feb 1923, m. 17 Apr 1946, William Preston Mabry.

2665. Kate[6] Willard (David[5], Elizabeth[4], David[3], John Uriah[2], Michael[1]) was born 11 August 1888 and died 20 March 1932. She married, on 8 December 1912, Robert

Jenkins, who was born 16 November 1884 and died 23 April 1954. Both are buried at Beulah Baptist Church in Union County, South Carolina. Five children:

3169 i. David Willard[7] Jenkins, b. 15 Oct 1913

3170 ii. Margaret Louise[7] Jenkins, b. 16 Sept 1916

3171 iii. Thomas Douglas[7] Jenkins, b. 21 Dec 1918

3172 iv. Robert[7] Jenkins, Jr., b. 16 Sept 1921

3173 v. Janie Sue[7] Jenkins, b. 16 Feb 1932.

2666. Mattie Louise[6] Willard (David[5], Elizabeth[4], David[3], John Uriah[2], Michael[1]) was born 23 July 1892 and died 1 August 1974. She married, on 12 December 1915, Charles Preston Bailey, who was born 18 January 1892 and died 18 March 1960. Both are buried at Sardis United Methodist Church in Union County, South Carolina. Five children:

3174 i. Charles[7] Bailey, Jr., b. 21 June 1919

3175 ii. Paul[7] Bailey, b. 15 Feb 1922

3176 iii. Morris Sanders[7] Bailey, b. 11 Apr 1926, d. 18 Jan 1978, unm.

3177 iv. Marion Eugene[7] Bailey, b. 19 Sept 1930

3178 v. Sue Catherine[7] Bailey, b. 5 Jan 1933.

2679. Lois[6] Willard (Joseph[5], Elizabeth[4], David[3], John Uriah[2], Michael[1]) was born 19 April 1900 and died 24 Aug 1982. She married John Lewis Hines, who was born 2 March 1896 and died 30 October 1971. Children:

3179 i. Joseph Lewis[7] Hines, m. Margaret Blackwood; child:

      3180 a. Jo Ann[8] Hines, m. Sonny Wood

3181 ii. Willard Montgomery[7] (Wishie) Hines, m. Margaret Clark; child:

      3182 a. Willard Montgomery[8] (Monty) Hines, Jr., m. Jan Jones; children:

          3183 (1) Matthew[9] Hines

          3184 (2) Ann Katherine[9] Hines

3185 iii. Helen[7] Hines, m. John Bradburn; children:

      3186 a. Jerrie[8] Bradburn

      3187 b. Sue[8] Bradburn

3188 iv. Edward Faye[7] Hines, m. Rita Vaughan; children:

      3189 a. Eddie[8] Hines

      3190 b. Rita Faye[8] Hines

      3191 c. Rhonda Kaye[8] Hines.

2681. Joe Barth[6] Willard (Joseph[5], Elizabeth[4], David[3], John Uriah[2], Michael[1]) was born 17 September 1904 and died 11 February 1963. He married Maggie Scott, who was born 3 July 1907. Joe Barth Willard is buried at Forest Lawn Cemetery in Union, South Carolina. Children:

3192 i. J. T.[7] Willard, m. Myrtle Helton

3193 ii. Hazel[7] Willard, m. Ray Nance

3194 iii. Frances[7] Willard, m. R. D. Mitchell

3195 iv. Joe Barth[7] Willard, Jr.

3196 v. William[7] Willard

3197 vi. Ned[7] Willard

3198 vii. Wayne[7] Willard

3199 viii. Dean[7] Willard

3200 ix. Dolly[7] Willard, m. David Murphy.

2682. Harry Baldwin[6] Willard (Joseph[5], Elizabeth[4], David[3], John Uriah[2], Michael[1]) was born 30 October 1912 and died 3 November 1991. He married, first, Bessie Mae

THE BEDENBAUGH-BETENBAUGH FAMILY

Robertson, and second, Ora Vick. Harry B. Willard is buried at Sylvan Abbey Memorial Park, Clearwater, Florida. One child:

3201 i. Patricia[7] Willard, married John D. Long, III, resides Union, SC, children:
    3202 a. Lou Ann[8] Long
    3203 b. Mary Jane[8] Long
    3204 c. Steve[8] Long
    3205 d. William[8] Long.

2683. John Clarence[6] Gregory (Sarah Ellen[5], John J.[4], David[3], John Uriah[2], Michael[1]) was born 4 September 1876 and died 24 February 1974. He married Bertha Young, who was born 28 November 1878 and died 18 January 1957, the daughter of J. Christopher and Sallie (Edge) Young. Both are buried Hebron Baptist Church in Union County. J. Clarence Gregory was the oldest living member of the family at the time of his death, and he was quite lucid and had an excellent memory when the writer first knew him in 1966. It is largely through his cooperation that some early graves were located and marked and some excellent information was preserved. Children:

3206 i. Lola Lawson[7] Gregory, b. 27 Oct 1897, m. Morris Douglas[6] Betenbaugh (see under him for descendants)
3207 ii. Ernest Talmadge[7] Gregory, b. 1902
3208 iii. Clyde Carlisle[7] Gregory, b. 1905
3209 iv. Ralph Gilliam[7] Gregory, b. 1907
3210 v. John Clarence[7] Gregory, b. 1918.

2687. Grover Cleveland[6] Gregory (Sarah Ellen[5], John J.[4], David[3], John Uriah[2], Michael[1]) was born 13 November 1884 and died 9 July 1960. He married Lollie Brooklyn Jolly, who was born 23 July 1893 and died 19 November 1977. both are buried at Hebron Baptist Church in Union County, South Carolina. Children:

+ 3211 i. Anita[7] Gregory, b. 16 Dec 1914
3212 ii. Annie Grey[7] Gregory, b. 2 May 1917, d. 16 June 1979
3213 iii. Douglass Leroy[7] Gregory, b. 6 Aug 1919, d. 10 Apr 1921
+ 3214 iv. Claude Cleveland[7] Gregory, b. 6 Dec 1921
3215 v. Mary Jo[7] Gregory, b. 5 Dec 1926
+ 3216 vi. John Wilson[7] Gregory, b. 29 Nov 1934.

2689. Eugene[6] Gregory (Sarah Ellen[5], John J.[4], David[3], John Uriah[2], Michael[1]) was born 2 May 1889 and died __ April 1976. He married, on 28 June 1908, Donna Ellen Turner, who was born 16 May 1887. They lived in High Point, North Carolina. Children:

3217 i. Charlotte Elizabeth[7] Gregory, b. 17 May 1911, m. Carl Lanier; children:
    3218 a. Malcolm Keith[8] Lanier, b. 19 Dec 1937
    3219 b. Martha Jean[8] Lanier, b. 13 March 1945
3220 ii. Rachel[7] Gregory, b. 21 May 1916, m. Charles Homer Prevost; children:
    3221 a. Sylvia Sue[8] Prevost, b. 12 March 1937, m. Ellis Brinson
    3222 b. Brenda LaLane[8] Prevost, b. 22 June 1940, m. D. T. Myers
    3223 c. Charles Gregory[8] Prevost, b. 23 June 1942, m. Judy Green
3224 iii. Joseph Loyd[7] Gregory, b. 4 Sept 1918, m. Otha Elnore Ellege; children:
    3225 a. Wayne Ray[8] Gregory, b. 25 Nov 1940
    3226 b. Alma Joyce[8] Gregory, b. 29 Jan 1950
    3227 c. Jerry Lee[8] Gregory, b. 23 Aug 1956
3228 iv. Leland Cozine[7] Gregory, b. 28 March 1920, m. Triva Inez Swaim, b. 8 June 1916; children:

3229 a. Barbara Jean[8] Gregory, b. 15 Nov 1939, m. E. T. Collins
3230 b. Donna Kay[8] Gregory, b. 22 Dec 1946, m. John David Harper
3231 v. Cornelius Earl[8] Gregory, b. 2 Jan 1921, m. Frances Grogan
3232 vi. Carolyn[7] Gregory, b. 21 Jan 1922, m. James Driver.

2693. Ida[6] Gregory (Sarah Ellen[5], John J.[4], David[3], John Uriah[2], Michael[1]) was born 20 April 1902 and died 2 January 1945. She married Leland Cunningham Young, who was born 25 September 1896 and died 29 September 1969, the son of James B. and Josie (Bailey) Young. They had four children:
     i. (infant)
3233 ii. Connie[7] Young
3234 iii. Ellen Jo[7] Young, m. Waylon Cagle; children:
          3235 a. Karen Lynne[8] Cagle, m. George Arthur Wilson
          3236 b. David[8] Cagle
          3237 c. Vickie[8] Cagle
          3238 d. Bonnie[8] Cagle
3239 iv. Morris[7] Young, m. Barbara Brown; child:
          3240 a. Gerald David[8] Young, m. Emma Ruth Bright.

2705. Horace Hughey[6] Beatenbough (Henry Estee[5], T. R.[4], Michael[3], John Uriah[2], Michael[1]) was born 23 March 1899 in Madison County, Georgia, and died 19 February 1977 in Shelby County, Alabama. He married, on 14 June 1921 in Clarke County, Georgia, Jane LaTrelle Hix, who was born 19 August 1897 in Madison County and died 30 August 1976. Both are buried in Pleasant Grove, Clarke County, Georgia. They had the following children:
+ 3241   i. Mary Kathryn[7] Beatenbough, b. 8 Aug 1922
+ 3242 ii. Hugh Jackson[7] Beatenbough, b. 29 Oct 1924
  3243 iii. James Estee[7] Beatenbough, b. 16 Feb 1928, m. 1st Guinette Strickland (div.); m. 2nd Lena _____
+ 3244 iv. Joan[7] Beatenbough, b. 4 Aug 1930.

2706. Charles Edwin[6] Beatenbough (Henry Estee[5], T. R.[4], Michael[3], John Uriah[2], Michael[1]) was born 30 October 1901 in Madison County, Georgia and died there 3 August 1974. He married, on 25 December 1921, Mary Allene Fowler, who was born on 23 August 1903 in Madison County, Georgia, and died 4 June 1974 in Athens, Clarke County, Georgia. Both are buried at Jones Chapel Church in Madison County. They had the following children:

+ 3245   i. Mary Rachael[7] Beatenbough, b. 10 Mar 1923
+ 3246 ii. Paul Kenneth[7] Beatenbough, b. 26 Mar 1926
+ 3247 iii. Charles Michael[7] Beatenbough, b. 29 Feb 1928.

2707. William Clifford[6] Beatenbough (Henry Estee[5], T. R.[4], Michael[3], John Uriah[2], Michael[1]) was born on 27 December 1905 in Madison County, Georgia, and died 12 December 1968. He married, on 5 September 1926, Minnie Will Fowler, who was born on 23 October 1906 in Madison County and died 5 March 1989. Both are buried in Evangelical Methodist Church, Madison County, Georgia. They had the following children:
+ 3248   i. Clifford Neil[7] Beatenbough, b. 14 May 1927
+ 3249 ii. William Doyle[7] Beatenbough, b. 12 Nov 1929
  3250 iii. Mildred[7] Beatenbough
+ 3251 iv. Shirley Jean[7] Beatenbough, b. 16 Apr 1936

+ 3252   v. Martha Elizabeth[7] Beatenbough, b. 25 Feb 1941.

2708. Clara Elizabeth[6] Beatenbough (Henry Estee[5], T. R.[4], Michael[3], John Uriah[2], Michael[1]) was born on 27 Dec 1905 in Madison County, GA. She married, on 9 November 1924, Paul Lee Fortson, who was born on 1 April 1904 in Madison County, Georgia and died 23 April 1980. They had the following children:
+ 3253   i. Gladys Evelyn[7] Fortson, b. 7 Sep 1925
+ 3254   ii. John Curtis[7] Fortson, b. 18 May 1928
+ 3255   iii. Martha Rachel[7] Fortson, b. 12 Dec 1933
+ 3256   iv. Rebecca Faye[7] Fortson, b. 16 Jan 1938
+ 3257   v. Barbara Jean[7] Fortson, b. 6 Oct 1945.

2709. Robert King[6] Beatenbough (Henry Estee[5], T. R.[4], Michael[3], John Uriah[2], Michael[1]) was born 23 July 1908 in Madison County, Georgia and died 26 October 1982. He married, on 4 December 1927, Orie Lee Dudley. He is buried at Shiloh Baptist Church in Madison County. They had the following children:
  3258   i. Mary Frances[7] Beatenbough, b. 18 Aug 1930, Madison Co., GA, d. 25 Jul 1983
+ 3259   ii. Delrea[7] Beatenbough, b. 26 Aug 1934
+ 3260   iii. John Buren[7] Beatenbough, b. 7 Aug 1937
+ 3261   iv. Robbie Sue[7] Beatenbough, b. 16 Aug 1941.

2711. Thomas Reeder[6] Beatenbough (Henry Estee[5], T. R.[4], Michael[3], John Uriah[2], Michael[1]) was born on 21 September 1912 in Madison County, Georgia and died in May 1991. He married, on 29 May 1931, Eula Mae Fowler who was born 31 December 1910 in Franklin County, Georgia, and died on 8 Feb 1974. After their divorce, Thomas Reeder Beatenbough married, second, on 3 July 1951, Reba Williams. He is buried in Athens, Clarke County, Georgia. Children:
+ 3262   i. Virginia[7] Beatenbough, b. 12 Nov 1931
+ 3263   ii. Jerry Ollin[7] Beatenbough, b. 29 Apr 1939.

2800. Carrie Sartor[6] Davis (Frank[5], Frances[4], Elizabeth[3], John Uriah[2], Michael[1]) was born 1 July 1903. She married, on 20 September 1936, Robert Marcus White, who was born 27 August 1900. They adopted two children:
  3264   i. Edward Marcus[7] White, b. 2 Apr 1941, m. Linda Williams; children:
        3265 a. Vickie[8] White, b. 14 Nov 1962, Ozark, AL
        3266 b. Robert Edward[8] White, b. 2 Apr 1970, Rock Hill, SC
        3267 c. Candice Lyn[8] White, b. 11 Nov 1974, Rock Hill, SC
  3268   ii. Charles Glenn White, b. 26 Aug 1943, m. Zendra Tollison.

2803. Sarah Francis Elizabeth[6] Brandon (Virginia[5], Frances[4], Elizabeth[3], John Uriah[2], Michael[1]) was born 2 September 1887 and died 20 July 1974. She married, on 25 January 1905, Almond Lee Garner, who was born 14 July 1883 and died 23 June 1930. Both are buried in Rosemont Cemetery, Union, South Carolina. Children:
+ 3269   i. John Rufus[7] Garner, b. 16 Dec 1905
  3270   ii. Paul Brandon[7] Garner, b. 29 May 1908, d. 21 Feb 1971, m. Mary Louise McGowan; child:
        3271 a. Michael Keith[8] Garner, b. 27 Oct 1945
+ 3272   iii. Thelma Virginia[7] Garner, b. 22 June 1910
+ 3273   iv. Joseph Woods[7] Garner, b. 17 July 1913
+ 3274   v. Daniel Bruce[7] Garner, b. 4 Nov 1915
+ 3275   vi. Ralph Lee[7] Garner, b. 20 May 1917

3276 vii. Ben Wilson[7] Garner, b. 23 Oct 1919, m. Cornelia Kelly
+ 3277 viii. Jennie Viola[7] Garner, b. 12 Feb 1922
3278 ix. William McBeth Garner, b. 25 Aug 1924, d. 11 May 1945, bur. Rosemont Cem., unm.

2807. Lovick Pierce[6] Brandon (Virginia[5], Frances[4], Elizabeth[3], John Uriah[2], Michael[1]) was born 16 August 1891 and died 25 July 1962. He married, on 19 December 1917, Jessie Hazel Sorgee, who was born 3 January 1898 and died 19 May 1980. Children:
+ 3279 i. Eva Mae[7] (Boots) Brandon, b. 13 Sept 1919
+ 3280 ii. Lovick Pierce[7] Brandon, Jr., b. 28 Aug 1921.

2810. Janie Musgrove[6] Brandon (Virginia[5], Frances[4], Elizabeth[3], John Uriah[2], Michael[1]) was born 1 November 1899 and died 22 September 1948. She married, on 14 March 1917, John McKinley Stutts, who was born 17 March 1898 and died 24 February 1970. Children:
+ 3281 i. Herbert Lindo[7] Stutts, b. 1 May 1918
+ 3282 ii. Johnnie Brandon[7] Stutts, b. 29 Dec 1920
+ 3283 iii. Roy Davis[7] Stutts, b. 22 Apr 1922
3284 iv. Robert Theodore[7] Stutts, b. 28 Nov 1924, m. Mary Frances Boozer, b. 7 Aug 1926, live Columbia, SC
+ 3285 v. Sarah Elizabeth[7] Stutts, b. 11 May 1927
+ 3286 vi. Fannie Louise[7] Stutts, b. 14 June 1929
3287 vii. Lewis Calhoun[7] Stutts, b. 25 Aug 1931, m. Edna Delilah Douglas, b. 17 July 1943; one child:
3288 a. Rhonda Darlene[8] Stutts
+ 3289 viii. Peggy Ann[7] Stutts, b. 22 July 1933
+ 3290 ix. Helen Mae[7] Stutts, b. 31 Oct 1935
3291 x. Ora Jane[7] Stutts, b. 9 Dec 1937, m. Wendell Armstrong; child:
3292 a. Wendell Stutts[8] Armstrong
+ 3293 xi. Errol Barry[7] Stutts, b. 15 Dec 1941.

2937. Ira Lee[6] Keenan (William[5], Nancy[4], Mary Ann[3], John Uriah[2], Michael[1]) was born 28 December 1900 and died 15 September 1975. He married Coralea Gardner, who was born 16 April 1899 and died 30 December 1984. They are buried in Frederick Memorial Gardens, Gaffney, South Carolina. Children:
+ 3294 i. Ida Velle[7] Keenan, b. 26 Aug 1923
+ 3295 ii. William Robert[7] Keenen, b. 24 Sept 1924
+ 3296 iii. Henry Donald[7] Keenan, b. 27 Oct 1929, m. Isabel Bolin, b. 3 Aug 1932
3297 iv. Shirley Joan[7] Keenan, b. 7 July 1935, m. Jack L. Coyle, Sr.
3298 v. Nancy Nadine[7] Keenan, b. 16 Nov 1937, m. Eugene Howard Bolton, b. 9 May 1935
3299 vi. Norma Gayle[7] Keenan, b. 22 March 1940, m. Joe Edward Porter
3300 vii. Iris Earle[7] Keenan, b. 31 Aug 1945, m. James Harold Burgess.

2941. Ida Mae[6] Keenan (William[5], Nancy[4], Mary Ann[3], John Uriah[2], Michael[1]) was born 24 August 1908. She married William Harold Friddle, who was born 19 August 1910 and died in 1946. Two children:
3301 i. William Harold[7] Friddle, b. 5 Dec 1932, m. Margie Ann Carter, b. 18 Aug 1936; child:
3302 a. Laura Ann[8] Friddle, b. 24 Nov 1965
3303 ii. David Clinton[7] Friddle, b. Jan 1935, m. Viston Tyler; children:

3304 a. David Clinton[8] Friddle, Jr.
3305 b. Allen Keith[8] Friddle.

2942. Coleman Blease[6] Keenan (William[5], Nancy[4], Mary Ann[3], John Uriah[2], Michael[1]) was born 1 July 1912. He married, on 8 February 1936, Gaynell Hall, who was born 18 February 1916. Children:
  3306 i. Jean Claudette[7] Keenan, b. 13 Sept 1937, m. John W. Cauley; children:
       3307 a. Jo Lynn[8] Cauley, m. Richard Lott
       3308 b. John W.[8] Cauley, Jr., m. Denise Kelly
       3309 c. Robert Anthony[8] Cauley
  3310 ii. Janet Yvonne[7] Keenan, b. 8 June 1939, m. Joseph Branson Stafford; children:
       3311 a. Karyn Lisa[8] Stafford, m. Randy Mattison
       3312 b. Kathy Lane[8] Stafford
  3313 iii. Dana Lynn[7] Keenan, m. Robert Hall
       3314 a. Travis Lee[8] Hall, b. 16 May 1975
       3315 b. Gregory Blake[8] Hall, b. 23 June 1978.

2945. James Talmadge[6] Keenan (William[5], Nancy[4], Mary Ann[3], John Uriah[2], Michael[1]) was born 3 November 1916. He married, on 23 Dec 1923, Louise Cook, who was born 5 November 1917. Children:
  3317 i. Patricia Ann[7] Keenan, b. 6 Oct 1936, d., 27 March 1988, m. 1 July 1960 Bill Cantrel; child:
       3317 a. Pam[8] Cantrel, m. Dennis Dyer
  3318 ii. Joyce Lee[7] Keenan, b. 21 Jan 1941, m. Wilford Enoch; children:
       3319 a. Michael[8] Enoch, b. 17 Apr 1960
       3320 b. Daniel[8] Enoch, b. 24 June 1964
  3321 iii. James Robert[7] Keenan, b. 2 Apr 1944, m. Judy ____; children:
       3322 a. Dale[8] Keenan, b. 21 Jan 1972
       3323 b. Neal[8] Keenan, b. 10 Jan 1977
       3324 c. John[8] Keenan, b. Dec 1977
  3325 iv. Richard Wayne[7] Keenan, b. 1950 m. Roxane Styles; children:
       3326 a. Christie[8] Keenan, b. 1973
       3327 b. Jennifer[8] Keenan, b. 1979
  3228 v. Mary Alice[7] Keenan, b. 9 Apr 1953, m. Steve Lynch; child:
       3329 a. Angela[8] Lynch, b. 20 Dec 1972
  3330 vi. Alan Dale[7] Keenan, b. 10 Oct 1954, m 1st Debbie Honnicut; 2nd Cindy Martin; children:
       3331 a. Susan[8] Keenan, b. 1 July 1973
       3332 b. Jeremy[8] Keenan, b. 23 Oct 1983.

2951. Clyde Webster[6] Keenan (James[5], Nancy[4], Mary Ann[3], John Uriah[2], Michael[1]) was born 6 November 1904 and died in January 1995. He married, first, Irene Brown (1905-1980). He married second, Emma Collins; third, Lucy Ellenburg; and, fourth, Pauline Kirkland. Children:
  3333 i. Hazel[7] Keenan, b. 16 March 925, m. 1st Robert Wilson; 2nd Wm. Mazwell Coursey; children:
       3334 a. Robert Lee[8] Wilson
       3335 b. Faye[8] Wilson, m. ___ Rushton
  3336 ii. Dorothy Louise[7] Keenan, b. Oct 1927, m. Gerold Smith (Sumter, SC); children:
       3337 a. Gerry[8] Smith

3338 b. Jenny[8] Smith
3339 iii. Arthur Lee[7] Keenan, b. 1930, m. Betty Hart; children:
    3340 a. Tony[8] Keenan
    3341 b. Sherry[8] Keenan
    3342 c. Lynn[8] Keenan.

2954. Mazie[6] Keenan (James[5], Nancy[4], Mary Ann[3], John Uriah[2], Michael[1]) married Garvin Chandler. Children:
    3343 i. Wilma[7] Chandler, m. ___ Fletcher
    3344 ii. James Walter[7] Chandler
    3345 iii. Arthur Boyd[7] Chandler.

2960. Paul Edward[6] Keenan (James[5], Nancy[4], Mary Ann[3], John Uriah[2], Michael[1]) was born 3 December 1923, and married, in 1948, Clara Elizabeth Garrison, who was born 7 June 1925. They reside in Easley, South Carolina. Two children:
    3346 i. Wayne Edward[7] Keenan, b. 16 June 1949, m. 23 Dec 1965 to Margaret Lena Fosett, b. 31 July 1950; children:
        3347 a. Paul Wayne[8] Keenan, b. 2 July 1966, m. Pamela S. Cooper
        3348 b. Terry James[8] Keenan, b. 18 June 1968, m. Crystal Diane Finley; child:
            3349 (1) Christopher James[9] Keenan, b. 14 Nov 1988
        3350 c. Candace Recquel[8] Keenan, b. 20 Jan 1972
    3351 ii. Nancy Mae[7] Keenan, b. 25 Dec 1956, m. 1st Jimmy Pressley, 2nd Phillip Aiken; children:
        3352 a. Maria Michelle[8] Aiken, b. 28 July 1978
        3353 b. Tabitha Cecelia[8] Aiken, b. 20 Jan 1980.

2978. Ira Kenith[6] Keenan (Ira[5], Nancy[4], Mary Ann[3], John Uriah[2], Michael[1]) was born 23 August 1917. He married Dorothy Magaline Woods, who was born 27 July 1924. Children:
    3355 i. Ira Kenith[7] Keenan, Jr., b. 18 Sept 1941, m. 1st Delores ___; m. 2nd Susan Denice Rankin; children:
        3356 a. Travis Steele[8] Keenan, b. 23 Feb 1983
        3357 b. Ira Kenith[8] Keenan, III, b. 10 Aug 1989
    3358 ii. Donna Rae[7] Keenan, b. 25 May 1943, m. 29 Apr 1962 Norman Carey Dacus, b. 17 Aug 1941; children:
        3359 a. Norman Carey[8] Dacus, Jr., b. 27 Apr 1966
        3360 b. Kenith Shane[8] Dacus, b. 8 Aug 1970
    3361 iii. Ronique Earline[7] Keenan, b. 14 Jan 1953, m. 1st Edward Emerson Smith, Jr., m. 2nd 14 Aug 1975 Dennis Edward Coleman; children:
        3362 a. Dennis Ryan[8] Coleman, b. 27 June 1977
        3363 b. Kimberly Ronique[8] Coleman, b. 17 May 1981.

2979. Alvin Decatur[6] Keenan (Ira[5], Nancy[4], Mary Ann[3], John Uriah[2], Michael[1]) was born 14 October 1919 and died 26 June 1984. He married, on 19 October 1940, Lillian Lee, who was born 5 June 1923. Children:
    3364 i. Sheila Lee[7] Keenan, b. 2 Nov 1941, m. 10 Feb 1962, m. Alvin Rich Babb, b. 12 May 1937; child:
        3365 a. Allison Lee[8] Babb, b. 30 June 1965
    3366 ii. Alvin Randle[7] Keenan, b. 27 July 1946, m. 2 May 1970 Carol Jean Dickerson; children:
        3367 a. Christi Joy[8] Keenan, b. 7 Feb 1974

3368 b. Victor Jason[8] Keenan, b. 7 Apr 1975.

2980. Duran Garrett[6] Keenan (Ira[5], Nancy[4], Mary Ann[3], John Uriah[2], Michael[1]) was born 22 February 1922 and died 15 February 1988. He married Nancy Reeves, who was born 9 February 1922. Children:
   3369 i. Patricia Gale[7] Keenan, b. 1945, m. 1st Murl Lee Moore; m. 2nd Jimmy Fowler; children:
          3370 a. Jeff[8] Moore, b. 19 July 1965, m. Felicia___; children:
             3371 (1) Amber Leigh[9] Moore, b. 1987
             3372 (2) Jason[9] Moore, b. 1990
          3373 b. Krista Caroline[8] Moore, b. 14 March 1967
   3374 ii. Linda Diane[7] Keenan, b. Nov 1947, m. 27 Nov 1965 Ronald Lewis Meredith; children:
          3375 a. Brad[8] Meredith, b. 19 Nov 1970
          3376 b. David Garrett[8] Meredith, b. 10 Nov 19--
   3377 iii. Mary Joyce[7] Keenan, b. 16 Apr 1949, m. 1st Larry Dean Meredith; m. 2nd Bill Connolly; child:
          3378 a. Kimberly Dawn[8] Meredith
   3379 iv. Joan Harriet[7] Keenan, b. 19 Apr 1951, m. Rev. Ronald Frank McManus, b. 19 Sept 1951; children:
          3380 a. Gregory Scott[8] McManus
          3381 b. Kevin[8] McManus
   3382 v. Deborah Lee[7] Keenan, m. 1st Jimmy Lewis Owens; m. 2nd Steven Andrew Anastos
   3383 vi. Judy Denice[7] Keenan, m. Charles Schwerdtfeger; children:
          3384 a. Eric[8] Schwerdtfeger, b. 21 Sept 1981
          3385 b. Jonathan[8] Schwerdtfeger, b. 19 July 1986.

2981. Evelyn Inez[6] Keenan (Ira[5], Nancy[4], Mary Ann[3], John Uriah[2], Michael[1]) was born 4 August 1925. She married, on 15 February 1943, Wallace Elford Knight, who was born 10 June 1921. Child:
3386 i. Sylvia Reene[7] Knight, b. 2 Jan 1956, m. 27 Sept 1980 Guy Red Smith, b. 16 Feb 1956.

2982. Theodore Roosevelt[6] Keenan (Ira[5], Nancy[4], Mary Ann[3], John Uriah[2], Michael[1]) was born 23 July 1927. He married Juanita Faye Gardner, who was born 28 October 1949. Children:
   3387 i. Teddie Faye[7] Keenan, b. 5 July 1954, m. 11 Nov 1972, Ronnie Earl Bates, b. 15 Dec 1949; children:
          3388 a. Ronnie Keith[8] Bates, b. 15 Oct 1974
          3389 b. Daniel Scott[8] Bates, b. 26 Aug 1977
   3390 ii. Aaron Keith[7] Keenan, b. 9 June 1957, m. 1st Tammie Jean Edwards; m. 2nd 21 March 1981 Kathy Lynn Owens, b. 6 Oct 1961; children:
          3391 a. Crystal Nicole[8] Keenan, b. 1 Nov 1971
          3392 b. Jessica Elaine[8] Keenan, b. 16 May 1983
          3393 c. Ashley Renee[8] Keenan, b. 24 Apr 1985
   3394 iii. Cynthia Marie[7] Keenan, b. 3 Nov 1960, m. 1 Sept 1978 Ricky Allen Johnson, b. 18 Oct 1957; children:
          3395 a. Richard Keenan[8] Johnson, b. 4 May 1982
          3396 b. Christopher Allen[8] Johnson, b. 4 Nov 1984
   3397 iv. Denice Michelle[7] Keenan, b. 4 May 1962
   3398 v. Samuel Paul[7] Keenan, b. 12 July 1963.

2983. Henry Junior[6] Kennan (Ira[5], Nancy[4], Mary Ann[3], John Uriah[2], Michael[1]) was born 19 November 1928. He married Elizabeth Wilson, who was born 3 January 1935. Children:
  3399 i. Kemberly Renee[7] Keenan, b. 6 July 1958, m. 1st David Joel Hawkins, b. 21 May 1955; m. 2nd Mike Wood, b. 26 June 1953; m. 3rd Joseph Russell Guzzetta, b. 9 Apr 1961; children:
      3400 a. Michael David[8] Hawkins, b. 12 March 1977
      3401 b. Adam Zachary[8] Wood, b. 14 Nov 1981
      3402 c. Brittany Nichole[8] Guzzetta, b. 11 July 1986
  3403 ii. Staci Nicole[7] Keenan, b. 24 Jan 1970.

2984. James Douglas[6] (J. D.) Keenan (Ira[5], Nancy[4], Mary Ann[3], John Uriah[2], Michael[1]) was born 4 May 1933. He married, on 23 May 1953, Betty Ann James, who was born 15 September 1935. Children:
  3404 i. Anthony Douglas[7] Keenan, b. 16 Apr 1954, m. 2 June 1979 Sylvia Louise Wood, b. 3 March 1978, dau. of Lewis A. and Bobby Nell (Page) Wood. [Lewis A. Wood has contributed most of the data on the McCreight descendants for this work.] Child:
      3405 a. David Anthony[8] Keenan, b. 17 Aug 1983
  3406 ii. Lisa Ann[7] Keenan, b. 25 Jan 1962, m. 21 March 1981 Joe Billy Honea, b. 17 Nov 1959; child:
      3407 a. Thomas Andrew Honea, b. 8 July 1988
  3408 iii. James Mark[7] Keenan, b. 18 Nov 1972.

2985. Dewey William[6] Quinn (Beulah[5], Nancy[4], Mary Ann[3], John Uriah[2], Michael[1]) was born 3 February 1904. He married, on 15 January 1923, Christine Williams, who was born 30 December 1905. Children:
  3409 i. Dewey William[7] Quinn, Jr., b. 23 Oct 1923, m. Margaret Washington; children:
      3410 a. Jane[8] Quinn
      3411 b. Martha Ann[8] Quinn
      3412 c. Nancy[8] Quinn
      3413 d. Billie Dell[8] Quinn
  3414 ii. Winston Andrew[7] Quinn, b. 24 Jan 1926 (twin), m. Dorothy Gamble; children:
      3415 a. Frances[8] Quinn
      3416 b. Kathryn[8] Quinn
      3417 c. Christine[8] Quinn
  3418 iii. Woodford Simpson[7] Quinn, b. 24 Jan 1926 (twin), m. Ellene Jordan; children:
      3419 a. (dau.)
      3420 b. Woodford Simpson[8] Quinn, Jr.

3000. Frances Elizabeth[6] Quinn (Beulah[5], Nancy[4], Mary Ann[3], John Uriah[2], Michael[1]) was born 19 July 1926 and died 13 Mar 1981. She married George Elliott Jewell, who was born 20 May 1925. Children:
  3421 i. Gary Anthony[7] Jewell, b. 6 July 1949, m. Rhonda Daniels, b. 16 Apr 1956; child:
      3422 a. Melody Elizabeth[8] Jewell
  3423 ii. George Timothy[7] Jewell, b. 8 Sept 1952
  3424 iii. Todd Elliott[7] Jewell, b. 18 Nov 1956, m. 1986 Cathy Higginson, b. 25 Jan 1958; child:

3425 a. Skylar Elliott[8] Jewell, b. 8 Jan 1990

3426 iv. Phillip Anderson[7] Jewell, b. 6 Feb 1960

3427 v. Suzanne Elizabeth[7] Jewell, b. 19 Sept 1966, m. 1989 Israel Olegnowicz.

3008. Rev. Paul Levi[6] McCreight (John Robert Levi[5], Herndon[4], Mary Ann[3], John Uriah[2], Michael[1]) was born 17 April 1909 and died c1962. He married, Marie Sloan, who was born 4 May 1911. Children:

3428 i. Marion[7] McCreight, b. 3 Jan 1928, m. Charles Calvert; child:
    3429 a. Dannie McCreight

3430 ii. Paul Levi[7] McCreight, Jr. (Rev.), b. 14 Sept 1930, d. Nov 1988, m. Shirley Christopher, b. 9 Dec 1938. Children:
    3431 a. Paula[8] McCreight, b. 27 Aug 1954, m. Donnie Ray Hayes, b. 7 Dec 1957; children:
        3432 (1) Anthony Ray[9] Hayes, b. 18 June 1975
        3433 (2) Brian Scott[9] Hayes, b. 7 Apr 1979
        3434 (3) Jason Eric[9] Hayes, b. 30 Oct 1983
    3435 b. Phillip Andrew[8] McCreight, b. 31 May 1968
    3436 c. Joel Nathan[8] McCreight, b. 14 Aug 1970, m. Misty Paxton

3437 iii. Mary Deloris[7] McCreight, b. c1931, d. unm.

3438 iv. Richard[7] McCreight, b. c1933, d. young

3439 v. William[7] McCreight, b. 19 Sept 1935, m. Jeannette Gancy; children:
    3440 a. Paul Levi[8] McCreight
    3441 b. Cathey[8] McCreight
    3442 c. Kim[8] McCreight

3443 vi. Doris[7] McCreight, b. 18 June 1942

3444 vii. Donnie[7] McCreight, b. 8 May 1947.

3009. Elsie Mary Lee[6] McCreight (John Robert Levi[5], Herndon[4], Mary Ann[3], John Uriah[2], Michael[1]) was born 30 September 1911, and died 6 June 1989. She married, first, Carl Price, who was born 21 December 1902 and died 18 May 1983. She married, second, Joe Price. Children:

3445 i. Alice Mettra Lea[7] Vassey, b. 25 May 1930, m. Paul Erskine, b. 29 June 1929 (div); children:
    3446 a. Sandy Kay[8] Erskine, b. 16 Oct 1950 m. Bill Jenkins, b. 31 Oct 1942; child:
        3447 (1) David[9] Jenkins, b. 22 Nov 1975
    3448 b. Mark Edward[8] Erskine, b. 15 Sept 1959, m. Margerie Boyd, b. 19 Apr 1957; children:
        3449 (1) Shawna Alyce[9] Erskine, b. 28 Dec 1989
        3450 (2) Katelyn Paige[9] Erskine, b. 28 Apr 1993

3451 ii. Valorie[7] Vassey, b. 28 Jan 1932, m. Berlin Loyd McAbee; children:
    3452 a. Phill Loyd[8] McAbee
    3453 b. Michael Dean[8] McAbee, m. ___; children:
        3454 (1) Joshua[9] McAbee
        3455 (2) Amelia Jean[9] McAbee
    3456 c. Cristal Jean[8] McAbbe, m. ___ Carter; child:
        3457 (1) Cassady Nichole[9] Carter
    3458 d. Kim Allice[8] McAbbe, m. ___ Lowery; children:
        3459 (1) Chase Paul[9] Lowery
        3460 (2) Taylor[9] Lowery.

3017. George Edward[6] McCreight (John Robert Levi[5], Herndon[4], Mary Ann[3], John Uriah[2], Michael[1]) was born 14 September 1923 and married Elaine Bryson, who was born 3 January 1928. Children:

3461 i. Larry Douglas[7] McCreight, b. 21 June 1959 m. Sandy Donohue
3462 ii. George Edward[7] McCreight, Jr., b. 14 Apr 1954, m. Ann _____
3463 iii. Mark Steven[7] McCreight, b. 21 June 1958, m. Synthia Denise Gile, b. 22 Sept 1957
3464 iv. Timothy[7] McCreight, b. 21 Nov 1961, m. Diane Derrick (div).

3030. Clarence[6] Foister (Alice[5], Herndon[4], Mary Ann[3], John Uriah[2], Michael[1]) was born c1912 and died 27 Dec 1960. He married Cora Whitt and had one child:

3465 i. Willard[7] Foster, b. 15 Feb 1931, m. Melvin Ansel Arms, b. 8 July 1925; children:
   3466 a. Melvin Dickie[8] Arms, Jr., b. 17 July 1948
   3467 b. Randel Steven[8] Arms, b. 11 June 1952, m. Patricia Jones; children:
      3468 (1) Christopher Steven[9] Arms, b. 5 Apr 1973
      3469 (2) Kevin[9] Arms, b. 1 June 1975
      3470 (3) Courtney Gene[9] Arms, b. 28 Feb 1989
   3471 c. Russell Lynn[8] Arms, b. 13 July 1971.

THE BEDENBAUGH-BETENBAUGH FAMILY

SEVENTH GENERATION

3083. Boyce Malcolm[7] Vise (Della[6], Thomas J.[5], Micheal R.[4], David[3], John Uriah[2], Michael[1]) was born 4 August 1900. He married, on 13 November 1925, Lunette Kirby, who was born 12 October 1907. One child:
  3472 i. Ernest[8] Vise, b. 12 June 1932.

3084. Jeanette[7] Vise (Della[6], Thomas J.[5], Micheal R.[4], David[3], John Uriah[2], Michael[1]) was born 22 August 1905 and died 15 May 1967. She married Richard Welch. One child:
  3473 i. Jean[8] Welch, m. Whit Plowden. Children:
      3474 a. Cynthia Jean[9] Plowden, m. _____ Goldberg
      3475 b. Richard W.[9] Plowden; child:
          3476 (1) Richard Shane[10] Plowden
      3477 c. Gerald W.[9] (Jerry) Plowden.

3086. Herman Douglas[7] Betenbaugh (James S.[6], Thomas J.[5], Micheal R.[4], David[3], John Uriah[2], Michael[1]) was born 27 December 1905 and died 6 June 1972. He married Lillie Linderman, who was born 11 September 1918 and died 27 July 1988. Both are buried at Sardis United Methodist Church in Union County, South Carolina. Children:
+ 3478   i. James Sanders[8] Betenbaugh, II, b. 24 July 1938
+ 3479 ii. Patricia Ann[8] Betenbaugh, b. 9 Aug 1939
+ 3480 iii. William Douglas[8] Betenbaugh, b. 23 July 1941
+ 3481 iv. Herman Donald[8] (Don) Betenbaugh, b. 14 Nov 1948
  3482   v. Thomas Michael[8] Betenbaugh, b. 5 July 1947, d. 17 Aug 1966
  3483 vi. Martha Susan[8] Betenbaugh, b. 23 Dec 1950, d. 6 Oct 1972
+ 3484 vii. John Roper[8] Betenbaugh, b. 20 Dec 1951
+ 3485 viii. David Robin[8] Betenbaugh, b. 22 Aug 1953

3096. Leila Mae[7] Young (Annie Lou[6], Thomas J.[5], Micheal R.[4], David[3], John Uriah[2], Michael[1]) was born 17 March 1920 in Union County, South Carolina. She married, on 1 October 1947, Wendell Phillip Bailey, who was born 31 December 1924. They reside in Asheville, North Carolina. Five children:
  3486   i. Philip Michael[8] Bailey, b. 13 Aug 1948, m. Benemma Bentley, b. 14 June 1958
  3487 ii. Stephen Thomas[8] Bailey, b. 24 Oct 1949, m. Nancy C. Williams, b. 8 July 1950; children:
      3488 a. Ryan Thomas[9] Bailey, b. 22 Aug 1983
      3489 b. Christopher David[9] Bailey, b. 12 June 1985
  3490 iii. William Ernest[8] Bailey, b. 28 June 1951, m. Elizabeth Robinson, b. 22 June 1953; children:
      3491 a. William Andrew[9] Bailey, b. 11 Aug 1990
      3492 b. Grayson Wendell[9] Bailey, b. 21 Feb 1994
  3493 iv. Kenneth Wendell[8] Bailey, b. 19 Oct 1954, b. 18 Oct 1954, m. Nancy Reside, b. 11 March 1955; children:
      3494 a. Scott Douglas[9] Bailey, b. 25 Feb 1987
      3495 b. Kelly Jane[9] Bailey, b. 1 May 1990
      3496 c. Jessica Lynn[9] Bailey, b. 15 Apr 1993
  3497   v. Daniel Anthony[8] Bailey, b. 5 Feb 1958, b. 5 Feb 1958, m. Tammy Foster, b. 5 May 1960 (div); children:
      3498 a. Annie Marie[9] Bailey, b. 22 Oct 1986

3499 b. Maggie[9] Bailey, b. 20 Apr 1990.

3114. Era Virginia[7] Littlejohn (Martha[6], John C.[5], Micheal R.[4], David[3], John Uriah[2], Michael[1]) was born 26 September 1912 and married Hulton Aden Stone. Children:
   3500 i. Alliene[8] Stone
   3501 ii. Shirley[8] Stone
   3502 iii. Sybil Virginia[8] Stone.

3115. Lavare Verbena[7] Littlejohn (Martha[6], John C.[5], Micheal R.[4], David[3], John Uriah[2], Michael[1]) was born 15 July 1916 and married, on 12 February 1935, Deloin Franklin Harris. She married, second, on 14 December 1957, Louis Tony Zupanic. Children:
   3503 i. Patricia Verbena[8] Harris, b. 12 Nov 1935
   3504 ii. Melvin Franklin[8] Harris, b. 4 Dec 1937.

3116. Lonnie Vernon[7] Littlejohn (Martha[6], John C.[5], Micheal R.[4], David[3], John Uriah[2], Michael[1]) was born 5 May 1919 and married, on 31 August 1940, Frances Margaret Tuck. Children:
   3505 i. Lonnie Darve[8] Littlejohn, b. 27 Apr 1945
   3506 ii. Frances Carole[8] Littlejohn, b. 24 Sept 1947.

3117. Edisto Edith[7] Littlejohn (Martha[6], John C.[5], Micheal R.[4], David[3], John Uriah[2], Michael[1]) was born 10 August 1921 and married, on 12 December 1939, Benjamin Felix Harris, who was born 4 July 1921. Children:
   3507 i. Edith Brenda[8] Harris, b. 19 Sept 1940
   3508 ii. Rebecca Amanda[8] Harris, b. 15 Nov 1943
   3509 iii. Deborah Lynn[8] Harris, b. 20 Sept 1956.

3129. Gary Hope[7] Holcomb (Mary[6], John C.[5], Micheal R.[4], David[3], John Uriah[2], Michael[1]) was born 30 November 1916, Union, SC, married Hazel Elizabeth Howard on 8 August 1942. Two children:
   3510 i. Brent Howard[8] Holcomb, b. 4 May 1950, Clinton, SC (compiler of this volume)
   3511 ii. Barry Milton[8] Holcomb, b. 19 Sept 1954, Clinton, SC, married 7 Aug 1977, in Atlanta, GA, Margaret Carol Eddings, b. 4 Jan 1956. Two children, b. Spartanburg, SC:
      3512 a. Nathanael Christopher[9] (Nathan) Holcomb, b. 27 Feb 1980
      3513 b. Adria Denise[9] Holcomb, b. 27 May 1983.

3131. Rufus T.[7] Holcomb, Jr. (Mary[6], John C.[5], Micheal R.[4], David[3], John Uriah[2], Michael[1]) was born 31 December 1924, married 13 Oct 1945 to Alma Frances Simpson, who was born 16 January 1927. They live in Charlotte, North Carolina. Two children:
   3514 i. Russell Dwight[8] Holcomb, b. 22 Jan 1947 Charlotte, NC, married Mary Jane Priest (live Fresno, CA); two children:
      3515 a. Teresa[9] Holcomb, b. 28 June 1969
      3516 b. Eric[9] Holcomb, b. 11 May 1973
   3517 ii. Mark Arnold[8] Holcomb, b. Charlotte, NC, 3 July 1957, d. 16 Sept 1979.

3132. Jessie Marie[7] Holcomb (Mary[6], John C.[5], Micheal R.[4], David[3], John Uriah[2], Michael[1]) was born 10 July 1932 in High Point, North Carolina. She married (1) Cole Blease Crook (2) Donald McCombs (3) Wayne E. Wolfe. One child:

3518 i. Lori Ann[8] Wolfe, b. 18 Feb 1966, Greenville, SC, m. 14 Feb 1992 in Memphis, TN, to James Edward McKinney, b. 19 Jan 1961. One child:
3519 a. Zachariah Brian[9] McKinney, b. 19 Sept 1992, Memphis, TN.

3155. Ralph[7] Phillips, Jr. (Margaret[6], Powell[5], Micheal[4], David[3], John Uriah[2], Michael[1]) was born 9 June 1942. He married, first, Michelle McLennan; second, on 18 December 1981, Barbara Blackwood; and, third, Susan (Young) Robinson. Children:
3520   i. Elizabeth Ann[8] Phillips, b. 8 Feb 1968
3521 ii. Evelyn Ashley[8] Phillips, b. 18 Dec 1974
3522 iii. Kyle[8] Phillips, b. 13 Feb 1985
3523 iv. Mark Hamilton[8] Phillips, b. 18 March 1993.

3211. Anita[7] Gregory (Grover[6], Sarah Ellen[5], John J.[4], David[3], John Uriah[2], Michael[1]) was born 16 December 1914 and married, on 6 March 1936, Clarence Berry Sanders. Children:
3524 i. Donald Ray[8] Sanders, b. 1 June 1937, m. 22 Sept 1957, Nancy Elizabeth Gerring; children:
3525 a. Donald Anthony[9] Sanders, b. 22 Oct 1958
3526 b. William Ray[9] Sanders, b. 13 Dec 1960
3527 c. Carl Edward[9] Sanders, b. 24 Apr 1969
3528 ii. Mary Ann[8] Sanders, b. 4 March 1939, m. 31 Aug 1957, Paul Thomas Bell; children:
3529 a. Paul Thomas[9] Bell, Jr., b. 1 Aug 1958, m. 6 July 1979, Tammy Brown; child:
3530 (1) Kristy Dianne[10] Bell, b. 21 Feb 1981
3531 b. Anita Elaine[9] Bell, b. 13 Feb 1961, m. 9 June 1979, Melvin Dale Lathem; child:
3532 (1) Geoffrey Dale[10] Latham, b. 17 Dec 1981.

3214. Claude Cleveland[7] Gregory (Grover[6], Sarah Ellen[5], John J.[4], David[3], John Uriah[2], Michael[1]) was born 6 December 1921 and married Virginia May. Children:
3533 i. Claude Cleveland[8] Gregory, Jr., b. 11 March 1962
3534 ii. Debra Jean[8] Gregory, b. 29 June 1966, m. 1984, Chester Duty.

3216. John Wilson[7] Gregory (Grover[6], Sarah Ellen[5], John J.[4], David[3], John Uriah[2], Michael[1]) was born 29 November 1934 and married Joann Hartle. They adopted one child:
3535 i. John Richard[8] (Ricky) Gregory, b. 19 May 1975.

3241. Mary Kathryn[7] Beatenbough (Horace[6], Henry Estee[5], T. R.[4], Michael[3], John Uriah[2], Michael[1]) was born 8 August 1922 in Madison County, GA. She married, on 27 March 1946 in Clarke County, Georgia, Joel Lee Carey, who was born on 21 Aug 1921 in Clarke County. They had two children, both born in Fulton County, Georgia:
3536 i. Bruce Joel[8] Carey, b. 8 Sept 1949, m. Cindy Ellsworth
3537 ii. Rebecca Kathryn[8] Carey, b. 17 Jan 1954, m. Robert Alan Hollingsworth.

3242. Hugh Jackson[7] Beatenbough (Horace[6], Henry Estee[5], T. R.[4], Michael[3], John Uriah[2], Michael[1]) was born 29 October 1924 in Madison County, Georgia, and died 19 November 1977. He married Annie Helen Fouche, who was born 9 August 1927 in Franklin County, Georgia, and died 26 July 1977. Both are buried in Evergreen

Memorial Park in Clarke County, Georgia. They had the following children, all born in Clarke County, Georgia:
    3538 i. Rita Carol[8] Beatenbough, b. 11 May 1955, m. 1st Jeffery Fitzpatrick; m. 2nd Carl Betzler
    3539 ii. Donna Sue[8] Beatenbough, b. 25 Mar 1958, m. Randall Monroe Smith; child:
            3540 a. Chad Jackson[9] Smith, b. 24 May 1982, Clarke County, GA
    3541 iii. Janiece[8] Beatenbough, b. 4 Mar 1961, m. Tim Smith (div); child:
            3542 a. Jennifer Helen[9] Smith, b. 27 Jul 1983, Clarke County, GA.

3244. Joan[7] Beatenbough (Horace[6], Henry Estee[5], T. R.[4], Michael[3], John Uriah[2], Michael[1]) was born 4 August 1930 in Madison County, Georgia. She married, on 24 October 1947 in Clarke County, Georgia, Keith Lamar Fowler, who was born 4 October 1925 in Madison County. They had the following children:
+ 3543 i. Linda Elaine[8] Fowler, b. 30 Aug 1948, Clarke County, GA
+ 3544 ii. Kevin Richard[8] Fowler, b. 11 Feb 1954, San Francisco, CA.

3245. Mary Rachael[7] Beatenbough (Charles[6], Henry Estee[5], T. R.[4], Michael[3], John Uriah[2], Michael[1]) was born 10 March 1923 Madison County, Georgia. She married, on 11 February 1950, Otho Morris Coffee, Jr., who was born 8 August 1922. They had the following children:
+ 3545 i. Michael Dennis[8] Coffee, b. 18 Jul 1951 in Duval County, FL
+ 3546 ii. Karen[8] Coffee, b. 13 Sep 1953, Austell, GA
    3547 iii. Mark Edwin[8] Coffee, b. 7 Mar 1955, Fulton County, GA, m. 15 Jun 1985 Sharon Long.

3246. Paul Kenneth[7] Beatenbough (Charles[6], Henry Estee[5], T. R.[4], Michael[3], John Uriah[2], Michael[1]) was born 26 March 1926 in Madison County, Georgia. He married, on 11 September 1949 in Jones Chapel Church, Madison County, Joyce Walton, who was born 23 May 1929 in Laurel, Mississippi. They had the following children:
    3548 i. Debra Joyce[8] Beatenbough, b. 16 Jun 1954, Kansas City, MO, m. 20 Oct 1989 in Seattle, WA, G. Ronald Payne
    3549 ii. David Walton[8] Beatenbough, b. 14 Nov 1957, Medina, NY.

3247. Charles Michael[7] Beatenbough (Charles[6], Henry Estee[5], T. R.[4], Michael[3], John Uriah[2], Michael[1]) was born 29 February 1928 in Madison County, Georgia. He married, on 1 July 1950 in Riverdale, Clayton County, Georgia, Clara Frances Camp, who was born on 23 Dec 1931 in Atlanta, Fulton County, Georgia. Charles Beatenbough has contributed much of the information on the descendants of Trusvan Reeder[4] Beatenbough for this work. They had the following children:
+ 3550 i. Charles Michael[8] Beatenbough, b. 10 Nov 1951, Atlanta, GA
+ 3551 ii. Susan Paula[8] Beatenbough, b. 4 May 1953 Atlanta, GA
+ 3552 iii. Helen Dean[8] Beatenbough, b. 24 Jun 1960, Burlington, NC
+ 3553 iv. John Clark[8] Beatenbough, b. 13 Mar 1964 in Burlington, NC.

3248. Clifford Neil[7] Beatenbough (William[6], Henry Estee[5], T. R.[4], Michael[3], John Uriah[2], Michael[1]) was born 14 May 1927 in Madison County, Georgia. He married, on 27 Aug 1949 in Fulton County, Georgia, Barbara June Hilburn, who was born 3 June 1930 in Atlanta, the daughter of Russell Bogart and Nora Mae (Ragan) Hilburn. They had the following children. all born in Fulton County, Georgia:
+ 3554 i. Brenda Gail[8] Beatenbough, b. 8 Feb 1952

+ 3555 ii. Sheryl Lynn[8] Beatenbough, b. 31 Oct 1955
+ 3556 iii. Clifford Neil[8] "Cliff" Beatenbough, Jr., b. 29 Apr 1959.

3249. William Doyle[7] Beatenbough (William[6], Henry Estee[5], T. R.[4], Michael[3], John Uriah[2], Michael[1]) was born 12 November 1929 in Madison County, Georgia. He married, on 17 June 1949 in Atlanta, Georgia, Helen Alice Strickland, who was born on 11 March 1930 in Fulton County, Georgia, the daughter of James Wade and Nettie Lee (Croom) Strickland. They had the following children, born in Jacksonville, Florida:

+ 3557 i. Susan Anne[8] Beatenbough, b. 14 Jul 1955
+ 3558 ii. Jennifer Lee[8] Beatenbough, b. 5 Mar 1958.

3251. Shirley Jean[7] Beatenbough (William[6], Henry Estee[5], T. R.[4], Michael[3], John Uriah[2], Michael[1]) was born 16 April 1936 in Madison County, GA. She married, first, Robert Smith and, second, George O'Quinn. Children:
3559 i. Donna Shan[8] Smith, b. 15 Feb 1959, m. Bobby Lee Patrick; children:
    3560 a. Bobby Ray[9] Patrick, bur. Evangelical Meth, Madison County, GA.
    3561 b. Brent Ashley[9] Patrick
    3562 c. Heath Aaron[9] Patrick, b. 10 Dec 1982
3563 ii. Robert[8] Smith, b. 15 Jan 1962, d. 18 Jan 1962, bur. Evangelical Meth Ch, Madison Co., GA.
3564 iii. Vicki[8] Smith, b. 23 Jul 1964, m. 1st Tim Fowler m. 2nd Ricky Drake; children:
    3565 a. Megan[9] Fowler, b. 7 Sep 1986
    3566 b. Will[9] Drake, b. 1992
3567 iv. Robin Regina[8] Smith, b. 7 Nov 1965, m. Kenneth Dean; children:
    3568 a. Michael[9] Dean, b. 1988
    3569 b. Brianne Nichole[9] Dean, b. Oct 1993
3570 v. Alice Elizabeth[8] Smith, b. 19 Jul 1968, m. Chris Harper; child:
    3571 a. Joshua[9] Harper.

3252. Martha Elizabeth[7] Beatenbough (William[6], Henry Estee[5], T. R.[4], Michael[3], John Uriah[2], Michael[1]) was born 25 February 1941 in Madison County, Georgia. She married, first, James H. Johnston and, second, John Wesley Petel. Children, born Fulton County, Georgia:
3572 i. James Alan[7] Johnston, b. 2 Aug 1962, m. Sue Jane Stowe; children:
    3573 a. James Russell[9] Johnston, b. 20 Apr 1984
    3574 b. Heather[9] Johnston
3575 ii. Elizabeth Paige[8] Johnston, b. 28 Dec 1965, m. 7 July 1990 Mickey Hilton Martin
3576 iii. John Wesley[8] Petel, Jr., b. 19 Dec 1970, m. 24 July 1993 Lori Hayes.

3253. Gladys Evelyn[7] Fortson (Clara[6], Henry Estee[5], T. R.[4], Michael[3], John Uriah[2], Michael[1]) was born 7 September 1925 in Madison County, Georgia. She married, on 9 November 1948, William Garnet Adams, who was born 9 September 1928 in Madison County. They had the following children:
3577 i. Charles Dabney[8] Adams; two children:
    3578 a. Shawn[9] Adams
    3579 b. Stacey[9] Adams
3580 ii. Robin Latrell[8] Adams, m. Randy Adams
3581 iii. Teresa Faye[8] Adams, m. Roy Russell; one child:

3582 a. Angie[9] Marie Russell
3583 iv. Ronnie Michael[8] Adams, b. 3 Jan 1952, Madison Co., GA, m. Geraldine Hill; two children:
    3584 a. Joe[9] Adams
    3585 b. Wesley[9] Adams
3586 v. Martha Dale[8] Adams, b. 27 Sep 1954, Madison Co., GA, m 1st a Rice, one son; m. 2nd Willie Jack Toole, b. 15 Feb 1943; child:
    3587 a. Derrick Mandel[9] Rice, b. 4 Jul 1977
3588 vi. Linda Gail[8] Adams, b. 21 Oct 1957, Clark County, GA, m. Rocky Brooks; child:
    3589 a. Karen[9] Brooks.

3254. John Curtis[7] Fortson (Clara[6], Henry Estee[5], T. R.[4], Michael[3], John Uriah[2], Michael[1]) was born 18 May 1928 in Madison County, GA. He married Blanche Leonia Porterfield on 22 May 1948 in Madison County, GA. Blanche Leonia Porterfield was born on 30 Aug 1928 in Madison County, GA. They had the following children:
3590 i. Wayne Curtis[8] Fortson, b. 12 Mar 1949, Franklin Co., GA., d. 16 Jan 1962, bur. Bethel Bapt Ch, Madison Co., GA.
3591 ii. Larry Randall[8] Fortson, b. 15 Feb 1951, Franklin Co., GA, m. 1st Carol Phillips; m. 2nd Connie Sexton. Child:
    3592 a. Todd[9] Fortson, b. 26 Feb 1973
3593 iii. Deborah Lanette[8] Fortson, b. 25 Aug 1955 in Franklin County, GA, m. Ronald Dove; children:
    3594 a. Kelly Amber[9] Dove, b. 13 Jun 1981.
    3595 b. Crystal[9] Dove, b. 22 Dec 1982
3596 iv. David Anthony[8] Fortson, b. 27 Apr 1957, Franklin County, GA
3597 v. Ricky Darrell[8] Fortson, b. 16 Jan 1959, Franklin County, GA, m. Joyce Martin
3598 vi. Cheryl Denise[8] Fortson, b. 1 Dec 1966 in Franklin County, GA, m. Kent ᵀⁱcks.

3255. Martha Rachel[7] Fortson (Clara[6], Henry Estee[5], T. R.[4], Michael[3], John Uriah[2], Michael[1]) was born on 12 Dec 1933 in Madison County, Georgia. She married, on 17 December 1949 in Madison County, Henry Thomas Haley, who was born on 22 June 1933 in Madison County. They had the following children:
3599 i. Thomas Jerry[7] Haley, b. 30 Oct 1950, Madison Co., GA, m. Carolyn Diane Anderson; child:
    3600 a. Laurie Anne[9] Haley, b. 21 Jul 1980
3601 ii. Doris Ann[7] Haley, b. 9 Oct 1953, Franklin Co., GA, m. Timothy Miller; child:
    3602 a. Jessica Lauren[9] Miller, b. 13 Feb 1983.

3256. Rebecca Faye[7] Fortson (Clara[6], Henry Estee[5], T. R.[4], Michael[3], John Uriah[2], Michael[1]) was born on 16 Jan 1938 in Madison County, Georgia. She married, on 16 January 1957 in Fulton County, Georgia, John Hampton Carson, who was born on 26 October 1934 in St. Petersburg, Florida. They had the following children:
3603 i. John Hampton[8] Carson, Jr., b. 9 Nov 1957, Fulton County, GA; he and wife Beth have one child:
    3604 a. Jonna Marie[9] Carson, b. 21 Feb 1982
3605 ii. Karen Lee[8] Carson, b. 21 Jan 1962, Clarke County, GA, m. Walter Lawrence Warren; children:

3606 a. Adam Branford[9] Warren, b. 15 Aug 1981
3607 b. Ivy Nicole[9] Warren, b. 27 Jul 1983
3608 iii. Stanley James[8] Carson, b. 27 Dec 1962, Calcasieu Parish, LA
3609 iv. Christine Elizabeth[8] Carson, b. 16 Jul 1971, Calcasieu Parish, LA.

3257. Barbara Jean[7] Fortson (Clara[6], Henry Estee[5], T. R.[4], Michael[3], John Uriah[2], Michael[1]) was born on 6 Oct 1945 in Clarke County, Georgia. She married, on 14 February 1965 in Madison County, Georgia, Emmett Guy Lloyd, who was born on 14 February 1945 in Newton County, Georgia. They had the following children, all born in Clarke County, Georgia:
3610 i. Alyse Ann[8] Lloyd, b. 1 Jun 1967
3611 ii. Mark Emmett[8] Lloyd, b. 22 Jun 1970
3612 iii. Jana Marie[8] Lloyd, b. 31 Jan 1973.

3259. Delrea[7] Beatenbough (Robert[6], Henry Estee[5], T. R.[4], Michael[3], John Uriah[2], Michael[1]) was born 26 August 1934 in Madison County, Georgia. She married, on 3 May 1951 in Hart County, Georgia, Marce Douglas "Bud" Kinley, who was born 15 April 1923. They had the following children:

3613 i. Charles Douglas[8] Kinley, b. 20 Jan 1952, Anderson, SC, m. Betty Sue Barnes; children:
        3614 a. Joshua Douglas[9] Kinley, b. 12 Dec 1975, Anderson, SC
3615 ii. Dennis Michael[8] Kinley, b. 17 Mar 1955, Anderson, SC
3616 iii. Don Robert[8] Kinley, b. 17 Sep 1960, Anderson, SC
3617 iv. Darrell Lee[8] Kinley, b. 17 Sep 1960, Anderson, SC.

3260. John Buren[7] Beatenbough (Robert[6], Henry Estee[5], T. R.[4], Michael[3], John Uriah[2], Michael[1]) was born 7 August 1937 in Madison County, Georgia. He married, on 14 November 1940 in Elbert County, Georgia, Myron Juanita "Nita" Smith who was born 21 March 1940 in Madison County. They had two children, both born in Anderson, South Carolina:
3618 i. John Bryan[8] Beatenbough, b. 7 May 1963, m. Kaye Byrd; child:
        3619 a. Kathie Beth[9] Beatenbough, b. 5 Aug 1992
3617 ii. James Barry[8] Beatenbough. b. 13 Feb 1968, m. Aug 1992, Thesa Crain.

3261. Robbie Sue[7] Beatenbough (Robert[6], Henry Estee[5], T. R.[4], Michael[3], John Uriah[2], Michael[1]) was born 16 August 1941 in Madison County, Georgia. She married, on 16 July 1959, Alton Wayne Hill. They had two children, both born in Franklin County, Georgia:
3618 i. Robert Wayne[8] Hill, b. 7 Jan 1960, d. 23 Aug 1983, bur. Madison County, GA., m. Sue Massey
3619 ii. Larry Michael[8] "Mike" Hill, b. 7 Jan 1960, m. Tamberlyn Gail Mulkey.

3262. Virginia[7] Beatenbough (Thomas[6], Henry Estee[5], T. R.[4], Michael[3], John Uriah[2], Michael[1]) was born 12 November 1931 in Madison County, Georgia, and died in March 1993. She married Clarence Mack Roberts and had the following children:
3620 i. Patricia Faye[8] "Pat" Roberts, b. 29 Apr 1950, Fulton County, GA
3621 ii. Thomas Michael[8] Roberts, b. 2 Nov 1951, Fulton County, GA, m. Linda Lee Johnson; children:
        3622 a. Daniel Lee[9] Roberts, b. 18 Nov 1969
        3623 b. Douglas Michael[9] Roberts, b. 6 May 1972
        3624 c. David Andrew[9] Roberts, b. 30 Aug 1975

3625 d. Darrin Matthew[9] Roberts, b. 7 Jan 1980
3626 e. Derrick Alan[9] Roberts, b. 16 Aug 1985.

3263. Jerry Ollin[7] Beatenbough (Thomas[6], Henry Estee[5], T. R.[4], Michael[3], John Uriah[2], Michael[1]) was born 29 April 1939 in Fulton County, Georgia, and married Katherine Cannon. They had the following children:
3627 i. Tony Ollin[8] Beatenbough, b. 6 Jul 1959
3628 ii. Scott Allan[8] Beatenbough, b. 14 Jan 1961
3629 iii. Thomas Jerry[8] Beatenbough, b. 4 Sep 1963.

3269. John Rufus[7] Garner (Sarah[6], Virginia[5], Frances[4], Elizabeth[3], John Uriah[2], Michael[1]) was born 16 December 1905 and died 17 June 1975 in Union, South Carolina. He married, on 18 September 1926, Gladys A. Greer, who was born 30 May 1909 in Union, the daughter of John C. Calhoun and Eva Elaine (Clark) Greer. Three children:
+ 3630 i. Carroll Bruce[8] Garner, b. 19 June 1928
+ 3631 ii. Gene Edward[8] Garner, b. 3 Dec 1929
+ 3632 iii. Jack Greer[8] Garner, b. 3 July 1933.

3272. Thelma Virginia[7] Garner (Sarah[6], Virginia[5], Frances[4], Elizabeth[3], John Uriah[2], Michael[1]) was born 22 June 1910 and died 18 May 1982. She married David Artice Crocker, who was born 9 February 1909 and died 8 June 1952. Both are buried at Rosemont Cemetery, Union, South Carolina. Child:
+ 3633 i. Bobby Maurice Crocker, b. 16 Aug 1932.

3273. Joseph Woods[7] Garner (Sarah[6], Virginia[5], Frances[4], Elizabeth[3], John Uriah[2], Michael[1]) was born 17 July 1913 and died 18 February 1965. He married Ruby Lee O'Dell, and they had two children:
3634 i. Donald Woods[8] Garner, b. 10 Sept 1938, m. Christine Cobb; children:
3635 a. Christy Lynn[9] Garner, b. 12 March 1964, m. Donald Ralph Cannon
3636 b. Donald Woods[9] Garner, Jr., b. 10 Apr 1967, m. Deborah Roberts
3637 ii. Ted McBeth[8] Garner, b. 12 Dec 1941, m. Marva Moody; children:
3638 a. Greg McBeth[9] Garner, b. 27 Feb 1967, m. D'Lynn Conners
3639 b. Joseph Moody[9] Garner, b. 26 Jan 1976.

3274. Daniel Bruce[7] Garner (Sarah[6], Virginia[5], Frances[4], Elizabeth[3], John Uriah[2], Michael[1]) was born 4 November 1915 and died 19 May 1992. He married Mary Ema Nichols, and they had one child:
3640 i. Susan Ann[8] Garner, b. 21 May 1945, d. 23 March 1973, m. _____ Alexander; children:
3641 a. Amy Elizabeth[9] Alexander, b. 20 July 1969
3642 b. Mary Catherine[9] Alexander, b. 23 March 1973.

3275. Ralph Lee[7] Garner (Sarah[6], Virginia[5], Frances[4], Elizabeth[3], John Uriah[2], Michael[1]) was born 20 May 1917, and married Carolyn Bullington. Three children:
3643 i. Joyce Lynn[8] Garner, b. 21 Sept 1945, m. 1st John League (div); m. 2nd "Corky Huey" (div); m. 3rd Kenneth Campbell; children:
3644 a. John Jay[9] League, Jr., b. 5 Dec 1967
3645 b. Micah[9] Huey, b. 5 July 1977
3646 ii. Jessie Carol[8] Garner, b. 30 March 1950, m. David Morris; child:
3647 a. Garner Morris, b. 17 Apr 1989
3648 iii. Ralph Lee[8] Garner, Jr., b. 21 Apr 1954, m. Sylvia Garrett; children:

3649 a. Garrett[9] Garner, b. 17 Nov 1987
3650 b. Jacqueline[9] Garner, b. 20 Feb 1993.

3277. Jennie Viola[7] (Vi) Garner (Sarah[6], Virginia[5], Frances[4], Elizabeth[3], John Uriah[2], Michael[1]) was born 12 February 1922, and married James Cecil O'Dell. They live in Union, South Carolina, and have one child:
  3651 i. James Cecil[8] O'Dell, Jr., b. 6 March 1948, m. Sharon Campbell (div); children:
    3652 a. Nathan Blair[9] O'Dell, b. 27 Feb 1973
    3653 b. James Allen[9] O'Dell, b. 9 March 1979.

3279. Eva Mae[7] (Boots) Brandon (Pierce[6], Virginia[5], Frances[4], Elizabeth[3], John Uriah[2], Michael[1]) was born 13 September 1919 and married, on 2 September 1939, Floyd Earnest Young. Children:
  3654 i. Raymond Brandon[8] Young, b. 9 Jan 1943
  3655 ii. Michael Floyd[8] Young, b. 17 Feb 1948.

3280. Lovick Pierce[7] Brandon, Jr. (Pierce[6], Virginia[5], Frances[4], Elizabeth[3], John Uriah[2], Michael[1]) was born 28 August 1921, and married, on 5 February 1955, Audrey Lois Bryan. Children:
  3656 i. Bruce O'Neal[8] Brandon, b. 30 June 1956
  3657 ii. Christopher Lee[8] Brandon, b. 21 Feb 1960, m. 23 Nov 1988, Patricia Sligh Gaddis; children:
    3658 a. Catherine McKenna[9] Brandon, b. 17 Apr 1990
    3659 b. Gracyn Gaddis[9] Brandon, b. 5 Nov 1992.

3281. Herbert Lindo[7] Stutts (Janie[6], Virginia[5], Frances[4], Elizabeth[3], John Uriah[2], Michael[1]) was born 1 May 1918 and died 14 September 1984. He married Vivian Ducker. Two children:
  3660 i. Sherry Lindo[8] Stutts, m. Lloyd Brigman; children:
    3661 a. Melissa[9] Brigman, m. Dr. Claude Shumpert; children:
      3662 (1) Ashton[10] Shumpert
      3663 (2) Melissa[10] Shumpert
    3664 b. Trudy[9] Brigman
    3665 c. Tammy[9] Brigman m. Tim Swygert; child:
      3666 (1) Joey[10] Swygert
    3667 d. Blake[9] Brigman
  3668 ii. Herby Kay[8] Stutts, m. Susan Little; children:
    3669 a. Brad[9] Stutts
    3670 b. Jonathan[9] Stutts
    3671 c. Lauren[9] Stutts.

3282. Johnnie Brandon[7] Stutts (Janie[6], Virginia[5], Frances[4], Elizabeth[3], John Uriah[2], Michael[1]) was born 29 December 1920, and died 14 September 1989. He married Katherine Thackston, who was born 23 October 1920. Child:
  3672 i. Dollie Jane[8] Stutts, m. H. E. Tuttle; child:
    3673 a. H. E.[9] (Trip) Tuttle.

3283. Roy Davis[7] Stutts (Janie[6], Virginia[5], Frances[4], Elizabeth[3], John Uriah[2], Michael[1]) was born 22 April 1922 and married Alice Warner. Children:
  3674 i. Marcia[8] Stutts, m. Richard Parrott; children:
    3675 a. Kim[9] Parrott

3676 b. Bryan[9] Parrott
3677 ii. Roy Davis[8] Stutts, Jr.; children:
    3678 a. Davis[9] Stutts
    3679 b. Allison[9] Stutts
    3680 c. Tracy[9] Stutts
3681 iii. Pamela[8] Stutts, m. George Pitts
    3682 a. Kelly[9] Pitts
    3683 b. Kevin[9] Pitts.

3285. Sarah Elizabeth[7] Stutts (Janie[6], Virginia[5], Frances[4], Elizabeth[3], John Uriah[2], Michael[1]) was born 11 May 1927 and died 8 May 1992. She married John Calvin Neel, Jr., who was born 17 December 1921. Children:
3684 i. John Calvin[8] Neel, III, m. Shirley Stewart; children:
    3685 a. J. C.[9] Neel
    3686 b. Elizabeth[9] Neel
    3687 c. Janie[9] Neel
3688 ii. Janie Elizabeth[8] Neel, m. Richard Douglas Medlin; children:
    3689 a. Jenna[9] Medlin
    3690 b. Jay[9] Medlin
3691 iii. George Daniel[8] Neel; children:
    3692 a. A. C.[9] Neel
    3693 b. Wiley[9] Neel
3694 iv. Peggy Ann[8] Neel.

3286. Fannie Louise[7] Stutts (Janie[6], Virginia[5], Frances[4], Elizabeth[3], John Uriah[2], Michael[1]) was born 14 June 1929, and married Rev. Wingard Berry. Children:
3695 i. Michael[8] Berry; children:
    3696 a. Blake[9] Berry
    3697 b. Whitney[9] Berry
3698 ii. David[8] Berry; children:
    3699 a. Dave[9] Berry
    3700 b. Brandon[9] Berry.

3289. Peggy Ann[7] Stutts (Janie[6], Virginia[5], Frances[4], Elizabeth[3], John Uriah[2], Michael[1]) was born 22 July 1933, and married Robert Fitzgerald Rutherford. Children:
3701 i. William Fitzgerald[8] Rutherford; children:
    3702 a. Will[9] Rutherford
    3703 b. Brannon[9] Rutherford
3704 ii. Robert Drayton[8] Rutherford; child:
    3705 a. Drayton[9] Rutherford
3706 iii. John Houseal[8] Rutherford.

3290. Helen Mae[7] Stutts (Janie[6], Virginia[5], Frances[4], Elizabeth[3], John Uriah[2], Michael[1]) was born 31 October 1935. She married Bobby Wesley Corley, who was born 15 May 1932. Children:
3707 i. Candace Louise[8] Corley, m. David A. Koshinki; children:
    3708 a. Cory[9] Koshinki
    3709 b. Cassie[9] Koshinki
3710 ii. Kevin Dean[8] Corley, m. Patricia G. Houston; child:
    3711 a. Colt Garrett[9] Corley, b. 19 May 1995
3712 iii. Russell Stutts[8] Corley, m. Carole Rhoads

3713 iv. Kriste Lynn[8] Corley, m. David Sexton.

3293. Errol Barry[7] Stutts (Janie[6], Virginia[5], Frances[4], Elizabeth[3], John Uriah[2], Michael[1]) was born 15 December 1941. He married Catherine Elizabeth Gordon, who was born 13 June 1942. They live in Columbia, South Carolina. Children:
  3714 i. Angela Lee[8] Stutts m. Richard Henry Lagroon; child:
      3715 a. Leanne Elizabeth[9] Lagroon, b. 10 May 1995
  3716 ii. Brandon Gordon[8] Stutts, m. Kimberly Marie Coker.

3294. Ida Velle[7] Keenan (Ira[6], William[5], Nancy[4], Mary Ann[3], John Uriah[2], Michael[1]) was born 26 August 1923. She married William Albert Horn, who was born 30 May 1915 and died 21 September 1968. She resides in Gaffney, South Carolina, and has two children:
  3717 i. Donna Velle[8] Horn, b. 29 March 1949, m. Charles Terrell Wilson, b. 18 Jan 1949; children:
      3718 a. Tessa DeAnne[9] Wilson, b. 10 Aug 1971
      3719 b. Jennifer Lee[9] Wilson, b. 4 July 1973
  3720 ii. William Albert[8] Horn, Jr., b. 20 Nov 1953, m. Cynthia Robin Craven, b. 9 Apr 1959.

3295. William Robert[7] Keenen (Ira[6], William[5], Nancy[4], Mary Ann[3], John Uriah[2], Michael[1]) was born 24 September 1924 and died 29 September 1975. He married Frances Jones, who was born 1 May 1931. Children:
  3721   i. Billy Dean[8] Keenan, b. 7 Feb 1947, m. Janice Parris; children:
      3722 a. Steven Dean[9] Keenan, b. 11 Mar 1971, d. 13 Sept 1985
      3723 b. Jeffery Scott[9] Keenan, b. 13 June 1975
  3724 ii. Arthur Lee Keenan, b. 16 Aug 1948, m. Barbara Burgess; children:
      3725 a. Brian Lee[9] Keenan
      3726 b. Jennifer Marie[9] Keenan
  3727 iii. Bobby Gene[8] Keenan, m. Carolyn Ogle; child:
      3728 a. Robert Andrew[9] Keenan
  3729 iv. Terry Francis[8] Keenan, b. 1 Jan 1952, m. Dorothy Waldrop; children:
      3730 a. Wesley Robert[9] Keenan
      3731 b. Marsha Annette[9] Keenan
  3732   v. Michael Ray[8] Keenan, b. 11 Oct 1856
  3733 vi. Joseph S.[8] Keenan, b. 5 Aug 1962
  3734 vii. Dale J.[8] Kennan, b. 13 July 1965
  3735 viii. David T.[8] Keenan, b. 1 Nov 1967.

3296. Henry Donald[7] Keenan (Ira[6], William[5], Nancy[4], Mary Ann[3], John Uriah[2], Michael[1]) was born 27 October 1929 and married Isabel Bolin, who was born 3 August 1932. Children:
  3736   i. Deborah Elaine[8] Keenen, m. 12 Sept 1954 Michael D. Griffith, live Niceville, FL; child:
      3737 a. Kelly Ann[9] Griffith
  3738 ii. Sharon Lynn[8] Keenan, m. Cecile G. Jenkin, live Blacksburg, SC; children:
      3739 a. Aaron J.[9] Jenkin
      3740 b. Paul R.[9] Jenkin
  3741 iii. Jeffrey Alan[8] Keenan.

THE BEDENBAUGH-BETENBAUGH FAMILY

EIGHTH GENERATION

3478. James Sanders[8] Betenbaugh, II (Herman[7], James S.[6], Thomas J.[5], Micheal R.[4], David[3], John Uriah[2], Michael[1]) was born 24 July 1938 and married, first, Jackie Garrison; he married, second, Judy _____. Children:
    3742 i. James Sanders[9] Betenbaugh, III, b. 17 Sept 1958
    3743 ii. Lisa[9] Betenbaugh, b. Aug 1959
    3744 iii. Carl Alvin[9] Betenbaugh, b. Apr 1961
    3745 iv. Michael[9] Betenbaugh, b. Sept 1963
    3746 v. Adam[9] Betenbaugh (twin), b. Sept 1975
    3747 vi. Jennifer[9] Betenbaugh (twin) b. Sept 1975
    3748 vii. Kirkland[9] Betenbaugh, b. Oct 1980.

3479. Patricia Ann[8] Betenbaugh (Herman[7], James S.[6], Thomas J.[5], Micheal R.[4], David[3], John Uriah[2], Michael[1]) was born 9 August 1939 and married Carol E. Sanders, who was born 30 May 1940. Children:
    3749 i. Kathryn Diane[9] Sanders, b. 14 Nov 1958, m. James L. Garner. Children:
        3750 a. David Christopher[10] Garner, b. 26 Nov 1977
        3751 b. Jamie Lee[10] Garner, b. 31 Jan 1980
    3752 ii. Carol E.[9] Sanders, Jr., b. 9 Oct 1961
    3753 iii. Kenneth Wayne[9] Sanders, b. 5 June 1964.

3480. William Douglas[8] Betenbaugh (Herman[7], James S.[6], Thomas J.[5], Micheal R.[4], David[3], John Uriah[2], Michael[1]) was born 23 July 1941 and married Eunice Fulbright. Children:
    3754 i. Carolyn Teresa[9] Betenbaugh, b. 15 Sept 1964
    3755 ii. William Douglas[9] Betenbaugh, b. 11 Dec 1967.

3481. Herman Donald[8] (Don) Betenbaugh (Herman[7], James S.[6], Thomas J.[5], Micheal R.[4], David[3], John Uriah[2], Michael[1]) was born 14 November 1948 and married, on 1 May 1967, Margaret Bailey, who was born 21 August 1950. Children:
    3756 i. Donald Richard[9] (Donnie) Betenbaugh, b. 23 Apr 1968, m. 31 Dec 1994 Crystal Wright, b. 26 Dec 1971. He was elected county supervisor for Union County at the end of 1994 and is presently serving in that capacity.
    3757 ii. Donna Sue[9] Betenbaugh, b. 23 Jan 1970, m. Scott Farmer; child:
        3758 a. Joni[10] Farmer
    3759 iii. Kimbrely Dawn[9] Betenbaugh, b. 13 Sept 1979.

3284. John Roper[8] Betenbaugh (Herman[7], James S.[6], Thomas J.[5], Micheal R.[4], David[3], John Uriah[2], Michael[1]) was born 20 December 1951 and married Wanda Payne. Children:
    3760 i. Misty Michelle[9] Betenbaugh, b. 5 July 1974
    3761 ii. John Michael[9] Betenbaugh, b. 23 Feb 1979.

3285. David Robin[8] Betenbaugh (Herman[7], James S.[6], Thomas J.[5], Micheal R.[4], David[3], John Uriah[2], Michael[1]) was born 22 August 1953 and married Mary Lee West. Children:
    3762 i. David Robin[9] Betenbaugh, Jr., b. 26 Apr 1971
    3763 ii. Cynthia Lynn[9] Betenbaugh, b. 4 Sept 1972.

3543. Linda Elaine[8] Fowler (Joan[7], Horace[6], Henry Estee[5], T. R.[4], Micheal[3], John Uriah[2], Michael[1]) was born 30 August 1948 in Clarke County, Georgia. She married, first, on 6 January 1966 in Carson City, Nevada, Monte Leroy Person, who was born 3 February 1945 in San Francisco, California, the son of Leonard and Violet Shirley Person. She married, second, on 21 November 1991 in Reno, Nevada, Joseph Lloyd Wayne, who was born 18 October 1941 in San Francisco, California, the son of Lloyd and Clarice (Sanguinetti) Wayne. Children:

3764 i. Noelle Christine[9] Person, b. 29 Oct 1969, San Mateo, CA, m. 16 Sept 1989 Douglas Allen Dillon, b 5 Jan 1968, San Mateo, son of Ronald and Diane (Battaglia) Dillon

3765 ii. Todd Jeremy[9] (T.J.) Person, b. 27 Jul 1973, San Francisco, CA.

3544. Kevin Richard[8] Fowler (Joan[7], Horace[6], Henry Estee[5], T. R.[4], Michael[3], John Uriah[2], Michael[1]) was born 11 February 1954 in San Francisco, California. He married, on 16 June 1974 in San Mateo, California, Karen Ann Kelley, who was born 13 May 1954 in San Francisco, the daughter of John and Frances (Lapachet) Kelly. He married, second, on 4 November 1984, in Reno, Nevada, Vonda Sue Leveque, who was born 23 June 1962 in Lebanon, Ohio, the daughter of Melvin Alford and Betty Jane (Bailey) LeVeque. Children:

3766 i. Kelley Marie[9] Fowler, b. 1 May 1978, Seattle, WA

3767 ii. Eric Lamar[9] Fowler, b. 22 Mar 1987, King County, WA

3768 iii. Anthony James[9] (A.J.) Fowler, b. 22 Oct 1989, King County, WA.

3545. Michael Dennis[8] Coffee (Mary[7], Charles[6], Henry Estee[5], T. R.[4], Michael[3], John Uriah[2], Michael[1]) was born 18 July 1951 in Duval County, Florida. He married, first, Renea Bartlet and, second, Cindy York. Children by first marriage:

3769 i. Tammy Renea[9] Coffee, b. 30 Nov 1969, Cobb County, GA, m. 3 Oct 1987 Kai Uve Lampe, b. 28 Mar 1964; child:

      3770 a. Christane Victoria[10] Lampe

3771 ii. Lisa Marie[9] Coffee was born on 18 Jul 1974 in Cobb County, GA.

3546. Karen[8] Coffee (Mary[7], Charles[6], Henry Estee[5], T. R.[4], Michael[3], John Uriah[2], Michael[1]) was born 13 September 1953 in Austell, Cobb County, GA. She married Larry Ralph Echols, and they had the following children:

3772 i. Andrew Jason[9] Echols, b. 12 Oct 1984, Rock Springs, WY

3773 ii. Kristen Day[9] Echols, b. 15 Jan 1987.

3550. Charles Michael[8] Beatenbough (Charles[7], Charles[6], Henry Estee[5], T. R.[4], Michael[3], John Uriah[2], Michael[1]) was born 10 November 1951 in Atlanta, Fulton County, Georgia. He married, on 14 June 1975 in Athens, Georgia, Karen Jane Anderson, who was born on 28 Oct 1953 in Amityville, New York. They had the following children, all born in Atlanta, Fulton County, Georgia:

3774 i. Cole Michael[9] Beatenbough, b. 5 Nov 1981

3775 ii. Dane Andrew[9] Beatenbough, b. 25 Jun 1986

3776 iii. Jesse Evan[9] Beatenbough, b. 28 Dec 1991.

3551. Susan Paula[8] Beatenbough (Charles[7], Charles[6], Henry Estee[5], T. R.[4], Michael[3], John Uriah[2], Michael[1]) was born on 4 May 1953 in Atlanta, Fulton County, Georgia. She married Kenneth Lee Morris, who was born on 23 Jul 1953. They had the following children, all born in Atlanta, Georgia:

3777 i. Steven Braden[9] Morris, b. 16 Jan 1984

3778 ii. Paul Kenneth[9] Morris, b. 20 Jun 1986

3779 iii. Philip Graham[9] Morris, b. Mar 1988

3780 iv. Michael Len[9] Morris, b. 21 Oct 1989.

THE BEDENBAUGH-BETENBAUGH FAMILY

3552. Helen Dean[8] Beatenbough (Charles[7], Charles[6], Henry Estee[5], T. R.[4], Michael[3], John Uriah[2], Michael[1]) was born 24 June 1960 in Burlington, Alamance County, North Carolina. She married, on 23 July 1983, Jeffrey Morris Farley, who was born 7 January 1953 in Gainesville, Hall County, Georgia. They had the following children:
3781 i. Jeffrey Ezekial[9] "Zeke" Farley, b. 19 Dec 1986, Atlanta, Fulton Co., GA
3782 ii. Evelyn Helen[9] Farley, b. 28 Oct 1989, Gwinnett Co., GA.

3553. John Clark[8] Beatenbough (Charles[7], Charles[6], Henry Estee[5], T. R.[4], Michael[3], John Uriah[2], Michael[1]) was born 13 Mar 1964 in Burlington, Alamance County, North Carolina. He married, on 8 November 1982 in Gainesville, Hall County, Georgia, Shelly Joan "Joni" Coalson, who was born on 4 Jan 1956. They had the following children:
3783 i. John Clark[9] Beatenbough, Jr., b. 16 Jun 1983, Gwinnett Co., GA
3784 ii. Julie Camille[9] Beatenbough, b. 13 Feb 1986, Gwinnett Co., GA
3785 iii. Joy Christine[9] Beatenbough, b. 21 Feb 1987, Gwinnett Co., GA
3786 iv. Joshua Calvin[9] Beatenbough, b. 3 Apr 1989, Fulton Co., GA
3787 v. Joanna Claire[9] Beatenbough, b. 7 Dec 1991, Forsyth Co., GA.

3554. Brenda Gail[8] Beatenbough (Clifford[7], William[6], Henry Estee[5], T. R.[4], Michael[3], John Uriah[2], Michael[1]) was born 8 February 1952 in Atlanta, Fulton County, Georgia. She married, on 23 Nov 1973 in Atlanta, Ronald Lee Henson, who was born on 13 December 1949 in Walton County, Georgia. They had the following children:
3788 i. Ronald Lee[9] "Beau" Henson, Jr., b. 25 Jul 1978, Indianapolis, IN
3789 ii. Julie Elizabeth[9] Henson, b. 10 Nov 1979, Fulton Co., GA
3790 iii. Joshua Neil[9] Henson, b. 31 Aug 1984, Fulton Co., GA.

3555. Sheryl Lynn[8] Beatenbough (Clifford[7], William[6], Henry Estee[5], T. R.[4], Michael[3], John Uriah[2], Michael[1]) was born 31 October 1955 in Fulton County, Georgia. She married, on 26 June 1982 in Fayetteville, Georgia, Hanson Gary Wright. Child:
3791 i. Garett Hanson[9] Wright, b. 29 Apr 1991, Portland, OR.

3556. Clifford Neil[8] "Cliff" Beatenbough, Jr. (Clifford[7], William[6], Henry Estee[5], T. R.[4], Michael[3], John Uriah[2], Michael[1]) was born 29 April 1959 in Atlanta, Fulton County, Georgia. He married, on 21 June 1986 in Atlanta, Lucia Eyzaguirre. They had the following children:
3792 i. Christin Nichole[9] Beatenbough, b. 6 May 1989
3793 ii. Nicolette Alexandria[9] Beatenbough, b. 11 Dec 1992.

3557. Susan Anne[8] Beatenbough (William[7], William[6], Henry Estee[5], T. R.[4], Michael[3], John Uriah[2], Michael[1]) was born on 14 July 1955 in Jacksonville, Duval County, Florida. She married, on 3 October 1981 in Orinda, California, Paul John Poletti, the son of Louis John and Natalia Jean Poletti. Child:
3794 i. Mary Spenser[9] Poletti, b. 20 Mar 1991, San Francisco, CA.

3558. Jennifer Lee[8] Beatenbough (William[7], William[6], Henry Estee[4], T. R.[4], Michael[3], John Uriah[2], Michael[1]) was born on 5 Mar 1958 in Jacksonville, Duval County, FL. She married, on 16 February 1985 in Burlingame, San Mateo County, California, Richard Louis Poletti, the son of Louis John and Natalia Jean Poletti. They had the following children:
3795 i. John William[9] Poletti, b. 30 Dec 1985, Jacksonville, Duval Co., FL

3796 ii. Natalie Alyse[9] Poletti, b. 18 Aug 1987, San Mateo Co., CA
3797 iii. Louis Richard[9] Poletti, b. 1 Nov 1989 (twin), Santa Clara Co., CA
3798 iv. William Wade[9] Poletti, b. 1 Nov 1989 (twin), Santa Clara Co., CA.

3630. Carroll Bruce[8] Garner (John[7], Sarah[6], Virginia[5], Frances[4], Elizabeth[3], John Uriah[2], Michael[1]) was born 19 June 1928 and died 11 November 1992 in Saluda, South Carolina. He married, on 1 October 1950, in Newberry, South Carolina, Jewel Louise Bouknight, who was born 7 March 1932. Issue:
3799 i. Carol Jean[9] Garner, b. 9 Nov 1951, m. 1st Terry Chapman; m. 2nd, 9 Apr 1994, Thomas Edward Fulmer; child:
    3800 a. Travis Garner[10] Chapman, b. 31 July 1970, m. 28 March 1992 Susan Kinard; child:
        3801 (1) Jessica Alaine[11] Chapman, b. 11 Oct 1992, Greenwood,SC
3802 ii. Kenneth Bruce[9] Garner. b. 8 July 1953, m. 12 July 1975, Sabrina Bedenbaugh, b. 25 Sept 1957; child:
    3803 a. John Ellerbe[10] Garner, b. 14 Jan 1976
3804 iii. William Mack[9] Garner, b. 28 Oct 1958, m. 23 June 1984, Leanne Brown, b. 23 March 1962; m 2nd Cynthia Thomas, Jacksonville, FL; children:
    3805 a. Jason[10] Garner, b. 7 Sept 1979, Jacksonville, FL
    3806 b. Jessie Bruce[10] Garner, b. 13 Dec 1984, Jacksonville, FL.

3631. Gene Edward[8] Garner (John[7], Sarah[6], Virginia[5], Frances[4], Elizabeth[3], John Uriah[2], Michael[1]) was born 3 December 1929 in Union, South Carolina, and married, first, Barbara Joan Young, and they had one child. He married, second, in Cleves, Ohio, Madelyn Miller, and they also had one child:
3807 i. Gladys A.[9] Garner, b. 29 Aug 1954, Union, SC, m. David Prouty, in Lynn, MA; children, all born Lynn, MA:
    3808 a. Shawn[10] Prouty, b. 20 July 1975
    3809 b. Shannon[10] Prouty
    3810 c. Tanya[10] Prouty
3811 ii. Gene Edward Garner, Jr., b. 4 March 1972, Lawrenceburg, IN.

3632. Jack Greer[8] Garner (John[7], Sarah[6], Virginia[5], Frances[4], Elizabeth[3], John Uriah[2], Michael[1]) was born 3 July 1933 in Union, South Carolina, and married on 25 August 1954, Myrtle Louise Kelley, who was born 25 October 1934. They had two children:
3812 i. Jack Turner[9] Garner, b. 20 July 1957, m. 17 Nov 1977 Teresa Allison
3813 ii. Elizabeth Louise[9] Garner, b. 1 March 1960, m. 13 March 1983, Bobby Knox, Jr., b. 13 Aug 1957; m. 2nd, 21 July 1994, David Allison.

3633. Bobby Maurice[8] Crocker (Thelma[7], Sarah[6], Virginia[5], Frances[4], Elizabeth[3], John Uriah[2], Michael[1]) was born 16 August 1932, and married Patricia Gist. Children:
3814 i. Mara Beth[9] Crocker, b. 12 Jan 1958
3815 ii. Bobby Maurice[9] Crocker, Jr., b. 9 June 1961, m. Carole Elaine Brigman; three children, all b. Columbia, SC:
    3816 a. Everett Maurice[10] Crocker, b. 16 Dec 1987
    3817 b. Rebekah Carol[10] Crocker, b. 16 Sept 1992
    3818 c. Andrew Gist[10] Crocker, b. 19 May 1995.

THE BEDENBAUGH-BETENBAUGH FAMILY

NOTES AND REFERENCES

1. Union County General Sessions Papers, No. 467, original at South Carolina Archives.

2. 1800 U. S. Census, Newberry District, S. C., p. 90.

3. General Assembly Petitions, 1792 #28, original at South Carolina Archives.

4. General Assembly Petitions, 1794, original at the South Carolina Archives.

5. Newberry County, SC, Deed Book I, p. 507, original in the Office of Clerk of Court, Newberry County Court House, Newberry, SC.

6. Richland County [Columbia District] Equity Rolls, 1812 #73, originals at SC Archives.

7. Brent H. Holcomb, *Memorialized Records of Lexington District, S. C. 1814-1825* (Easley, S. C.: Southern Historical Press), page 90.

8. Union Deed Book O, p. 188

9. Union County Common Pleas, 1817, #557, Box 127, Package 2: McGraw vs Betenbaugh.

10. Union County Court of General Sessions, Coroner's Inquisitions, Box 1, originals at the South Carolina Archives.

11. 1810 Federal Census, Lexington District, South Carolina, p. 71.

12. 1820 Federal Census, Union District, South Carolina, p. 153.

13. 1830 Federal Census, Union District, South Carolina, p. 195.

14. Union County Deed Book H-26, pp. 252, 254, 491, 493, and 495, originals in the Office of the Clerk of Court, Union, South Carolina.

15. 1850 Federal Census, Union District, South Carolina, page 36 (all were children still living in the household of their parents).

16. Franklin County, Georgia, Judge of Probate, Will Book 1867-1889, pp. 236-238.

17. 1850 U. S. Census, Union District SC, page 55.

18. 1860 U. S. Census, Union District, SC, page 202.

19. 1850 Census, DeKalb County, Georgia, page 109.

20. 1860 U. S. Census, Campbell County, Georgia, p. 343.

21. 1870 Federal Census, Campbell County, Georgia, page 139.

22. Abbeville County, South Carolina, Estates, Box 142, Package 3999.

23. Union County, SC, General Sessions, Roll #1472, original at South Carolina Archives.

24. J. S. G. Richardson, *Reports of Cases at Law and in Equity Argued and Determined in the Court of Appeals and Court of Errors in South Carolina,* Law Vol. XIII- Equity Vol. XII (Charleston, SC: E. J. Dawson & Co., 1866), pages 42-46.

25. Union County, South Carolina, Records of the Clerk of Court as other than register of mesne conveyance, estrays (loose papers), original at SC Archives.

26. Union Deed County Book Z-18, p. 236.

27. Union County, SC, Estates, Box 71, Package 5.

28. Obituary notice in the *Weekly Union Times,* issue of April 19, 1889.

29. 1870 Federal census, York County, South Carolina, #448, p. 235.

30. 1880 Census, Union County, South Carolina, Union Township, page 418.

31. Tommy J. Vaughan, *Union County, South Carolina, Death Notices from Early Newspapers, 1852-1914,* page 92.

32. Union County, South Carolina, Records of the Clerk of Court as other than register of mesne conveyance, estrays (loose papers), original at SC Archives.

33. A clipping of an obituary notice for Mrs. Elizabeth (Betenbaugh) Willard was found pasted in the journal of John F. Brandon. This notice indicates exact birth and death dates for her. The notice has been found to come from the *Southern Christian Advocate,* issue of 9 June 1910, page 15.

34. In a ledger book of Rev. John Gibbs is an entry that he married John Whitton and Elizabeth "Beatenbough" in the latter part of the winter of 1850. The writer has a photocopy of the page from that ledger. Since it was an entry made well after the fact, the name of John Whitton may have been an error for John Willard. However, the obituary notice of Elizabeth (Betenbaugh) Willard in 1910 states that she married John Willard fifty-five years earlier, which would have been in 1855. The marriage year of 1855 is also supported by the 1900 census (Union County, p. 163), which states that John and Elizabeth Willard had been married for 55 years. In any case, if Elizabeth Betenbaugh was indeed married to a John Whitton/Whitten, there were no children by that marriage, and Mr. Whitten probably did not live very long.

35. Union County, South Carolina, Records of the Clerk of Court as other than register of mesne conveyance, estrays (loose papers), original at SC Archives.

36. Randolph J. Kirkland, *Broken Fortunes,* page 25.

37. Information on Trisvan Reeder Beatenbough and his descendants was contributed by Charles Beatenbough of Buford, Georgia, in 1995.

38. Based on family in the 1860 U. S. Census, Union District, p. 197.

39. Death Certificate of John Henderson Gregory, 1924 #18713, DHEC microfilm at SC Archives.

40. Data on this family is from the F. E. Davis Bible, found on pages 52-53, *South Carolina Bible Records,* published 1994 by the Pinckney District Chapter of the South Carolina Genealogical Society. The journals of John F. Brandon indicate the

data on the death of Frances Davis and states that Hiram, Frances, and Jeff Davis are buried at Mt. Vernon Presbyterian Church in Union County. However, no gravestones have been located for them.

41. Death Certificate, 1925, #17939.

42. Obituary notice in *The State*, issue of 15 July 1907, page 1, column 2.

43. Marriage notice in the *Weekly Union Times*, issue of 3 January 1879.

44. 1880 Census, Union County, South Carolina, Union Township, page 418.

45. *Cemeteries in Chickasaw & Surrounding Counties*, Volume 2, page 140.

46. Pontotoc County, Mississippi, Marriage Records 1893-1897, page 424, microfilm at Mississippi Archives in Jackson.

47. Death Certificate of Mrs. Nancy Keenan, 1930 #2432, DHEC microfilm at SC Archives.

48. Death Certificate of David Andrew McCreight, 1940 #17540, DHEC microfilm at SC Archives.

49. Death Certificate of Nelia Humphries, 1933 #16789, DHEC microfilm at SC Archives.

50. Marriage date from obituary notice of T. J. Betenbaugh, *The Progress*, issue of 19 October 1915.

51. News item in *The Progress*, issue of 24 January 1911.

52. Union County Marriage License Book A, page 3. This was the third marriage license issued in Union County, the law having taken effect 1 July 1911.

53. Marriage Notice in the Union *Progress*, issue of 29 October 1909.

54. A brief obituary notice for John Betenbaugh appeared in *The State*, issue of 26 August 1911, page 3, column 4.

55. Marriage notice in the *Weekly Union Times*, issue of 1 March 1889.

56. Register of Deaths, City of Union, page 9, microfilm at South Carolina Archives.

57. The obituary notice of Mrs. Sallie Wilburn in the *Union Daily Times*, issue of 3 September 1946, page four, states that she was survived by a brother W. T. Faucette.

58. 1900 Federal Census, Union County, South Carolina, Santuc Township, p. 163-B.

59. 1900 Federal Census, Union County, South Carolina, Santuc Township, p. 163-B.

60. Marriage Notice in the Union *Progress*, issue of 17 August 1909.

61. Death Certificate, J. B. Betenbaugh, 1937 #1128, microfilm at SC Archives.

62. Death Certificate, 1924 #9514, microfilm at South Carolina Archives.

63. Union County, South Carolina, Marriage Book I, page 447, original at Office of Probate Judge, Union County Court House.

64. Union County, South Carolina, Marriage Book A, page 220, original in Office of Probate Judge.

65. Death Certificate of William Alexander White, 1921 #19872, DHEC microfilm at SC Archives.

66. Death Certificate of Rev. E. B. Foister, 1940 #12859, DHEC microfilm at SC Archives.

67. Data on this family supplied by Mr. Bob Cartee, Spartanburg, South Carolina.

68. Data on this family supplied by Mr. Bob Cartee, Spartanburg, South Carolina.

69. Marriage notice in the *Union Daily Times*, issue of 14 July 1905.

Armstrong (cont.)
Mavis (Ritter) 66
Metta A. (Conwill) 66
Michelle (Calloway) 84
Ora Jane (Stutts) 165
Wendell 165
Wendell Stutts 165
Arnold, Lillian Divola
(Bedenbaugh) 54
Ruby (Bedenbaugh) 49
Arrington, Suzanna (Be-
denbaugh)(Myers) 67
William B. 67
Arseneau, Linda Marie
(Conwill) 99
Atkinson, Mary Kathleen
(Bedenbaugh) 108
Aull, Arverene (McGee)
52
Carrell A. 52
Clarence Jacob 42
Gula (Bedenbaugh) 42
Lula Mary (Bedenbaugh)
52
Margaret (Cook) 20
Auman, Betty (Betenb-
augh) 159
Delmar Burch 159
John Andrew 159
Kathy (Ackers) 159
Richard Curtis 159
Robin Marie (Clement)
159
Tamara Lynn (Siler) 159
Austin, 10
Auton, Alicia Carol (Cro-
mer) 92
Dana Michele (Blancher)
92
Henry Tillman 92
Phyllis Carol (Shealy) 92
Tammy (Kunkle) 82
Avery, Jacqueline Delores
105
John William 105
Phyllis Ann 105
Tolula Mary Jane (Be-
denbaugh) 105
Ayers, Doris (Dyer) 152
John 152
Babb, Allison Lee 167
Alvin Rich 167
Sheila Lee (Keenan) 167
Bailey, Andrea Lynn (-
Sims) 83
Annie Marie 172
Benemma (Bentley) 172
Betty Jane (LeVeque) 184
Charles Jr. 161
Charles Preston 161
Christopher David 172
Christopher M. "Kit" 83
Daniel Anthony 172

Dovie Marie (Beten-
baugh) 143
Elizabeth (Robinson) 172
Grayson Wendell 172
Jeff Eugene 83
Jessica Lynn 172
Josie (Young) 163
Judy Lynn (Bedenbaugh)
83
Kelly Jane 172
Kenneth Wendell 172
Leila Mae (Young) 172
Maggie 173
Margaret (Betenbaugh)
183
Marion Eugene 161
Mattie Louise (Willard)
145, 161
Melvin Eugene 83
Morris Sanders 161
Nancy (Reside) 172
Nancy C. (Williams) 172
Paul 161
Philip Michael 172
Preston 145
Ryan Thomas 172
Scott Douglas 172
Stephen Thomas 172
Sue Catherine 161
Tammy (Foster) 172
Wendell Phillip 172
William Andrew 172
William Ernest 172
Willis Andrew 143
Baker, Clifton Samuel Jr.
116
Retha Cheryl (Cotney)
116
Balcomb, Patricia (Be-
denbaugh) 78
Baldwin, Sallie J. (Willard)
145
Ballentine, Clara Armenia
(Cumalander) 102
Clay 51
Dorothy May (Boozer) 51
Evelyn Jeannine "Jenny"
(Bedenbaugh) 102
Helen (Dennis) 80
William Arthur 102
Bannister, Frances (Dan-
ielsen) 73
Bantum, John William Jr.
93
Lucia Merle (Sum-
mer)(Turner) 93
Barclay, Tina J. (Silva) 78
Barnes, Betty Sue (Kinley)
178
Clarence 97
Dorothy Jean (Werts)-
(Smith) 102

Elizabeth (Bedenbaugh)
45
Jason 102
Josephine Katherine
(Bedenbaugh)(Frye) 97
Nettie (Mills) 103
Nettie Julian (Mills) 72
Robert 102
Tony 102
Barnett, Nannie (Beten-
baugh)(Johnson) 143
Barnoe, Alvan A. 121
Calhoun 121
Carrie J. 121
Bartlet, Renea (Coffee)
184
Bashore, Allen S. 50
Anne (Boozer) 50
Bates, Daniel Scott 168
Ronnie Earl 168
Ronnie Keith 168
Teddie Faye (Keenan)
168
Battaglia, Diane (Dillon)
184
Beachem, Matilda (Chap-
man)(Bedenbaugh) 14
Beadebaugh, 10
Beadenbaugh, John 127
Beard, Don Steven 93
Margaret Ann (Summer)-
(Harrison) 93
Pamela Anne 93
Tana Michelle 93
Beatenback, Adam 13
Beatenbaugh, Adam 126,
127
Annie (Miller) 137
Caroline 127
Elizabeth (Anderson) 137
George 137
George Washington 127,
137
Ida (Haney) 137
Inez (Parlier) 137
Irene (Holbrook) 137
John 127
John Uriah 124
Joseph Jackson 127, 137
Josie 137
Lilla Mae 137
Mary (--) 124
Michael 124-126
Minnie Lee (Ledbetter)
137
Nancy (--) 126, 127
R. A. 137
"Rezia/Reesy" 127
Sarah F. (Carter) 137
Theressa (--)(Nance) 127
William Pinckney Jesse
Jackson 137
William Pinckney Jr. 137

192

Bedenbaugh (cont.)
Elizabeth 13, 14, 16, 17, 29, 41
Elizabeth A. (Boozer) 24
Elizabeth Armada (Nettles) 105
Elizabeth Armada 75
Elizabeth Teryl 94
Ella (Mundy) 28
Ella (Rhinehart) 68
Ella (Wright) 58
Ella 122
Ella Caroline (Morris) 19
Ella Florence (Gilliam) 49
Ella Ruth (Boozer) 71, 80
Elleene Ann (Hilton)-(Wilson) 110
Ellen (Outzs) 66
Ellen (Warner) 44, 80
Ellen R. (Moore) 36
Ellen R. 20
Ellie Anna (Miller) 97
Elliott Hurley 37
Elmer Ernest 44
Elmina Novice (Roberts)-(Covington) 45
Eloise (Drake) 48
Elsie (Nichols) 70
Elsie Ernestine (Fry) 39
Elva Mae (Skipper) 64
Emily Christine Susannah (Nichols) 34
Emily Kay 103
Emma 32
Emma Elizabeth 18
Emma Katie Bell (Douberley) 76
Emma Maybelle (Witt)-(Burns) 48
Emory Hayes 78
Epsie (Stewart) 14
Eris Naomi (Frye) 83
Ernest 34
Ernest C. 29
Ernest Day (Campbell) 32
Ernest Doyle 97
Ernest Wyche 35, 61
Ernestine (Livingston) 63
Esmond Denny 67
Esta Mae (Taylor) 107
Estelle (Bouknight) 56
Ethel (Fellers) 69
Ethel Elizabeth (Adams) 69
Ethel Lester (Bedenbaugh) 34
Ethel Nannie 61
Ethel Nannie Mary 68
Etta (Abrams) 73
Etta 47
Eugene Holland 56
Eula Belle (Joiner) 70
Eula Lillie (Bowers) 71

Eula Lillie 44
Eula Melissa (Bedenbaugh) 71, 83
Eula Melissa 55
Eunice (Chapman) 59
Eva 49
Eva Lois (Callaway) 43
Eve (Boozer) 18
Eve 14
Evelina 40
Evelyn 42
Evelyn Jeannine "Jenny" (Ballentine) 102
Everett 29
Fannie E. (Dominick) 20
Fanny Alethie (Eargle) 37
Faye Annelle (Shealy) 64
Flora Belle (Wilson) 69
Florence (Harman) 41
Florene (Noegel) 106
Forrest 35
Frances (Moore) 79
Frances 25
Frances Austin 67
Frances Caroline "Fannie" (Ruff) 41
Frances Christine (Zimmerman) 49
Frances Drury 26, 43
Frances Elizabeth "Bessie" (Wheeler) 32
Frances Elizabeth (Earhardt) 32
Frances Soffie (Marks) 109
Francis "Frank" Pickens 27, 48
Frank 28
Frank Pickens 76, 110, 111
Frank Pickens Jr. 111
Frank S. 119, 120
Frank Willoughby 48, 76
Franklin S. 16, 24, 28
Fred L. 42
Fred Lester 50
Fred Shields 39
Frederick L. 68
G. A. 17
Gabriel Lewis 109
Gail (Bruce) 79
Garnett Franklin 66
Garnett Franklin Jr. 66
Garrett Alexander 83
Gary King 79
Gayle (--) 82
Geneva (Oswald) 37
George Allen 97
George Anderson 16, 17, 27, 28
George Clarence 64
George Elton 59
George Julian 60, 96

George L. 48
George Pettus 19 34
George Robert 91
George Robert Jr. 92
George Roscoe 81
George Simeon 34
George Stephen Julian 96
George Steve 96
George W. 67, 122
George Washington 13, 16
George Willis 36
Georgiana (McCollough) 41
Georgie (Fulmer) 100
Georgie 68
Gerald 37, 56
Geraldine (Riley) 71
Gerhard Day 32
Gertrude (Chapman) 57
Gladys (Berry) 66
Gladys (Shealy) 36, 37, 60, 95
Gladys 49
Glenda (Melton) 82
Glenn Shealy 79
Grabilla Adeline (Venable) 31
Grace (Hendrix) 70
Grace Beryl (Holcombe) 56
Grace Edith Leone (Richards) 37
Grace Edith Leone 23
Gregory Adam 110
Gregory Alvin 110
Gregory Owens 101
Gula (Aull) 42
Gussie (Miller) 44
Gwynne (Sandel) 79
H. E. 28
Halie Ann 110
Hall 41
Hannon William 81
Harmon M. 72
Harold E. 40
Harold Oxner 63
Harold Stanley 83
Harold Thomas 71, 83
Harold Timothy 63
Harry 29
Haskel L. 37
Hattie Elizabeth 23
Hattie Virginia (Thomas) 39
Hawkins 55
Hawkins Kinard 19, 34
Hawkins S. 56
Hazel Inez (Cotney) 55
Hazel Mae (Smith)(Blair) 94
Hazel Mae 60

Bedenbaugh (cont.)
Hazel Ruth (Campbell)
63
Heather (Bright) 82
Helen (Burton) 78
Helen (Cloaninger) 67
Helen (Stribble) 49
Helen (Weir) 32
Helen 122
Helen Beatrice (Schumpert) 59
Helen Louise (Frier) 110
Helen Ruth (Martin) 84
Helen Ruth 55
Henry 13, 14
Henry Boston 135
Herbert Hayne "John" 50
Herman Michael 82
Hester (Stephens) 16, 17
Hettie Hodges 35
Horace Nichols 35, 59
Hosea G. 42
Howard Elmore 43
Howard King 50, 79
Howard Levi 66
Hubert Murchison 71
Ida Beatrice (Hope) 38
Ida Beatrice 23
Ida Mae (Hayes) 50, 78
Irene (Warren) 34
Iris Elizabeth (Kibler) 81
Isabelle (Oxner) 36
Isadore (Addy) 66
J. Todd 103
J. Willie 32
Jackson 41
Jacob 13, 15, 16, 118
Jacob Asbury 16, 26, 72
Jacob Belton 15
Jacob Calvin "Cally" 35
Jacob Calvin "Jake" 35
Jacob Calvin 20, 97
Jacob Hawkins "Bud" 34,
56
Jacob Hazelius 25
Jacob Kibler 19, 34
Jacob Moody 44, 71
Jacob P. 25, 41
Jacob W. 26
Jacob Warner 102
Jacquelyn (Cox) 106
Jakie Lee 56
James Arthur 32
James Carey 64
James Carey Jr. 64
James Edwin 75, 106
James G. 72
James H. 42
James Henry 43
James Ira 32, 120
James Kleckly "Jim" 26
James Lawrence 40
James Luther 27, 47

James Lyttleton 16, 27
James Manly 50
James Ralph 82
James Roscoe 55, 81
James Simeon Jr. 55
James Simeon Simpson
34, 55
James T. 25, 40
James Timothy 94
James W. 56, 122
James Wade 41, 67
James Wendell 57
James Wendell Jr. 57
James William 35
Jana 72
Jane (North) 104
Janice (Bradley) 72
Janice Leigh (Blackwell)
102
Janie (Bedenbaugh) 56
Janie Louise (Raulerson)
110
Janie [or Frances] 16
Janis (Rauch) 94
Jean 102
Jean Ruth (Oxner) 45
Jeanne Marie 107
Jeannette (Law) 106
Jeannette Eileen 66
Jed Willoughby 108
Jefferson Holland 34, 56
Jeffie Gerald 68
Jeffie Otto 68
Jeffrey Artemas 108
Jeffrey Austen 108
Jeffrey Furman 101
Jeffrey Thomas 83
Jeffry Allen 64
Jennie Beardon (Miller)
35, 59
Jennifer 104
Jennifer Lynn 108
Jennings Read 48
Jeremy Elton 59
Jerry Hugh 75, 107
Jerry Wayne 91
Jerry Wayne Jr. 91
Jesse Levi 39
Jesse P. 36
Jessica 83
Jessie Mae (Dobbins) 47
Jimmie Sue (Trotter)(Matthews) 68
Jimmy 68
Jimmy Byrnes 71, 102
Jno U 124
Jo Rosemary (Moore) 96
Jody Alan 83
John 13, 15, 16, 24, 29
John Adam 14, 15, 18, 20,
55, 64, 83, 119
John Adam Jr. 20, 36, 64
John Allen 36

John Bachman 23, 37
John Benjamin 57
John Bennett 37
John Clinton 40
John Denniston 28, 49
John Gilbert 40
John Holcombe "Jack" 56
John Hugh 108
John L. 26, 42
John Michael 82
John Nicholas 27, 48
John Preston 41
John Q. A. 16
John Roscoe 34, 55
John Simpson 19, 34
Johnny Clarence 56
Jones Edward 60
Jones Mathias 35, 60
Joni Rene 83
Joseph Ballenger 30
Joseph Falls 26, 45, 72
Joseph Guy 68, 101
Joseph Ira Cronk 35, 60
Joseph Moody 72, 103
Joseph Worth 45, 71, 80
Josephine (Lipscomb) 37
Josephine K. (Addy) 61
Josephine Katherine
(Frye)(Barnes) 97
Josephine Lula (Law) 107
Joshua Lee 94
Josie Henrietta (Schumpert) 76
Josie Henrietta 49
Joyce (Vorwaller) 111
Joyce 76
Juanita (Fulmer) 57
Judith Ann (Milton) 110
Judy 59
Judy Diane (Godwin) 83
Judy Lynn (Bailey) 83
Julia (Clary) 50
Julia Ann (Stockman) 96
Julia Ann 63, 61
Julian 66
Julian Watt 104
Julius Ray 61
June Levonne (Minick)-
(Stevenson) 60
June Willimena (Christian) 43
Justin Hugh 108
Juvernia (Ward) 66
Kaleb Wilson 110
Karen (Steele) 96
Karen 97
Karen Leah (Birmingham) 94
Karen Nikole 94
Karen Renee 72
Karman Jay 81
Kate (Taylor) 34
Katherin 15

197

213

English, Leon P. 48
Melba Syble (Bedenbaugh)(Williams) 48
Enoch, Daniel 166
Joyce Lee (Keenan) 166
Michael 166
Wilford 166
Epting, Allison Elizabeth 86
Amanda Catherine 87
Amy Elizabeth (Kimbrell) 86
Andrew Kenneth 56, 86
Andrew Kenneth Jr. 86
Benny 34
Bonnie Lou (Reagin) 86
Bonnie Lou 56
Brooks 50
Catherine Lucille (Solomons) 86
Cynthia Ann (Petty) 86
Eliza Jeannette (Bedenbaugh) 56
Gregory Scott 86
Harold 50
Jacob Dewey III 113
Jacob Dewey Jr. 113
Janet Solomons (Shook) 87
John Adam 12
Killian N. 56
Kimberly Tina Lilie 113
Lee Renee (Koon) 103
Lydia (Farr) 86
Marie Belle (Bedenbaugh) 50
Mattie Wytche (Bedenbaugh) 34
Merle (Bedenbaugh) 103
Olivia (Addy) 50
Ralph 50
Randall 50
Robert F. 50, 103
Rodney Farrell 103
Rodney O'Nelia 113
Sheron F. 103
Theresa Elizabeth (Nagy) 86
Timothy James 113
Toye (Bedenbaugh) 55
Trudie (Bedenbaugh) 50, 103
Vinnie Izora (Bushardt) 86
Violet M. (Counts) 86
Violet M. 56
Voight Milton 56, 86
Voight Milton Jr. 86
Zoe Jeannine (Wells) 86
Erskine, Alice Mettra Lea (Vassey) 170
Katelyn Paige 170
Margerie (Boyd) 170

Mark Edward 170
Paul 170
Sandy Kay (Jenkins) 170
Shawna Alyce 170
Etheredge, Charlotte (Dominick) 63
Alley James 62
Arna (Hinton) 62
Edgar Marvin 62
Frances (Cannady) 62
Frances Cornelia (Cathcart) 62
Lila (King) 62
Marvin E. 62
Nancy Ophelia (Ross)-(Dominick) 62
Eubanks, Emma (Gregory) 135
Everhart, Clyde 140
Margaret Aurelia "Maggie" (Betenbaugh) 140
Ewing, Mamie (Conwill) 39
William 39
Eyzaguirre, Lucia (Beatenbough) 185
Fairbanks, Mary Bell (Norris)(Bragg) 43
William Cash 43
Fant, Lucille Anderson (Dominick) 63
Farley, Evelyn Helen 185
Helen Dean (Beatenbough) 185
Jeffrey Ezekial "Zeke" 185
Jeffrey Morris 185
Farmer, Donna Sue (Betenbaugh) 183
Joni 183
Scott 183
Farr, Alley Pearl (Conwill) 65
James 15
Johnnie Lee (Conwill) 65
Lydia (Epting) 86
Mamie Lou (Bedenbaugh) 60
Mary (Conwill) 15
Farris, Jerry Rufus 98
Micheal William 98
Rufus Lafayette 98
Wanell (Conwill) 98
Faucett, Sallie T. (Willard)(Wilburn) 144
Victoria "Victory" (McCreight) 138
Faucette, Sallie (Wilburn) 189
W. T. 189
Feagle, Catha Lee (Bedenbaugh) 48
Fears, Doris Lillian (Minga) 65

Maxine Oclay (Minga) 65
Fellers, Ethel (Bedenbaugh) 69
Glenn 70
Jacob L. 20
Joy (Hunter) 70
Lyon Calhoun 70
Mary (Buzzard) 20
Myra Rebecca (Bowers) 70
Susan (Crim) 70
Terry 70
Finger, Rose (Burgess) 156
Finken, Courtney Marie 58
Debra Sue (Smith) 58
Scott 58
Finley, Angela 82
Cecil 82
Crystal Diane (Keenan) 167
Dale (Vasser) 82
Debbie 82
James 82
Jerry 82
Kay (--) 82
Lynn 82
Mae (Bedenbaugh) 82
Michael 82
Roscoe 82
Finney, J. Hunter 145
Nelle (Gregory) 145
Fisher, Vera Catherine (Bragg) 43
Fite, Doxie (Bedenbaugh) 31
Matthew S. 31
Fitts, Georgia Willie (Beatenbo) 148
Johnnie Mell (Beatenbo) 148
Fitzpatrick, Dorcas (Carey) 147
Jeffery 175
Rita Carol (Beatenbough)(Betzler) 175
Flanery, Hazel Modean (Riser) 90
Fleming, Violet (Bedenbaugh)(Aaron) 50
William 50
Fletcher, Wilma (Chandler) 167
Floyd, Azelle (Bedenbaugh) 67
Collette 113
Elvin 113
Gene Gordon 113
Geneva Ruth (Bundrick) 113
J. Y. 67
James Norman 113
Leonard 113

Fuller, Angela DeCarolus
(Bedenbaugh) 59
Betty (Smith) 58
Dovie (Betenbaugh) 143
Fulmer, 31
Alice (Morris) 30
Anna "Annie" Caroline
(Bedenbaugh)(Kinard) 18
Annie Grace (Beden-
baugh) 100
Annie Vernetha (Ren-
wick) 100
Beth (Haggard) 96
Carol Jean (Gar-
ner)(Chapman) 186
Clarence 100
Daniel Walter 92
Dora Bell (Mills) 72
Elizabeth (Phelps) 96
Georgie (Bedenbaugh)
100
Gerald Duane 100
Geralyn (Brooks) 100
Gladys (Bowers) 100
Guerry Alvin 60, 96
Guerry Harvey 60
Jerry Thomas 60, 96
John 18
Joseph Edward 66
Juanita (Bedenbaugh) 57
June (Moore) 96
June 100
Lillie (Bedenbaugh) 66
Linda Suzanne (Shealy)
92
Lori Danielle 92
Mary Ethel (Whiteley)
100
Monroe E. 57
Nancy Elizabeth (Amick)
96
Noah Calhoun 100
Ola (Mills) 46
Pamela Gayle (Berrian)
96
Ruby Velma (Beden-
baugh) 60
Stephen Luther 96
Thomas Edward 186
Valerie 96
William Jennings 100
Willie Maytrude (Katz)
100
Gamble, Dorothy (Quinn)
169
Ganey, Jeannette (Mc-
Creight) 170
Gant, Allison (Hagan) 105
Gardner, Coralea (Kee-
nan) 165
Juanita Faye (Keenan)
168
Garlick, Bonnie (Riser) 90

Garner, Almond Lee 164
Barbara Joan (Young)
186
Ben Wilson 165
Carol Jean (Chapman)-
(Fulmer) 186
Carolyn (Bullington) 179
Carroll Bruce 179, 186
Christine (Cobb) 179
Christy Lynn (Cannon)
179
Cornelia (Kelly) 165
Cynthia (Thomas) 186
D'Lynn (Conners) 179
Daniel Bruce 164, 179
David Christopher 183
Deborah (Roberts) 179
Donald Woods 179
Donald Woods Jr. 179
Elizabeth Louise
(Knox)(Allison) 186
Garrett 180
Gene Edward 179, 186
Gene Edward Jr. 186
Gladys A. (Greer) 179
Gladys A. (Prouty) 186
Greg McBeth 179
Jack Greer 179, 186
Jack Turner 186
Jacqueline 180
James L. 183
Jamie Lee 183
Jason 186
Jennie Viola "Vi" (O'Dell)
180
Jennie Viola 165
Jessie Bruce 186
Jessie Carol (Morris) 179
Jewel Louise (Bouknight)
186
John Ellerbe 186
John Rufus 164, 179
Joseph Moody 179
Joseph Woods 164, 179
Joyce Lynn
(League)(Huey)(Campbell)
179
Kathryn Diane (Sanders)
183
Kenneth Bruce 57, 186
Leanne (Brown) 186
Madelyn (Miller) 186
Marva (Moody) 179
Mary Ema (Nichols) 179
Mary Louise (McGowan)
164
Michael Keith 164
Myrtle Louise (Kelley)
186
Paul Brandon 164
Ralph Lee 164, 179
Ralph Lee Jr. 179
Ruby Lee (O'Dell) 179

Sabrina (Bedenbaugh) 186
Sabrina (Bedenbaugh)-
(Manning) 57
Sarah Francis Elizabeth
(Brandon) 164
Susan Ann (Alexander)
179
Sylvia (Garrett) 179
Ted McBeth 179
Teresa (Allison) 186
Thelma Virginia (Croc-
ker) 179
Thelma Virginia 164
William Mack 186
William McBeth 165
Garrett, Betty (Dominick)
73
Ernest T. 73
Faye 73
George 73
John 73
Lois 73
Robert 73
Sara 73
Sparta (Nichols) 73
Sylvia (Garner) 179
Vernon 73
Zilla 73
Garrison, Clara Elizabeth
(Keenan) 167
Jackie (Betenbaugh) 183
Gaskins, Cathy (Beden-
baugh) 78
Ron 78
Gasser, John 12
Gatens, Beverly Ann (Har-
ris) 93
Gault, Eva (Betenbaugh)
150
Mable 150
Mamie (Hughes) 150
Marie (Hollingsworth)
150
Vernon 150
Gauthier, Robin Ann
(Williams) 108
Gay, Angelia F. (Beden-
baugh) 103
Bertie Sue (Bedenbaugh)
135
James 135
Phyllis (Boozer) 71
Gennoe, Horace Lenord
43
Mary Julia (Bragg) 43
Gentry, Lena Estella (Be-
tenbough) 148
George, Lewis 124
Gerring, Nancy (Elizabeth)
174
Gessler, Margaret (Werts)
55

216

Geyler, Catharine (Bidenbach) 1
Philipp 1
Gibbs, John 188
Gibson, Andrew Chase 94
Billy Riser 90
Carole Elizabeth (Shealy) 90
Cornelia (Bedenbaugh) 42
Debra Lynn (Abrams) 90
Dora Opal (Riser) 90
Edith Lynn (Bedenbaugh) 94
Ernest 73
Ernestine (Riddle) 73
Evelyne 73
Frank Woodrow III 94
Frank Woodrow Jr. 94
Helen Meredith (Marsh) 90
Henrietta (Warren) 73
James Corbett 90
James Ira 90
Jeoffrey Corbett 91
Joel Marsh 91
Lisa Ann (Kinard) 90
Mary Varie (Kibler) 73
Mattie Sula (Hipp) 73
Sarah Ruth 73
Sylvia (Boozer) 90
Violet (Boozer) 50
William Michael 90
William Newton 73
Gilbert, Leola (Bedenbaugh) 135
Gile, Synthia Denise (McCreight) 171
Gill, Lorrilee Gay (Bedenbaugh) 108
Gilliam, Alyce (McIver) 112
Arnold Moore 112
Barbara Jean (Miller) 92
Ella Florence (Bedenbaugh) 49
Ina Celeste (Morgan) 112
Ina Sandra (Shealy) 112
Jacquelina Elaine (Taylor) 92
Lacee Devin 112
Lauren Ann (Collins) 112
Marion Todd 92
Mark Alan 92
Ralph Cedric 92
Sanford Moore 112
Gilligan, Dan 88
Patricia Lynn (Riser) 88
Gintz, Thelma (Beatenbough) 135
Gist, Patricia (Crocker) 186
Glaser, Charlie 158

Susan Earle (Strahley) 158
Susan Fair (Moss) 158
Glenn, Barbara (Dominick) 63
Glisson, Marlene Derryl (Hagans) 108
Godfrey, Clara (Dennis)(Stroud) 90
Rita (Burnsed) 107
William Drayton 90
Godshall, Grace (Willard) 160
Godwin, Judy Diane (Bedenbaugh) 83
Goff, Dianne (Boozer) 71
Douglas M. 71
Lois (Bedenbaugh) 59
Mattie Pearl (Bedenbaugh) 42
Nancy (Bedenbaugh) 41
Goforth, Sarah "Sallie" (Betenbaugh)(Young) 146
Sarah Elizabeth (Davis) 137
Goldberg, Cynthia Jean (Plowden) 172
Gomez, Nora Louise (Bedenbaugh) 66
Goodman, Tillie (Betenbaugh) 156
Goodwin, Tenny Lee (Conwill) 38
Thomas A. 38
Gordon, Catherine Elizabeth (Stutts) 182
Grant, Andrea Mills 90
Barbara Elaine (Keason) 53
George Mills III 90
George Mills Jr. 90
Mary Permelia (Harrell) 53
Olive Elaine (Boozer) 53
Reuben Herbert 53
Reuben Humphrey 53
Ruth Elizabeth (Johnson) 53
Sue Andrea "Andi" (Stroud) 90
Graves, Ella Rae (Shealy) 53
Huber 53
Green, Barbra Joan (Conwill) 99
Bellzora (Conwill) 38
Charlie 65
Frankie Dianne (Hopkins)(Welford) 154
Jack 154
Judy (Prevost) 162
Kathleen (Cowan) 65

Liza Melverda (Conwill) 65
Lizzie (Norris) 43
Martha (Conwill) 25
Michelle (Guinn) 154
Ruby Mae (Tarver) 65
Sarah C. (Conwill) 38
Scott 154
Greer, Angelia (Foister) 154
Aurelia Adell (Betenbaugh) 140
Charner Sanders 140
Eva Elaine (Clark) 179
Gladys A. (Garner) 179
Jason Martin 146
John C. Calhoun 179
Kyle 154
Mary Ann (Malone) 140
Sarah (Sanders) 146
Sarah Ann "Sallie" (Betenbaugh) 146
Gregory, Alma Joyce 162
Anita (Sanders) 174
Anita 162
Annie Grey 162
Barbara Jean (Collins) 163
Bertha (Young) 162
Carolyn (Driver) 163
Charlotte Elizabeth (Lanier) 162
Claude Cleveland 162, 174
Claude Cleveland Jr. 174
Clyde Carlisle 162
Colene (Scott) 146
Cornelius Earl 163
Debra Jean (Duty) 174
Della (Foster) 145
Donna Ellen (Turner) 162
Donna Kay (Harper) 163
Douglass Leroy 162
Emma (Eubanks) 135
Ernest Talmadge 162
Eugene 145, 162
Frances (Grogan) 163
Gilliam 145
Gilliam Maurice 146
Grover Cleveland 145, 162
Helen (Sweeney) 146
Ida (Young) 163
Ida 146
Jerry Lee 162
Joann (Hartle) 174
John Clarence 145, 162
John Henderson 135, 188
John Richard "Ricky" 174
John Wilson 162, 174
Joseph Loyd 162
Lavinia "Viny" (Koon) 135
Leila Pearl 145
Leland Cozine 162

226

Lybrand, Barbara (Bedenbaugh) 36
Casey Shealy 112
Denise (Shealy) 112
Erika Dawn 112
Toy Randal 112
Lynch, Angela 166
Lynda (King) 115
Mary Alice (Keenan) 166
Steve 166
Lynn, Marie (Dyer) 152
Mabry, Dorothy Sanders (Willard) 160
William Preston 160
MacDonald, Kelly Denise Burnsed 107
Mace, Vivian Annalle (Cartee) 155
Mack, Carolyn Davis "Judy" (Bedenbaugh) 83
Mary Ann (Jolly) 160
Thomas 160
Mackey, Deborah Lynn (Bedenbaugh) 81
Majette, Bradley Lynn 160
Helen Claire 160
Helen Tate (Bradley) 160
John Fox 160
Louis Dean 160
Malone, Mary Ann (Greer) 140
Manning, Gary 57
Sabrina (Bedenbaugh)-(Garner) 57
Manship, Mary Ann (Bedenbaugh) 63
Marks, Frances Soffie (Bedenbaugh) 109
Marsh, Helen Meredith (Gibson) 90
Martin, Albert 47
Anna Marie (Betenbough) 149
Beverly (Sweezy) 84
Birdie Orine (Danielson) 47
Brittany 84
Cathy (Holloman) 54
Cindy (Keenan) 166
Heather 84
Helen Ruth (Bedenbaugh) 84
Helena Stewart 84
Horace Clyde Jr. 81
James Horace 84
James Horace Jr. 84
Joyce (Fortson) 177
Judy (Jolly) 160
Martha Elise (Hawkins)(Bedenbaugh) 81
Michael 84
Mickey Hilton 176

Pamela Alynn (Bedenbaugh) 110
Patti Denise (Suber) 84
Rachel (Simmons) 84
Randy Stewart 84
Rebecca (Wicker) 84
Robbie 84
Robert Harry 84
Robert Harry Jr. 84
Sheila Ryan (Dickert) 84
Massey, Bernice Beatrice (Bedenbaugh) 135
Carrie (Bedenbaugh) 30
Claudia Ann (King) 135
Ernest 135
John 30
Pamela Ernestine 135
Rosilend Paulette (Mayo) 135
Sue (Hill) 178
Mathias, Alice L. (Moore) 36
J. Cephus 36
Mathis, Charity Alisa (Keen)(Smith) 109
Charity Michelle 109
Wyndell 109
Matthews, Carrie J. (Bedenbaugh) 41
Corria J. 121
Jimmie Sue (Bedenbaugh)(Trotter) 68
Nannie Harmon Bedenbaugh 44
Mattison, Karyn Lisa (Stafford) 166
Randy 166
Maxie, Brenda Maxine (Bedenbaugh) 64
May, Virginia (Gregory) 174
Mayer, Ann (Bedenbaugh) 34
Francis Ronald 104
Susan (Bedenbaugh)-(Elinoff) 104
Mayo, Larry 135
Rosilend Paulette (-Massey) 135
McAbbe, Cristal Jean (Carter) 170
Kim Allice (Lowery) 170
McAbee, Amelia Jean 170
Berlin Loyd 170
Joshua 170
Michael Dean 170
Phill Loyd 170
Valorie (Vassey) 170
McAllister, Elizabeth Kate (Boozer) 51
McBride, Mary (Bedenbaugh) 26
Patrick 26

Phoebe Ann (Bedenbaugh) 25, 26
McCartha, Angelina Elisha 115
Brenda Diane (Coppock) 115
Clarence Wayne 115
Edith (Whiteman) 115
Helen Doneria (Bledsoe)-(Carver) 114
James Bernard 115
John Clarence 103, 114
Joyce (Hutchinson) 115
Lila Mae (Leopard) 103
Lucy (Bradley) 115
Martha Frances (Hembree) 115
Mary Frances 103
Mattie Mae (Mills) 103
Randy Lee 115
Ruby (Lake) 115
Ruby 103
Willie John Silas 103
McClish, Isa Belle (Betenbough) 135
Lloyd Edisto 135
Martha (Woodside)(Hogan) 135
R. E. 135
Velma Lee 135
McCollough, Georgiana (Bedenbaugh) 41
McCombs, Donald 173
Jessie Marie (Holcomb)(Crook)(Wolfe) 173
McConnell, Debra (Bedenbaugh) 72
McCool, Leila (Dominick) 62
McCraw, Edith (Keenan) 151
McCreight, Albertha 138
Alice Gertrude (Foister) 153
Alice Gertrude 139
Ann (--) 171
Ann (Brown) 153
Annie Belle (Harris) 153
Bernice (Yokum) 153
Cathey 170
Clarence 153
Cornelia "Neely" 128, 139
Cornelia 138
Dannie 170
David Andrew 128, 139, 189
Diane (Derrick) 171
Donna 138
Donnie 170
Doris 170
Elaine (Bryson) 171
Eleanor "Ellie" (Halsell) 138

www.ingramcontent.com/pod-product-compliance
Lightning Source LLC
Chambersburg PA
CBHW060453290526
45791CB00001B/99